Working with
Religious Issues in Therapy

Working with Religious Issues in Therapy

Robert J. Lovinger

𝒜

Jason Aronson, Inc.
New York and London

The author gratefully acknowledges permission to reprint excerpts from the following sources:

Alter, R. (1981). *The Art of Biblical Narrative*. Basic Books, Inc., Publishers, New York, p. 33. Copyright © 1981 by Robert Alter. (p. 218)

Boulding, K. (1980). Science: Our Common Heritage. *Science* 207: 831-836, 22 February 1980. Copyright © 1980 by The American Association for the Advancement of Science. (p. 8)

Frankl, V.E. (1973). *The Doctor and the Soul: From Psychotherapy to Logotherapy*, 2nd ed, p. 139. Translated by Richard and Clara Winston. Copyright © 1973 by Alfred A. Knopf, Inc. (p. 190)

Fromm-Reichmann, F. (1950). *Principles of Intensive Psychotherapy*. pp. 33-34. Copyright © 1950 by The University of Chicago. All rights reserved. (p. 37)

Kluckhohn, F.R., and Strodtbeck, F.K. (1961). *Variations in Value Orientation*. p. 11. Copyright © 1961 by Row, Peterson & Co., New York. Reprinted by permission of Florence R. Kluckhohn. (p. 128)

Lazarus, A.A. (1971). *Behavior Therapy and Beyond*. McGraw-Hill Book Company, p. 8. Copyright © 1971 by McGraw-Hill. (p.38)

Rogers, C.R. (1951). *Client-Centered Therapy*. Copyright © 1951, renewed 1979 by Houghton Mifflin Company, pp. 149-150. (p. 37)

Jacket drawings: from *Oskar Kokoschka: Drawings 1906-1965*. Translated by Heinz Norden from the German edition, *Oskar Kokoschka Handzeichnungen 1906-1965*. Copyright © 1966 by Ernest Rathenau, New York, formerly Euphorion Verlag Berlin. Copyright © 1970 by the University of Miami Press.

Copyright © 1984 by Jason Aronson, Inc.

10 9 8 7 6 5 4 3 2 1

Library of Congress Cataloging in Publication Data

Lovinger, Robert J.
  Working with religious issues in therapy.

  Bibliography: p. 277
  Includes index.
  1. Psychotherapy. 2. Psychoanalysis and religion.
3. Psychotherapy patients—Attitudes. I. Title.
RC445.4R4L68 1984   616.89'1487   84-6198
ISBN 0-87668-727-3

Manufactured in the United States of America
Printed on acid-free paper with a life expectancy of 250 years.

To Sophie, for making it possible

Contents

Preface

As a supervisor in a clinical psychology training program, I once received a call from a colleague in another department who wanted to secure treatment for his youngster, who sounded quite troubled. I assured him that I would arrange for a good student therapist and he asked, "Is he [the student] a Christian?" I felt considerable irritation and thought, "Do you want to help your child or not?" but I said, "I don't know. If that is important to you, you should take it up with Mr. A. in the intake interview."

Another companion question a therapist faces is "Have you been saved?" Whether the therapist has a positive religious orientation, is disinterested in religion, or is anti-religious, such questions are often experienced as intrusive or irritating. What should one say? Should I ignore or deflect this question ("Why do you want to know?"), say that I do not discuss religion (or answer personal questions), or should I disclose my attitudes to religion? I do not think that a simple answer will suffice, since it depends a great deal on the therapist and how the task ahead is conceived. Tact and a reasonably clear view of the issues are very important, since the religious ideas and beliefs of the patient contain material that is highly useful to therapy, if properly understood. I do not believe, however, that a patient who is not religious is lacking something therapy should provide. But whatever the eventual stance regarding religion, a person who becomes a psychotherapist typically travels one of three main academic routes: psychiatry, psychology, or social work. Less common paths include pastoral counseling, psychiatric nursing, educational psychology, special education, or teaching. With the exception of pastoral counseling, the training encountered in these programs tends either to discourage or undermine a religious orientation (Gartner 1982, Sollod 1978); alternatively, people who are nonreligious initially may self-select such training programs. Rarely, if ever, do such programs attend to religious matters in patients, leaving most therapists unprepared on both a conceptual and practical basis.

How can religious issues be used in psychotherapy? Let us look at the question from the side of the therapist. At one time, I supervised a talented student, Mr. B., who was treating an obsessive patient employed in the physical sciences. Therapy was moving slowly and the patient's feelings were bottled up. In supervision, the therapist reported that the patient said he prepared for the therapy session by going over in his mind the matters he wanted to take up in the forthcoming session. Both the patient and the therapist were Catholic, and the therapist had gone to parochial school for many years. I asked, "What is he [the patient] doing?" The therapist was aware that the patient's "organizing" prior to the session functioned as a resistance, but he could take it no further. I asked, "Do you know what an examination of conscience is?" Although he was no longer religious, the therapist immediately flashed back to the preparation incumbent upon a Catholic prior to confession and replied, "Oh God, you're right." "How come you missed that?" I asked, and this led to a fruitful discussion of some of the therapist's countertransferences. Therapy began to move forward again.

Religious issues develop from the patient's side, too. Adults often have negative memories of the religion of their childhood, in part because they learned it as children. Of course, such learnings are also bound up with significant experiences with important adults, but if intellectual growth in religion ceased as the person entered adolescence, retrospective views look childish and embarrasing. Late in therapy, another patient (Mr. C) had worked through many of his earlier difficulties with his parents but his feelings and understanding about his religion were still painful and clouded. Although he might have liked an adult relationship with his church and God, he could neither reject nor accept what he remembered. I suggested he take out some books on the topic, which seemed to free him enough to do so. He looked at several books in the library and chose one unfavorable to the Early Fathers of the Church, which supported his need to reject his early indoctrination.

These examples are from early in my experience, when I thought of religion as significant but secondary to what seemed to be the main thrust of therapeutic work. As I continued, I realized that religious issues, like transference and resistance, presented the therapist with opportunities to learn about the patient's life and to move therapy forward.

> For example, when Mr. D. first entered therapy, he was deeply beset with doubts about the stability of reality and was making strenuous efforts to retain a modicum of positive relations with others, including his wife and God. Later in therapy, as we had begun to get some grip on his hallucinations, he recounted how as a young adolescent he had run away one winter night and, as the temperature was dropping, set out across a field looking for shelter. He found an abandoned house without windows, but with a cot, where he spent the night and saved himself from frostbite or possibly death from exposure. Earlier in this session he had been struggling with deep feelings of worthlessness and then began to talk of his puzzlement as to whether events had meaning. Finding this abandoned house could not have been an accident when he needed it so desperately—what did it mean? Was God real? Did He care? I replied that I knew he felt worthless and sinful, but I thought that God cared more for good than bad people.[1] He agreed. I said that since he had found this shelter at such a desperate time, and felt that this was God's doing, maybe God knew something he didn't. By pitting one imperative in his life against another in his own idiom, I was able to allow him to modify his crushingly negative self-image.

Therapists are understandably cautious about entering into the domain of a patient's religion, and for good reason. This is not part of our training and we usually have a limited background in other religions. Most therapists have had some exposure to religion in childhood and whether their attitude is positive or negative, they usually recognize the risks of countertransference. Values and beliefs are difficult personal issues, and many therapists are opposed to inflicting their own values on other people. In contrast, without trying to force values on a patient, a basic assumption undergirds this entire effort: a patient's religious beliefs and experiences contain important meanings about past experiences and can characterize the quality of the patient's relationships with others. When these issues emerge in therapy, they can aid therapy if approached with

---

[1]This is a common idea, but it is not really correct. In Christian theology, salvation (repentance, reconciliation with God and humans) for the sinner is a central goal. Judaism holds a roughly similar position.

interest and respect. None of this requires any change in the therapist's own attitudes to religion, other than relinquishing the idea (if held) that religion is silly or meaningless. No phenomenon can be usefully approached this way.

The definitions of religion used here will emerge over the course of this book, but in essence, religion is one way to give order and meaning to the world. The patient's denominational memberships (past and present), however, form the frame of reference in which to appraise and interpret individual meanings and symbol systems. That is, the person's individual religious sentiment (Allport 1950) is seen in a denominational context that has both normative and variant qualities, so one can go on to understand the very personal meanings as well. Such an approach is inherently limited, but this is not a text on psychotherapy, religion, or the psychology of religion, as such. Rather, the aim of the book is to develop ways to understand and respond to the problems religious patients present in psychotherapy and the problems religions present to therapists.

There are limitations to this approach. Although the therapist cannot become an expert theologian, he or she should be aware that patients often misunderstand the theology of their own religion. Before this can be dealt with, the therapist should deal with some of his or her attitudes and values; these are addressed in the first two chapters. The next three chapters deal with various religious issues, personality factors, and specific denominations. In Chapters 6 and 7, therapy and alternative translations as a way to deal with certain religious issues in therapy are discussed. Supplementary material on various religions is included in the appendices. Bibliographic sources follow the references. This is not a general text on therapy, and it is assumed that the reader has had some actual experience as a therapist—at the minimum, a semester or two of practicum. Although presented in a general psychodynamic framework, the theoretical approach here is an object-relations, ego-psychological one. Technique is regarded as flexible, but I am reluctant to do more than is needed to obtain a good therapeutic result. With the issues of concern here, there will be times when one is directly dealing with values, so caution is needed. Religious issues will be viewed in terms of psychodynamic functions: defense, adaptation, growth, and regression. For the religious therapist who experiences "something more," this may have a cold, reductionistic ring; for the nonreligious therapist, the attempt to view the patient's meanings with sympathy may seem too approving. Overall, my aim has been to inquire into the meanings and functions of a patient's religious beliefs and experiences to improve understanding without taking a position on "ultimate" questions.

Since this book is primarily for the North American reader, the range of religions is restricted. "Mainline" American religious groups, such as the main Catholic divisions (Roman Catholic, Greek Orthodox), the main Protestant denominations (Lutheran to Methodist and Baptist through Unitarian), and the Pentecostal and Holiness churches, will receive major attention. The three main divisions within Judaism (Orthodox, Conservative, and Reform) will be reviewed, as will several special denominations, such as Jehovah's Witness, Mormon, and Christian Science. The Black churches are not discussed here because I have no experience with them. This is regrettable because Black churches are powerful and important factors in the lives of their parishioners and the equivalent white denominations (e.g., Methodist, Baptist) are rather different. A therapist working with a Black patient with religious issues related to one of these denominations should be cautious in making assumptions about these churches. Certain modern cults (Hare Krishna, "Moonies") are not discussed because their members are unlikely to be seen in therapy, although their ex-members may be. The transplanted Eastern religions (Buddhism, Zen, Bahai, Yoga, Transcendental Meditation), as well as Islam, are not discussed, but the "Black Muslim" (properly called The American Moslem Mission) is. Although one might quarrel with some of the choices, I am reluctant to present on those denominations I have had no experience with unless they are bounded by similar denominations I have had some contact with.

Finally, a word about reading this book. Most therapists, myself included, want practical help with the complex, often puzzling work of therapy. First are discussed a number of fundamental issues in the background of psychotherapy with religious patients so that specific issues and strategies in therapy with patients who express their problems in a religious idiom can be seen in context. As well, the specifics offered should indicate how to approach those matters and problems not covered here.

Acknowledgments

Many people have graciously contributed to this effort. In addition to her generous support, encouragement, and tolerance of my burrowing at my typewriter, my wife Sophie freely took time from her own professional labors for candid and helpful critiques of the ideas and organization of this book. I am grateful to her beyond words. Joseph Frankenfield, Fr. Mark Glidden, Jefferson Stewart, and Paul Vitz were most helpful in reading much or all of the manuscript in one or more of its various stages. A sabbatical leave from Central Michigan University helped provide time to do much library work and about one-half the writing. A number of other people were also helpful. My thanks go to Karen Beehr, Donald Beere, George Del Grosso, Katherine Epperly, Robert Garrels, Ronald Johnstone, Rabbi Jossef Kratzenstein, Jeanette Munn, and Mary Roberson. The faculty of the Religion Department at Central Michigan University critiqued an early draft. In particular, William Reader scrutinized part of the text in very helpful detail. Joan Langs' careful and tactful editing contributed to clarity, readability, and organization at many points, and I record here my debt to her. Finally, I am grateful to Calman Levich who contributed more to this book than he knows.

1

The Secular and Religious Background of the Therapist

Training in education, nursing, psychiatry, psychology, and social work—founded in a secular, rational, liberal arts and natural science tradition—is at odds with the religious orientation and background of many Americans. For example, a liberal education usually includes an introductory course in psychology. What does such a course say about religion? Very little! Beit-Hallahmi (1977) reviewed a number of introductory texts and found that most completely ignored religion, although a few mentioned religion once or twice. He also summarized studies that showed that academics are generally less religious than the general population, whereas psychologists are typically less religious still (Ragan, Malony, and Beit-Hallahmi 1980). Meehl et al. (1958) examined the areas of agreement and disagreement between conservative Lutheranism and dynamic psychotherapy. From their declared faith position they asserted that "scientific naturalism (philosophically underpinned by logical empiricism) . . . is today the strongest intellectual enemy of the church" (p. 173). This opinion is not in the least contradicted by the Humanist Manifesto II (1973), which stated "we find insufficient evidence for belief in the existence of a supernatural; it is either meaningless or irrelevant to the question of the survival and fulfillment of the human race" (p. 4).

Although psychology's roots are in philosophy and religion, religious traditions are often seen as incompatible with the sciences and the humanities. This incompatibility can be summarized as follows:

1. The religious assertion of non-material (spiritual) factors collides with the scientific emphasis on public verification of directly or

indirectly observable events (Meehl et al. 1958). Perhaps not all events are even indirectly observable, but this principle supports a common mythology used to distinguish between science and religion.

2. The religious emphasis on belief and faith is inconsistent with the scientific emphasis on curiosity and questioning. Authority is also used in science, sub rosa (Shapin 1980), but it is more vulnerable to challenge.

3. The acceptance of intuitive or non-rational (not *ir*-rational) sources of data by religion contravenes the convention of scientific culture of rational procedures. Intuitive processes in science are acknowledged (Broad 1979), but are rarely made explicit to undergraduates.

Even if the educational experiences of the therapist do not include direct critiques of religious beliefs or practices, the overall intellectual atmosphere of higher education and professional training militates against a religious orientation. There are more overt selective processes as well. Observations of the reactions of admissions committees reviewing an applicant with strong, overt religious beliefs for entry to a graduate psychology program show that some faculty regard these expressions of belief as neurosis, poor judgment, or "bad taste" (Gartner 1982; Sollod 1978).

It is not surprising that students in such training programs already have or will acquire one or more of the following orientations:

1. A scientific *Weltanschauung*
2. A humanist orientation
3. A liberal political outlook

A *scientific Weltanschauung* (or world-view) can be characterized by an empirical or a fact-oriented approach to problems, confidence in investigation and/or technology as solutions to problems, and a rational rather than an intuitive or affective approach to many aspects of life. A *humanist orientation* is probably more diffuse, but seems to emphasize a primary concern for people, rather than things or goals, and to value human growth (Humanist Manifesto II 1973). Although there may be more emphasis on, or at least acceptance of, intuitive methods than in the scientific *Weltanschauung*, a humanist orientation is not incompatible with, and is generally comfortable following rational methods as well. The *politically liberal outlook* tends to agree with the humanist emphasis on human growth and human concerns and with the scientific emphasis on rational, technologically based solutions; but it sees application of these concerns in the political arena and favors intervention by government.

It might be concluded from the above that religious feelings and values are more important to many patients than to most psychotherapists. The therapist needs to be as free as possible of constraints stemming from emotional limitations and informational deficits. The academic study of religion is rarely an aspect of the therapist's training and the overall attitudinal matrix of a psychology-oriented education tends to foster a negative attitude toward religions.

THE NONRELIGIOUS THERAPIST

Within the overall stance of being nonreligious, roughly three groups may be identified: *nonaffiliation*, *anti-affiliation*, and *former affiliation*.

The Nonaffiliated Therapist

The nonaffiliated therapist is defined as one who is largely indifferent to religious rituals, belief-systems, values, and cultural and social activities oriented around a church or synagogue. This does not mean that such a therapist has no rituals, beliefs, values, culture, or social life, but only that an explicit religious tone or orientation is essentially absent. Occasional appearances in a church or synagogue for various reasons are not precluded, but there is a conscious attitude of indifference to various aspects of religion; unconscious attitudes at variance to the conscious attitude may or may not exist. Although some of the strongly held secular beliefs (theories), practices (therapies), and values (ethics) of psychotherapists may be equivalent in psychological function to similar processes in religion, they are not experienced as religious by the therapist. Such parallels have been used as a special argument in favor of religion, but they extend the concept of religion to the point of uselessness. Genuine indifference to religion is probably rare. Although most people have some feelings about religion, the indifference of the nonaffiliated therapist does not mean deep repression. The definition here is consistent with such conventional attitudes as "religion is okay because it helps some people feel better," or "religion is kind of silly because it isn't believable."

The family background of the nonaffiliated therapist is also likely to be nonaffiliated; his or her parents were also indifferent. Attendance at church or synagogue was sporadic and more for social or family reasons, and religious instruction in Sunday school, or its equivalent, was either absent or inconsistent. However, unless children grow up in a like-minded community, they will be exposed to friends' questions about religious affiliations and beliefs. By the age of four or five, a child will be trying to understand death, the universe, and other such matters. To have nothing in the way of a structuring belief or explanation is not consistent with how children think. To the question, "Do you believe in God?" a spontaneous answer of "I don't know and I don't care" puts the child in the position of experiencing an internal deficit. Some protective covering will be acquired in either a superficial believing or unbelieving stance. Only late in high school or college will other values or philosophies be acquired, so the person will be comfortable with indifference to religion.

The Anti-affiliated Therapist

There are many critiques of the religious position and organized institutional religion. A good sample may be found in Humanist Manifesto II (1973) and Ellis (1970). In Ellis' description of his own personal development and that of rational-emotive therapy, he noted "that personality disturbance is little more than another name for devout religiosity, intolerance, dogmatism, magical thinking and anti-scientism" (1974, p. 197). The background of many anti-affiliated therapists is similar to that of the formerly affiliated therapist, but here only the anti-affiliated therapist whose background as a child was also antireligious will be considered. As an adult, the therapist continues with values learned as a child and elaborated upon as an adult. This therapist has a belief-system or at least a set of axioms about the world and its people. These beliefs are not only nonreligious in origin, but also have a clear, antireligious orientation. The scientific or humanist position is compatible with the anti-affiliated therapist's stance on religion. An anti-affiliated therapist might hold one or more of the following attitudes:

1. A sharply disparaging attitude toward most or all religions
2. A view of religion as destructive or severely confining to people
3. A view of religion as an unprovable myth a sensible person should ignore
4. A view of religion as the support of emotionally crippled people

Other than the Soviet work summarized by Cullen (1974), little has been written on the antireligious person in the psychological literature. More has been written on the religious person: Bowers (1963) reported on the therapy of a number of clergy, and Helfaer (1972) studied psychological development in theology students, but there appears to be little in-depth, empirical psychodynamic study of the personality of the religious person.

The Formerly Affiliated Therapist

In describing the "religious" background of psychotherapists so far, we have assumed a continuation of their orientation from childhood through adulthood. Many psychotherapists in this group have changed from a religious affiliation to a nonaffiliated stance. As with any cultural change, cross-currents of ideas and feelings will be present and people who have changed are less likely to feel entirely comfortable in their new stance. Formerly affiliated and anti-affiliated therapists have reported various reasons for changes in attitude, including

1. The desire to escape oppressive demands and prohibitions
2. The wish to be free of others' control of their beliefs
3. The subjective experience that the answers provided by a specific religion were incompatible with subsequent experiences, i.e., the answers failed
4. The world-view provided in early religious education was incompatible with the world-view provided by later secular education
5. The rewards for doubt and skepticism inherent in many vocational areas, such as scientific research, provided substantial gratification

The differences between the anti-affiliated therapist and the formerly affiliated therapist may not be great. Unless the person's childhood religious experiences are reflected upon and worked through by personal self-scrutiny, by discussions with a third party, or in psychotherapy, this aspect of childhood will leave a residue of bitterness, anger, guilt, or rejection.

Both from conversations with a number of therapists and the psychotherapy of several, the history of anti-affiliated and formerly affiliated therapists contains one or more crucial experiences. Specific, and usually repetitively hurtful experiences with clergy or religious teachers were reported; or the parents, clergy, or teachers were unable to answer important questions; or there was a lack of understanding on the adult's part, leading to the use of force or pressure. One therapist recalled that, as a child, she had asked her mother about the Cain and Abel story. "After Cain killed Abel, he crossed the desert and got married. How could he, if Adam and Eve were the first people?" The mother's reply of "Just accept it" discouraged the child from reading further.

Since religion is mediated through psychological processes (McFadden 1969) and involves significant identifications, the religious attitude that eventually develops may well reflect the specific developmental course and resolution of the person's identifications. Although not everyone with problems in parental identification will express this in a religious idiom, this is certainly one arena in which the issue may be played out. This might appear to suggest that an anti-affiliated, or a formerly affiliated, orientation reflects developmental difficulties, and that a religious orientation does not. This is not the position taken here. A person may evince adaptive or maladaptive resolutions in many ways, but a very strong antireligious orientation *may* indicate a set of experiences that are only partly resolved. It also follows that a very strong proreligious orientation may indicate the same.

Religion for the Nonaffiliated Therapist

Nonaffiliated therapists may have been able to recognize some parts of their development in the previous discussion. Indifference or rejection are difficult attitudes to change, but they are obstacles to apprehending the experiential and conceptual world of the patient. The following material is directed at these cognitive and attitudinal issues so that the patient's religious orientation can be viewed with genuine respect without altering the reader's personal belief system. This is not a form of apologetics for religion, but rather, an attempt to understand a patient's religious beliefs. Such beliefs are not silly, even if they are inconsistent or destructive or obstacles to personal growth. It is easier to regard these beliefs seriously, however, when the therapist sees their purpose, grasps their meaning, and finds a basis for respecting them, even though the therapist holds other beliefs.

The Scientific Weltanschauung and Religion

It is believed that religions arose from early magical practices (Ostow 1958). Malinowski's work on the Tobriand islanders indicates that empirical methods for dealing with adaptive problems were readily employed, but magic was used when empirical methods failed (Allport 1950). A popular theory holds that magic was a form of early technology that was subsequently replaced by religion with its ethical foundation, which was, in turn, supplanted by technology. This has been thoroughly and sharply critiqued by Douglas (1966, 1970). In her very critical assessment of Frazer's *Golden Bough*, and particularly his division between magic and religion, she attacked his "false assumption about the primitive view of the universe worked by mechanical symbols, and another false assumption that ethics are strange to primitive religion" (1966, p. 28). Reviewing a number of primitive societies, she countered the common view of all primitive peoples being highly religious and magic-ridden. Instead, "all the varieties of scepticism, materialism, and spiritual fervour are to be found in the range of tribal societies" (1970, p. x). Further, she noted that magic and sacrament are not distinct and far apart, and although some primitive groups emphasize magic and ritual, others (such as the Pygmy) emphasize affect and internal states, with little if any magic or ritual involved. Without disputing the ethical substrate of Roman Catholic teaching about the Mass, Douglas (1970) pointed to the magical, sacramental aspects of the Eucharist in the transubstantiation of the bread and the wine into the body and the blood of Christ.

In addition to the magical components of Judaism and Christianity, both also contain traces of pagan influences as is, for example, seen in Christmas and Hanukkah (Beit-Hallahmi 1976). "Pagan" is derived from the Latin *pagus* for peasant (i.e., civilian), since early Christians considered themselves soldiers for Christ. "Heathen" (of Anglo-Saxon origin) referred to the people who lived in the country, or heath, and thus not greatly influenced by urban Christian activity. These etymologies are not word-games, however; they reflect ancient conflicts and adjustments between competing ways of life.

Although both primitive and modern magical practices may be expected to have instrumental value, what should not be overlooked is the symbolic value of magic that expresses a person's or a culture's view of the world and what is important about that world. For example, although most people employ modern technology to a greater or lesser extent, how many people repair their own color television? The following statement on the clock radio in my office is a measure of our alienation from the "life-support system" our appliances represent: "Caution—To prevent electric shock, do not remove cover. *No user-serviceable parts inside*. Refer servicing to qualified personnel" (emphasis added). The current rise of interest in the occult and in witchcraft suggests that some people are alienated from the "magic" of modern technology. Pruyser (1974) has observed that this rise in interest may be, in part, a response to the deprivation of myths because of society's technological orientation. This response may be another way of expressing a loss of continuity with the past and the disruption of community so often characteristic of urban life.

Pruyser's suggestion is intriguing, when it is considered that modern technology is instrumentally efficacious, whereas magic is only symbolically so, and without reliable impact on the world. This interest in magic and the occult indicates that other motives are active in the face of the culture's powerful scientism.

Science is conceptually founded on a solidly deterministic expectation that certain events have a regular, lawful, causal relation to certain other events. Most ancient peoples saw events as caused by local, often inexplicable deities. Other peoples had different deities and, hence, different rules. The nature of reality was fragmented. Although a primary conception running through the Bible is monotheism, competing views still exist. In Genesis, after Jacob has stolen his father's blessing, he flees and stops somewhere for the night where he has the famous dream of "Jacob's ladder." The story continues in Genesis 28:16: "Jacob awoke from his sleep and said, 'Surely the Lord is present in this place, and I did not know it!'" (JPS 1967, p. 50). This expressed the concept of local gods with a defined "turf." Jaynes' (1976) thesis on the effects of the breakdown of the bicameral mind, with the consequent loss of the voices of the gods, may relate to this fragmented view of the world that seemed extant in the second millennium B.C.E.[1] Monotheism made reality whole and came to imply a deterministic world regulated by universal law, even if stated in terms remote from modern scientific usage.

Boulding (1980) elaborated on this idea in his surprise that science arose in Christian Europe rather than in China, which was technologically more advanced, or in Islam, which preserved the Greek heritage. He stated:

> it was not wholly an accident that science arose in a Christian society. Christianity was a proletarian religion founded by a carpenter and propagated by a tentmaker and fisherman. . . . This legitimated the world of work and matter in a way that the more aristocratic and "spiritual" religions of the East could not. (p. 832)

Although a monotheistic world-view would, in itself, be unlikely to lead to a scientific method and philosophy, it would contribute to a basic set of presuppositions and assumptions about the world that could foster the development of science. Boulding's analysis is open to dispute, and other factors were also operative, such as the disruption of feudal society by the

---

[1]Jews date their calendar from the assumed date of creation so that 1983 would be about 5743. Christians date theirs from the birth of Jesus. The Christian dating will be used here, but instead of B.C. and A.D., the more neutral B.C.E. (Before the Common Era) and C.E. (Common Era) will be used.

Black Plague, the relearning of Greek thought and Arab advances, and the impact of exploration fueled by a desire for spices and silk. Still science (as distinct from technology) was a stunning invention in thinking about and in organizing perceptions of the world. Ironically, Western religions strongly opposed science at times, so science may have been an unanticipated side effect of monotheism. In brief, then, it is suggested that science may have originated, in part, in the structuring of reality implicit in Judaic and Christian monotheism.

The Humanist Orientation and Religion

The modern concept of separation of church and state dates to the American and French revolutions, and it is still a matter of struggle and disagreement. Many functions that were once church-based, such as welfare aid, have been gradually secularized (Pruyser 1974). Before the Renaissance in Europe, the state, in the modern sense, hardly existed, even though the king, army, Church, peasantry, and merchants were reasonably distinct groups. During the high Medieval period, the Doctrine of the Two Swords was superficially analogous to the separation of church and state, with the Church responsible for defending the spiritual realm and the princes and the nobility the temporal realm; in the ancient Middle East, however, the religious life *was* the political life. In Hebrew, there was no direct word for religion because it was not needed, although the word usually translated as religion more nearly means "way of life." Modern Hebrew does contain such a word, *religia*, clearly an import.[2] Thus, although the development of monotheism served to unify the conception of the physical world progressively, the same monotheistic ideas (more exactly, ethical monotheism) made human concerns increasingly more central to communal living because of the intertwining of religious, ethical and social matters.

It is worth citing some specific instances in which this is so because religious law is so commonly regarded as harsh and inhumane.

Fugitive Slave Legislation. In Deuteronomy 23:16 it is stated "You shall not turn over to his master a slave who seeks refuge with you from his master" (JPS 1967, p. 367). Although traditionally dated to the Exodus, it more likely was written in the reign of King Josiah, some 2,600 years ago. In either event, this law is in advance of the U.S. Supreme Court decision

[2] I am indebted to Rabbi Jossef Kratzenstein, Ph.D. for this.

in the Dred Scott case of 1857 in which fugitive slaves could not escape their owners.

Human Sacrifice.   Abraham's attempt to sacrifice his son Isaac (Genesis 22) and the sacrifice of the lamb or kid for the first Passover (Exodus 12) may symbolize the prohibition of human sacrifice (Beit-Hallahmi 1976; Hertz 1960). What it actually meant to the ancient Hebrews is open to debate, but compared with surrounding cultures, prohibition of child sacrifice was quite unusual. Human sacrifice was substantially suppressed some 1,000 to 1,500 years later, with the rise of Christianity.

Personal Responsibility.   In Exodus 21, there is a section regarding a dangerous ox that gores people. If the owner knew of the animal's propensity and failed to keep it penned up, he had to pay damages if someone were injured, and he could be stoned if someone were killed. Then it goes on to say "whether it have gored a son, or have gored a daughter, according to this judgment shall it be done unto him. (i.e., the owner)" (Hertz 1960, p. 310). This odd stipulation was only understood when the Code of Hammurabi was discovered, for that code required that the owner's child be punished if another child were injured. Hammurabi's Code is dated about 400 years before the usually accepted date of the laws in Exodus.

Social Legislation.   Exploitation of hired labor was prohibited, humane treatment of slaves was required, cruelty to animals was forbidden, noncitizens had the same civil rights as citizens, welfare aid was a person's right, and one could not be forced to testify against oneself for a capital crime.

If all this is so, then what accounts for the oppressive reputation many religions have? The knowledgeable person who holds a humanistic orientation might well be skeptical of these assertions as characterizing religion as he or she knows it, since careful selection of material from the Bible can justify nearly any position. Two points can be made. Like most important human activities, religion is variegated and complex. First, compared with most of the religions they replaced, Judaism and Christianity represented a real advance in humaneness. Second, there *is* harsh and restrictive law in the Bible. The slave laws ameliorated the lot of many slaves, but although the owner's killing of a slave on the spot was punishable, if the slave lived for a day or two after being beaten, the owner was not to be punished. Permanent injury to a slave meant the slave should be freed, but corporal punishment for discipline was assumed to be restrained by financial interests. Flogging, limited to 40 lashes, was a non-capital means of punishment. As recently as the end of the eighteenth century, British sailors could be "flogged 'round the fleet" and receive 500 lashes, which, if not fatal, left the sailor crippled for life. Forms of execution permitted in the Bible were not pleasant, but they were not designed to maximize agony as were disembowelment, impalement, or crucifixion. However, working on the Sabbath, speaking harshly to one's parents, and adultery were capital crimes, so one must understand these laws in the context of the practices of surrounding societies. Thus, one may conclude that the concern for human rights had its origins in these ancient writings, but the standards and specific issues differed considerably from ours.

The Liberal Political Outlook and Religion

The value of separation of church and state is widely but by no means unanimously accepted in this country; this has, however, a long and often bloody history. It is hard to imagine life when political and religious structures were essentially indistinguishable, yet the roots of modern Western religions were the political/social "glue" of past societies. The gods were the guarantors and enforcers of contracts and treaties and the providers of such environmental necessities as the rain and the sun, and the engineers of the fruition of field and herd. The gods gave the social order through the king, priest(ess), and army and protected the community from pests, disease, and invasion.

If the nation were invaded, the army defeated, and the land conquered, then the gods had failed. Often the conqueror's gods were incorporated into the local pantheon, but not unknown was the practice of the people destroying the shrines and images of their own gods as revenge for the gods' failures. The sickness and premature death of a person, among ancient peoples, was often a sign that a god was angry with that person, and the loss of a war was interpreted similarly. Propitiation of the gods was the usual procedure if the gods were not to be rejected for their failure. When the kingdom of Judaea finally fell to the Babylonians in 586 B.C.E., the prophets had already declared that the nation *deserved* punishment. The traditional act was to offer sacrifice, but they did something new; *they changed their behavior*. This may be understood as the effective start of public or national morality or conscience, entailing internalized responsibility. In contrast, when Sumer's political life was destroyed around 2000 B.C.E., a series of lamentations were written for the goddess of the cities, in which she complained of her lack of support and the unfairness of the great gods An and Enlil, who had caused this destruction without cause (Kramer 1983). Private morality was surely extant much earlier and not the invention of the Jews of that time.

Although not generally recognized, the concept of a constitutional monarchy is advanced by the circumstances of both Saul's and David's elevation to king. A lottery was involved in Saul's selection (presumably to signify God's choice), but he was both anointed (anointment is still used in coronations) by Samuel (1 Sam. 10:1)[3] and acclaimed by the people (1 Sam. 10:24). The constitutional quality of the monarchy may have been rudimentary by modern standards, but it is revealed in the account of Samuel telling the people of the nature of the kingdom and writing it in a book (1 Sam. 10:25), which has not survived. Similarly, when David became king (2 Sam. 5:3), he entered into an agreement with the political leaders (elders) of Israel. The constitution referred to consisted partly of the agreement between the leader and his followers and partly of the king's continuing to hold office based on his good behavior. He should act in conformity with the law in the first five books of the Old Testament (the *Torah*), for a king who violated this law would incur God's displeasure and be punished. These are the rudiments of the concept of a ruler subject to external, ethical restraints. Neither the written "constitution" set down by Samuel, nor the covenant between David and the elders, has been recovered in written form, but it is well to remember that the Magna Carta only survived because it was necessary to re-issue it on several occasions. Perhaps at other times, similar forms of government developed, but no record was left. A constitutional monarchy was not typical of Middle Eastern governments; absolute, and often cruel, despotism was the general rule, and retention of the biting criticism of kingship in general (1 Sam. 8:11–18) is startling in the political context of its time.

Of course this was not the only time and place a checks-and-balance form of government obtained. The two-consul system of the ancient Roman Republic (Muller 1961) and the Greek city-states with their dominant assemblies represented attempts to govern other than through a tyrant or god-king. The transmission and study of the Bible ensured the survival of these concepts and may have contributed to the slow development of a public conscience (commonly lacking in imperial Rome), separation of church and state (king and high priest were not supposed to be the same person in Israel), and a form of constitutional monarchy. The

[3]References to the Bible are given for those who wish to review them in detail. The usual style will be followed, giving the name of the book, the chapter, and the verse. In this case, it is the first book of Samuel, chapter 10, verse 1. Biblical abbreviations are listed in the Appendix.

pattern of the Supreme Court, involving a panel of judges with a majority and a minority opinion, may have been influenced by the Sanhedrin, still visible in the Talmud,[4] which recorded both majority and minority opinions.

This discussion is aimed at providing alternative ways to understand certain roots of modern Western religions, transposed into terms compatible with the world-views and interests of many nonreligious psychotherapists. The purpose here is twofold. First, it is useful to grasp some of the nonreligious functions religions have served in the course of societal development. Second, it is difficult to take seriously a matter one is misinformed about or has no respect for. For the therapist without a religious affiliation, lack of respect is a handicap if one is to enter the experiential world of the patient. Respect, here, does not mean that religion is off-limits for scrutiny in the therapeutic process. On the contrary, the purpose is to make that inquiry astute, incisive, and useful.

The Discrepancy between Concept and Application

The scientifically, humanistically, or liberally oriented therapist might well now ask, "If monotheism implies determinism, how do you explain Creation science?" or "If religion is concerned about people, how can you explain the attempts of specific churches to intrude their own values into secular life?" In other words, there is a disparity between what has been said here about the origins, functions, and principles of various religions and how religion is put into practice.

This inconsistency between concept and application, or precept and behavior, is readily observed and has several aspects. One aspect is analogous to the gap between some scientific theory and its application in a laboratory by a nonscientist. For example, the mathematical theory of networks was developed in the last century by the Russian mathematician Markov. This theory has direct applications to electronics, and electrical engineers often think that these mathematics were developed expressly to solve circuit problems. Instead, this is an unexpected benefit of pure mathematics, and the origin of the theory that dictates circuit measurements and required circuit values is not likely to be known by the engineer.

[4]The Talmud is a collection of legal decisions, stories, history, and other material. It dates back more than 2,300 years and was finally edited and closed about 500 C.E. Its primary purpose was to record the then current interpretations of the original law in the *Torah*.

Analogously, when a Jew recites a prayer called Kaddish on the anniversary of the death of a parent, there may be no awareness that this represents an ancient custom whereby this yearly memorial was observed by spending the day in public study. This was a sign that the parents had provided the son with a good education and the Kaddish prayer was the conclusion of such study. This is why the Kaddish makes no mention of death, since it was not originally connected with death rituals. Similarly, in the Roman Catholic mass (pre-Vatican II), the elevation of the Host when the priest faced the altar was similar to ancient sacrificial rituals in the Temple in Jerusalem. Although many Catholics will be aware of the sacrificial symbolism regarding Christ, few will be aware of the derivation from ancient Israelite worship.

These examples typify the simplest discontinuity between concept and application, but they are not the only ones. A second discontinuity arises from distortions or variations introduced by personal needs. This gap is not specific to religious issues in therapy, but rather is generally seen as a conflict between behavior or impulse, and ego-ideal. A simple example would be when a person is unable to protect himself or herself in the face of aggression. A woman may endure considerable abuse from her husband and explain this endurance as based on the injunction to "love your neighbor" (Lev. 19, Matt. 5) or "submit to your husband" (Eph. 5). Exploration in therapy often reveals that the patient had an abusive parent and that therapeutic work on these experiences is regularly accompanied by a decline in the acceptance of abuse and increased resistance to it. The therapist, however, may be misled when there is a more complex interaction between religious and therapeutic factors.

A third discontinuity can be seen when the development of an individual denomination is at variance with the overall normative trend in Christianity or Judaism, or when the Bible is used idiosyncratically. Judaism is based on a written collection of canonical literature (the Old Testament),[5] although the Talmud and later sources have canonical or near-canonical status for many Jewish communities. For some Christian churches, the New Testament is historically later than the canonical revelation contained in the death and resurrection of Jesus; for others, the New Testament is taken as canon. Some Pentecostal churches are "unitarian" in the sense that Jesus is regarded as God and the Trinity is largely disregarded, although this is not a normative Christian tradition. Some Christian denominations have additional writings of near-biblical

---

[5] Jews regard what is often called the Old Testament as their Bible, although they recognize that Christianity has additional authoritative Scripture.

status. In modern usage, however, a core question is what does the canonical literature say and how can it be applied.

In Genesis, it is stated that the earth was created in six days, Adam and Eve were the first man and woman, they sinned, and were punished by expulsion from the Garden of Eden. How may this be viewed? It can be:

1. An allegorical tale of the lost bliss of early infancy
2. An early attempt to develop a cosmology
3. A justification for the subordinate place of women as an outcome of the victory of a patriarchal religion over a matriarchal one
4. A description of man's relation to agricultural work, his wife, and God
5. A literal description of the events of Creation and the fate of Adam and Eve and their descendents

None of these alternatives (and there are others) are likely to be of more than passing interest unless they have modern relevance and application. When this part of Genesis is taken literally, and understood in a religious framework as both a description of actual events and as an exemplar of the basically sinful nature of human beings (i.e., original sin) (Rom. 5:12), then there are considerable implications for perceptions of the nature of humanity.

Other positions beside the literal may be held on Genesis. Jews, along with many Christians, will likely regard Genesis as an allegory, and take the position that "God speaks in the language of men." Rather than emphasizing original sin, which is a central Christian concept, Jews talk of the "evil impulse" (Gen. 8:21) or *yetzer hara*.[6] These two concepts lead to somewhat differing perspectives on the nature of humanity, theological issues, and how one deals with problems in human behavior in the context of a religious community. Neither the "evil impulse" nor "original sin" positions absolve the person of responsibility, but the former is less likely to see the person as inherently bad. These two views lead to somewhat divergent approaches to guilt, responsibility, and behavioral control, which flower in subtly different ways in patients whose origins are in one or the other community.

Finally, it is difficult to maintain a serious, inquiring attitude on religion while war, rebellion, terrorism, and oppression continues in the name of religion. There are two replies to this. First, as therapists we do not have to like, agree with, or approve the values of our patients in order to try to help them, nor is a direct attack on values helpful. Such an attack

[6]Transliteration of Hebrew follows the accepted practice.

does not seem to differ from efforts at religious conversion. If the therapist's aversion to a patient's values is too strong, the patient should be referred elsewhere. Second, the differences between Judaism and Christianity, and the differences among Christian denominations, are matters over which much blood has been shed, but *these differences are basically minor* when one's frame of reference includes those religions contemporaneous with early Judaism and Christianity. Many of these religions practiced child or adult human sacrifice, ritual sexuality with people and/or animals dedicated to the religion, fertility rites of a most explicitly symbolic nature, consumption of flesh cut from still living animals, worship of animal or insect images, and celebration of fratricidal, patricidal, adulterous, or incestuous relations within the Pantheon. The differences among modern religions are not primarily attributable to religion, but rather represent a much broader human propensity. On one level, Freud (1930) referred to the narcissism of minor differences. On another level, the diversity of religious forms permits one to choose the cosmology best suited to the way one has resolved and organized one's life.

The discrepancies discussed here, plus others that may come to mind, have been used as grounds to dismiss religion as a topic for serious consideration or as reasons why one cannot do anything with religious issues in therapy. The position taken here is the reverse: these and other gaps or contradictions offer therapeutic leverage for the exploration and resolution of problems in living expressed in a religious idiom. Cognitive dissonance produces discomfort and anxiety, and anxiety can be used to expose and resolve conflict in therapy.

Religion for the Anti-affiliated and Formerly Affiliated Therapist

The task for the nonaffiliated therapist vis-á-vis religion is by no means simple or easy, since the therapist is dealing with value-systems that differ significantly from his or her sources and modes of expression, even if the values themselves are not so different. For the therapist who at one time had a religious affiliation, and now no longer has one, the problems posed by religion encountered in therapy are even more challenging. Here the therapist has to return to scenes that are at least partly familiar. Pulls occur if the feelings are not walled off or well worked through via personal therapy or searching self-scrutiny. Guilt over desertion, apostasy, or heresy are often experienced. There may be anger toward former beliefs and practices and toward those who hold those beliefs and practices. In addition to the problems caused by conflicting emotional pulls in the therapist, many adults who received some religious education in childhood now view religion as childish, and for good reason. Much religious education stops at about age 13 to 14. This is just about the time Piaget's Stage of Formal Operations is being entered, when the young adolescent is beginning to acquire the capacity for abstract thinking. What remains is a view of religion as childish because the instruction received was designed for children. Also, a goodly amount of religious instruction slides over serious intellectual and moral challenges, leaving the person to discover them later, and this may add to a residue of bitter feelings over having been deceived.

Certain parts of the Bible are quite difficult to grasp because of difficulties in translation and problems in understanding ancient cultures. Sections of the Old Testament are regarded by some as quite unsuited to children. The Song of Songs appears to be erotic wedding poetry; David and Bathsheba committed adultery, and David then arranged to murder her husband to conceal her pregnancy; Lot offered his daughters to be raped by a mob in order to protect two strangers, and Lot's daughters arranged to commit incest with their father after the destruction of Sodom. Since the religions we will consider emphasize their sacred writings as a source of authority, teaching sexual and aggressive material in the Bible to children is troublesome for teachers, parents, and clergy. In part, they may have difficulty handling the children's questions, and in part, they may fear the apparently negative aspects of their religion. Thus, the residue of the child's religious instruction is seen by the adult to have glaring defects in the light of retrospective intellectual scrutiny.

Control of Behavior

Prominent in the childhood experiences of those who have rejected or relinquished a particular religious affiliation are issues related to the control of their behavior, belief, and thought. Regulation of behavior often relates to pleasure and aggression. Pleasure is a potent force in human behavior and *may* have deleterious consequences: Alcohol is associated both with cheerful times and alcoholism; food is connected both with family closeness and obesity; sex can enhance the marital bond and lead to children born outside a family system. Pleasure is a powerful force in shaping human activity, and the principles that govern behavior are perhaps only beginning to be understood. The patterns and requirements of various religions flowed out of their suppositions about human character (e.g., original sin or the evil impulse) and the interventions devised to modify behavior. One possible conclusion is that if certain behaviors lead to unwanted outcomes, then prohibiting the activity is the most direct way to deal with the problem. However, prohibition is not the only method available. Other forms of control could include making the activity available, permissible, or even required, but with built-in limits. Thus those human activities that powerfully affect other members of a society are regulated in a variety of ways; these include prohibition, ritual outlets, enhancement through association with sacred matters, and sublimation.

Aggression also affects society greatly, for it may have either destructive or constructive ends. A number of sociological, historical, and personal factors (as chronicled in the Bible) have contributed to the strong constraints against violence, many of which are transmitted to children without provision for future modification. We then have a solution (to the destructive effects of aggression) causing its own problems (overinhibition).

This perspective is not available to the person who, in childhood, receives a body of rules, requirements, and prohibitions. These rules are said to come from God and are reinforced by teachers and parents who threaten dreadful consequences if they are violated. Oddly enough, similar values obtain in an essentially secular context, even when they are expressed quite differently. The point here is that the main tenets of religions represent adaptive efforts to structure and facilitate human society. The impact and eventual outcome on the young child is mediated by the skill and insight of the adults who convey these rules. However distorted or damaging overcontrolling forms of training have been to individual people, when properly structured, they *do* work (often for those not our patients) and they *are* aimed at important purposes.

Control of Belief

Closely related to the regulation of behavior is the governance of belief. Belief as "assent to or acceptance of a proposition, statement, or fact, as true" (Onions 1955, p. 165) is often closely linked to a faith that is defined as "confidence, reliance, trust" (p. 670). An important difference between belief and faith appears to be more of an intellectual content in belief and an attitudinal component to faith. Belief and faith are so commonly linked with contemporary religions as to be ubiquitous. The source for the emphasis on belief in Christianity seems to be expressed in a famous line from Acts (16:31), which, in the King James version, states "believe on the Lord Jesus Christ, and thou shalt be saved. . . ." *Belief* or *faith* in anything like their modern sense do not appear in the oldest part of the Old Testament, but there are signs of them somewhat later, as in Psalms 10 and 14. Perhaps assuming that one's internal state would alter behavior, the early Christians went beyond the concerns of the Jews of that day about specific behaviors and devoted considerable attention to belief, faith, and attitude. This emphasis carried forward to the present day and is particularly acute when modern religions are seriously challenged by such alternative systems as science and politics. Those who once had and eventually rejected their religious attachment often report that the demand for belief in doctrines was especially intrusive, and they may retain considerable anger and resentment.

Although the consequences of undesirable social behavior may provide a rationale for a community's efforts at regulation through religion, what can be said of the more personally intrusive experience regarding control of belief? The answer may lie partly in the nature of the historical development of early Christianity out of its Jewish (and Greek) matrix. Judaism of that time, although now commonly understood as a religion, might better be seen for our purposes as a folk-culture. Prayer and religious observance in the modern sense were only a small part of life in which everything was recruited into what we would call religion: agricultural practices from plowing to ecology; personal hygiene; child-rearing; commercial transactions; communal association; type, composition, and construction of clothing; drinking; eating; education; labor regulations; law and justice; sanitation; sexuality; social welfare (charity); warfare; and so on, in great detail. As a culture, Judaism was relatively successful in its regulatory mechanisms because the community was highly self-contained even when dispersed around the Mediterranean.

Paul deleted the detailed behavioral requirements of Judaism when he conveyed the Christian message to his pagan contemporaries. His emphasis on the spirit over the law connected with then current Greek concepts and gave Christianity a wider appeal. Since Christianity relinquished the detailed Jewish behavioral system to a major degree, it is proposed here that the belief system that evolved also operated as a form of community "glue," and faith integrated an increasingly mobile Christianity. Spreading rapidly as it did through its missionary effort across many cultures, Christianity did not rely on inculcating a detailed behavioral code, perhaps because of the time needed to learn it. Belief and faith became the functional equivalents of the Jewish prescriptive pattern of conduct, and both operated to perpetuate social cohesion. Although Christianity tended to stress belief more than behavior, Judaism's reversed accent was a matter of emphasis, not a dichotomy. The conflicts between orthodoxy and heresy may be seen as historical derivatives of Christianity's rise and mode of propagation. These behaviors and beliefs and their means of instruction were not invented to bedevil children, even if some teachers have been poorly equipped to transmit them. They promoted cultural survival.

Truth and Validity

Belief hinges on the question of truth. This is a very troublesome question, since the claims of Christianity seem to pivot on the truth of certain key events. This is also true, to a much lesser extent, for Judaism. For Christianity the central event is usually the death and resurrection of Jesus, although several denominations include additional historical events. For Judaism, the primary historical occurrences are the exodus from Egypt and the revelation at Sinai, but because belief is not really an issue, their historicity is less important. For some, the historical truth of these events is essentially undisputed and is the cornerstone of their religion. Others regard these accounts as little more than fairy tales exploited by Cecil B. DeMille and his Technicolor cameras. What follows is a useful way to regard issues of belief in the patient.

The likelihood that incontrovertible historical evidence will be found that Moses stood on Sinai and received the Ten Commandments from God and chiseled them on two stone tablets seems vanishingly small, although as Wouk (1960) noted, *the historical effect is the same as if he did.* Proof that a Jew named Yeshua was crucified some 1,950 years ago seems equally unlikely to be forthcoming, and clear evidence that having died or having been taken for dead, he returned to life seems even more unlikely to be found (essentially because of the privacy of the latter event). The question of whether these accounts are true or not is fruitless to pursue because they have the most minute possibility of being proven. Even if they were proven, this would likely have little effect on those who do not now believe in them, since belief is largely independent of proof. If the probability of proving these root experiences (Fackenheim 1970) is minute, the probability of disproving them is even more so, so whether these events are true or not may well be irrelevant.

There *are* questions that can be addressed even if they are not the usual ones on truth. Is this or that way a *valid* (not the *true*) way to live? Does a particular pattern of living have specifiable effects, does it promote or get in the way of certain goals, does it promote group or individual survival? These are questions that, although lacking the grandeur, finality, sweep, and ultimateness of inquiries about truth, are nevertheless theoretically answerable if the thought, effort, and skill necessary to find the answers are mobilized. With this redefinition in mind, it is proposed that religions can provide valid patterns of life that are desired by large numbers of people. However these models can also cause problems and difficulties in the life of an individual or the survival of a group. Thus, if a patient's life has a religious configuration, this is one of several modes of adaptation (such as choice of vocation or spouse) that provide meaning and coherence. In therapy, a patient's insistence on the historical truth of the biblical accounts may symbolize other issues. The therapeutic inquiry is normally directed toward whether the patient's way of life strikes a reasonable balance between competing motives.

Truth and Miracles

Miracles present a somewhat different problem. Not all miracles are of the same order, since some are clearly natural phenomena. The description (Exod. 14) of the crossing of the Red Sea (actually the Sea of Reeds, a place of relatively low water) is clear enough. A strong wind blowing over shallow water can substantially alter water levels. Some miracles do not appear to be natural phenomena, but are nevertheless. The burning bush involved a native plant with a volatile sap of so low a vapor point that on hot days it could ignite without destroying the plant. A more general question is What do we mean by miracles? Most often a miracle is taken to mean some supernatural interference with the general order of nature. But did it mean that to a people whose concept of nature was very different from ours and whose understanding of the functioning of the world was very much less buttressed by scientific method and data? The natural–supernatural dichotomy seems not to be a useful aid to understanding, but it is not parsimonious to dismiss biblical accounts of miracles because they do not fit within a natural science framework. The usual juxtaposition of myth versus reality is misleading. Myths are symbolic representations of real experiences, historical events, or aspects of the social structure. They are often problematic because they are commonly depicted as actual occurrences, but without the symbolic quality being made explicit. Thus, beliefs and practices, which often have a mythic substrate, have significant meanings in the lives of patients and the intent here is to find ways to regard, comprehend, and respond to these meanings. As therapists, we are accustomed to deal with myths on a regular basis, only we call them fantasies, transferences, screen memories, or the like. Further, we understand that these "myths" have important dynamic purposes in the life and adaptation of the patient. Without making the analogy too precise, myths may be seen as having similar functions for societies.

Eliade (1959) and Douglas (1966, 1970) discussed a variety of myths in various primitive societies and showed how they expressed facets of a culture's internal structure and relations with other societies and the physical environment symbolically. Douglas (1970) held that the human body was a metaphor for a community and vice versa. If the experience of social reality involved a weak structure or lack of control in the society or of forces in the environment, then the form of religious expression would favor less control, such as speaking in tongues (glossolalia). A highly structured society, or one under external stress, would have a religion favoring strong self-control. Although Douglas did not make the point, it seems reasonable to expect myths to be consistent with ongoing rituals and a society's view of its world.

The Failed Answer

The education provided to children and the answers given to their questions about the world, life, people, God, sex, marriage, good, and bad may become inadequate and be replaced by other answers as the person matures. McFadden (1969, p. 495) noted "a man may become an unbeliever because belief failed him, psychologically." In this vein, many years ago, a friend described his conversion to being a devout atheist. As a youngster he was raised as a Christian Scientist and believed that God loved everyone, that the world was good, and that right behavior was rewarded. Drafted late in World War II, he was sent to Burma and when his plane landed, he had to "hit the dirt" because Japanese soldiers in the jungle at the edge of the airstrip were shooting at him. Shocked that someone would want to kill him when he was full of love and goodwill toward humanity, he re-evaluated his life and his attitude changed dramatically. Undoubtedly other dynamic forces were at work, but the world-view he had been raised on and believed in had failed, and his life was shockingly and unexpectedly at risk. The teachings of his childhood had not undergone the needed gradual updating and expansion and their collapse was immediate and total.

A similar dramatic turnabout was reported by Ellis (1974) who discovered at age 12 that the earth was formed millions of years ago hence

"I immediately surrendered my belief in Old Testament cosmology and became an atheist" (p. 197). Maimonides gave a generally acceptable reconciliation (*c.* 1190) between the science of his day and Jewish cosmology, so these kinds of changes arise from other motives and thoughts, which are then expressed through dramatic alterations.

Answers also fail because of the obvious failures of the teacher, with the outcome being that the solution is no longer valid for the person. One patient, seduced by her pastor, had a residue of distrust along with a yearning for a good, unselfish relationship. In another instance, it was observed that a child was being taught a Lutheran catechism with the father's belt for an incentive. He was beaten when he could not remember to answer the question "What is God?" with "God is Love."

When the demand for acceptance or belief does not coincide with available data, the inability to find an acceptable rationale often invalidates the explanatory system. Not untypical is the experience of the eight-year-old described earlier who questioned the story of Cain's marriage after Abel's murder. Her mother's reply of "Just accept it" disrupted this precocious girl's independent study of the Bible.

An activity that has not been made comprehensible or that elicits inconsistent messages about its value leads to a fourth type of breakdown of an explanatory system. A Latin mass or a synagogue service in Hebrew will likely have little meaning to most children unless the origins and meanings of the elements of the service are explained simply. If the child is sent to the synagogue or church on Saturday or Sunday, while the parents sleep in, the message to the child is clear. But if the parents accompany the child and willingly participate, this facilitates the child's identification with the parents' values and behaviors. If the meaning of the service is also explained, the child is better able to apprehend and participate in the activity. Parents and teachers may have difficulty explaining the service because they themselves do not clearly grasp enough of its symbolism. One colleague described his son's First Communion. As the boy approached the altar railing, the priest was announcing the cup contained the blood of Jesus. The youngster looked distressed and needed much encouragement to essay a sip. Clearly, the service had not been adequately explained beforehand. Children can ask embarrassing questions that require a considerable degree of aplomb to answer. Further, doubt is ubiquitous, and some of the aversive reactions children have may have been fueled by adult discomfort with their own unresolved doubts.

One assumption that underlies the characteristically empirical American approach is that if something does not work, it must be wrong or untrue. When we consider the possible variations in societies that appear to function for a major proportion of its members, it is an overgeneralization to assume that the failure of a culture for an individual indicates that the society's answers are wrong, unless one has applied the rigorous and infallible test of one's own personal prejudices. Explanations fail for some people and essentially similar explanations succeed for others. Therapists who have decided that their religious upbringing ceased to provide what was needed have made an indisputable personal decision, but this individual determination does not illuminate the question of the general validity or invalidity of that cultural solution. Thus patients need not be "cured" of the presence or absence of religion. The therapist faces the more difficult task of helping the patient discover what is or is not personally valid. The therapist examines religion in the life of the patient as if it were any other aspect of the person's functioning, and its meanings and operations are collaboratively unraveled in the course of therapy. Since meanings are often conveyed to the patient through interpretation, the therapist should engage in careful self-scrutiny and self-discipline.

Finally, the general tenor of the above discussion may sound as though it parallels Gibbon's (1776/1946, p. 22) elegant remark that, in Rome, all religions "were considered by the people as equally true; by the philosophers as equally false; and by the magistrate as equally useful." Rather, it is suggested that different religious orientations are valid ways to structure lives, but any decision as to whether one is more valid than another might well have to wait for more solid data. That different religions have different effects is fairly certain; what these are is a good deal less certain.

The Joy of Skepticism

No book with the above title is likely to be written to join Schutz's *Joy*, Rombauer and Becker's *Joy of Cooking*, or Comfort's *Joy of Sex*. Nevertheless, some degree of pleasure is associated with skepticism. The young child grows up in an environment largely controlled by powerful adults. As the child's own powers grow, annoyance or anger with the parents becomes somewhat less risky as the child's need for parental approval lessens. Still, the child may prefer safer ways to irritate the parents, if they are available. Religions contain contradictions more obvious to children than do politics or history, particularly in contrast to parental behavior. Skepticism, doubt, and challenge become ways for the child to "needle" the parents with less risk than open defiance. My older son, a somewhat reluctant attendee of the synagogue instructional program, was learning about the dietary laws and kosher slaughtering. He challenged us on our sincerity, since we did not use kosher meat. Although there was no real supply of kosher meat nearer than 150 miles, we nevertheless undertook semiannual trips to purchase kosher meat.

If religion is important to the parents and belief is emphasized, then skepticism or doubt can be a significant weapon. Vulnerable to this mode of attack and perhaps sensitive to their own uncertainties, parents or teachers may react with suppressive answers, such as "It's a sin not to believe." The adult therapist who rejected this demand may look back with anger and a sense of betrayal. This can then become injected into the therapist's appraisal of the role of religion in the life of the patient.

Doubt or skepticism are survival traits, since accepting, without testing, whatever one is told is to be vulnerable to exploitation. The normative religious position on the issue of belief is largely confined to specific doctrinal matters not open to empirical tests. Notwithstanding, most religious denominations make a significant effort to present at least part of their doctrinal position logically. The recent discovery of evidence in support of the "big bang" hypothesis was welcomed in some religious circles. The "big bang" was consonant with the biblical account of creation and it also cast doubt on the "steady state" hypothesis, which clearly was not. Nevertheless, the demand for belief may be generalized far beyond specific doctrine and invade other areas, or it may lead to an overly critical stance wherein proof is required before the person will accept anything. McFadden (1969, p. 495) described such people as those who "will believe anything so long as it is not in the Bible." Inquiry into overly credulous or overly skeptical attitudes may open up important personal dynamics.

Acceptance in psychotherapy is sometimes misunderstood, with the therapist believing the patient's recital rather than the therapist receiving or accepting the communication as representing some aspect of the patient's experience. Therapeutic skepticism is most appropriate as is exemplified in Sullivan's (1954) statement, "the psychiatrist, the interviewer plays an active role in introducing interrogations, not to show that he is smart or that he is skeptical, but literally to make sure he knows what he is being told" (p. 21).

The Freedom of Inquiry

For those with one of the three orientations (scientific, humanist, politically liberal), the right to follow one's interests and curiosity in inquiry, research, or study is "sacred." Many without one of these specific orientations would also agree. A villain in all this is clearly identifiable as the "Church" and such an attribution has historical warrant. Giordano Bruno was burnt at the stake as a heretic by the Inquisition; Galileo was forced to recant his teachings of Copernican thought (as modified by his own discoveries); and Darwin was subjected to a veritable storm of abuse for his *On the Origin of Species*. In this country, the trial of John T. Scopes in 1925 in Tennessee and current disputes over the teaching of the theory of evolution attest to the continuation of efforts to set limits on the freedom of human thought and inquiry.

There are some remarkable ironies in all this. The collision between the Roman Catholic Church and Bruno and Galileo was based on the Church's incorporation of Aristotelian physics and astronomy into monastic teaching and eventually into Church dogma (Bixby 1964). There was no need for the Church to do this, since Aristotle was irrelevant to the Church's concerns. Galileo, the hero of freedom of inquiry, was actually a loyal Roman Catholic who was attempting to move his Church forward (de Santillana 1955). Furthermore, Galileo was close to Pope Urban VIII and many members of the Italian political and religious establishment, which would have been impossible had he been a real outcast or heretic. But a still further irony about evolution is that the fossil record mostly parallels the sequence of creation laid out in Genesis, although the time scales are different.

If this were all, no further comment would be needed, comforted as we would be by the clear distinction between the "good guys" and the "bad guys," but in the words of Pogo, "We have met the enemy and they is us." The wish to suppress unpleasant information no doubt antedates the custom of beheading messengers who brought bad news, but the reaction is enduringly human. As therapists, we recognize this reaction in our patients (and ourselves) as a defense. The esteemed freedom of inquiry is not necessarily an unalloyed benefit and prudent questions can indeed be asked. The recent start on gene splicing provoked a major debate over recombinant DNA, and safeguards were instituted. There was speculation that exploding the first atomic device might start a chain reaction in the earth's oceans. A therapist is understandably cautious in exploring material with a patient in whom a psychotic decompensation might be possible. The point to be made is that the fear of free inquiry is widespread and attributing a monopoly on this to religion is an error. That specific denominations have been, and are, active in attempting to suppress threatening views is well known. What is less well known is that some churches have learned from these encounters and now recognize "the harmony that exists between scientific truth and revealed truth" (Pope John Paul II 1980, p. 1166).

The fear of free inquiry exists in other domains, too. To what degree do we evade or brush aside children's inquiries because they touch upon uncomfortable or sensitive areas or just areas we, as adults, are ignorant of? To what extent are therapists withholding in self-disclosure to patients to maximize the evocation of fantasy and to what extent is it personal discomfort? Discouragement of certain types of inquiry by various denominations protects what is perceived as important. This is really not different from the patient's defensive strategies, although the social consequences may be considerable.

THE RELIGIOUS THERAPIST

Counseling by clergy is an ancient function (Adams 1970; Jackson 1975; Wise 1980), but it is only in this century that therapeutic aid has been provided through systematic techniques set into coherent theoretical structures, and these have been secularly based. The interest evinced by pastors in psychotherapy led to the rise of pastoral counseling as a definable field with literature, training programs, and accrediting bodies (Moss 1977). Secular training institutions are also beginning to see students who are devout, and many of these students declare their intent to combine their therapeutic training with their religious investment. This linkage between religion and psychotherapy is not new; rather the separation is a modern Western development (Feifel 1958), and it has been remarked that a significant proportion of psychologists and psychiatrists have close relatives in the clergy (Feifel 1958; Lowe 1976). Curiously, in empirical studies, most clinical psychologists, social workers, and psychiatrists have no significant religious affiliation (Henry, Sims, and Spray 1971; Ragan, Malony, and Beit-Hallahmi 1980). It thus appears that only a distinct minority of secularly trained professionals with a strong religious orientation would like to combine their training and their personal religiousness. Therapists (and students) with an overt religious orientation meet a number of problems not encountered by their nonreligious colleagues. An open expression of religiousness is likely to be characterized as peculiar, if not actually neurotic (Gartner 1982; Sollod 1978). The discomfort I have observed among both faculty and students regarding overtly religious clinical psychology students supports this. Modern personality theories conflict with traditional Christian doctrine regarding "obedience, humility, and self-sacrifice" (Vitz 1978, p. 4). Although such collisions could test the assumptions behind both scientific and Christian theories of personality, a mutual exchange of hostile or snide comments is more likely (Bergin 1980a,b; Ellis 1980; Walls 1980). One patient who had a religious vocation left the order and entered graduate school. In therapy, the patient angrily reported a former professor's remark that equated the cloistered religious life with neuroticism. Even though this life had been relinquished, the patient was not willing to disparage this experience or to agree to so simple an equation.

Student therapists who are religious are often perceived by faculty as being less likely to suspend personal judgments, and personal experience with a few students has tended to support this perception. Williams and Kremer's (1974) work, however, suggested the opposite. They studied 90 secular and 58 pastoral counseling students prior to their practicum experience. Testing for degree of Christian belief, dogmatism, and counselor attitudes, they found that the pastoral counseling students were much more religious and somewhat more dogmatic on Form E of the Dogmatism scale than were the secular students. On a test of counselor attitudes, which is a series of client statements with multiple choice responses, the pastoral counseling students were less likely to choose evaluative or interpretive statements and more likely to choose statements indicating understanding.

These differences are unexpected and, post hoc, might be explained as follows. The students in the Williams and Kremer study were already in seminary training and were, although deeply religious, also professionals in training. This may have firmed up those parts of their identities that would otherwise be more vulnerable in the religious student in a secular training institution. Both religious and nonreligious students usually have to work through their judgmental attitudes, so the differences are not dichotomous. For the overtly religious student, the quality of supervision and the student's work can be seriously affected if the supervisor's feedback is tinged with disdain for religion. Dealing with the effects of the student's religious training requires tact and a basic attitude of goodwill, especially if the student and supervisor have differing attitudes. One student had no access to his feelings or reactions to interviewees or test subjects during his first year of training. This blocking seemed partly the result of an intense Catholic upbringing. Conferences did not help this man penetrate his own internal blocks, so at one meeting, I asked him about the nature of his seminary training. Since he had never mentioned this, he was startled that I could know (it was only a guess). He accepted my assurance that I did not read minds, but that I was more open to certain subtle aspects of his functioning that led me to hypothesize his background. The conference seemed to help convince him that feelings could be important. Further conferences, supervision, and work on his part were accompanied by increasing openness to and use of his more available emotional reactions. By the end of two years of training, his basic religious orientation was intact, but he was able to discern how his friends used their religion to deal with problems he had found more effective ways to deal with.

The "Unconverted" Therapist

Psychodynamically, conversion refers to a defense mechanism. From a religious point of view, most simply it means a change of mind. Meehl et al. (1958) noted that "the man who becomes a Christian does not acquire a faith, but changes one faith for another faith" (p. 28). Conversion will be used here in its religious senses. In current conservative usage, even though one has been raised as a Christian and regards oneself as seriously Christian, such a person is unconverted until Jesus has been accepted as one's personal savior (Adams 1970). This is specifically within a Christian tradition in which the internal quality of the experience is paramount, but not all Christian denominations apply Adams' standard and many churches will accept members without requiring signs of conversion in this fashion.

Conversion in Judaism has a rather different quality. The internal quality of the experience is deemed very important, but it is not usually inquired into directly. Rather, what is determined is that the person has converted freely and without hope of personal gain and that the person knows and understands some minimum amount of Jewish concepts and ritual. The topic of cultural differences among religious groups will be discussed in detail in Chapter 5.

The term "unconverted" is used here in a conservative Christian sense to denote a person who grew up with a religious orientation that has continued at approximately the same level of intensity into adulthood. Temporary flirtations with other positions would not exclude someone from this category, nor does the term unconverted connote a lack of seriousness or sincerity. The question of whether one can be a Christian without being converted (Adams 1970) is a matter of theological debate outside the scope of this book. If one were born and raised a Roman Catholic and became Episcopalian, such a person would be regarded as having maintained approximately the same orientation, in spite of denominational differences. Someone who grew up as a Southern Baptist and became a Unitarian, or vice versa, has made a major move; such persons will be considered below.

A therapist grounded in a particular religious orientation that was maintained from childhood will likely be more at ease with that stance than will someone who has moved from one position to a significantly different one. The intensity with which the denominational affiliation is held, as well as the nature of the original religious training, will affect the salience of the therapist's religious feeling as it relates to other facets of his or her life. A strong Baptist background will have a more likely impact on attitudes and behaviors than will a similar degree of Methodism. Further, some religions emphasize more active missionary efforts than do others. Even if the therapist is not impelled to present personal faith convictions to a patient, a therapist whose background emphasized missionary work may feel more impelled toward (or away from) therapeutic intervention than one whose background was less activist. Again, religious identification has important implications for the character, direction, and integration of the therapist's life. Beit-Hallahmi (1979) suggested that it is a major aspect of identity for many and serves as a support system for the ego, a control function for the superego, and a structure for interpersonal relations. As a support system for the ego, Beit-Hallahmi saw religion as aiding adaptive efforts to deal with the world. The control function strengthens the superego's impact on the ego in the regulation of impulses, while the defining process provides appropriate behavioral patterns, distinguishes between permissible and impermissible relations, and offers solutions for interpersonal problems. Beit-Hallahmi did not see psychotherapy as having a basically different message from most religions. Rather, psychotherapy proffered another, more flexible set of regulatory mechanisms and behavior patterns, but not ones that basically differed from the core of most religiously based configurations. These support, control, and defining functions are important, and if the therapist has to rely on religion to provide these structures because of deficits in other systems, then religious issues will acquire increased salience in the therapist's life. One consequence is that such a therapist will probably have greater difficulty in separating personal values from those of the patient in the intensity and intimacy of psychotherapy.

The "Converted" Therapist

Here conversion is simply a significant change from little or no religious affiliation or from the religion of childhood to a strong, different faith position and includes, but is not limited to, being "born again." Although one could argue the matter, it seems confusing to include people who have changed to being an agnostic, an atheist, or even a devout atheist.

The obvious differences among religions relate to their doctrines, beliefs, and practices. Less obvious are the social and cultural configurations, but the implications for personality are broad. As Hux (1979) has persuasively argued, if he were to convert to Judaism from Christianity, it would be a rearrangement of intellectual furniture, just as it would be if he changed from one Christian denomination to another. But for him to *be* Jewish would mean a cultural change on the order of an immigration, and as an adult, he would not be part of the culture because he was not raised in it as a child. Writing from a position of comfort and self-acceptance, Hux may have underestimated the degree of alteration required to move to a quite different denomination even within Christianity. A major revision in stance to the world, as in a religious conversion, requires more than a rearrangement of the intellectual furniture, since such shifts are instituted by impelling needs. Important cultural and social factors are involved, and the person has to make more strenuous efforts as an adult than as a child to acquire the characteristic patterns. Hence, religious patterns are less likely to be as thoroughly and comfortably integrated into the personality, and the person will be less secure in the new identification. More rigid, dogmatic, or enthusiastic attitudes are also probable. When a therapist has recently converted (within several years), there will be a need to "practice" the newly acquired stance and this can intrude into therapy. If the patient's religion is important and diverges substantially from the therapist's, the discussions of religion can lose a therapeutic aim and quality. But if the patient has a similar orientation, the therapist may overlook the patient's conflicts expressed in a religious idiom, or may deal with them only as religious problems and not treat them psychodynamically. Knowing the therapist's orientation, the patient may seek the therapist's collusion to insulate certain problems because of a shared denominational membership. The religious therapist discussed here may find it easier not to venture into religiously based matters when the patient's problems are straightforward dynamic conflicts than when the patient both lacks and seeks some overall way of life.

Religious Issues for the Religious Therapist

The religious therapist's specific denominational affiliation provides both a cognitive and an affective understanding of that community. Generalizations to other, rather different religions may not apply nor does such a background automatically allow the therapist to grasp various religions in a way that has therapeutic applicability. The discussion of denominational experiences and religious upbringing earlier in the chapter may help the therapist understand the experiences of certain patients.

Any social system can have more or less deleterious side effects. Pruyser (1977) cogently summarized the seamy side of religious beliefs, paying most attention to the more florid forms of pathology in religious life. He also mentioned several basic problems. Notable talent in religious expression, like ability in other areas of existence, is not so broadly distributed that a leader will not attract followers. The obscurity but great importance of religious matters facilitates the surrender of independence and the reliance on the authority and power of the leader. Pruyser saw this as neurotic, but common, although this abandonment of autonomy has the quality of a division of labor. It is not so typical among some certain religions, such as Japanese Zen, as Kopp's (1972) *If You Meet the Buddha on the Road, Kill Him* has suggested. In Western culture, reliance on authority is normative in religious life, partly because there is a set of authoritative writings, and religion has not been traditionally recognized as a process fostering personal growth. There are exceptions to this in certain aspects of the cloistered religious life. In therapy, the patient seeking instruction and guidance is an initially appealing figure. In the religious sphere, solutions exist and if the therapist yields to the temptation to offer these, then growth can be truncated.

Although religions offer support, directions for living, and consolation or reparation for loss, these qualities are also the bases for criticisms of religion. Since political ideologies, philosophies, and the display of financial success can also be so utilized, the issue is whether religion is used for regressive, infantile purposes or in the service of mature object-relations.

Responsibility or free will is a central problem for theology. If God is all-powerful and the world exists through God's intervention, then humanity is powerless and God is the source of both good and evil. But if God is also the source of evil, then one can evade responsibility. One resolution is to hold that God's omnipotence applies to everything but human responsibility. Even in the older parts of the Bible there is some recognition that a person may not always have self-control or control over events in a situation. The concept of the Devil permits an easy evasion of one's responsibility ("the Devil made me do it"). The therapist whose religious affiliation takes this position faces the problem of helping a patient to nevertheless assume the task of struggling to bring behavior within the range of ego-control and to understand the rationalizations involved.

The encouragement and support for group cohesion and individual identity offered by a religion leads to comparisons (usually favorable) between one's own denomination and the "other one." This narcissistic support for self-esteem offers a ready humor, but impedes apprehending the more profound qualities of the patient's denominational attachment. Psychotherapists who are serious about their religious commitment will have as patients people who use their religion for self-serving purposes without recognizing the high ethical, intellectual, spiritual, moral, and emotional qualities of the religion that the therapist appreciates. The therapist may be offended by the patient's exploitation of religion, but since religions are readily available for such uses, it may be more useful to scrutinize what patients *do* with a religious orientation rather than what they *should do*.

2
Ethics, Morals, and Values in Psychotherapy

The problem of values in psychotherapy is persistent, but interest and attention to values seem to occur cyclically. The underlying theme seems to be that, in the good old days, values were clear cut and well understood, but that today, values have come adrift. Concurrent with this is the marked difficulty in defining ethics, morals, and values. The surveying of the range of disagreement and confusion is an unpleasantly humbling experience when it used to seem that at least the definitions were clear.

Many psychologists who write on value issues in psychotherapy seem more or less uncomfortable. There are exceptions (Frankel 1967; Menninger 1973; Mowrer 1961), but overall, psychologists seem to have forgotten that one of the field's parents was moral philosophy. This has made it difficult for psychotherapists who have had the standard scientific training in Psychology Departments operating in the scientist-practitioner Boulder model to regard values openly and objectively. The activist orientation of many social workers yields a similar difficulty, although perhaps for somewhat different reasons. Even if values are studied in research, there seems to be a fear of their affective, motivational aspects. Perhaps one outcome has been the tendency for the same issues and questions to recur in about a 20- to 30-year cycle, although with elaborations and variations.

VALUES, PSYCHOTHERAPY, AND PARALLELS TO SOCIAL STRUCTURES

Value is the term most consistently used in the psychological literature, but definitions vary widely. Green (1946) simply equated values with standards of morality, whereas Hartmann (1960) saw moral values as a dynamic part of the personality and called them "direction-giving facts" (p. 41). Mallenbaum (1973) remarked on the complexity and confusion in definitions, whereas Peterson (1970) pointed out that values can include motives, attitudes, and customs, among many other qualities, and that the word *values* is used as an abstract or a concrete noun or as a verb, which compounds the confusion.

Values in psychotherapy were an early problem. Breuer abruptly terminated the "talking cure" with Anna O. because she developed a passionate transference to him and he dropped his discomfiting discovery with alacrity. Since modern psychotherapies have their primary methodological and conceptual roots in psychoanalysis, a brief retrospective glance may help provide a historical perspective.

Values in the Historical Development of Psychotherapy

Hysteria was a "disease" commonly confronted by neurologists as well as other physicians, and when Joseph Breuer disclosed to Freud his remarkable breakthrough in treating Anna O., Freud recognized the utility of this technique for the treatment of this disease. In essence, the patient suffered from memories no longer available to consciousness and if, through hypnosis (and later, free association), these memories and their associated affects could be recovered—presto, a quicker, more permanent cure than was available by the then current methods was obtained.

Implicit in this early formulation was the notion of skilled treatment by a physician, with results like the treatment of syphilis with Salvarsan, malaria with quinine, or heart disease with digitalis. Unfortunately it was not to be so simple. Freud soon realized that the physician was much more a part of the cure than he was for physical disorders. Further, he realized that values were inevitably implicated in psychoanalytic treatment when he commented that one would "forfeit this primary success (rapport) if one takes up from the start any standpoint other than that of understanding, such as a moralizing attitude" (1913, p. 152), or "the patient should be educated to liberate and fulfill his own nature, and not to resemble ourselves" (1919, p. 188).

Freud necessarily moved from the development of a medical technique to a treatment that involved values, such as a choice of vocation, spouse, or life-style. Rieff (1959) made this more explicit by characterizing psychoanalysis as a "science of morals" based on "the ethic of honesty" (p. 300). Honesty was essential to Freud's therapeutic method—he had set out to recover the memories of events hidden behind evasions, denials, motivated forgettings, and rationalizations. With his instruction in the "basic rule" of free association, treatment became a struggle between truth and concealment. Tolerant of ambiguity, incompleteness, and conflict (Holt 1973), Freud did not react to the patient's "dishonesty" with morality. Rather he sought to strengthen the ego, to show interest in the patient's reality, and to persist in efforts to uncover, face, and understand with the patient what was so terrifying.

Similarly, Fromm-Reichmann (1950) noted

> In early psychoanalytic literature, some authors claim that the psychiatrist should be free from any evaluational goals while dealing with his patients. To my mind, this holds true only for those personal evaluational systems of the psychiatrist which pertain to religion, philosophy, political viewpoints, and other questions of *Weltanschauung*. . . . It is not correct to say, however, that there is no inherent set of values connected with the goals of psychotherapy. (pp. 33-34)

From a Sullivanian perspective, Fromm-Reichmann saw the goals of psychotherapy as related to the patient having sufficient self-understanding and freedom from past irrational patterns to function effectively.

Rogers (1951) extended the position of insulating values from therapy when he stated

> As therapy progresses, the client comes to realize that he is trying to live by what others think. . . . But if he is to relinquish these introjected values, what is to take their place? There ensues a period of confusion and uncertainty as to values. . . . Gradually this confusion is replaced by a dawning realization that the evidence upon which he can base a value judgment is supplied by his own senses, his own experience. (pp. 149-150)

One outcome of psychoanalysis was the replacement of an unconsciously motivated repression with a conscious act of rejection, expressed in the famous dictum "where id was, there shall ego be." Similarly, Rogers saw a shift from values introjected from others to those values that were self-derived, which implied that the patient developed values freer of unintegrated prohibitions and imperatives.

Bugental (1965) applied existential thinking to the issue of values in psychotherapy when he asserted that "authenticity is the primary good or value of the existential viewpoint" (p. 32) and "neurosis consists in the denial or distortion of authenticity" (p. 41). Although his view resembled Hartmann's (1960) on authenticity, Bugental's language diverged considerably from that of more standard psychotherapeutic approaches. His discussion made it clear that although there were values in his therapeutic and conceptual course, these too were held to the minimum necessary to advance treatment.

In an applied, concrete discussion of behavioral treatment techniques, Lazarus (1971) demonstrated an acute awareness of value issues when he declared

> When expressing the virtues of personal integrity as opposed to hypo-critical modes of social intercourse, therapists will be hard pressed to justify their actions in S–R terms. The same is true when faced with moral issues involving divorce, sexual practices, business ventures and other such daily or indeed *hourly* therapeutic topics. (p. 8)

Segments from his interviews make it clear that Lazarus had values that applied to the therapeutic situation and included the therapist as being "*sensitive, gentle,* and *honest*" (p. 19).

So far, the theorists cited have tended to support the necessity or utility of some values in psychotherapy. Although Rogers (1951) eschewed values more than most, his position was value oriented in that it included nonjudgment. The main emphasis so far has been on the therapist's effort to *understand* the patient. Related to understanding is the idea of *neutrality*. Neutrality is commonly understood as not siding with one or another person in a dispute. In psychoanalytic terms, it means not favoring the ego, id, or superego (A. Freud 1946). De la Torre's (1977) extensive review of this concept made it clear that neutrality is a complex, shifting stance on the part of the analyst and does not preclude spontaneity, personal openness, activity, gratification, or other interventions on the analyst's part if aimed at the furtherance of treatment. What is precluded is "a lack of genuine commitment" (p. 367). In addition, neutrality in de la Torre's discussion is clearly both a value as a "respect for the patient's individuality" (p. 367), as well as a technique that, by withholding the analyst's reaction, brings the patient's own emotional patterns or transferences more clearly to the surface for understanding and resolution.

These proposed values were seen as instrumental to therapy. Their primary purpose is to help patients arrive at their own solutions and not have them superimposed. These *values* are also therapeutic *techniques*. Hartmann (1960) observed that some patients will adopt these therapeutic value/techniques as values with concrete behavioral outcomes in the patient's life. Although Hartmann regarded the maintenance of these value/techniques after an analysis was concluded as perhaps an unresolved identification with the analyst, he may have confused the mode of transmission of the values (identification) with their eventually acquiring a functional autonomy by becoming part of what Hartmann (1951) called the conflict-free ego-sphere. Thus, therapy can alter values even when there is an earnest and sincere wish to avoid doing so, and when the therapist's training devotes substantial attention to avoiding untoward therapist influence in the form of countertransference.

Another aspect of neutrality as a value/technique is not as commonly attended to and yet is in the background of most therapists' awareness. In the course of treatment, demands, offers, threats, and opportunities are regularly presented to the therapist. Some are most attractive in emotional or physical terms. In regard to this, Eissler (1971) observed

> psychoanalysis would have been impossible in antiquity or in the Middle Ages. In those times the discussion of such "lurid" subjects as are inescapably dealt with during . . . psychoanalysis would have aroused excitement of a sort that would have driven both participants toward sexual actions. . . . It is one of those impressive paradoxes of history that psychoanalysis needed Victorianism to be born. . . . (p. 306)

Neutrality, then, in addition to its therapeutic function, serves to reduce the emotional stress of therapy for the therapist and to restrain behaviors damaging to both patient and therapist.

It could be concluded that such benign values as understanding, honesty, neutrality, and commitment are a natural and necessary part of successful therapy. The matter is not so simple, and objections have been raised, which we will consider in turn. The first set of objections has to do with the systematic effects of the theories and/or values of *therapeutic systems*. The second set deals with the effects introduced by *therapists*; the third group relates to *alternative viewpoints* that emphasize rather than minimize the introduction of values in therapy.

Systematic Effects Produced by Systems of Therapy

Since all therapeutic procedures acknowledge that one purpose of treatment is to produce change, one may ask What changes occur? What are the consequences? In the first decade of this century, "Freud's theories were interpreted as direct incitements to surrendering all restraint, to reverting to a state of primitive license and savagery" (Jones 1955, p. 109). Such notions are still encountered, but they are less prevalent. However, our task here is not to deal with misconceptions, but rather to look at the actual impact produced by psychodynamic therapeutic systems.

Some of the commonly desired effects of psychotherapy would likely include more awareness of feelings, increased consistency between conscious and unconscious ideas and affects, and increased concordance between thoughts and feelings and behavior. Although this may sound mild enough, when put into practice, *honesty*, *understanding*, and *commitment* are likely to have a considerable effect on the patient's behavior and interpersonal relationships. The following case is illustrative:

Mrs. E. was about 23 when she was first referred to me by her husband for severe anxiety and deep feelings of insecurity based on her strong belief that she was disliked by her co-workers and friends. What emerged early in therapy were serious problems with her husband, who was also in therapy with a colleague. She felt emotionally and sexually unsatisfied, very angry, and afraid to either examine her relationship to her husband and family or to accept her angry feelings. She strongly denied clear indications of her husband's extramarital sexual activity. Therapy focused on support to accept the realistic needs she had, to understand and accept her anger as having real roots, and to develop more appropriate expressions of assertiveness; domestic Frisbee with the dishes was unhelpful to her marriage. Although there were ups and downs in her relationship to her husband and her own family, as she became stronger and was able to express her needs more directly and appropriately, her marriage temporarily improved but then deteriorated. She was able to work out a satisfactory and more adult relationship with her family, but her husband left her and began an open affair in such a way that she had to notice it. For Mrs. E., separation and eventual divorce were no longer avoidable. Continuing in therapy, she was able to overcome her conviction of stupidity and she entered college, eventually acquiring specialized professional training.

At the end of therapy, we felt that it had been reasonably fruitful. Mrs. E. had overcome much of her insecurity, the diffuse and dreadful anxiety was reduced to specific problematic events, her relationship with her family was congruent with her chronological age, she was increasingly effective in her studies, her relationships with men were more satisfying, and the men were more suited to her by virtue of age and accomplishment. Nevertheless, the collapse of her marriage was at least partly attributable to therapy, and interposing the fact that her husband was considering leaving her when he first arranged for her to enter therapy is not the issue. He might well have continued the marriage nevertheless. In a later discussion, her husband's therapist was of the opinion that the marriage collapsed partly because the husband could not deal with Mrs. E.'s increased strength and assertiveness.

Therapeutic intervention brings consequences that are partially attributable to the underlying value/techniques discussed here. To help a patient break free from a damaging sadomasochistic relationship has outcomes the sadistic partner will not desire. Szasz's (1965) proposal of "autonomous psychotherapy," wherein it is made clear at the beginning that the therapist will in no way intervene in the life of the patient is not a solution. Therapy is intervention and it affects values (Bergin 1980a); only the form and degree of impact may be modifiable.

Buhler (1962) summarized some of the values inherent in various psychotherapeutic systems and methods and proposed the following tripartite division of value/techniques:

1. The opportunity to think matters through clearly and honestly
2. Authoritarian or advisory directives
3. Mystical or philosophical speculations

Apparently not enamored of either directive counseling or Jungian theory, her study group agreed that the first value of therapy was the patient gaining freedom of choice, but thereafter there was little agreement about values.

Moving away from such values as honesty and neutrality, which are rather generally regarded as necessary for psychotherapy, there are value/techniques that begin to tilt toward the technique side. *Insight* may be one such. Repeatedly emphasized as the sine qua non of psychoanalytic therapy, its primacy has been repeatedly challenged (Ellis 1973; Glasser and Zunin 1973; Hobbs 1962, 1981; Perls 1969; Wilson 1981). Even from a sympathetic perspective, Appelbaum (1977) provocatively considered the negative effects produced by the "dangerous edge of insight" and asked whether it is an appropriate ingredient in all therapies, and if so, to what degree. Kernberg (1975) did not reject insight as a part of therapy, but rather cautioned against early interpretations connecting past and present in therapy with borderline patients. Since interpretation is regarded as important to the development of insight, this implied a constraint on the early promotion of insight. As a value, insight can be seen as related to understanding as discussed previously, but has the more specific technical meaning in dynamic psychotherapy of connecting past experiences and events with present attitudes and behaviors in a way that will lead to changes in present thoughts, feelings, and actions.

Still within the general position of not trying to communicate and instill a *specific* set of values, Samler (1960) nevertheless argued explicitly for value change as a goal in counseling when he proposed

> for the demanding and infantile—assumption of responsibility . . .
> for the guilt-ridden—tolerance of himself and life's reality;
> for the unloved and unloving—self-acceptance and kindliness;
> for the achievement- and power-ridden—appreciation for the rich resources in human beings;
> for the highly controlling—reduction of anxiety and a more trusting and optimistic outlook. (p. 36)

Samler recognized, however, that values and techniques were to some degree independent of one another. To tell a person to start to feel is probably ineffective, but approaching feelings more slowly and indirectly has a greater likelihood of allowing access to feelings.

The value/techniques discussed so far are used more or less generally in a number of psychotherapeutic systems. An example of more focused and specific value/techniques is seen in the psychoanalytic concept of the vaginal orgasm as an indicator of psychosexual maturity. The original Masters and Johnson reports of the clitoral basis for orgasm renewed some angry attacks on psychoanalytic theory. However, Kaplan's (1974) discussion of the clitoral basis of orgasm detailed some of the complexities involved and indicated the physiological basis for the reported experience of some women of a clitoral–vaginal orgasm. Some of the discrepancy related to different sources of data: physiological versus experiential. One may question whether the clitoral versus the vaginal orgasm is a value matter at all. Since the issue deals with the quality of pleasure and its worth in how one's life is organized, value seems implicated, although this is not how it is usually construed.

What makes the different types of orgasm important is how these data are interpreted. The analytic view that a woman who achieves only a clitoral orgasm has retained too strong an attachment to her infantile sexual life is damaging *if* the type of orgasm is not related to significant issues of psychological development, *if* therapy is prolonged, and *if* a needless sense of failure is conveyed. This would then be a systematic distortion produced by a therapy system because of an error in the theory. A theory is necessary in therapy, however. Because the material a patient produces is of so vast an array, the emotions so varied in range and intensity, the demands on the therapist so complex, and the nature of what will be helpful so often uncertain, a theory is needed to reduce the cognitive and emotional burdens on the therapist. A theory aids therapy by, at the very least, reducing the *therapist's* anxiety and confusion to manageable levels so that it is possible to continue to hear the patient.

The Effect of the Therapist

It has not been demonstrated, even in careful studies (Lieberman, Yalom, and Miles 1973; Sloane, Staples, Cristal, Yorkston, and Whipple 1975), that effects in psychotherapy are directly attributable to the theory used. Therapists do differ in effectiveness, and therapist style or personality may fit more or less well to patient personality or diagnostic category. Lazarus (1971, p. xii, quoting Perry London) noted, "it is techniques, not theories, that are actually used on people." We might substitute *therapist* for *technique* and be in a position to examine value issues derived from therapist effect.

One of the early accusations against Freud's theory, particularly regarding infantile sexuality and the oedipal complex, was either that it was derived from "sick" people and therefore not related to normality or that it was an expression of Freud's own personality and thus not generalizable. Like many myths, there is some truth here. Freud stated that he tested his theoretical concepts on himself, and Sullivan similarly commented that the inability to understand something in a patient meant that the therapist had not yet been able to locate the experience in himself. Szasz (1965) declared that a therapist's mode of functioning is an expression of personality and cannot be otherwise. Eclecticism, in his view, was "a pretentious hoax" (p. 40). In the same vein, Stolorow and Atwood (1979) demonstrated connections between specific life experiences and the metapsychologies in the theories of Freud, Jung, Wilhelm Reich, and Rank. Thus it is probable that the therapist's framework for understanding and intervening in therapy is affected by the therapist's personality.

The research literature is not ample, but there is no shortage of opinions about the relationship between the therapist's values and changes in the patient's values. Rosenthal (1955) studied twelve patients (nine were hospitalized) who were seen for a mean of five months and were assessed for improvement through blindly rated interviews. He found that Q-Sorts by patients regarding sex, aggression, and authority tended to shift toward those of the therapist in more improved patients and away from those of the therapist in less improved patients. There was no such shift with the Allport-Vernon-Lindsay Study of Values. Therapists were psychiatric residents, but otherwise undescribed.

This provocative, oft-cited report was followed by one from Nawas and Landfield (1963), who studied 20 clients seen at a University Mental Hygiene Clinic by six therapists (not otherwise described, but who may well have been graduate students). Clients were given an inventory assessing constructs or personal language at the start of therapy and again at the end of therapy. Compared with the therapists' constructs or personal language assessed at the start of therapy, more improved clients (based on comparisons of pre- and post-therapy typescripts) were a iittle *less* likely to use their therapist's personal language at the end of therapy, whereas less improved clients were a little *more* likely to. The differences were not significant.

Although the Nawas and Landfield (1963) study looked at therapist impact, it did not assess values directly. Welkowitz, Cohen, and Ortmeyer (1967) did attempt to assess value acquisition in patients relative to therapist perception of improvement, without trying to assess improvement objectively. Using 38 therapists in training at two postdoctoral institutes, with 44 patients having one to nine months of therapy, they measured patient values through the Morris "Ways to Live" scale and the Strong Vocational Interest Blank. They found that similarity in values increased as a function of time in therapy and that patients rated as improved were more similar to their therapists in values than those rated non-improved. The therapists used in the study varied in values, and the patients did not seem to resemble the other therapists.

In two other related studies (Mendelsohn 1966; Mendelsohn and Geller 1963), the number of sessions a client saw a counselor was studied as a function of client-counselor similarity on the Myers-Briggs Type Indicator. The latter yields a measure of four Jungian dimensions. Although dissimilarity led to few sessions (one or two), similarity led to either few or more sessions. Both studies dealt with short-term counseling (up to six sessions) at a university counseling center, which involved both personal and academic counseling. The experience of the staff was reported to have varied, but was not described or studied as a variable, although counselor sex was noted (no interaction).

In assessing the import of these studies, one runs afoul of a real but common problem. These five studies used, or appeared to use, available, captive samples of therapists in training; psychiatric residents (Rosenthal, 1955), postdoctoral trainees (Welkowitz et al. 1967), or undescribed therapists at a university clinic (Mendelsohn 1966; Mendelsohn and Geller 1963; Nawas and Landfield 1963). In contrast, Farson's (1961) report is notable because it used experienced therapists (five of the six were doctoral-level faculty), who employed the same, client-centered approach. Overall, clients did not resemble their own therapists after therapy or at follow-up more than the therapists as a group. Farson concluded that gain in therapy can occur without introjection of the therapist's values, as measured by either a Q-Sort or the Allport-Vernon-Lindsay Study of Values. Curiously, he found that therapists rated by colleagues as less competent and well-adjusted tended to have clients who resembled their values more, whereas the clients of the better-adjusted therapists did not resemble them.

It is difficult to draw clear inferences from these studies. Rosenthal's study dealt with a central issue in his moral values Q-Sort; however, his use of partly trained psychiatric residents with patients, many of whom did not complete therapy, raises questions about the quality of therapy in his study. Nawas and Landfield's report with unknown therapists examined therapist impact indirectly, but did not find an effect. Welkowitz et al. also used trainees (probably advanced) and did not assess the effect of therapy, but only therapist perceptions in relation to values in patients. The Mendelsohn studies used mixed client problems and treatments with yet another instrument, which yielded results subject to alternative interpretations. Except for the weak experimental control, it could have been an analogue study. Farson's much more carefully controlled study suggested that the therapist's competence and ability (the two were essentially the same on his ratings) were *inversely* related to alteration of values. Although not replicated, Farson's results are consistent with long-held ideas that training, competence, and relative freedom from personal problems are important both to the outcome of therapy and to avoiding unnecessary and/or damaging influences on the patient. Similar findings were suggested by the results of Lieberman et al. (1973).

Beutler (1979) reviewed a large number of studies on the complex variables of therapist influence in individual, group, and marital therapy. The results are less than clear cut, since attitudes frequently change in therapy, but the therapist is not always the cause of the change. Beutler addressed an important question when he asked "Do patients acquire a more 'mature' set of attitudes *or* specifically those of their therapists?"

(p. 434, emphasis added). A number of articles have suggested that patients may acquire some of the values of the therapist in the course of therapy. There is an implicit assumption that there is a general set of mature values, but if the patient merely acquires some of the therapist's values, this is only exchanging sets of values of equal utility and maturity.

There is no reason to assume that there is a *general* set of mature values. Rather there are probably *specific* sets of mature values, so that if a patient alters values, in part, to resemble those of the therapist, a more mature set of specific values may be acquired. Hobbs (1962, 1981) discussed factors influencing gain in psychotherapy and noted that the patient may be suffering from a world-view (a set of values) that does not work any longer and the therapist's world-view is acquired because it does. Similarly, Buhler (1962) indicated that value conflicts are quite common, but this is not an indicator for therapy unless the person is not managing these value conflicts effectively.

An implicit assumption to Beutler's question seems to come out of the democratic ideal embedded in many psychotherapies. This is that it is wrong to influence another person, perhaps partly a reaction to the discomfort attendant upon the nearly life-and-death responsibility of some aspects of therapeutic work. This ideal is probably an extension of a more generally accepted ideal that it is improper to exert an exploitative, injurious influence on someone with whom you have a fiduciary relationship. Ginsburg (1950), a medically trained analyst, flatly asserted the need for the therapist to confront personal values, and he was candid about the importance of undermining those values in the patient he saw as destructive. All this is not an argument for prescribing values to the patient in psychotherapy. Rather, it is necessary to face the bases of the fear of influence that seems partly founded on a fear of awful responsibility. Therapy makes an impact; it is better to face it than back into it with closed eyes.

Despite the lack of consistency in design, instruments, and therapist training in these studies, one may infer that patient values can be affected in the course of therapy. Not all values are equivalent, however. A person who holds that one should never respond to aggression may enter therapy to deal with the consequences of such a value, or if attention is directed to this behavior and the underlying stance, the patient may change spontaneously. On the other hand, a person may esteem their personal altruism and not wish to change it.

Any discussion of values needs to be clear on which values are at issue. Rosenthal's (1955) study was sophisticated in some ways. He compared change on a Moral Values Q-Sort (*sex, aggression,* and *authority* were the areas) with changes on the Allport-Vernon-Lindsay Study of Values. He did find systematic changes in patients on the former, but not on the latter, which suggested that although values can change in therapy, those values that change may well be the ones that bring the patient into treatment in the first place. Values might change for other reasons. The changes may be a secondary phenomenon, wherein the patient identifies with the therapist's values secondarily to the changes wrought in therapy.

Parallels between Psychotherapeutic and Political Systems

The original reason for a didactic or training analysis was to prevent the therapist's personal life from intruding into therapy. So far, we have considered the individual therapist's impact and the associated value/techniques on the patient's values. Other influences not generally in the therapist's awareness saturate the therapeutic structure and parallel current political ideologies.

Bockoven (1963) retrieved a startling bit of early American psychiatry in *Moral Treatment in American Psychiatry*. "Moral treatment" arose in the late eighteenth and early nineteenth centuries in the United States as a result of the then current political experiments in freedom, democracy, and the more humane treatment of citizens. This was extended to felons, lunatics, and paupers on the basic assumption that psychological or emotional stresses (i.e., "moral causes") could cause lunacy. The treatment involved small facilities (up to 200 patients), kindly and personal care by physicians and attendants, group and individual discussions between patient and physician, and many, varied activities. Success rates that would be envied today were regularly reported. There were many reasons for the breakdown of moral treatment, including an increasing cultural dissonance between patient and physician, the failure to train followers, and the lack of a coherent theory, but it is important to note the parallel that existed between the political ideology and treatment practices.

More recently, Green (1946) commented that, with the exception of psychoanalysis, "all modern psychotherapy incorporates a democratic ideology: therapy should be nonauthoritarian, individualistic, aimed to promote self-help, independence and self-achievement" (p. 221). Some 16 years later, Patterson (1959) said much the same thing. Commenting specifically about psychoanalysis, Redlich (1960) saw analysis as a scientific tool, not a world-view or religion, but he also stipulated that psychoanalysis is incompatible with rigid, dogmatic, authoritarian, or repressive political systems, such as those of the USSR and Nazi Ger-

many, and certain religions. Going a step further, Beit-Hallahmi (1974a)
offered a sharp critique of the values inherent in psychotherapy and how
treatment tended to bring about adjustment to damaging social systems
rather than to direct people to change these systems. A good deal angrier
was Agel's (1971) edited collection *The Radical Therapist*, which offered a
wide selection of commentary in this vein. Beit-Hallahmi and the writers
Agel collected generally have an "either–or" orientation. If the structure
of a society has caused or contributed to emotional difficulties in a
person, then changing the structure is the appropriate intervention
(assuming we know what the effect of this sort of social surgery will be).
Will that change really help those persons now emotionally troubled to
feel happier or function better, or will the emotional troubles remain
embedded and still need psychotherapy? Is the choice *either* social change
or psychotherapy?

If the values operative in psychotherapy are consistent with the political structure, well isn't that fortunate? But have these values merely
paralleled the political structure? In a little-noticed commentary, Ekstein
(1962) drew some striking parallels between theory and society. The early
conception of the unconscious as a boiling cauldron of impulses kept in
check by a doorkeeper or censor was a striking image. Ekstein pointed
out that in the late nineteenth century this image paralleled, to a remarkable degree, the reality of the Austro-Hungarian Empire and many Central European countries with their repeated revolutions. After World
War I, there were a number of new, untried, somewhat shaky and
insecure democracies in Europe, and Freud's tri-partite model of the mind
cast the ego as an executive agency, without real power of its own except
what it could acquire by balancing off various competing impulses and
demands. Ekstein went further to note that ego psychology, with its
emphasis on ego functions and structure, is very popular in this country,
which has a long history of a stable, increasingly powerful central government, with many agencies, commissions, and departments. That psychotherapy in the United States, with its emphasis on independence,
achievement, self-help, and non-authoritarianism, should parallel current political ideology could be merely a flattering reassurance of the essential rightness and wisdom of our leading theorists. If, however, our
political life "writes" our theories, we have a drastically different situation.
We may have to consider as well the nature of our infra-theories, i.e., our
theories about what theories are, how they arise, and how they are tested.
As an anthropologist, Douglas (1970) demonstrated how natural symbols,
such as the body, are often symbolically representative of a particular
social environment. It is beyond the scope of this book to follow this

intriguing concept very far, but if our society emphasized community responsibility to a much greater degree and saw happiness as primarily based on concern and service to others, while rejecting self-fulfillment as selfish, would our psychotherapies be different in techniques and theories? If our society were much more authoritarian, how would theories and therapies be structured? The issue of values, society, and psychotherapy seems to contain much more subtle and pervasive connections than has been generally recognized. Theories and values can symbolize the experienced nature of the society, both in its internal organization and in its external environment, such as international relations. Heightened awareness regarding values is needed and a "neutral" refusal to consider such matters does not avoid the difficulty. Neutrality, too, is a value.

ALTERNATIVE VIEWPOINTS ON VALUES

Standard forms of psychotherapy typically may have powerful effects on the lives, feelings, thoughts, attitudes, and values of patients. Since many patients early in the history of psychoanalysis suffered from paralyzing inhibitions, liberation from unlivable restraints was an understandable analytic stance. Recognizing the seductive effects of the patient's positive transference, Freud rejected the imposing of most limits, the offering of advice, or the providing of instruction as therapeutic tools beyond the minimum necessary to conduct the analysis. These strictures have been followed in broad measure by most of those who came after him; expanded by some, such as Rogers, and modified by others. More recently, there have been efforts to rethink the issue of direct action and the nature of interventions in psychotherapy. Not all who have dealt with the problem have sought to minimize the impact on values. Some theorists have called for an increased emphasis on values.

The Value-Oriented Psychotherapies

Rational-emotive therapy (Ellis 1973) set itself the task of persuading and directing the patient to alter behavior and personal attitudes to the self, the world, and significant others. With its beginning in the fifties, it was one of several approaches to therapy that emphasized changed patient values and insisted on attitudinal/value/cognitive changes as well as behavioral ones. Ellis (1973) regarded much of a person's emotional difficulties as a function of erroneous ideas and beliefs that the individual generated, based on ideas about *shoulds* or *oughts* or about *awful* or *catastrophic* events that will occur if certain needs or wishes are not met. These beliefs, which the person continually re-indoctrinates himself or herself with, need to be exposed, attacked, and altered. In their place, rational approaches, empirically based data and evaluations, and altered behavior need to be developed in the patient, and with hard work, practice, and discipline, the patient is expected to improve rather quickly.

Not too dissimilar to rational-emotive therapy is Glasser's reality therapy (Glasser and Zunin 1973). This rejects the past as an "excuse for behaving in an irresponsible manner" (p. 292). What is emphasized is a basic need in all people for an identity that is greatly affected by their ability to love and be loved and to accomplish things that give a feeling of worth. Therapy focuses on the necessity for individuals to accept responsibility for their behavior and to look for alternatives to current behavior. With reality therapy's attention to the present and to realistic planning for successful accomplishment of the patient's goals, value judgments are encouraged. These judgments are aimed at the individual's own contribution to personal success or failure, and to the individual's affective states. Further, "the value of behavior has to be decided, not in the limited context of the person alone, but in the broader context of himself and those around him. The reality therapist should not shrink from moral judgments" (p. 301). Although reality therapy appeared to place less emphasis on the distortions induced by the imperatives of conscience than did rational-emotive therapy, it underscored behavior, responsibility, planning for oneself and effects on others, the importance of the present, and plans for the future. Values, attitudes, and their immediate behavioral correlates are major issues directly addressed in this therapeutic modality.

Both these methods are still within the psychotherapeutic mainstream. Other psychotherapy systems make values even more central. Integrity therapy (Frankel 1967), based on the importance of responsibility, guilt, choice, and values, stemmed from Mowrer's work (1960, 1961). Although not detached from the more standard psychodynamic methods, integrity therapy concentrated on values related both to individual behavior and interpersonal relations. Frankel, Mowrer, Glasser, and others have held that standard dynamic approaches (and sometimes the behavior therapies, too) relieved the patient of responsibility and encouraged free and unrestrained self-gratification of aggressive and sexual impulses.

The values dealt with in rational–emotive, reality, and integrity therapy are those that relate to the patient's relationship to significant people, to activity or work, to choice and responsibility, and to guilt. Logotherapy goes beyond this. Frankl (1968) would likely find reality therapy and integrity therapy quite compatible, but went further by conceiving of logotherapy as signifying concern with spiritual values, although without a religious connotation. The spiritual values he concerned himself with seemed to center around the meaning of life, the capacity to bear suffering with courage, and the interaction between responsibility and freedom.

Logotherapy does not replace psychotherapy but rather complements it. Frankl amplified his position with two specific techniques: paradoxical intention, and de-reflection. He also noted the need for careful diagnosis and warned against the dangers of misapplication of technique.

The four approaches reviewed so far seem representative of a set of conceptions that progressively emphasize values and move in a roughly linear fashion from Ellis (1978), who is more or less explicitly opposed to most religions, to Frankl (1968), who advocates spiritual, but nonreligious values. Jung is not included here because he did not seem to fit in a linear development and his stance with regard to religion is much more complex.

The Biblically Based Counseling Value System

We now turn to the most extreme of the alternative positions to be considered: biblical or Christian counseling as proposed by Jay Adams (1970, 1973). Although pastoral counseling or parish counseling (Jackson 1975; Moss 1978; Wise 1980) is ancient in its roots and function, it is only in the past 50 to 75 years that the field has been reorganized and drastically altered both by competition from, and infusion of, secularly based psychotherapeutic techniques. Historically, one of Freud's early associates and supporters was Oskar Pfister (Jones 1955), the Swiss clergyman, but psychoanalysis had a limited impact on pastoral counseling in the first few decades of this century. Pastoral counseling was heavily influenced by Rogers' nondirective methods (May 1939; Rogers 1942, 1951), which came to exert a prominent influence. There was considerable variability, however, since pastoral counseling ranged from the use of some modern procedures by clergy in the context of their regular work to intensive, largely secular psychotherapy conducted by ordained clergy (Moss 1978). Rather than survey this entire field, the focus here will be on one vigorous counterattack by Jay Adams; called Christian counseling, it represents a major challenge to the more established pastoral counseling methods and to the secularly based psychotherapies.

The extensive writings of Adams are a vigorous and persuasive attack on nearly the whole range of psychotherapies from rational–emotive therapy through psychoanalysis to client-centered therapy. Mowrer's integrity therapy and Glasser's reality therapy were approved in part, but little else was. Adams held that original sin means that people are basically sinful, hence the solution to personal problems lies in repentance, confession, and expiation of sin with salvation through Jesus Christ. Modern psychotherapy and counseling have failed because they have encouraged people to

1. Act irresponsibly by blaming others for their troubles
2. See their guilt as mere guilt feelings instead of as real guilt
3. Regard themselves at the center of their lives instead of putting God at the center

Therapy or counseling techniques have failed because they encouraged self-reliance instead of dependence on God and God's Word as disclosed in the Bible.

This extremely condensed summary would not be regarded as more than another attack on contemporary psychotherapies from a conservative religious perspective (Adams' own self-description), were it not supplemented by an extensive and detailed set of counseling methods and a coherent and authoritative rationale. The *nouthetic* counselor was Adams' term for Christian counseling involving authoritative instruction and directive, confrontive techniques. In his polemical review of "the traditional Freudian and Rogerian ideas" (Adams 1970, p. 13), he concluded that "he [Freud] has sanctioned irresponsible behavior and made it respectable" (p. 17) and went on to characterize Ellis as a modern application of Freud's theories. Although there is some accuracy to this characterization, it is not in the way Adams proposed.

After his sweeping critique of current psychotherapies, behavior therapies, and psychiatry, Adams presented his methodology. He urged

1. Taking the counselee seriously
2. Providing hope
3. Admitting an error if the counselor has made one
4. Providing homework
5. Being aware of too great an emotional involvement with the counselee (though full commitment is urged)
6. Securing a detailed history to seek out characteristic patterns
7. Paying attention to the counselor's feelings to understand those of the client
8. Using role playing
9. Using a team approach (two or three counselors)

It would be easy to assert that Adams is disqualified from further consideration because of his misunderstanding of psychological theories (which have not been detailed here) or because his techniques are similar to many of the procedures derived from the systems he inveighs against. It would be an error to dismiss Adams because (1) his approach has sufficient power to work with certain types of people and (2) there are real, but subtle differences between Adams' personality theory and those in the mainstream of counseling, psychotherapy, and behavior therapy.

A variety of evidence has accumulated to indicate that some powerful effects in therapy are not specific to any particular method (Lieberman et al. 1973; Sloane et al. 1975; Smith and Glass 1977), but do relate to therapy in some way. Hobbs (1962) made a persuasive case for seeing psychotherapy as effective in helping people whose view of the world has failed, by providing them with an alternative, coherent perspective believed in by the therapist. Using methods generally thought to be effective, and housed in an organized world-view for which there is ample societal support, it is reasonable, if not very palatable, to hypothesize that this kind of Christian counseling does work. As for the differences between Adams' conceptions and those of mainstream theorists, a major point of divergence is his position that people are basically sinful, as contrasted with Rogers' view that people are basically good. Although Adams assumed that people are basically sinful, he went on to indicate that there are strivings toward doing the right thing, living a better life, being more productive, and obeying God's commandments. Thus, his perceptions, with some translations and adjustments, were not inconsistent with Freud's view of the person as basically in conflict with id impulses, on one hand, and reality demands and superego imperatives, on the other. Adams' stance on the basic nature of people does not appear crucial, although, in practice, it may lead to counseling that starts in a very different manner. The basic divergence revolves around the issue of autonomy and the perception of self.

For Adams, emphases on autonomy and concern with self-actualization are inherently wrong because they deny the importance of God in the lives of human beings and because they generate self-concern, self-interest, and selfishness, as well as irresponsibility for one's behavior and a lack of involvement with others. Adams' intemperate, sweeping, and blundering criticisms obscured a point that may have been better made by Vitz (1977). Vitz, in his pointed critique of Werner Erhard (née Jack Rosenberg, and founder of Erhard Seminar Training—EST) and many of the other do-it-yourself kits on the "pop" psychology market, pointed to the self-gratifying, exploitative emphasis of these approaches and argued for the consideration of a conservative Christian perspective of humanity with a different psychological understanding of people. Self-actualization, he declared, needs to be replaced with love of God and of others. To the implicit all-goodness of people of Rogers, Fromm, Maslow, and May, with its corollary of unlimited growth and free choice, Vitz countered with a sharp sense of human limits and a duality of human character (good and evil). Some of the conflict between these positions may parallel the still unresolved problem of free will versus determinism. Roughly speaking, self-actualization emphasizes the free will position; Vitz's conservative Christian stance is somewhat more aligned with deterministic views.

DETERMINISM AND FREE WILL

Historically, the physical sciences have been marked by a progressive commitment to an increasingly strict conceptualization of causality in the physical world. Immergluck (1964) summarized the similar development in the biological sciences and the current incomplete status of this concept in psychology. He succinctly reviewed the current uncertainty and sense of paradox between free will and determinism and then disposed of attempts to use modern physics as a support for the concept of free will when he pointed out that the Heisenberg Uncertainty Principle was not an indeterminism principle. Similarly, probability theory did not, in principle, refer to indeterminism, but only to our inability to specify the active causal factors in complex situations sufficiently. Having shown that determinism was the only scientifically defensible position, Immergluck did not reject free will as an epiphenomenon, but rather found a place for it as a necessary illusion. This was supported by Lefcourt's (1973) later summary of research, which demonstrated that the perception of having control had a major influence on response to stress. Immergluck concluded that if a deterministic position is fully accepted, "we will (must?) still persist to behave *as if* inner freedom were a fact, if not for those around us, then at least for ourselves" (p. 280). This is an unsatisfactory solution, since Immergluck was saying, in effect, that the experiential aspect of free will is outside the explanatory framework of scientific thinking.

Responsibility and Choice

Immergluck's theoretical analysis of the free will/determinism issue was followed by Silverman's (1969) analysis of expert testimony. His discussion of the professional issues is not germane here, but he agreed with Immergluck and concluded, "a person *can* be held responsible for his behavior, whether it is determined or not" (p. 6), even if this position is a useful fiction for the benefit of the person and the social group. Silverman did not note that if you *hold* a person responsible, this changes the set of determining factors from what they would be if you *don't hold* the person responsible, but this idea would be consistent with his thinking.

Silverman went further, however, and proposed some guidelines for deciding whether or not it is reasonable to hold a person responsible for a criminal or civil illegal act. From an ego-psychological position, he proposed that a person's ego controls may be traumatized sufficiently to be rendered nonfunctional for varying periods of time. He suggested that such variables as degree of external stress, range of effective responses in a person's repertoire, degree of preparedness for stress, physiological state, and amount of energy tied up in defenses were worthy of consideration in evaluating a person's capacity for responsible behavior. Although sensitive to the complexities of the theoretical issues involved and aware of the problems and ambiguities in such important practical assessments, Silverman could not resolve the tangle posed by the collision between the scientific insistence on determinism and the phenomenological report of free will any more than Immergluck could. Although Lefcourt (1973) only examined the *experience* of control of aversive stimulation, his review suggests that one could add the perception of control to Silverman's list.

Freedom of the Will

Although a thoughtful deterministic position did not dismiss free will as a non-topic, Immergluck's (1964) review of the issue, from the free will side, mirrored similar discomfort and puzzlement. Tomkins' (1962) term *freedom of the will* reflects the concept that freedom is a function of the complexity of the system and that yields a step toward resolution. Tomkins, in his discussion, spelled out that determined behavior referred to actions with sources that were based on drives or the interaction between motivational and control systems. He pointed out the confusion between "the drives, a motivational system of little freedom, with the affects, a motivational system of great freedom" (p. 108). Thus, although drives lead to affects, drives are relatively specific with regard to satisfiers and have limits with regard to biological tolerance for delay, with breathing being the most specific and with the least biological tolerance for delay, whereas sex is the least specific and has the most biological tolerance for delay. Drives cannot substitute for each other; water will not satisfy hunger, but affects are much more variable and one can control another (fear may inhibit aggression, anger may displace anxiety). Affects can combine with each other, be molded along a time dimension, be modified in terms of intensity or choice of object, and so on. Tomkins saw drives as not very amenable to control by the person, although this varied according to the drive satisfaction required. This difficulty in control gives the affects upon which they are based some of their imperative quality. Display of affect is a learnable control, but control of the experience of affect is much more difficult; being able to deliberately evoke the experience of an affect on demand (especially a positive one) is even more rare.

Tomkins made the important point that since affects are not highly specific (unlike drives), there is much more possibility for error and thus for learning. Affects combine not only with each other but are also intimately involved with cognition, whereas the adaptive patterns developed to avoid unpleasant affects and acquire pleasant ones are readily automated. Such automated patterns, if relatively efficient, free the cognitive system for new learning, but automated patterns are resistant to revision in new situations. This is a very condensed summary of Tomkins' tightly woven analysis, but his concepts permit the free will–determinism controversy to be approached in a manner that does not lead to indefensible opposing positions. Although maintaining a clearly deterministic stance, Tomkins nevertheless saw freedom of the will as a function of

1. The complexity of the cognitive and affect systems
2. The relative lack of specificity built into these systems
3. The long period of time in which learning of highly complex patterns of thought, behavior, and feeling was possible
4. The capacity to develop automated affect/cognition/behavior patterns that could free the person for new learnings

Tomkins attenuated the free will–determinism tangle by construing free will as degrees of freedom and made it possible to consider the phenomenological report of choice without discarding determinism or acting only *as-if* free will existed (Immergluck 1964). It may be possible to go a step further.

Separating Free Will and Determinism

The argument for determinism has been made in many ways, but it is simply unprovable. Rather, it is an axiom that makes it possible for scientists to apply themselves to their work without continually wasting energy wondering if this or that case is an exception. The position taken here is that all behavior is determined and that there are no qualifications or exceptions. *The free will–determinism controversy is quite simply an error because what is juxtaposed here are two issues that are not on the same level.* Thus, the experience of freedom is indeed a real phenomenon, but it does not contradict determinism nor is it necessary to pretend about freedom or choice. Instead, the experience of freedom reflects the *experienced location of control* of behavior. It is an error, of course, to equate, without qualification, the experience of freedom with an objective evaluation of one's capacity to indeed do what an individual feels can be done, but the experience of freedom has a considerable effect on the organism even if it does not, in fact, exist (Lefcourt 1973).

The experienced location of control refers to some of the determinants of behavior and to consciousness. The following two clinical examples may be illustrative.

In the first case, a man in his early forties consulted me because of increasing agoraphobia. Always vigorous, he led a life typical of people in rural communities, including hunting and fishing. His fears typically occurred when he was away from his accustomed path, as when he was hunting alone. The onset, traced to age 34, was insidious, but his anxiety had increased to the point where he could barely get to work and return home, although he was comfortable in either place. He openly expressed his chagrin in being unable to control his feelings and behavior. I pointed out that his fear of being alone in a strange place began when he was the same age as his mother was when she died and left him an orphan at about 2½ or 3. I suggested that he was remembering her, his fear over her early loss as well as his living in a strange place (the home of a relative). This was promptly followed by a decline in his symptoms. He had previously experienced no free will or control in dealing with his agoraphobia, but he now experienced choice or freedom to engage in preferred activities.

In the second case, a young man entered treatment because his marriage was in serious trouble. His wife, a very hostile and disparaging woman, continually derogated him, which led to considerable conflict and a diminution in affectionate feelings. In investigating how he first came to be attracted to her, it became clear that although he believed that she was his choice, he had dropped relationships with warm, supportive women if he should be so unfortunate as to stumble into one accidentally. Discovering his lack of free choice and his actual avoidance of situations the lack of which was being lamented in therapy startled him and opened a major field of therapeutic inquiry. After termination of his marriage and further therapeutic exploration, he began a new relationship with a young woman with the determination not to repeat the past. The repetition did not occur, since his choice was no longer actuated by the same unconscious determinants. This case exhibits the experience of apparent freedom in which unconscious determinants are the decisive influences.

In both these examples, each patient's behaviors, thoughts, and feelings were steered by unconscious factors, or to use Tomkins' phrase, the behaviors, thoughts, and feelings were partly determined by automated neurological programs. When these automated neurological programs are made conscious, as in therapy, alternative choices become possible to an increased degree because consciousness appears to be inconsistent with the automated behaviors. This is a brief summary of a complex process, but, in accord with Tomkins, psychotherapy increases the patient's degrees of freedom *in the sense that* the determinants of behavior are more extensively conscious. In no way is it implied that the person's choice is undetermined or that impossible choices now become available. Instead, the *location* of the determinants of behavior are partly altered. Choices occur that are both more under ego control and more consistent with the current and future needs of the person.

How does all this relate to free will and determinism, or perhaps to the narrower problem of choice and responsibility? Among the outcomes of successful therapy are the patient's increased capacity to make selections based on a greater awareness of

1. The available possibilities
2. The patient's current and future needs rather than automated (unconscious) past needs
3. The impact of the patient's behaviors on significant people
4. The patient's own capacities seen in a more realistic light

In this context, responsibility means being able to perceive and "own" the impact of one's behavior and to have access to energies and behaviors to deal with the consequences of these choices.

A New Determinism

Psychotherapy has, as one of its basic goals, the freeing of the patient from crippling constraints on the capacity (in Freud's felicitous phrase) "to work and to love." To help the patient acquire the capacity to choose has sometimes been assumed to mean that the individual is now freed from all restraint (Adams 1970). Rather, my experience has been that in those therapies both the patient and the therapist agree is successful, a typical, but not certain outcome has been behavior patterns that could be characterized as "moral." This means changes in the direction of consistent, responsible behavior in humanely meeting both the patient's needs and those of other important people, appropriate assertiveness, and an increased capacity for persistent and effective work. There is a decline in, or termination of, extramarital sexual activity, temper outbursts, over-tolerance for abusive situations, and the inability to enjoy sexuality.

It would be tempting to assert that therapy makes people moral, and in view of the discussion of values earlier in the chapter, one cannot overlook the possibly quite subtle influence a therapist may have in spite of a desire for neutrality. This outcome may derive from the introjection of the therapist's values (Cf. Rosenthal 1955 and Farson 1961). It may be hypothesized that a regular, but not universal outcome of therapy is realignment of the determinants of behavior. In a person freed from crippling, inappropriate, past-determined behavior patterns, choice or free will can be understood *not* as selecting anything at all, but rather as selecting what is *now* useful for happiness and fulfillment. To choose to be unhappy as a random choice would indeed be "free will," but it is not credible as "free" choice. An individual will not freely choose to avoid good interpersonal relationships when they are available, for such a choice is incompatible with our social and biological foundations. The choices open to the person are in the range of which relationships one will have, how they shall be constructed, and what limits will be "freely" chosen. Many religious denominations assume "free will" in the person for sinful behavior. The therapeutic position here is that such an assumption depends on the locus of the determinants of behavior and this discussion of issues may help if one has to deal with a pastor or relative concerned with the effects of therapy.

ETHICS, MORALS, AND VALUES

Up to this point, the discussion has been almost exclusively focused on values, partly because of the currency of this term in the psychotherapy literature. It may be useful to consider two related terms, ethics and morals; the former because psychotherapists concern themselves with this, too, the latter because many patients will bring similar kinds of concerns into therapy under that heading. A patient may enter therapy

because of a wide range of unpleasant internal states, interpersonal difficulties, or external pressures. If therapy continues for a while, questions
of goals, good and evil, or right and wrong are likely to arise whether we
wish it or not. When religious issues are also included, value problems
may be intensified. Nor is this all. Liefer (1964) reviewed the issue of legal
testimony regarding criminal responsibility and showed that psychiatry
has been willing to assess the issue of right and wrong, but has also
progressively moved the courts to view matters from a psychiatric rather
than a legal perspective. The McNaughten Rule of 1843, which was based
on intellect (or reason), was moved in the Durham Decision of 1954 to
consider both reason and emotion in tests of responsibility. Thus "the
effect is that the *moral* decision is placed more firmly in the hands of the
psychiatrist" (p. 828, emphasis added). This has been generalized to other
professions with the increasing frequency that workers in diverse fields
offer expert testimony.

Ethics

The various human services professions have codes of ethics partly
shaped to the particular needs and issues of each field. Nevertheless they
overlap in major ways and the discussion that follows is of the American
Psychological Association (APA) ethics code only because of my greater
familiarity with it. The American Psychological Association first published
its specific code of ethics in 1953. In the *Casebook on Ethical Standards
of Psychologists* (1967, revised 1974), the Introduction noted that the
Standards had originally been developed in an empirical, deductive fashion
using specific incidents, but it then went on to note that the Casebook
reflects "the values of the times in which we live. Professional standards
are not, after all, fixed and immutable for years to come" (p. ix). Rather
than work from abstract principles in an inductive fashion, the original
committee sidestepped the problems of an inductive approach, but left the
reader to determine what, if any, are the underlying principles of the Code
of Ethics.

To some real degree, however, the Code does imply some basic
principles in the Preamble and elsewhere with such phrases as "the dignity
and worth of the individual" (p. 1) or "high value on objectivity and
integrity" (p. 3) or "regard for the social codes and moral expectations of
the community" (p. 13) or "acts with integrity in regard to colleagues"
(p. 47). However, by not addressing the issue of underlying principles
squarely, the reader or user of the Code can neither assess whether a

particular item in the Code conforms to the principles, nor can he or she be in a position to evaluate the principles because they are underground— in a sense, part of the professional unconscious.

Turning to the Oxford Universal Dictionary (Onions 1955), *ethics* comes from the Latin *ethicus* and the Greek *ethikos*. The latter, formed on *ethos*, means character. Part of the definition is "1. . . . a science of morals . . . 3b. The rules of conduct recognized in certain limited departments of human life. 4. The science of human duty in its widest extent, including besides ethics proper, the science of law whether civil, political, or international" (p. 637). In the sense used here, science probably means "a particular branch of knowledge or study" (p. 1806). These dictionary definitions parallel the APA Code of Ethics, both as a set of rules of conduct "in certain limited departments of human life" and as morals. In Principle 3 of the Code of Ethics, entitled *Moral and Legal Standards*, one finds such statements as "the practice was not only illegal but also unethical" and "the practice was unprofessional and unethical" (APA 1967, p. 11). The term morals in professional and scientific conduct seems to have been partly replaced by the term ethics. Both deal with questions of right and wrong, with matters of behavior, and with sanctions imposed for violations. Ethics tend to be confined to a more circumscribed area than morals and are generally seen as somewhat more flexible.

Morals

In addition to the Code of Ethics, there is a moderate amount of material on specific ethical issues (Geiser and Rheingold 1964; Liefer 1964; Siegel 1979; Smith 1978). There is a larger body of literature on values, but the topic of morals is largely absent, with a few exceptions (Menninger 1973; Mowrer 1961). Morality as an indicator of divine influence in the form of conscience is no longer a part of psychology (moral philosophy), whereas studies of superego formation (Fisher and Greenberg 1977) and moral behavior (Kohlberg 1964; Piaget 1948) are. Moral development and behavior are certainly important topics for study, but morality in its cognitive, affective, and motivational aspects rarely receives the attention that ethics receives. Morality appears to make psychologists professionally uncomfortable.

Again turning to the dictionary, we find that *moral* comes from the Latin *moralis*, a rendering of the Greek *ethikos*. It is defined as "1. Of or pertaining to character or disposition; of or pertaining to the distinction between right and wrong, or good and evil in relation to actions, volitions, or character; ethical" (Onions 1955, p. 1280). Thus, although there are definite overlaps between ethics and morals as defined, it would appear that one of the differences between these terms relates to the narrower scope of ethics as contrasted with the broader range of morals in terms of right and wrong. In Greek there seems to be only *ethikos,* whereas in Latin there were two words, *ethicus* and *moralis,* so that there was some divergence in underlying concepts requiring two related but distinct words.

Values

The word *values* is derived from the Old French *valoir* and is defined as "1. To consider of worth or importance; to rate high; to esteem; to set store by" (Onions 1955, p. 2332). There are some clear similarities and differences among these three words. Both values and morals address a wide range of topics; ethics, a narrower one. Morals and ethics are bipolar and specific (right or wrong, professional or unprofessional); values, unipolar (the values of the individual human being, the worth of democracy). Thus, it may be that the concept of morals has been effectively split into two terms: ethics (specific and bipolar) and values (less specific and unipolar). The history of the place of values in psychotherapy previously presented indicates some reasons for avoiding the term morals. Most of the people who were originally treated by the first form of modern psychotherapy (psychoanalysis) suffered from a clash between conscience and impulses, and the conscience, the custodian of morals, was commonly the victor. The term morals carried such a freight of meaning as to make the substitution of ethics and values desirable.

To summarize what appears to be the major similarities and differences among ethics, morals, and values, Table 2-1 shows five dimensions derived from this discussion. The Central Way of Expression is related to Dimensionality (bipolar or unipolar). The Range of Behaviors refers to the extent or numbers of diverse kinds of behaviors or issues addressed. The Experienced Source of Code refers, roughly, to the experience that morality, even if well accepted by the person, is usually experienced as impelling and as imposed from outside the person (conscience), whereas ethical codes are likely to be experienced as more structured and as having been learned. Values are more likely to be experienced as if chosen.

This rather simple scheme may be quarreled with. For the person who feels that he or she has worked through and rejected conventional moral

Table 2-1
Similarities and Differences between
Ethics, Morals, and Values

	Ethics	Morals	Values
Dimensionality	Bipolar	Bipolar	Mostly unipolar
Central way of expression	Right–wrong	Good–evil	Good–not good
Specificity of behavior	Relatively specific	Both specific and general	Relatively general
Range of behaviors	Circumscribed	General	General
Experienced source of code	Learned	Imperative	Chosen

judgments and is now guided by an ethical code, the Morals column may be irrelevant or the Ethics column may have acquired some of the characteristics of the Morals column. To the extent that this table usefully summarizes typical patterns found in a person's experiences, it offers a guide to the therapist in evaluating whether what a patient describes as a Value, for example, might not better be understood as an Ethic or a Moral. If a patient has transposed or mislabeled a facet of their experience, increased clarity may lead to increased understanding of important developmental experiences or current dislocations in the individual's interpersonal environment.

Redlich (1960) differentiated between institutional values as myths or beliefs and instrumental values as the tools and instruments used by society. Psychoanalysis emphasized instrumental values, although Redlich grudgingly conceded that there were institutional values, too. Hartmann (1960) used a different terminology, but supported instrumental values as the exclusive values of psychoanalysis. Peterson's (1970) distinction between intrinsic and instrumental values seemed to parallel Redlich's, whereas a somewhat similar bifurcation was offered by Buhler (1962), who distinguished between normative values (those people "ought" to have) and factual values (demonstrated preferences, desires, or judgments).

In an effort to establish an overall theory in the social sciences, the General Theory of Action (Parsons and Shils 1951), a great deal of attention was given to systematizing the concept of values. Clyde Kluckhohn's (1951) extensive contribution to this joint effort of the Department of Social Relations at Harvard distinguished among *normative, existential,* and *aesthetic* values. These three aspects were set in terms of a society's conception of "the structure of the universe, the relations of man to the universe (both natural and supernatural), and the relations of man to man" (p. 410). *Normative* refers to the culture's standards or "oughts," whereas *existential* refers to the society's conception of the way the world really is, although Kluckhohn indicated that what "ought to be" and what "really is" tended to overlap considerably. *Aesthetic* seemed to relate to the culture's conception of what is beautiful.

This very condensed summary reflects the consensus that values that are normative are viewed within the group as standards or "oughts." Differentiations from these norms occur in various directions, including what people really do (factual), how they accomplish certain values (instrumental), and how they construe the physical and social universe (existential). Kluckhohn took up the topic of cultural relativity and rejected the concept that values are completely culturally determined, noting that, in spite of the diversity across cultures, murder, lying, and stealing within the in-group are not condoned by any known society. Florence Kluckhohn (Kluckhohn 1956; Kluckhohn and Strodtbeck 1961) expanded the issue of values, detailing five problems common to all cultures and the methods of patterning solutions to obtain a scheme for analyzing the dominant and variant value orientations in any culture. This led to methods for the analysis and assessment of values within societies. Spiegel (1959) described a beginning application of Florence Kluckhohn's scheme to psychotherapy, which we will take up in Chapter 4.

Another quality of values is that they "are motivational concepts and specify goals for the individual's behavior or life" (Beutler 1979, p. 433). Variously characterized as expressing needs, interests, and criteria for the selection of goals (Patterson 1959), preferred goals (Buhler 1962), and direction-giving facts (Hartmann 1960) or involving needs, goals, beliefs, attitudes, or preferences (Peterson 1970), values are rather consistently seen as having strong affective characteristics. These commentators also more or less clearly demonstrated that a cognitive component to values exists. They involve evaluation, judgment, choice, alternatives, or comparisons. Thus, *values are motivations toward goals and ways to structure or order the physical and social environment, and they can be studied empirically.*

As previously mentioned, ethics, morals, and values tend to be handled a bit gingerly by most psychotherapists. Not untypical is Hartmann (1960), who, in *Psychoanalysis and Moral Values*, stated that the aim of psychoanalysis "is the aim of every therapy, and the value of this therapeutic aim is not questioned; moral considerations are kept from inter-fering with it" (p. 20). This aim was health; there was no other for Hartmann. He went on to make clear that although psychoanalysis did not reject moral values as such, nor was the aim to eliminate moral imperatives, the study of moral values was a scientific enterprise. He noted that the technical procedures of analysis

> may become a moral demand for the patient. Deep interpretation, the broad range of communication, unlimited self-revelation, widest per-missiveness, the discarding of every consideration which stands in the way of full psychological understanding . . . all these are then regarded as the only "right" ways to deal with interpersonal problems. (pp. 74–75)

Hartmann saw this development as a transference identification with the analyst, which was expected to end with the conclusion of analysis, although this did not always happen. Hartmann seemed to have missed the "moral" content of psychoanalysis, as did Redlich (1960), although others (Küng 1979, Rieff 1959) did not. The syllogism seems to be: Since science deals with questions of "what" or "how" and not "why," and since psychoanalysis is a science, therefore moral values can be studied objec-tively, but only as natural phenomena. "Why" was an animistic question progressively excluded by nineteenth-century science. When one recalls the struggles over vitalism or the inheritance of acquired characteristics, it is reasonable to regard the progress of modern science as inversely related to teleological reasoning.

It may be asked whether the social sciences should properly be con-ducted under exactly the same set of rules as the physical sciences. Lepley (1943) cogently raised this question when he argued that fact and value statements are regarded separately by scientists because valuative state-ments are less verifiable than factual ones, but this separation is a con-vention. Means–ends relations (valuative statements) and cause–effect relations (factual statements) Lepley held to be transposable from one system to the other. Ethics, morals, and values may then be admissible not only as matters for empirical study (which has already been done), but may also guide certain facets of scientific investigation. To exclude ques-tions of "why," meaning, or purpose in the social sciences risks sterility in investigation, on the one hand; to include these questions uncritically courts metaphysical diffusion, on the other. Psychotherapy, based on a theory (or theories) of human personality development and functioning and as a method of treatment may be able to explore the development and function of ethics, morals, and values, but may also move cautiously in the direction of becoming a science of morals (Rieff 1959). Values may be investigated not only as to sources and modes of development, but also appraised as to worth and consequences.

A clinical example may be useful here.

This concerns a married couple; the husband had become involved in an extramarital affair some years previously and had found it so enhancing to his ego (as reported in the initial session) that he indicated to his wife he would not object if she engaged in an affair during a previously scheduled upcoming separation for educational purposes. Although he did not disclose his own activity, she unconsciously recognized the meaning of the suggestion and started an affair that threatened to end the marriage by the time I was consulted. Later, in individual sessions with the wife, we uncovered and then explored the significance of her parents' separation at about the time that autonomy was probably the major developmental issue. Difficulty with autonomy, problems in being able to resist intrusions and control by others, the emotional cost to her independence in getting her dependency needs met had been recurrent topics in previous sessions. The therapeutic issue at this point seemed to be the damage to her capacity for autonomy in her second year when she was left with her grandparents because of her parents' separation.

In one particular session, she was agonized by the sense that she was causing her husband and family much pain by her wish to divorce. I also felt torn because marriage is a personal value for me, and although there were indications of some degree of difference between them in their interests and values, they did not seem unbridgeable in light of their prior marital history. My interpretations were aimed at the autonomy issue that seemed paramount, but the selection of autonomy as a focus paralleled my personal valuing of independence and individuality as well. The desire for rapprochement could have been attended to instead, since it also appeared to be a concern, and this might have tilted matters toward a reconciliation with her husband. Other material suggested that a reconciliation was not too probable, in spite of many years of a relatively satisfactory marriage, but the confluence of value and therapy was striking. Further, my countertransference was clear to me, and I could not be very confident that my choice of which therapeutic issue to interpret was free of this influence.

Countertransference will be considered in more detail in Chapter 6, but it is an ever present problem.

What is most disturbing here with regard to problems of values is that the decision as to whether to be silent, or how and in what way to intervene, did not appear to be clearly directed by data on which value was "better." Although there have been some suggestions that scientific investigation can provide such answers (Rieff 1966, Samler 1960), the spirit of current scientific attitudes does not seem prospective, nor is it clear what the questions are. An alternative position of neutrality in which one just analyzes what is "there" seems to beg the question, since what is "there" has to filter through cognitive–affective structures in the therapist that depend, in part, on values.

It is commonly assumed that ethics, morals, and values are associated with religion because (1) that is what religion is all about (a circular definition) or (2) God commands it. Although religion has many components, partly it gives order and meaning to the social and natural world. In the same sense, ethics, morals, and values also provide order and meaning to the world whether in a religious or a nonreligious framework. To varying degrees, ethics, morals, and values also deal with very important matters. Thus, in dealing with ethics, values, morals, or religion in therapy, one works not only with neurotic conflicts, but also with goals and how one should live one's life. Further, this latter part of the work is done when there are no clear guidelines, and it is not easy, and sometimes not possible, to disentangle neurotic from non-neurotic values. In dealing with one, the therapist likely affects the other.

A Way to Deal with Values in Psychotherapy

It may therefore be concluded that values pervade psychotherapy on several levels: the technical constructions of the theory, the person of the therapist, and the parallels between theory and concurrent political/social processes. In *An American Dilemma*, Myrdal (1944) appended a section entitled "A methodological note on facts and valuations in social science." Although it was directed to social science researchers, it is highly relevant to the dilemma of values in psychotherapy. Myrdal sharply critiqued three usual ways to avoid bias in the social sciences:

1. Avoiding practical implications of research
2. Reporting only "facts"
3. Giving a "balanced" picture

With only slight modifications, these three solutions parallel many thera-peutic ideas about "neutrality." Myrdal held that none of these techniques work in the social sciences and one may ask if they work in therapy. He emphasized that "there is no other device for excluding biases in social sciences than to face the valuations and to introduce them as explicitly stated, specific, and sufficiently concretized value premises" (p. 1043, italics omitted). Internally, the therapist must be as clear as possible on personal value premises. The communication of these to the patient, particularly without regard for the patient's needs or situation, may rightly be regarded as insensitive and is not being urged.

Myrdal's statement encompasses an ideal, and some of the issues raised so far are, one hopes, a move in the direction he recommended. Myrdal (1944) noted that the social scientist cannot become entirely free "from dependence on the dominant preconceptions and biases of his environ-ment" (p. 1035), but commended the effort to *try* to do so. However, it may be asked that if psychotherapy is so open to value influences, then why not "let our values all hang out?" Reveling in values in psychotherapy can have other unintended consequences, however. Lefcourt (1973) reviewed a number of studies that indicated that perceived control over a situation enables an organism to endure much greater stress. In an interesting therapy analogue study (Kanfer and Grimm 1978), it was demonstrated that certain improvements in reading were a function of the degree of control by subjects over treatment procedures, and comparisons to client response to therapy were made. Although Kanfer and Grimm saw their study in terms of behavior therapy, there was probably relevance to psychotherapy as well.

Patterson's *Counseling and Psychotherapy* (1959), which is regularly cited in the counseling literature for its extensive discussion of values, was itself an interesting mixture of support for client-centered methods, opposition to "depth psychology," and a naive expression of direct value judgments without much self-awareness. Still, Patterson noted that direct attempts to influence values were less likely to succeed than were procedures aimed at avoiding the exertion of influence. Support for this position was provided by Silverman (1976) whose review of a substantial body of studies showed that significant responses to emotionally relevant stimuli occur when stimuli are presented well below threshold, but those responses are absent when stimuli are above threshold. The therapist's effort to be genuinely neutral may have, paradoxically, a greater effect than trying to influence the patient directly. The situation is probably more complex, since directly active therapies also seem to bring about change. However, if therapy begins with direct efforts at influence, considerable opposition may be encountered. Even the very active therapies begin with the patient's definition of the problem, which allows the patient a significant measure of control over the treatment.

Another complicating factor has to do with the nature of the patient's personality organization. A more fragmented client may actively seek direction or guidance from the therapist, and to strictly insist on the principle of noninterference in a rigid fashion may leave the patient feeling abandoned. Here the therapist may wish to raise alternatives for discussion if the patient has none available, or even educate the patient as to the consequences of a course of behavior if the patient's background is sufficiently restricted (Simkin 1962). Buhler (1962) was relatively willing to discuss or even introduce values in therapy, but she indicated that this development usually came late in therapy. When the patient brought up the matter, she preferred to explore the issue thoroughly before disclosing her own position.

The matter of values comes more sharply to the fore when the patient is religious and asks about the therapist's religious stance in the early phase or poses other questions that derive from the patient's fear that a personal religious orientation will be attacked. What I have found helpful is to indicate my orientation briefly and state that I have no interest in having other people see it my way. If their religion is important to my patients, then I would certainly be interested in understanding it, as I am interested in anything they would want to tell me.

In summary, a number of aspects of therapy that have qualities of both values and techniques has been discussed. Honesty, neutrality, understanding, and commitment were seen as making it possible to proceed in therapy, enabling the patient to change and tending to induce changes in certain aspects of the patient's value system. The effort to generate an increased capacity for choice in the patient is both a treatment goal and a value. Along with increased freedom to choose, many therapists see as a concomitant an increased capacity for responsibility in that the patient functions in a coherent and effective fashion, rather than in a disjunctive, impulse-ridden one. Beit-Hallahmi (1979) offered a persuasive argument that a major difference between religious and psychotherapeutic modes of regulating behavior is that therapy offers another, more flexible path. It seems reasonable to take a cautious position to values deliberately introduced into therapy. Values can have a strong impact, and their introduction into therapy should further therapy in some reasonably clear way. It should be kept in mind, however, that it rarely happens that the therapist says something and the patient is completely changed. The usual problem in therapy is getting the patient to hear what the therapist has to say. Caution about our influence should not conceal therapeutic grandiosity.

What, then, about the alternative perspectives discussed in this chapter? Do they represent the expression of the therapist's own unresolved personality needs, as has sometimes been charged? Do they work and should they be accepted on empirical grounds? A reply that attacks alternatives based on motivational factors in the theorist is an alteration of the level of discourse and, thus, not a reply that responds to the issues. The core issue in alternative therapies seems to revolve mainly around modes of construing the world and actively choosing values for living. Rational-emotive therapy seems to concentrate on superego matters and empirically based decision-making, whereas reality therapy tries to avoid excuses and aims at generating concern for others and responsibility for oneself and one's behavior. Adams' (1970) Christian counseling pivots on issues of autonomy and a primary relationship with the divine. Many of the newer therapeutic techniques tend to be evaluation oriented (the "new kid on the block" syndrome), so the question of utility must be considered. With relatively bright, urban people, rational-emotive therapy is probably effective, as is reality therapy with delinquents or Christian counseling with conservative Christians. The test comes when the approach is extended beyond its original field of application. If values are to be accepted as a factor, then utility may be balanced against other qualities of a new technique.

Ethics, morals, and values are important to consider in therapy because they are important to many patients and therapists. "Human life is—and has to be—a moral life precisely because it is a social life" (Kluckhohn 1951, p. 388). Those patients without a functioning conscience we call psychopaths or sociopaths, and the joy and simplicity of treating them is well recognized. This is not a warrant for readily inculcating values into patients, but only for the therapist to admit such topics into therapy for scrutiny.

3

Some Religious Issues
Met in Therapy

As therapists, we may feel discomfort or guilt when we experience countertransference reactions, although we are often aware that they can also be useful (Epstein and Feiner 1979; Kernberg 1975; Yassky 1976). Training, supervision, and personal psychotherapy all help us to deal with, and even use these feelings, to hear, accept, and experience erotic, aggressive, dependent, or grandiose feelings in ourselves and in our patients. We learn to understand disparate life-styles and political orientations, but we rarely receive the same training in religious values and feelings; these tend to be lumped with a political and philosophical *Weltanschauung* and are thought of as private and outside the purview of psychotherapy (Fromm-Reichmann 1950). This is highly problematic. It has been pointed out (Bowers 1963; Morris 1955; Pruyser 1971) that if a patient's religion is prominent, an understanding of the patient's religious background and symbols may be essential to adequate diagnosis and treatment.

When we speak of a person's religion, we are actually referring to a complex process, with roots in antiquity and a long historical development that is far removed from the professional concerns of most practicing psychotherapists. How may the patient's religious expressions be understood? Can we grasp their psychological meanings without acidic disparagement or insulating reverence? This chapter will survey selected aspects of the historical development of Judaism and Christianity, so as to translate the patient's religious idiom into terms compatible with the issues and conceptions of psychotherapy.

HISTORICAL ANTECEDENTS OF
AMERICAN RELIGIONS

Some of what follows depends on a historical record that, in part, appears only in the oldest part of the Bible. The writers of the Bible did not intend to write history in the modern sense of the term, although their accounts were often quite accurate. However, Alter (1981) demonstrated that facets of the biblical narrative, which are often taken literally, actually reflect literary conventions of the time. One must be careful to differentiate historical from literary aspects of a passage for a fuller grasp of the meaning. It is reasonable to set the start of the historical section with the story of Abraham. The land purchases, the pastoral wanderings, the family arrangements, and such are consistent with what is known of life in the Fertile Crescent in the early second millennium, B.C.E. Did Abraham exist? Probably, for some of his behavior is far from admirable, so it is unlikely that such an ancestor was invented.[1]

Origins

God promised Abraham that his descendents would inherit a land not theirs and become a great nation after being oppressed by another people. This story has unusual qualities. Instead of setting the history of the eventual nation of Israel in the mythological past of their own land, they were given a lease as newcomers, contingent upon their good behavior. At that time, slavery was a stain upon the person, not a history one would want to recount. The origin of this people, whose religious descendents include followers of modern Judaism, Christianity, and Islam, had an historical rather than a legendary base, a contingent title (Lev. 20:22) to the land they eventually settled, a shameful past (slavery), and a peculiar conception of the divine (monotheism). One may speculate that this set of elements eventually had psychological derivatives, including an emphasis on an accurate knowledge of reality (the historical orientation), a developing emphasis on public, communal morality (the contingent title), an interest in one's historic past as it actually was (slavery), and a propensity toward a coherent and lawful conception of the universe (monotheism). If this is roughly correct, it was a long, slow, imperfect development.

[1] I am indebted to Dr. Calman Levich for this interpretation.

The Development of a Nation

The descendents of Abraham's grandson, Jacob, renamed Israel, left Egypt, received their national constitution in the form of a contractual or covenantal relationship with God, and arrived at the land of Canaan, which they infiltrated, entered, conquered, and settled. In contrast to the centralized, despotic, and bureaucratic governments common to that area, they established a loose confederacy for several centuries under the occasional leadership of chiefs we call "judges." Both inner and outer forces led to the development of a kingship, but with limitations as mentioned in Chapter 1. With the establishment of the Davidic line, a centralized worship system was focused on the Temple in Jerusalem and the Israelites then had a fixed place for sacrificial worship. In many ritual aspects, they resembled their neighbors with a god with a defined "turf," sacrifice as the primary form of worship, and an established and hereditary priesthood. Civil war divided the kingdom after Solomon's death into the northern kingdom of Israel, which eventually vanished into the Assyrian maw in 722 B.C.E., whereas the southern kingdom of Judaea lasted until Nebuchadnezzar of Babylon destroyed it in 586 B.C.E.

Exile, Dispersion, and Survival

The national leaders and many of the people were displaced persons in Babylon and would have been lost to history, as were their northern brethren, some hundred-odd years before except for a remarkable invention. The Temple was destroyed and the priests could not offer sacrifice anywhere else. Prayer (speaking and singing) was substituted for sacrifice as the central form of worship. A special sacred place (the Temple) was no longer needed and ritual became essentially liturgical. What is now called religion became portable and the society did not require a land in which to live; it existed and was transmitted by the cultural group (Dimont 1962).

Even before the development of religious portability, there was a leavening agent: bands or guilds of itinerant preachers who considered themselves spokesmen for God. Although fortune-telling was probably among their activities and some were involved in government, much of the vigorous social criticism and the light shed on the economic practices of post-Davidic Judea and Israel comes from these men. For them, all of life was contained in the modern definition of religion, so economic practices and political structures were as "religious" as ritual procedures.

This kind of independent critique had historical roots (Num. 11:27) and sanction.

Although the Jews were able to return to their land some 50 years later, many did not, continuing their communal life wherever they lived. A key theme throughout the Old Testament was religious decay and reform, for the Jews were repetitively attracted to the practices of the surrounding cultures. Sacrificing your child to Moloch was so much more meaningful than sacrificing your goat's kid. Although Jews were again in control of the land of Judaea, the height of their political power had passed; they were successively under the influence of Persia, Greece, and Rome. They were, however, able to reconstitute some of their national life, so that the priesthood, known as the Sons of Zadok or Zadokites (hence Sadduces in the New Testament), was again functional.

The substitution of prayer for sacrifice led to another stream in Jewish life, known as the Pharisees (from *perush*, meaning separate), who were the originators of normative rabbinic Judaism. These groups were two among many competing for political and religious power, as they attempted to shape the Judean world into their world-view. This turmoil, plus the increasing exactions of the Romans, intensified the misery, despair, and rebelliousness of the Jews and increased hopes for an anointed leader or *mashiach* (messiah) to aid and lead them. There were probably many individuals and groups trying to lead the Jews and thus hasten help from God. One such was Yeshua or Joshua, or as we now know him, Jesus (the Greek of the New Testament did not have an *sh* sound).

The New Israel

The group that formed around Jesus did not disband with his execution by the Romans. A powerful teacher, he brought hope, encouragement, and a meaningful idiom to express the despair and longing for rescue in those people for whom the available forms did not suffice (Sandmel 1957). The target of hostility from part of the community, this small band continued to grow within the Jewish community, but expanded greatly when Paul freed this Jewish sect from the strict requirements of Jewish ritual law. For reasons of political control, the Romans prohibited the formation of new cults, sects, or religions, and these early Christians were persecuted. They, like the Jews of their day, were successful in attracting sympathizers and converts among upper-class Romans. The Jews were none too popular with the authorities after the desperate Roman struggle to subdue them, which mainly ended with the destruction of the Temple in

Jerusalem in 70 C.E. Both Jews and Christians were unpopular because of their narrow and intolerant view that all other gods were frauds. This flew in the face of a long-standing tolerance by the populace. Rooted in Jewish thought, literature (the Bible and other writings), and liturgical practices (Werner 1959), early Christianity also was a historical, portable, monotheistic, ethically based religion. Understandably, early Christians saw themselves as the New Israel.

Two subtle themes seem to have emerged. Judaism emphasized community, culture, and behavior as their basic identity and so Judaism was vulnerable to attrition when individuals assimilated to the larger and often more attractive society. Concern for community integrity was, and is, a pervasive theme. This theme is likely to be seen in therapy. The New Covenant that developed between Christians and God implied that the older one was superseded, or so it was read. Thus, Jews should disappear, but they failed to fulfill their allotted place in history, and a certain discomfort between Jews and Christians may still be seen. The long historical conflict between Christianity and Judaism may be a vehicle for transference or countertransference when the therapist is Jewish and the patient Christian, or vice versa.

Development and Divergences

A persecuted, but increasingly important sect, Christianity took a major turn when it was adopted by Constantine early in the Fourth Century, C.E. Soon it was to suffer the dangers of successful adoption by the government as had the tribal practices and ideals of Abraham when they became the foundation of Israel and the Davidic monarchy, but there was an important and far-reaching difference in that Christianity emphasized belief and trust in doctrines. Caporale (Caporale and Grumelli 1971) declared that Christianity is about the only major religion with a cognitive base, noting that Oriental religions did not develop a rational belief-system.[2] Beliefs as internal states are much harder to observe, but because of their importance they were the focus of recurrent desperate disputes in the first few hundred years of Christian development.

There were many competing doctrines among Christians on the nature of God, Jesus, and humanity in these early centuries. The Gnostics felt that a much greater knowledge of God was possible through a mystical

[2]This seems in error (cf. Smith 1958), but may refer to the Christian insistence on acceptance of doctrine for community membership.

approach, whereas the Nestorians held that Jesus had two natures; one human and one divine and only the human one was crucified. The Donatists insisted that those who administered the sacraments had to be morally superior to their congregants, which undermined the religious–political authority of the bishops; the Arians, however, held that the Son was inferior to the Father. These are only a few of the controversies, but they indicate that the eventually successful trend of Christianity did not develop in a simple linear fashion. Many of these issues re-emerged at and after the Reformation in various Protestant denominations.

For complex political, geographical, and theological reasons, the Catholic Church split in 1054 C.E. into the eastern branch or Holy Orthodox Church and the western branch or Roman Catholic Church. Muller (1958) suggested that the Orthodox Church held somewhat closer to the early New Testament conceptions of Jesus, whereas the Roman Church, in order to lend more coherence to its theology, departed some-what from its early Scriptural sources. Without overdrawing the distinc-tion, it would appear that the mystical and emotional aspects of religious activity have a broader breadth in the Orthodox Church, whereas schol-arly, intellectual activities are more at home in the Roman Church. Since right belief is crucial, the tension between orthodoxy and heresy can lead to schism, but for a variety of reasons, the Roman Church was the dominant political force in the Western world for centuries, until the Reformation in the sixteenth century.

A Partial Retrospect

Christianity, originally a Jewish sect, owed much to its Jewish origin, including a literature, an ethical code, ritual, liturgy, and portability. The hereditary priesthood did not survive in either Judaism or Christianity, except in vestigial forms. Christianity also drew from Greek, Roman, and other sources for imagery, thought forms, and legal and governing struc-tures. Cardinals, for example, are unscriptural, but rather are derived from the Latin *cardo* or hinge, a Roman "hinge-man" or expediter. For Jews, the key historical events are God's promise to Abraham, the exodus from Egypt through God's intervention, and their agreement to the Ten Commandments at Sinai in a contractual relationship with God. For Christians, the key historical events are the Incarnation, wherein an aspect of God appeared in human form in the person of Jesus, the Atonement when the death of Jesus sacrificially atoned for Original Sin (Adam's disobedience and fall), and the Resurrection of Jesus after the crucifixion. The similarities between Judaism and Christianity are real in their sense of God's presence as an actual event that affects the course of history, the emphasis on ethics, and a coherent view of the universe.

The differences tend to be more implicit. The concept of an afterlife is a relatively late addition to Judaism, whereas it was an essential part of Christianity from its beginnings; thus, Judaism focused more on the present world than did Christianity. This appears to be changing among a number of Christian denominations. Both Judaism and Catholicism view humanity as a mixture of good and evil; the concept of Original Sin in Christianity is roughly matched by the Evil Impulse in Judaism. Although the former is inherent and may be perceived as an irreparable defect, the latter belongs to the individual and must be struggled against. The evil impulse locates control within the person, whereas original sin and the devil permit a more comfortable externalization. The concept of original sin was accompanied by a more thorough redemption, cleansing, and reunion with God. This "good news" was and is of great psychological power and reparative effect. The permitted satisfactions of Judaism in this world are not matched by the promised satisfactions of Christianity in the next.

Jewish emphasis on behavior as a central factor probably helped retain a sense of community among the widely scattered Jews and schisms were largely avoided. Even when there were bodies able to formulate a uniform code of belief, this was never done and no creed exists even now in the Jewish worship service proper. The detailed code of ritual and ethical behavior required careful study, which fostered an intellectual tradition of considerable freedom and daring. The Christian emphasis on correct belief (there are significant elements of the reverse in both groups) as a core of the Christian experience led to a tendency to split over doctrines, more invasiveness of the person's internal experience, but also had a potential for increased certainty and confidence. Because of the importance of beliefs, much energy was poured into intellectual matters, leading to the intense development of theology (and philosophy) and great subtlety of thought. By contrast, Jewish theology is relatively rudimentary. The concept of Jesus as God made manifest is entirely unacceptable to Jewish thought, which can be stated on this point as "anything that can be created is not God."[3] This is a core difference between normative Judaism and normative Christianity (Sandmel 1957).

Without overdrawing the differences between Judaism and Catholicism, certain modal differences in the psychological implications of these

---

[3]I am indebted to Rabbi Jossef Kratzenstein for this concise contrast.

two religions are suggested. Judaism may be somewhat more likely to
lead to difficulties in areas of being able to resist family demands, guilt
over involvement outside the ethnic group, and internalization of guilt.
Catholicism may be somewhat more likely to lead to problems over
doubt, unacceptable thoughts, difficulties in intimacy, and/or resentment
over feelings of being controlled by external influences. Brock (1962), in
an ingenious study, asked Yale non-Catholic undergraduates to write
essays in favor of their conversion to Catholicism. Those in a high-choice
condition showed more favorable attitudes than those in a low-choice
condition, and those who saw the change in behavioral terms were more
favorable in attitudes than those who saw the change in terms of belief.

The Shattering of Western Catholicism

The issues of the Reformation were precipitated by Martin Luther's
nailing of his 95 theses to the door of the Wittenberg Castle church in
1517. Beginning as an invitation to debate questionable Church practices,
this act rapidly exploded into a political and theological revolution, no
doubt much to Luther's surprise. Finally, in intransigent opposition,
Luther proposed to substitute the authority of the Bible for the authority
of the Church; the individual's understanding replaced the teachings of
the Church; for the Church's view that humanity was both good and evil,
Luther proposed a view of mankind as totally depraved.[4] Other theological changes included predestination, the irresistibility of grace, and salvation that depended solely on faith in Jesus. Salvation originally meant
physical healing (Hegy 1978), as well as help from God, but in the
development of Christian thought, it came to mean rescue from the state
of sin because of the sacrificial, atoning death of Jesus (Rahner 1975).
Predestination derived from the concept that if God is omnipotent and
omniscient, how could human behavior affect God's decisions about
salvation. The Roman Church's position was that a person could participate in his or her salvation through both faith and good deeds; Luther
and Calvin held that faith alone was the key, but good deeds were valued
as a sign of salvation, even though they were not enough to produce it.
Grace was God's action on a person to confer salvation. Modern Lutheran
and Calvinist views vary from these positions in practice, but at that time,
their political, social, and religious impacts were revolutionary.

---

[4]"Total depravity" did not mean people had no good qualities; it rather was an extreme way
of saying that one could not rely on oneself alone to achieve grace and salvation, but needed
to rely totally on faith in God.

The main lines of the Protestant tradition emphasized individual responsibility for religious self-direction, as well as degrees of literalness in the interpretation of the Bible. That complex of experiences of worth, reunion, and esteem that may be called salvation and grace was, for Protestants, more freely available without being bound to Catholic rules, ritual, tradition, sacrament, and ecclesiastical authority. It was also less certain, since it was more a matter of individual effort (at faith) and/or chance (predestination) without the traditionally efficacious ritual and sacraments. The Methodists and other Protestant denominations that arose subsequent to the Reformation brought more hope of salvation, but their impact came later. First came the Thirty Years War.

It seems reasonable to conclude that the Reformation led to greater religious and personal freedom in the long run, but it also increased insecurity about salvation and led to a more severe conscience for those concerned with such matters. The Protestant reduction in the number of sacraments from seven to one or two and their being more or less emptied of (there is no other word for it) "magical" efficacy, as well as the loss of clearly defined ritual channels for discharging guilt (confession, penance, absolution, unction), left the Protestant less controlled, but also less secure. This insecurity may also have affected the acceptability and permissibility of pleasurable satisfactions. The Roman Church had a structured and defined asceticism in the religious orders of priests, nuns, and monks; the laity had less to worry about because of established and Church-guaranteed vehicles of divine aid. Protestants were less certain and this may have intensified preexisting trends in Christianity of self-denial. The increased freedom probably contributed to commercial and intellectual expansion without the pervasive control of the Roman Church. There are contrary trends, but a shift in the overall balance is suggested. Spanish and Portuguese Catholics actively explored and conquered the New World, founded colonies, and exploited natural resources. Whether their relatively less creative colonization and development of Central and South America was due to the climate, the dulling effects of too much gold, or the kinds of subtle differences suggested here is debatable.

Protestant Developments after the Reformation

The main Protestant churches that arose at, and after, the Reformation cover a span of more than three centuries and can be construed as being derived from various strands of ritual, intellect, sacrament, mysticism, and affective expression that were more or less prominent within both the

Roman and the Orthodox churches. These developments will be covered in more detail when these churches are considered both in Chapter 5 and Appendix 3. Only a few points will be made here. The Reformation gave rise to two groups of churches almost immediately. In the first group, there were the churches that broke with Rome, such as the Lutheran and the Presbyterian, but did not turn their backs on the wider society. The second set comprised the more radical churches, such as the Mennonite, Amish, and Baptist, which tended to turn within their communities and avoided contact with, much less success within secular governments or the larger society. These churches were much more like sects in the sociological meaning of the term (see Sects below).

After this initial ferment, the next main development was the English break with Rome, leading to the Church of England, which is the Episcopal Church in this country. Coming later and propelled by partly different motives, it was more nearly similar to the Roman Church. The Methodist Church arose from this church, although for a long time it was a group within the Church of England and not a separate entity. The Methodist Church, in its turn, experienced an internal division giving rise to the Holiness churches, which again, in turn, yielded the numerous Pentecostal churches. The religious ferment intensified in this country after the Declaration of Independence and led to a variety of smaller, but important denominations with intense concerns about doctrine, eschatology (End of Days), salvation, and modes of religious expression; these are described in detail later. This trend was partly offset by the Christian churches, which attempted to set most doctrine aside in favor of greater unity, but they were only partly successful. They remain a significant, though quiet force in American Protestantism. Although most of the denominations mentioned here had their origins in Europe, American religious expression seems subtly different in ritual, variety, governance, and enthusiasm. Since there has never been a national Established Church, the competitive "supermarket" has had significant effects.

Later Jewish Development

Let us briefly return to the destruction of the Jewish state in 70 C.E. Recognizing the disaster facing Jewish communal life, Yohanan ben Zakkai escaped Jerusalem on a pretext and flattered the besieging general Vespasian into permitting him to found a school at Yavneh. This intensified the portability of Judaism that developed after the fall of the Davidic monarchy in 586 B.C.E. To preserve the accumulated cultural–religious practices, the *Talmud* (or Oral Law) was eventually put into written form and codified in the first several centuries of the Common Era. After another violent and bloody rebellion was finally put down in 135 C.E., Jews fitted quietly into European life for the first ten centuries but eventually, the separation between Jews and Christians became greater and greater. This political weakness and military impotence led Jews to turn inward, emphasizing community relations and intellectual activity devoted to study of *Torah* and *Talmud.* When conditions were less repressive, Jews were more likely to be active in the wider community's political and social life. An effective system of public education having been established at about the time of the start of the Common Era, learning was widespread and was one area in which anyone (but almost always male) could achieve status if he had the ability. Competent scholarship brought social standing equal to wealth or a distinguished family background and was the link between widely scattered communities. In 1648 one of the most severe and devastating massacres or pogroms occurred in Poland, in which hundreds of communities were destroyed and up to one-half a million Jews were killed. This fractured the communal system of education and led to a serious division between learned men and the mass of the community. Synagogue activities became rote for many, and learning was no longer the common possession of the mass of Jews, leading to a greater sterility in Jewish life. To a considerable degree, the damage to the wider community was repaired by an inspired leader, Israel ben Eliezer (called the Baal Shem Tov or Master of the Good Name), who reintroduced both study and joy back into Jewish life, although his innovations also led to communal strife.

Divisions in Modern Judaism

By the end of the eighteenth century, life was slowly becoming better for Jews in Western Europe, and some were venturing forth into the wider society outside the Ghetto. Efforts to adapt traditional Jewish practices to the opportunities that were opening up followed and led to the Reform movement. The Conservative movement, which came later, restored some of the sweeping deletions made by Reform Judaism and produced the three main divisions that came to the United States; Orthodox or the original pattern, Reform, and Conservative. The Hasidic movement, founded by the Baal Shem Tov, is generally grouped with the Orthodox, although there are real differences. Such terms as Reform or Orthodox have different connotations than they have in Christianity; they refer to the degree of adherence to the detailed ethical–ritual code laid down in the *Torah* and elaborated over the following 2,500 years. Basic concepts and practices, such as the value of study, views of God, concern for others, and the importance of ethics and the family were not in dispute.

What are the implications of this? The sense of family and the importance of children is strong, but the affectionate vehicle of family and cultural expectations can also be experienced as subtly controlling. The use of intellect is consonant with the emphasis on study, but can also indirectly express rebellious feelings. The activist concern for social justice has ancient roots, but is also a vehicle for hostile feelings. Bodily self-control and discipline is valued, but monastic asceticism is not, since the enjoyment built into most religious observances is mandatory.

Modern Religions
and the Historical Perspective

In modern Western societies, religion is only one of many areas of experience, so that most definitions of religion resonate with other facets of life. At one time, religion was just about co-equivalent with the whole of society, but a progressive secularization and compartmentalization has resulted in religion having indirect connections with apparently distant areas of the general culture (Pruyser 1974). Bellah's (1967) discussion of civil religion reflected a cycle of development through secularization to the point where a form of religion has silently pervaded civil life in the United States. The history briefly sketched has had multiple effects on modern American religions. Some of those that seem to impinge on therapy follow.

Diversity. With the progressive erosion of the power of a central authority, more room is provided for individual variation and development of alternative life-styles. With increased freedom, there is increased uncertainty (Fromm 1941), which is countered by the conservative denominations' offer of structure and confidence through strict, clear demands and expectations. Patients from high-demand denominational backgrounds are more likely to bring overt religious issues into therapy because these issues are pervasive in their lives. Denominations with low demands (e.g., Unitarianism) may have a strong impact, but not be as apparent.

Root Seeking. A result of the uncertainty brought about by diversity seems to be a seeking for roots. It may be expressed as an effort to recover the most accurate biblical texts or meanings. It may be partly responsible for various efforts to recover the "true" or "original" religious community seen in various charismatic and holiness groups seeking intense religious experiences.

Scientism.   The rise of the physical and the social sciences have strained the traditional bases of Christianity, and Judaism, to a lesser degree. An emphasis on the literal reading of Scripture and efforts to give instructional time to Creationism in science classes have been used to counter this. On its own terms, the Bible is not a physics or biology text, and sciences have not asked questions of why or what is the value of something, so this conflict has other bases. To the extent that psychotherapy has a scientific basis, it may be seen as an attack on religion and it is sometimes used that way by individual psychotherapists.

Intellectualism.   The increased openness of society to intellectual activity has led to a rise in good, modern scholarship, which attempts to recover original texts, events, and meanings recorded in the Bible and archaeological records. Many religious persons have acquired a better understanding of their origins, but one result has been pseudo-intellectual activities that cloak religious arguments (Balsiger and Sellier 1976).

SELECTED GENERAL RELIGIOUS CONCEPTS

These concepts and definitions can provide the therapist with a view of the client's experiential and conceptual world that can advance the therapeutic endeavor. They are not offered to reduce religion to yet another explanatory system, so that it will vanish, but rather to apprehend some of the alternative meanings that inhere in a number of religious concepts.

A Working Definition of Religion

Two of the more usual definitions are substantive (Berger 1974) and hold that

1. Religion is a structured pattern of relations (beliefs and rituals) to some divine (superhuman, other-worldly) power(s)

2. Religion is centrally concerned with ethical relations among individuals and groups in a society

Berger's (1974) discussion of functional versus substantive definitions clarified their potentially ideological elements, but for our purposes, both types are useful. Three functional definitions may be added.

3. Religions provide ways to resolve conflicts between people or between conflicting imperatives within an individual
4. Religions serve an integrative function to help restore community spirit as an aftermath of the resolution of interpersonal or intergroup conflict
5. Religions provide ways to resolve contradictions between conflicting concepts in the religion's view of divine power(s)

In essence, religion *gives order and meaning to the physical, social, and interpersonal world.*

The range of available definitions is wide. Argyle and Beit-Hallahmi (1975, p. 1) offered a "straightforward, everyday, limited definition of religion as a system of beliefs in a divine or superhuman power, and practices of worship or other rituals directed towards such a power," which is similar to (1) above. In contrast, Bonnell (1969) approached religion from the opposite direction when he elaborated on Tillich's well-known definition of religion as that which is of "ultimate concern." Bonnell's perspective was psychotherapeutic, and he argued that "the way we choose to handle existential anxiety *is* our religion, because this is our 'ultimate concern'" (p. 386). If health is our ultimate concern, will we worship medication? Bonnell's use of Tillich's "ultimate concern" is too far from concrete referents and diffuses the meaning of religion.

Ritual

The evaluative, conceptual, and affective facets of religion are expressed in concrete, systematic, and repetitive forms called rituals. Elkind (1971) characterized three levels of religion.

Institutional.   The formal aspects of theology, dogma, ritual, and church or synagogue structure are included here.

Personal.   This refers to the cognitive, emotional, and behavioral meanings the institutional components have.

Prepersonal. These meanings are similar to the personal ones that arise prior to substantial contact with the institutional aspects, such as meanings that arise in early childhood.

At the personal level, Elkind distinguished between *acquired* (arising by instruction) and *spontaneous* meanings (arising from a child's limited understanding of abstract concepts). Thus, ritual has an institutionalized form of expression, but with personalized meanings. An individual may have fragments of belief and/or ritual that are highly individualized and idiosyncratic, but to be called a religion, a community with a shared *system* of beliefs and/or behaviors is needed. There are, as well, prepersonal aspects to most people's religious life, which begin in early childhood as well as later.

Rituals that are distant from modern thought are vulnerable to misunderstanding both by outside observers (such as therapists) and by the practitioners themselves. They are often the product of long historical development and their basic, original meanings are subject to loss and distortion. For example, Jewish dietary practices, which prohibit pork and shellfish, have long been the subject of efforts of explanation and rationalization. The usual explanation is hygienic (trichinosis in pork, shallow polluted waters where most shellfish live). Other explanations emphasize the value of separation of the Hebrews from the surrounding cultures through diet restrictions or of discipline through abstinence. Harris (1977) has offered a number of modern rationalized explanations that ignore the meanings stated in the original texts.

Such explanations require a separate one for each ritual and ignore how early peoples saw these rituals. In contrast, Douglas' (1966) analysis of the "abominations of Leviticus" took the text of Leviticus as her starting point. She showed that the word for holy in Hebrew (*kadosh*) means set apart, but it also means whole or complete. Since the Hebrews considered the essential parts of their lives (their grazing animals; the rain and grass; and their grain, olives, and wine) as blessings from God, these aspects of their world were seen as blessed and orderly. What was in the wrong category or what did not fully fit within one or another category was *dis*orderly and thus unfit, or not *kosher*. Pork was not specifically singled out. Instead an animal had to have a cloven hoof and chew its cud to be acceptable, which characterized their grazing animals. Four animals are specifically mentioned as unfit or unclean: the camel; the rock-badger; the hare, which chews or appears to chew its cud, but lacks a cloven hoof; and the swine, which has a cloven hoof, but does not chew its cud. The specific mention of these four animals seem due to their incomplete fit within the acceptable category; hence they needed to be specifically excluded. The pig was no more loathsome than the rabbit. Similarly, for shellfish, it is probable that the ancient Hebrews perceived fins and scales as characteristic of most sea life. Other sea creatures did not fit and whales were no more acceptable than shrimp. This points up the dangers in regarding ahistorically the meaning of these concepts to peoples whose world-view was quite different from ours.

Assessing Religious Attitudes

Frequency of church attendance is a common index of religiousness, in the view of many researchers, as well as the devout communicant. Using this and similar measures, there has accumulated a consistent body of literature that indicates a correlation between religious behavior, conservatism, and prejudice (Dittes 1971). Allport (1950) had discussed maturity and immaturity of religious outlook, and a later empirical study (Allport and Ross 1967) divided religious motivations along an intrinsic-extrinsic dimension. A similar concept was proposed by Allen and Spilka (1967), who distinguished between committed (or personally meaningful) and consensual (or social or institutional) motivations toward religion. Allport and Ross argued for a greater complexity of religious attitudes and characterized three types: *extrinsic*, or religion in the service of some other motive, such as comfort or reassurance-seeking; *intrinsic*, or religion valued more for itself as a perspective on life; and *indiscriminate*, or pro-religious without differentiation. They found that people in the indiscriminate group were most likely to be prejudiced, followed by those in the extrinsic group and then by those in the intrinsic group. Allport and Ross attributed greater prejudice to the indiscriminate group because of a greater tendency to generalize, but the lack of other cognitive measures or an indiscriminately anti-religious group made their suggestion about a cognitive style speculative.

The intrinsic–extrinsic dimension proved attractive, perhaps in part because it exculpated religions in general from the accusation of contributing to prejudice. A later review (Hunt and King 1971) supported the conclusion that prejudice tended to be more highly associated with the extrinsic than with the intrinsic attitude. Their review also indicated methodological problems with these scales. A subsequent report (Batson, Naifeh, and Pate 1978) indicated that the negative correlation between the intrinsic scale and prejudice measures diminished or disappeared when social desirability was parceled out. The matter is by no means settled.

A number of points may be made here. First, religious attitudes and behaviors have complex determinants and tightly woven affective and cognitive roots (Hunt and King 1971). Simple indices of religious orientation, such as frequency of church attendance, do little to illuminate central processes of meaning and motive. Second, from scrutiny of their content, the scales just discussed are primarily useful with Protestant denominations. They may be somewhat less applicable with Catholics, and still less with Jews. Third, the interpretation that extrinsic people are more likely to exploit their religion than those in the intrinsic group is to be viewed cautiously. The data seem to show that extrinsic and intrinsic refers to differing modes of structuring a religious attitude, instead of one mode being utilitarian and the other unselfish.

For the therapist, a patient's assertion of a religious or a nonreligious stance should be regarded as one bit of information to be matched against other expressed attitudes. Church attendance is not a reliable measure for Christian patients, and synagogue attendance is even less useful for Jewish patients. This latter reflects the degree to which Judaism is home-centered in its religious activities.

Belief, Disbelief, and Unbelief

The religious lexicon often contains words defined more in context than otherwise. What makes such usage a special problem is that rather common words are often given special meanings and one may easily be misled. *Belief* is one such word with a heavy burden of meanings. In specific religious use, belief can be a codeword meaning religious adherence. *Unbelief* is often used to connote a rejection of religion, whereas *disbelief* is not as common and refers to the rejection of some specific item of doctrine or ritual. Although *atheism* is used in polemics and tracts, it seldom appears in serious writing. It is a narrow term indicating the rejection of the concept of God. Belief and unbelief are specifically Christian terms; Jews will use observant or nonobservant to refer to behaviors and attitudes that are only partly similar to belief and unbelief.

Interest in the psychology of religion has been uneven, although it dates from about 1882. A search of the psychological literature over the past 30 years did not yield a psychology of nonreligion, except in some reports of Soviet literature in the study of atheism. What was surprising was the almost complete silence on the topic of unbelief. Except for scattered and varied material (Campbell 1971; Caporale and Grumelli

1971; Helfaer 1972; Rümke 1962), a good portion of which was in the sociological literature, little has been reported. The silence indicates the degree to which American psychology tacitly views a nonreligious position as normative and a belief position as worthy of study, if not pathological. Since the bulk of the American population is at least conventionally religious, this is indeed a curious stance.

Belief

In order to understand belief in its religious implications better, we will first consider it more generally and with regard to personality. The *Oxford Universal Dictionary* (Onions 1955) gives the etymology of belief as derived approximately from meaning thoroughly dear or conspicuously esteemed. In general usage, belief is defined as "mental assent to or acceptance of a proposition, statement, or fact, as true on the ground of authority or evidence; the mental condition involved in this assent" (p. 165). Thus, belief can be seen as an internal representation or record of an expected durable reality based on direct data (observation) or indirect data (authority). Why is belief held in such low esteem by the scientific and the generally educated community? Pruyser's (1974) review of this process noted that in the course of freeing themselves from ecclesiastical authority and from theology as a discipline, Western intellectuals developed traditions that opposed extrinsic authority and valued originality and freedom of inquiry. The recent interest in the sociology of scientific knowledge has helped illuminate the ways in which "facts are invented" (Shapin 1980, p. 1065); that is to say, how authority functions in science. Still, belief in authority among scientists is subject to more rapid correction than was true regarding ecclesiastical authority at the time traditions regarding belief developed.

Some Functions of Belief in the Person

Belief may be seen as a statement of probability, such as "I believe it is four o'clock." As such, belief will not be our concern. Instead, we will consider belief as referring to a person's confidence or hope about matters that are at once important, but also unconfirmed. Thus the statement that one believes in someone's honesty is said with the possibility that the individual may not be honest in a particular instance, or the person may regularly be dishonest and one is in error. Belief, then, refers to intersections of needs and uncertainties in an individual's life. Beliefs, like religions, help order or structure a person's life, provide reassurance about matters that are important, but uncertain, and permit the person to work with more concentration and efficiency because worry or concern is reduced. The etymology of the word is suggestive: *be-lief.* The prefix comes from Old English and means by or about, which was weakened in prepositions and adverbs into *at* or *near.* The stem means dear or esteemed, whereas *lief* as a whole word means love (Onions 1955). Thus, from belief we can derive one definition, *by love,* indicating its origins and connotations.

Pruyser (1974) discussed beliefs in a specifically religious context and showed a language usage characteristic of loving relationships; faith is *embraced,* beliefs are *cherished* or *held dear,* one is *reborn,* and so on. Thus, strong beliefs may express the quality of one's relationships with others and beliefs may function as representations of loved and hated figures in one's life. Pruyser argued that relations with parents or other significant persons may well be reflected in the nature of the beliefs acquired and the beliefs rejected. He also proposed that when there is a dominant negative belief pattern, when what the person is against is clearly articulated, while what is believed in is vague or poorly formed, then a dominant negative identity is to be expected. The lack of a stable and relatively benign belief-system in a person is likely to connote transient and empty interpersonal relations. Religious beliefs are not being referred to per se; what is being referred to is whether or not the individual has the capacity to retain the experience of significant others when they are absent. In object-relation terms, beliefs are clues to object-constancy and the quality of object-relations. A similar point was noted by Ostow and Scharfstein (1954) who likened belief to eating. They stipulated that not all food nor all beliefs were necessarily nourishing.

Doubt

Doubt is sometimes a codeword for a defect in religious faith, whereas for others doubt or skepticism is valued as a basis for a scientific or critical attitude. Doubt has been defined (Onions 1955) as "1. The (subjective) state of uncertainty as to the truth or reality of anything . . . the condition of being (objectively) uncertain. . . . 2. A doubtful matter or point; a difficulty. 3. Apprehension, dread, fear; danger, risk" (p. 555, dates and sources in original omitted). The latter two definitions were obsolete, but will still be considered here because of their relevance to religious issues. From the dictionary, it may be seen that doubt has both subjective and objective meanings, roughly corresponding in a way to object-permanence and to reality-testing, respectively. Etymologically, doubt derives from two words in Latin: *dubio* or *dubius* and *duo*—that is, from dubious and two. Further, doubt in Norwegian and German may, in an intensified form, mean despair.[5] Thus, alternatives (two choices) may lead to a dubious state of affairs and even despair.

Allport (1950) argued that doubt is important in the development of intelligence. He discussed doubt at length in *The Individual and His Religion*, where he listed seven types. His discussion of types of doubt was largely framed in terms of the person's stance regarding his or her religious *sentiment* (a term he used to denote both feeling and meaning). His list of types of doubt suggest the range of emotional and cognitive issues that may be implicated. Regarding intelligence, Allport noted that doubt fosters the full use of intelligence and that intelligence is needed to develop a mature religious sentiment. Although the main thrust of Allport's discussion was aimed at his ideas regarding maturity and immaturity in religious development, the suggestion of the value of doubt for cognitive development is intriguing. Butcher's (1968) review of human intelligence discussed the issue of problem-solving and concept attainment in which the effect of varied experimental instructions affected flexibility in thinking and the ability to maintain options. Doubt, or flexibility (the two are not necessarily equivalent), can thus be seen as a means of discovering new solutions and exploring choices. However, exploration of choices and discovery of new solutions have a price: error and attendant loss, or expense, which has to be balanced against their costs. The introduction of new agricultural methods in impoverished areas has frequently foundered on the conservatism of farmers who would die if the methods failed, since they lacked a food reserve. The value of doubt, or flexibility, assumes adequate cushions against loss or failure.

Another facet of doubt is contained in its verb form of *to call into question* (Onions 1955), so doubt may be the label for the subjective experience of reality-testing. Since the value of doubt for the avoidance of error, or the correction of error after its occurrence, is clear, how can one make a case for the avoidance of doubt? In the usual religious usage, doubt involves choices about matters of great importance, such as believing true teachings on pain of great loss. As with the primitive farmer at subsistence level, choice depends upon a capital reserve. A patient troubled by the need to fight off doubts may be struggling not just with religious

[5] I am indebted to Dr. George Stengren for this information.

questions, but also with subsistence in a marginal and tenuous interpersonal environment that may be occurring in the present or may have existed in early childhood with threatening or unavailable parents. Catholics are often bothered by the sin of doubt, but many are unaware of the correct, technical meaning of doubt and take its common meaning instead. In the authoritative *New Catholic Encyclopedia* (McDonald 1967, v. 6, p. 1069), the definition is "doubt in this context is to be understood as the deliberate suspension or withholding of assent and is by no means to be confused either with indeliberate hesitation of mind that may occur when one considers a particular truth or with temptations, even vehement temptations to disbelief." Such a definition provides adequate room for intellectual scrutiny and hesitation, for here doubt is withholding assent in the knowledge that a doctrine is true.

Unbelief

Although unbelief is defined as "absence or lack of belief; disbelief; incredulity" (Onions 1955, p. 2284), *unbeliever* does specifically indicate "one who does not accept a particular (esp. the Christian) religious belief" (p. 2284). As before, it may be useful to retrieve this term from its specific religious usage. The third term in the generic definition given above, "incredulity," may help solve the problem. Primarily defined as "a disbelieving frame of mind; unwillingness to believe; disbelief" (p. 985), the reverse (credulity) is defined as "readiness to believe on weak or insufficient grounds" (p. 420). In this sense, unbelief is closely related to aspects of doubt as a check on validity. However, unbelief is a slippery term, since the form of the word indicates an absence of belief(s), but the boundaries of this absence are not specified. When used with a religious connotation, the unbeliever is, by implication, bereft and empty. This is a comforting thought, which may make the believer feel a pleasant and benevolent superiority. It seems more precise and less pejorative to see unbelief as

1. Skepticism about some domain or area
2. A dominant style of articulated rejection and suspicion
3. An emptiness and inability to accept anything not more or less currently being experienced

When used in a specifically religious sense, unbelief has a negative connotation for the believer. It need not, for both belief and unbelief can have neurotic and non-neurotic forms. Beliefs of a specifically religious nature are often regarded as psychological projections of strong and impelling needs from childhood for comfort and protection, reunification with a loved parental figure, or repair of an inadequate or damaging childhood. Several writers (Allen and Spilka 1967; Allport 1950; Allport and Ross 1967; Hunt and King 1971; Pruyser 1974) have indicated that religious feelings and concomitant attitudes may distribute along a maturity–immaturity dimension. Although unbelief has not been studied in the same fashion, Pruyser (1974) suggested four forms of unbelief:

1. Relinquishment of wishes for comfort and protection derived from early childhood
2. Neurotic rejection of God as a father-image or other neurotic, drive-determined, and primitive solutions
3. Opposition to the thought control of doctrinal religions and an emphasis on science as a liberation from taboos on thought and investigation
4. Sophisticated religious feelings and values without doctrine; an ethical or philosophical system

A fifth point may be added. Unbelief may derive from an emotional emptiness and inability to invest in or trust others.

Overall, then, unbelief has several qualities. Although commonly used in this country as a term of opprobrium, this is not its only meaning, and the reverse value is applied in official Soviet society (Cullen 1974). Unbelief may be related to doubt as a form of reality-testing or skeptical attitude. The religious patient who rejects the therapist as an unbeliever may be helped to see the therapist as inquiring rather than rejecting or ridiculing.

Sacred and Profane

Even more than belief and unbelief, sacred and profane have strong religious connotations. Sacred or holy most centrally means set apart or exclusively appropriated for some use, but these terms have acquired a strong, almost inseparable religious connotation. Generally defined as the reverse of sacred, profane is also defined as "secular, lay, common; civil as dist.[inguished] from ecclesiastical" (Onions 1955, p. 1592). Although sacred does mean set apart, Eliade (1959) showed it meant a good deal more in *The Sacred and the Profane*. In many primitive societies, making a place sacred was linked to a people's creation of their own cosmos from the surrounding chaos. The creation of a sacred place gave order and meaning to the world.

Eliade gave a striking example in a nomadic Australian tribe, the Achilpa, whose world centered about a sacred pole that supported the world and ensured communication with the heavens. This pole was carried by the tribe in their wanderings, sacralizing the space they occupied as they moved. To the Western mind, it may seem incredible that the axis of the world could be carried around as one moved. For a wandering desert tribe for whom fixed geographical markers were relatively few, water and other necessities scarce, and a stable and safe abode nonexistent, possessing the center of the world symbolically was comforting and important.

In therapy, matters sacred to the patient represent deeply important parts of their existence. Some things are sacred to therapists, too. One colleague, for whom religion was irrelevant, recounted a situation where he was being pressured by an outside party to disclose confidential information. He declared that confidentiality was "sacred" without this having a religious connotation for him. He felt deeply about it; it contained important values for him, and so he set such communications apart from the "secular, lay, common; civil" world.

SELECTED SPECIFIC RELIGIOUS TERMS AND ISSUES

A patient may sometimes bring in a specific religious term or issue, such as the devil, grace, or the role of women. Since these terms have common meanings that may differ from their religious meanings, the therapist can be misled. The patient, too, may be misusing a concept and some difficulties can be reduced by correcting a misunderstanding. Some two dozen specific concepts are reviewed here. The discussion is pointed, when possible, toward therapeutic issues, but if more detail is needed, a standard reference may have to be consulted and some are given in Bibliographic Sources. Some of the following is specifically Christian, some specifically Jewish, some have a Jewish origin with partly different Christian meanings, and some terms vary in meaning across denominations. Specific application of these definitions may still need to be further qualified to apply to a specific patient's meaning system.

Angels and the Devil

Angel comes from the Greek meaning messenger, a direct translation of the Hebrew *malach*. As God's messenger (Gen. 24:7), this simple meaning was elaborated in such post-Exilic (after 586 B.C.E.) writings as Job or Daniel, with names and characters attributed to specific angels. In the Common Era, the concept was elaborated further. This was consonant with the prevailing demonology of surrounding cultures, but angels are largely of diminished current interest to Christians.

Devil has a similarly humble beginning. Satan was not a proper name in Hebrew, but originally meant adversary (1 Chron. 21) and was translated in Greek as *diabolos* (accuser, slanderer) and eventually into English as devil. As an externalization of unacceptable impulses, the patient's ideas about the devil can offer useful information about his or her impulse life and the structure of the superego. For Jews, the idea of the devil as a supernatural power, even of lesser stature than God, is largely foreign and the equivalent concept is the evil impulse, which is seen as internal to the person. For a Jewish patient to emphasize the devil suggests a specific need to externalize. For Christians, the term varies from a figure of speech to a real personality or semi-deity, but its usage has to be considered in the context of the patient's denomination. A positive or worshipful attitude toward the Devil is probably ominous.

Bar Mitzvah

Literally meaning "son of the commandment," a better meaning is that the boy is now considered an adult for purposes of a religious quorum (*minyan*). Traditionally, as part of a regular service, the young man is called up to the reader's stand in the synagogue to read from the hand-lettered *Torah* scroll. The ceremony itself is without efficacy (see Priests, below), even if it is the object of considerable celebration. When a Jewish boy reaches the age of 13, he is *bar mitzvah*, with or without his participation in a worship service. As a ceremony, it is a late development, dating back some 500 years.

For many 13-year-olds, the experience becomes an aversive cram course in chanted, memorized Hebrew devoid of meaning, whereas for others it is meaningful, depending on the teacher's and the family's attitude. The girl is *bat mitzvah* (*bat* or daughter) at age 12 and in the past century or so, this has become a ceremony for girls in some Reform and Conservative congregations. Either in addition to, or as a substitute for, confirmation ceremonies are observed in many Reform and some Conservative temples (Ausubel 1964; Wigoder 1974).

Charism

Charisma, implying excitement or sex appeal, differs from the religious meaning where it marks a spiritual ability to be used for the benefit of others. This includes such abilities as teaching, helping, governing, healing, effecting miracles, prophesying, and speaking in tongues. The presence of any of these charisms is understood as the individual having received grace (see below) from God. In Pentecostal and charismatic churches, glossolalia is often prized as a gift of the Holy Spirit (see below). Since the usual diagnostic standards will regard some of these behaviors as pathognomic, the therapist may be misled as to the degree or even the presence of pathology if the activity is not set in the social context of normative behaviors.

Chosen People

Although referring to the idea of the Israelites as being chosen by God and their agreeing to accept the commandments and a special relationship with God, the term appears relatively late in the Old Testament (Daniel, second-Isaiah, 1 Chronicles, Psalms). It is based on a characterization of the Hebrews as a holy nation and a treasure (Exod. 19:5-6, Ausubel 1964). It was often offensive to Christians who, in the primitive Church, considered themselves the New Israel. The concept is often misunderstood to indicate that Jews are somehow better than other people, an idea that has been severely criticized in the Old Testament (Amos 9:7) and in the *Talmud* and rabbinic commentary. For a Jew to see this as meaning that Jews are better than other people reflects ignorance or some sort of defense.

Circumcision

The practice of circumcision is quite widespread and is performed regularly by Moslems, the Copts of Ethiopia, several South American Indian tribes, a number of tribes in Equatorial Africa, and others (Ausubel 1964). For Jews, the *brit* (or *bris*) *milah* (circumcision) is a covenant marking the agreement between the Jewish people and God, going back to Abraham. As with other Jewish rituals, it is a memorial and does not alter the Jewish boy's spiritual state. The circumcision is performed on the eighth day after birth, but will be deferred if the infant is ill. Explanations of the practice involving hygiene or reducing penile sensitivity to increase female sexual pleasure have been offered, but these are speculative.

Clean and Unclean

The dietary laws of the *Torah* and their subsequent elaboration are commonly explained in hygienic terms. Douglas (1966) regarded this as a modern overlay and remarked "dirt offends against order" (p. 2). Spring-cleaning can well be a reaction to a house closed up and cluttered by the confinement of winter snows, rather than a specific, rational cleanliness measure. As far as may be discerned from the Bible's injunctions on cleanliness, what was offensive were bodily issues (skin infections, ulcers, menstrual discharges) and contact with corpses and animals considered ritually unfit (not kosher). In some Greek Orthodox congregations, a woman is not allowed in church for 40 days after giving birth. The prohibition of male contact with a menstruating woman is commonly interpreted as male discrimination against women in biblical times, but a careful reading of the associated text (Lev. 15) makes it clear that the issue is bodily discharges (see Women, below).

Similarly, the detailed procedures for the ritual slaughter of animals included draining the blood, salting and washing the meat to remove residual blood, and inspecting the internal organs for blemishes (which were probably tubercular nodules). The meat had to be eaten promptly, nor could an animal that died of natural causes be used for food. Although it is reasonable to argue the hygienic basis for these practices (and they are consistently hygienic), there is no evidence to suggest any such awareness. For a Jewish patient to insist on a sanitary explanation may conceal a discomfort with Jewish identity by trying to rationalize an ancient and barbarous-appearing practice.

Creeds

Creeds were used in the early Church to encapsulate the key historical events central to the Christian movement, and later, for instructional purposes. Still later, creeds came to mean official, concise statements of orthodox (in Greek, correct opinion) belief. At times an object of veneration, creeds may be a verbal coat of arms, expressing the spirit of a community.

Dogma

This word is the same in Greek and can mean (1) an individual opinion, (2) a decree, and (3) a teaching. In the Septuagint (a Greek translation of the Old Testament) and in the New Testament, it meant a decree of the state. For Catholics, dogma now means those concepts held to be true, revealed by God that the faithful must believe, and the rejection of which is heresy. Although Protestantism was partly founded on the concept of the Bible as the supreme authority, and dogma and heresy were theoretically dropped as operative ideas, violation of group standards was often severely punished. Today, Protestant churches differ widely with regard to doctrinal adherence.

Eschatology

Again coming from the Greek, *eschatos* (last) and *logos* (word or thing), "last things" in both the Old and New Testament are the fulfillment of God's plan or promise. Other terms include the "End of Days" and "Day of the Lord." Jews expect the arrival of the *mashiach* or God's designated or anointed leader when the world will be perfected, whereas Christians who are concerned with this expect the End of Days with the return of Jesus. In the New Testament, Jesus expected the fulfillment of God's plan soon, as did Paul. When this did not happen, reinterpretations eventually modified this expectation. Although the Roman Church and most Protestant churches do not expect an immediate End of Days, millennialist churches, such as Jehovah's Witnesses and Seventh-Day Adventists, do. This concept seems to attract great dissatisfaction and anguish. Some of the imagery has a world-destruction quality, wherein the saved group member will be recompensed for suffering experienced and the wicked (others) will be punished or killed.

Festivals and Holidays

Reviews of these are readily available, so only a few points will be made here. Hanukkah celebrates the rededication of the Temple in Jerusalem after the Macabees defeated the armies of Antiochus IV in 168 B.C.E. It was a minor holiday in Jewish life, but became more important in the United States as the assimilation of Jews into the mainstream of American life left Jewish children envious of the Christian child's pile of Christmas presents. The reaction was to emphasize Hanukkah, which lasts eight days and, typically, the child is given a present each day. Christians sometimes confuse Hanukkah with Christmas, and those Jews who are uncomfortable with being different may bring a "Hanukkah bush" into the home, which confuses the child.

Christmas celebrates the birth of Jesus and about all that one can say about the date is that Jesus was probably born in the Spring (Luke 2).

New Year's Day comes eight days later and celebrates the circumcision of Jesus. Some later accretions to Christmas, such as burning the Yule log, were originally pagan practices. Most modern religions contain formerly pagan elements that were taken over and given new meanings. Easter, which celebrates the Resurrection of Jesus after his crucifixion, is probably the most important and powerful Christian holiday and occurs near the time of Passover (*Pesach*), hence the term Paschal. The association between Easter and Passover reflects the likelihood that the Last Supper was a Passover feast, though some think it may have occurred the day before.

Governance

There are three main forms of church governance: episcopal, presbyterian, and congregational. The episcopal form (Latin *episcopus*, or bishop) is a hierarchical system in which one person is charged with the supervision of a number of churches in a district or diocese. In many denominations, the bishop is elected under a constitutional system for a fixed term, so the system may be more democratic than it appears. The presbyterian form (Greek *presbyteros*, or elder) utilizes a governing council. In the early Church, the bishop functioned rather like the modern priest and the presbyter was an assistant, with the duties of a second-rank priest. Not all churches that use a presbyterian governing system are Presbyterian (i.e., derived from Calvin's teachings). Last, there is the congregational form (Latin *con*, with and *gregarius*, flock); the literal meaning is with the flock. In many American denominations, each congregation is more or less autonomous. Although apparently democratic, some of these churches, which are not restrained by a written constitution or an outside review body, can abuse or oppress individual members. In general, the form of church government is not a good indicator of tolerance for doctrinal disagreement.

Grace

Derived from the Latin *gratia*, or pleasing, it has more the Greek meaning given by Paul to *charis*. For Catholics, it means God's salvation (or spiritual aid) given to a person, but does not depend solely on individual merit. Grace is related to justification. It is assumed that all people are tainted by original sin, and justification is the change in a person from a state of sin or injustice to a state of righteousness or justice through the intervention of divine grace. In the Catholic view, the person must "freely accept and cooperate with the grace that justifies him" (Piepkorn 1977, p. 180), whereas the central Protestant view, arising from the Reformation, is that grace is irresistible. Luther felt that faith alone would bring grace, but Calvin held that nothing a person did would bring grace, although the presence of faith and good deeds was often taken as a sign that grace was present. Although grace is commonly referred to in some Old Testament translations, it has the simpler meaning of someone's approval. In the latter part of the Old Testament, grace begins to have more of a divine quality.

Grace and justification are both related to salvation. One of Paul's essential concepts was that following the Law (*Torah*) would not bring salvation. Rather, salvation was derived from faith in Jesus, although Paul did not seem to say that the Law was bad or wrong, but rather that one could not achieve salvation solely by one's own efforts. This condensed summary cannot convey the intensity of feelings and conflict these issues aroused. For some churches, the matter is relatively settled, but it is often a very live issue in newer denominations. In most Christian denominations, it is held that God's grace or love is available to all, and this is a central theme. Dynamically, grace seems to parallel a sense of acceptance from one's superego and contact with an effective and loving parent. Thus, grace is no small matter.

Hell

Hell originated from a Teutonic name for the place where all the dead went, like the Hebrew *Sheol* or the Greek *Hades*. The present meaning is a place for those damned by God. An afterlife is thought to exist in both Judaism and Christianity, but with quite different emphases. The concept of an afterlife did not appear until late in the Old Testament for Judaism, but for Christianity the Resurrection was a key motif. It occurred not only for Jesus, but for all those saved through him. The emphasis on an afterlife in Christianity is a core element, but many denominations have increased their attention to the present, both concretely and theologically.

Heresy

Derived from the Greek *airesis* (school or party), its meaning varies among denominations. If a Catholic rejects some doctrine for which there is a Church or divine injunction to believe, that person is a *heretic*. If all Church doctrine is rejected, the individual is an *apostate*, and the person who never accepted Church doctrine is an *infidel*. The final step in Catholic life regarding heresy is excommunication, which puts the person outside the community. It is often thought that excommunication interrupts access to God, but this is incorrect. It only means that the individual has to find their relationship to God outside the Catholic community. Although Protestantism holds that there are no intermediaries between God and man, and thus no heresy in the Catholic sense, doctrinal conformity has been required and is enforced by the social equivalent of excommunication from the community, and there have been heresy trials in a number of Protestant denominations. For Jews, people whose behavior has exceeded acceptable standards are called *apikoros* (from Epicurean), *minim* (Hebrew for species), or *kopher* or denier. Excommunication or *herem* (related to harem) meant roughly "off limits" and was uncommon. Excommunication could be applied to other than people and a *herem* was pronounced in May 1968 against California grapes because they were produced through the exploitation of labor, which is forbidden by a talmudic extension of a law in the *Torah*.

Holy Ghost (Spirit)

Holy ghost may seem an incongruous juxtaposition of terms, but ghost is an older translation of a word now rendered as soul or spirit. The Holy Spirit was a relatively slower development in early Church thought, but was eventually seen as the Third Person of the Trinity, equal to the Father and the Son. The term implies agency in that God acts through the Holy Spirit. One implication is the general sense that God's effects are through the Holy Spirit, as in conveying grace or salvation. When a person talks of experiences with the Holy Spirit, this is in accord with a common idiom in use in a number of denominations. When a direct experience with God is reported, this is more idiosyncratic and outside customary usage, perhaps indicating pathology. One psychotherapist of my acquaintance regularly makes this differentiation when doing a mental status examination.[6]

Infallibility

This means that error is ruled out when the Pope, acting officially as the head of the Church, states a doctrine about faith or morals the whole Church is to accept. It does not apply to everything the Pope says.

---

[6]I am indebted to Mr. Larry Warner for this.

Although thought to exist for some time, papal infallibility was made a matter of faith only in the late nineteenth century at the first Vatican Council. For the Orthodox Church, only the Ecumenical Councils can issue infallible pronouncements.

Miracles

This topic often irritates nonreligious, empirically oriented people for whom the claims of Christianity based on the reports of miracles are just not credible. This is another instance of a modern construction, since there is no word in the Bible for miracles. *Miraculum* appeared in the Latin Vulgate Old Testament translation, but not in the translation of the New Testament. The word *miracle* appeared in other translations, thereafter. Two words in Hebrew, *ot* (sign) and *mopet* (wonder), and two words in Greek, *semeion* (sign) and *dunamis* (act of power), were often translated as miracle, but their actual meanings were a good bit different.

Some miracles are understood in Scripture as literary devices, such as Jonah and the great fish. In some, the physical basis for a "sign" or "wonder" is clear from the description, as in the crossing of the Red Sea (actually the Reed Sea, Exod. 14:21–24). Sometimes the physical basis is not apparent, as with the "burning bush," which is actually a shrub of the region with a volatile sap that ignites at a relatively low temperature. Some have tried to explicate the physical bases for all miracles, either to explain them away or as a form of apologetics, whereas others have dismissed miracles as legendary, unreal events. Both approaches miss the point. For these peoples, whose view of the world was quite different from ours, the world had meaning, events had meaning, dreams had meaning. One asked not what something *was* as much as what it was *for* (Küng 1976). A sign was a matter of purpose, not a suspension or alteration in the laws of nature. Thus for the Israelites, it was not that a combination of wind (and perhaps tide) produced low water at the Reed Sea, but rather that it occurred *then* when it was needed.

For some patients, an unexpected event becomes a miraculous sign of God's love and aid. The world becomes less uncertain and more orderly, anxiety is reduced and confidence is increased, loneliness is reduced and God's care is experienced. The psychological functions are not hard to see. For therapy, the question may better be: How is this patient using this "sign?" Is this a regression to an infantile dependency, an indicator of an increased sense of worth meriting an indicator or divine favor, or is it something else? The response in treatment will be determined by the therapist's grasp of the meaning.

Original Sin

Like a goodly number of other concepts, original sin is developed out of texts (Gen. 3-5; Rom. 5:12-21) and passages that can be read more than one way. Early in the Catholic Counter-Reformation, the Council of Trent (1546) defined original sin as an inherent alienation between God and man because of Adam's "fall," and baptism was prescribed as the way to remove original sin. In therapy, original sin is usefully understood in this context as alienation from the acceptance and love of significant others.

Although early Protestant leaders, such as Luther and Calvin, took even more severe views of humanity's total depravity (see footnote 4), these positions have mellowed over time. If a Lutheran or Presbyterian patient takes a hard-line stance on this topic, then it is likely to be of considerable dynamic importance, and particularly so if the common but incorrect meaning is used. Similarly, Methodists seem generally more optimistic, so such a position on original sin is unusual and significant. When I have encountered this in therapy, a strong sense of original sin seemed connected with fairly early disruptions in the mother–child relationship. This is sometimes overlaid by later damaging experiences, such as incestuous or near-incestuous encounters coupled with parental rejection and blame.

Prayer, Observance, and Faith

Prayer in Jewish and Christian worship has petitionary, confessional, adorational (communion), and self-instructional facets. In Jewish thought, there is an inward quality of intense concentration (*kavanah*); if *kavanah* is missing, the prayer is considered worthless. An essentially similar concept exists in the Roman Church. For a time this was not a prominent attitude among mainline Protestant denominations, in which a more instrumental approach to prayer was taken, but a similar stance is now seen among these churches. Sacraments do not exist in Jewish practice (cf. *Bar Mitzvah*), but the lack of *kavanah* in the leader of a worship service is considered serious. Prayer and study in Jewish life are largely equivalent, so a similar attitude toward study holds. On a practical level, Christian and Jewish congregations regard insincerity or indifference in clergy in largely the same way.

The tendency to see prayer as having magical efficacy is general and is reinforced by the rituals used. The use of silence by some Quaker churches and their avoidance of almost all ritual may partly reduce this tendency, but it is probably inherent in the human proclivity to invest such significant activities as prayer with special meaning and power.

Observance in the Old Testament comes from a Hebrew word meaning to guard or protect, and for Jews it is the commandments or *mitzvot* (*mitzvah* is the singular) that are to be guarded. In common Jewish usage, *mitzvah* generally means a good deed and lacks much of the burdensome connotation of commandment in English. Adherence to the detailed *mitzvot* does not make life less complicated for the observant Jew, and for many Jews, the attractions of American life have outweighed the imperatives of Jewish observance. Diligent observance of the *mitzvot* may be integrating, in the service of obsessive defenses, or a way to elevate self-esteem by being better than the next person. One cannot tell just by the behavior.

Faith may express an intense, personal experience of communion and trust or the following of a received body of belief. In general, faith is the Christian path to achieving salvation and communion with God and attaining God's standards (Sandmel 1957). These standards are embodied in the ethical sections of the Old Testament, as well as in relevant sections of the New Testament. Faith, then, is the obverse of observance, but this is a matter of emphasis rather than differences in kind. Christian patients may express in their "lack of faith" or longing for faith a symbolic representation of early parent–child deficiencies. One lonely, empty-feeling patient who found her therapist to be reliable and consistent, announced her acceptance of Jesus as her personal saviour whose love she could experience—after two and one-half years of intensive therapy. The therapist eventually came to see this as, for the first time in the patient's adult life, her being able to experience a positive relationship.

Priests, Ministers, and Rabbis

Priest is derived from *presbyteros*, originally a second-rank priest after the bishop. Priest in Latin was *sacerdos*, but a member of the principal college of Roman priests was *pontifex*, hence the Pope as Pontiff. This latter relates to *pons* or bridge, suggesting the idea of a bridge between the worshipper and God. The Roman Church sees Jesus Christ as the only priest of the New Testament without successors (Heb. 5), but others can share the unique priesthood. The development of the priesthood was complex in the early Church, but priests are now ordained by an effective ritual or sacrament that leaves an irrevocable spiritual mark, and ordination is traced back to the Apostles through a successive handing down. For Protestants, all believers form a priesthood, so those designated functionaries who *minister* the Bible and sacraments are not intermediaries between people and God, although the minister may, in practice, appear in an intercessionary role to the parishioner.

The title *rabbi* (literally, my master, as in schoolmaster) is some 2,000 years old. The Zadokite priesthood ended with the destruction of the Second Temple in 70 C.E., and the teaching function of the rabbis linked the separate Jewish communities. The rabbi served as teacher, judge, and ritual advisor, but not preacher (although most rabbis do preach in this country). He also earned a secular living, since, until a few hundred years ago, it was forbidden to earn a living by being a rabbi. Protestant and Jewish views are similar in that there are no functions that a minister or rabbi performs that a knowledgeable adult cannot. It is a state requirement that marriages be performed by designated persons, such as clergy; hence, priests, ministers, and rabbis will officiate at marriages. Such marriages may not be recognized as valid within the denomination if not performed by clergy, nor will a Jewish conversion or divorce not issued by a rabbinic court be recognized elsewhere.

Sacraments

The word comes from the Latin *sacramentum*, meaning to consecrate, and was the translation of the Greek *mysterion*. Sacraments include religious rites, symbols, and revealed Christian teachings. The focus of considerable strife, crucial distinctions between various Christian denominations may be embedded in their view of sacraments. For Roman Catholics, seven sacraments have been observed since the twelfth century, a number fixed at the Council of Trent. For the Orthodox Church, there are also seven sacraments, but with some differences. In the Roman Church, *baptism* and *matrimony* can be performed by anyone who has been baptized and is able to marry. Although not regular, baptism or marriage can be performed without a priest in an emergency if the proper forms are followed. The other five sacraments can only be given by someone in holy orders. These are *confirmation*, which spiritually strengthens the child and, psychologically, may supplement infant baptism; *Eucharist* or the *Lord's Supper*, which is a thanksgiving for, and celebration of the life, death, and resurrection of Christ; *penance*, when, after confession with the sincere desire to change, sins are forgiven; *Holy Orders*, when the man enters the priesthood, which leaves an indelible mark on the soul; and *extreme unction* or (the current term) *anointing the sick*. In the Orthodox Church, *chrism* (anointing with a mixture of oil, balsam, and ointments) replaces confirmation; in *penance*, the priest is a witness to the confession and not a vehicle for absolution.

For non-Catholic Christians, the attitude toward the sacraments varies considerably. Quakers and Unitarians among others observe no sacraments at all, although in most denominations, baptism is practiced as is sometimes the Lord's Supper. These sacraments usually have a memorial or symbolic quality. Those churches that arose most nearly at the time of the Reformation (Episcopal, Lutheran, Presbyterian) were more likely to retain more of the sacraments given by the Roman Church, although with varying interpretations and emphases, whereas those that came later diverge more. The churches of the Radical Reformation (Baptist, Mennonite, and others), which also arose at the time of Luther and Calvin, retained few sacraments. Although Jews engage in a variety of activities that look like sacraments and are sometimes characterized as such (e.g., circumcision, *Bar Mitzvah*), they are not properly understood as such.

Sacrifice

In the Old Testament, sacrifice was the standard form of worship throughout that area and time, as prayer is now. Although not the only interpretation, Abraham's attempted sacrifice of Isaac may have symbolized the prohibition of human sacrifice, which was otherwise common. In any case, it came to be interpreted that way, although there is nothing to indicate that Abraham did not intend to sacrifice Isaac. Agamemnon's sacrifice of his daughter to secure favorable winds in Euripides' play *Iphigenia at Aulis* may have typified attitudes and practices then. Oil, cereals, fruits, birds, and animals were common offerings and became part of a sacred communion meal in many instances, with part of the offering used to support the priesthood. Tithing or giving 10 percent to support the priesthood was standard among the Israelites. Since Jesus preached largely to other Jews, and considering the intense Jewish aversion to human sacrifice, the idea of Jesus's death as an atoning sacrifice for reconciliation with God must have been powerfully attractive or repulsive to the Jews of his day. To non-Jews, the impact would also have been strong.

The embodiment of the death of Jesus as a sacrifice in the Eucharist can cause no small amount of difficulty, especially for children who are usually concrete in their understanding. Many Catholic children have encountered severe prohibitions against biting the Communion wafer, which was also the body of Jesus. Drinking the wine, which is also the blood of Jesus, can arouse cannibalistic fears and early oral aggressive impulses. I once commented on the literal meaning of the Eucharist to a graduate student for whom this service was very meaningful and the shock of recognition was very sharp and disturbing. She had always known what the service said, yet she had insulated herself from the literal meaning. Of course, the symbolic meanings are regarded as most important theologically, but the literal meanings can also exist unconsciously in mature adults.

Another measure of the difficulties that can be aroused are seen in the "blood-libel" cases, which occurred mostly in Europe. Here Jews were accused of kidnapping and slaughtering a Christian child to use the child's blood to mix with flour to make *matzoh* (unleavened bread especially required for Passover). Given the strict, pervasive Jewish dietary prohibitions against even the consumption of animal blood, such accusations are most ironic. Since the *matzoh* was the prototype of the communion wafer, and since the Last Supper was probably a Passover *seder* or feast, the revulsion against cannibalism for some Christians was facilitated.

Sects, Cults, and Churches

These three terms are variously defined. Sociologically, "a church is a religious group that accepts the social environment in which it exists. A sect is a religious group that rejects the social environment in which it exists" (Stark and Bainbridge 1979, p. 123). They added that a cult was an innovative group, whereas a sect had split off from a church. These distinctions are useful in appraising the nature of a patient's denominational membership, but the term sect or cult is often applied loosely to smallish groups with a pejorative intent, connoting a distorted, unhealthy, and perhaps exploitative quality. Because these connotations are so common, these terms will not be used in spite of their technical descriptive advantages. Instead the terms church, denomination, or group will be employed because of their greater neutrality.

Sin

Sin is defined as "a transgression of the divine law and an offence against God; a violation (esp. willful or deliberate) of some religious or moral principle" (Onions 1955, p. 1897). Sin is so strongly linked to intentional and thus supposedly controllable behavior that it is surprising to know that in the Old Testament the most frequent word for sin (*chet*)[7] comes from archery and means to miss the mark. A sin is most simply an error. Two other words were also used; *pesha*, which is translated as transgression and implied rebellion against God, and *avon*, which is translated as iniquity and connoted "sins committed from evil disposition" [impulse] (Hertz, 1960, p. 365). New Testament usage was similar. The Greek *hamartia* is translated as sin or error, whereas *paraptoma* is translated as offense or trespass. The former is the predominant usage. Venial and mortal sins seem to be later developments and are often misunderstood. To avoid venial sin means to not sin at all and is regarded as nearly impossible. A venial sin is one that strains the person's relation with God, but does not sever it. A mortal sin can be avoided; it interrupts the individual's relation with God; and it is thought to exclude a person from heaven unless penance is done.

For many therapists, the term sin is problematic because of its implication of evil, punishment, and an oppressive conscience. Many patients suffer from an overly strict, punitive, and inflexible superego and a benign, nonmoralizing attitude in the therapist is often therapeutically beneficial. Nevertheless, certain difficulties can develop from this. The usual therapeutic aim is to help the patient develop an efficient, flexible control system that allows for adequate, nondestructive satisfactions, not to dispense with these controls. To uncover and help modify the irrational, maladaptive aspects of the superego may require that the therapist take a strictly neutral stance in therapy much or most of the time. If the therapist's attitude is described by the patient to others, it may sound like encouragement to act out and may be utilized by the patient for that purpose. To the clergy, who may also be a significant figure in the patient's life, such apparent encouragement by the therapist to "sin" can be understandably troubling.

There is a further complication in that the therapist works with guilt *feelings*. Typically these are affective states (either free-floating or attached to some specific ideas or events), which appear inappropriate or inexplicable. The therapist knows that such feelings may be displaced from their original impulses or actions, defenses against other affects (such as helplessness), or methods to control or defend against unacceptable motives. As such, taking guilt feelings at face value is nontherapeutic. One patient was terrified by a hallucinatory image of a devil-like face and repeatedly expressed the feeling that he had done some terrible things long ago. It seems he had; primarily, his sin was to be born in the right

---

[7] Pronounced "het" with a strongly aspirated "h."

position in his family to become the target of parental projections of unacceptable impulses. For the clergy, guilt is a theologically definable objective state, which involves alienation from God and/or specific behaviors. Cooperative work with the clergy will be dealt with in a subsequent chapter, but it should be noted that sin is particularly subject to miscommunication because it can mean very different things to the patient, the clergy, and the therapist.

Synagogue

Synagogue, of Greek origin, in Hebrew, refers to places (literally, houses) of prayer, study, or assembly. The service can be conducted in any language known to the congregants, although Hebrew is often preferred. The structure of the service is often regulated by a committee of congregants. Community prayer requires a quorum (*minyan*) of 10 adults (aged 13 or over). In Orthodox synagogues, men and women are seated separately and women are not counted in the *minyan*. In Conservative and Reform synagogues (sometimes called temples), women are counted and are more active participants. Since the governing structure is congregational, there is a good deal of variation in this, as in other aspects of Jewish life. The Reform seminary has graduated a number of women rabbis. A central aspect of a synagogue is the presence of two hand-lettered scrolls of the *Torah*, which are traditionally read aloud on Monday, Thursday, Saturday, and at certain other times. More typically, they will be read only on Saturday, or sometimes Friday night.

Women

The role of women in Judaism and Christianity is highly complex and not amenable to simple or concise treatment—nor is their role unchanging over time or within different groups. A few main points may be sketched in. In Judaism, the mother had a powerful role within the intense and inward quality of family life. A child's religious membership was that of the mother, not the father. In theory, the father ruled the home, but the mother ran it when the father was away and, not infrequently, when he was home, too. Traditionally a wife could not divorce her husband, but she could compel him to grant her a divorce for cruelty, not satisfying her sexually, or having a loathsome disease or occupation. Nevertheless, divorce, although easy to obtain, was uncommon. For the duration of her menstrual period and seven days thereafter, a husband could not touch his wife because she was "impure" or in *niddah*. Offensive to modern attitudes, "impure" carried no connotation of infection or disease, but rather indicated that something, in the ancient Israelite view, was not in order (Douglas 1966). When this time was ended, the woman went to a ritual bath (*mikvah*) and completely immersed herself. Men would also go to the bath for ritual reasons, but not at the same time. Although *niddah* has been used at times to denigrate women, this is not the intended meaning.

There was much sexual tension between men and women in Jewish life in the cramped and crushing conditions of ghetto life in Europe, but sexuality was never rejected. The crowded conditions led to increased barriers between men and women to prevent impermissible sexual contact, but although sexuality was regulated, it was not only permissible, but also necessary. An unmarried adult man was pitied and often regarded as a "boy."

In Christianity, the role of women was probably both more exalted and more degraded (Walker 1976), which both fit the early theology and was consistent with Greek philosophical dialectics of material versus ideal. At first, women held significant roles in the Church, functioning as deacons, but not as priests or bishops. As the early Church became more structured and organized, their roles were restricted, although monastic orders for both men and women were established early on. There are some strong statements supportive of equality between men and women (Gal. 3:28, Eph. 5:32), and some supportive of women having a subordinate relation to men (Eph. 5:22-24), so one can find what one wishes to find.

The role and position of women has changed considerably over time, and in some ways, seems now to be moving toward what it was in the early Church. In current Roman Catholic practice, the role for women still has limits, but women now serve as readers and as ministers of the Eucharist when Communion is offered. This varies from parish to parish. In other denominations, women have been ordained as priests (Episcopal) or ministers (various Protestant denominations) and, recently, a woman was ordained as a Methodist bishop. Typically, conservative churches tend to ascribe more traditional roles for women, but there are numerous vehicles for significant religious involvement in their churches, which may entail preaching or other substantive activities. Denominations and ethnic groups vary considerably, so general statements are necessarily imprecise. Inquiring as to the normative pattern within a particular denomination may be useful if a female patient's role is at issue, since this may indicate whether the role is normative or idiosyncratic.

A Final Comment

A youngster entered a library with a large book and returned it to the librarian saying, "This told me much more about penguins than I ever wanted to know." Perhaps the reader has a similar feeling. Much of what has been presented in this chapter may not apply to a particular patient, but it may help connect the religious beliefs of the patient with the ongoing work of the psychotherapy. Inevitably, there are selections and omissions, and a problem not covered here may send the therapist to other resources. If nothing else, these materials should demonstrate that none of these ideas are fixed in stone, but are the product of long development, so that earlier, or alternative meanings may be applicable to a particular therapeutic situation.

4

Religion and
Personality Organization

The general religious concepts dealt with in Chapter 3 and the examination of the various denominations to be considered in Chapter 5 are pivotal to the dynamic conceptions of personality reviewed here. Although religion, in general, and specific religions, in particular, are not viewed as reducible to some other explanatory system, they certainly have important relations to and impacts on the personality. The psychology of religion as a specialty can be dated to 1882 with an article by G. Stanley Hall (Beit-Hallahmi 1974b), and it was a vigorous and flourishing field by the turn of the century because of the creativity of such people as James, Starbuck, and Leuba. The development of the psychology of religion, however, was affected by the shift to a behavioral emphasis in American psychology, by naive data collection methods, by an insufficient theoretical structure, and sometimes by insufficient independence from theology. Pruyser (1968) pointed out how James and others did pioneering work on the religious *experience* of the person, but they only confronted the problem of God in personal experience. This problem of God still exists, as reflected in Hodges' (1974) attempt to obtain testable propositions from a set of hypotheses about the supernatural. Although I think Hodges' proposal foundered on an insufficient grasp of the theory he used, it indicates that the problem of God in theories of the psychology of religion is very much alive.

Freud's incisive critiques of religion offended many theologians without attracting serious attention from most academic psychologists. Recently, this has begun to change (Homans 1970; Küng, 1979), but misunderstandings and vilifications have continued, and a goodly sample of these are found in Adams (1970). In *The Future of an Illusion*, Freud's (1927) critique of religion reflected, in large measure, the eighteenth- and nineteenth-century European debate on Christianity from the viewpoints of the Enlightenment and of natural science. He added some psycho-analytic observations regarding parallels between obsessive acts and religious practices, as well as some speculations on God being the projection of infantile paternal images and on the origins of religion based on the anthropology of his day. Although Freud drew such parallels, he did not flatly equate obsessive acts and religious practices. The illusion of religion was not that it was false (which Freud did not assert); rather, an illusion is derived from wishes and the wishful aspects in religion were the focus of his critique.

More positively, Allport (1950), in his classic discussion of religious sentiment, proposed that religion arose from a sense of self and a valuing of those things related to the self that became objectified as outside the self, such as Truth, Justice, and Love. This parallels Winnicott's (1951) concept of transitional objects, which we will consider later in this chapter. Allport suggested that religion lent meaning to the universe, but perhaps troubled by the irrationality and floridness of some forms of religious expression, he devoted a good part of his discussion to developing notions of religious maturity and immaturity. This all eventuated into the intrinsic–indiscriminate–extrinsic dimensions discussed in Chapter 3 (Allport and Ross 1967). His discussion of the psychological functions of religions was exalted by a preference for the "high road," but a good corrective is to be found in Pruyser (1977).

Control and Change

Ostow (1958) focused on the control factor in religion, in a symposium on religion and mental health. He noted four primary functions for religion:

1. A form of technology (magic)
2. Relief for psychological distress
3. Esthetic gratification not otherwise available
4. Stabilization of society through increased ethical emphasis

This list is consistent with the functions noted by others, but it reflects a concrete attitude toward magic. In contrast, Douglas (1966) noted that magic is a much more symbolic representation of experience than is commonly thought, and although there are instrumental aspects, too, these are not the entire and perhaps not the primary meanings for primitive peoples. Ostow's discussion seemed to criticize control as a function of religion. This was more carefully addressed by Pruyser (1974), who noted the common view of religion as stabilizing the social order, even to the point of oppression. He counterposed the thinking of Max Weber in *The Sociology of Religion* and *The Protestant Ethic and the Spirit of Capitalism* and remarked on the role of religion "in changing social institutions and conditions and in creating new belief systems" (p. 26) as well.

THEORIES OF PSYCHOLOGICAL FUNCTIONS OF RELIGION

A good sampling of theories on the psychological functions of religion was presented by Argyle and Beit-Hallahmi (1975), who grouped them into theories of *origin*, or beginnings; *maintenance*, or what sustains the religion; and *consequence*, or outcomes. Under theories of origin, they listed three subgroups: *cognitive needs, father-projection*, and *superego projection*. The first deals with issues of a partly intellectual nature formed around six groups of questions, such as What is the meaning of life? or What is the explanation of death or evil? or What should my life goals be?

The *father-projection* theory is derived from Freud's suggestion of a parallel between one's own father and the Divine Father. Argyle and Beit-Hallahmi relabeled this the *parent-projection* theory, since males tended to use their mothers as the pattern for their images of God, whereas females tended to use their fathers. Jones (1951) made a similar suggestion when he saw the family rather than the father as the model for the person's cosmic or divine representations or symbolizations. Tamayo et al. (1969) reported rather complex interactions that suggested different patterns as a function of nationality (Belgian versus American) and gender. More specific to therapy, Oetting (1964) pointed out that Protestant theology (and especially fundamentalist thinking) tended to restrict the number of figures available to the client, whereas Catholic theology made a much larger number of divine figures available. Rizzuto's (1979) study of the images of God as a function of diagnostic assessment demonstrated that the nature of the images reflected the type of object-relations characterizing the patient's personality organization.

The *superego projection* theory is related conceptually to the *father-projection* theory and holds that the superego, which was originally formed through an internalization of parental commands and prohibitions, is projected or externalized onto God, the clergy, and/or the church. Further, the commands or prohibitions are attributed to God, whereas impulses or temptations are attributed to the Devil.

Argyle and Beit-Hallahmi (1975) listed six individual *maintenance* theories: *social learning, deprivation and compensation, relief of guilt, fear of death, sexual motivation,* and *obsessional behavior.* The *social learning* theory describes how religion is transmitted through instruction and family relationships, but the motivations for a religion and the reasons for its rise or decline are outside the purview of the theory. Religions as ways to explain *deprivation* and offer *compensation* have been commented upon. Surprisingly, Argyle and Beit-Hallahmi found in their review that the more privileged were more likely to enter into organized church activity, but the more deprived emphasized religious behaviors of "devotion and traditional beliefs" (p. 192). In addition to being compensatory, churches that appealed to more deprived people tended not to be interested in social reform. When a person's view is fixed on eschatological visions, reforms of the tax code or busing patterns are not very important. Nor are such persons likely to have had the experience of affecting their world.

Relief of guilt is often considered to be one of the attractions of religion, but it seems that although people who are likely to feel strong guilt may be attracted to religion, religion may also foster guilt feelings. Some people may be attracted to certain religious denominations because they intensify guilt and gratify a need for punishment. Argyle and Beit-Hallahmi concluded "that fear of death is a basis for religious beliefs" (p. 197), but the data they cited suggested that religions were increasingly used to combat a *fear of death* as the person ages and that fear of death did not initiate religious beliefs. The fifth theory within this cluster saw *sexual motivation* as a force in the origin of religion (specifically, sexual repression) and that "religion and sex are alternative forms of commitment, and that sexual indulgence is a form of self-integration which is competitive with religious activities" (p. 198). Last, the connection between *obsessional behavior* and religious behavior has often been commented on. While reviewing the similarities, Argyle and Beit-Hallahmi also noted the differences and pointed out that there was little clear support for the connection between obsessions and ritual other than anecdotal or retrospective studies.

Finally, Argyle and Beit-Hallahmi reviewed two theories of *consequence* or outcome: *individual integration* and *social integration.* Religion in these theories was seen to have a positive role in improving individual integration and personal adjustment. However, they also cited data to the contrary and noted that society requires a concern for others and self-sacrifice. Religions tend to foster this, but this can also be at the expense of other human capacities, such as scientific creativity. The ambiguous results linking personality and religion (Dittes 1969), which are often compounded by social class and education variables, may well reflect the presence of hidden assumptions, as illustrated by two studies. Deeply religious believers are generally assumed to be dogmatic, particularly if they come from a conservative church. Gilmore (1969) studied a group of 62 Pentecostal church members who were differentiated on Rokeach's Dogmatism scale. She found that the low dogmatism group did significantly better on such scales of the California Personality Inventory as Sociability, Social Presence, Intellectual Efficiency, and Achievement via Independence than the high dogmatism groups. A number of points may be made. The low dogmatism group was at approximately the national norms, so overall, these Pentecostal believers were relatively higher on the Dogmatism scale, but the group was by no means homogeneous with regard to this measure. Further, simple comparisons between groups may obscure rather than illuminate the processes at work.

In another study, Hood (1974) found a negative correlation between Barron's ego-strength scale and a measure of intense religious experiences ($r = -0.31$, $p < 0.01$), suggesting a negative relation between ego strength and religiousness. However, when the religious items on Barron's scale were removed, correlation dropped to near zero. Thus, simple group comparisons in which religiousness is taken as a unitary variable are, at the least, likely to prove unfruitful, and at the worst they may hide biased conceptualizations of the problem.

Although religion is commonly seen as a mechanism for *social integration*, Argyle and Beit-Hallahmi (1975) correlated the decline of religion's control function with the secularization of control through the mass media and other devices. The secularization of formerly religious controls as part of the general secularization of society has been counterbalanced by the largely unnoticed (except in the sociological literature) phenomenon of civil religion. Bellah's (1967) seminal paper described the incorporation of a web of moral purposes in general civil life and ideals in this country that has many of the characteristics of a religion, including a set of rituals, images, and ideals. The decline of the political and social impact of liberal churches, and the rise of conservative churches with a primarily other-world emphasis, has made it appear that religions are on the decline. Instead, these functions may be diffused throughout the culture, and their religious character blurred.

Specific churches can have a sharp impact on social integration. Dearman (1974) studied 20 male members of a "Oneness" Pentecostal church who had been very thoroughly indoctrinated with an effective work ethic. Their consistent work and family orientation was at odds with a reported pre-conversion history of delinquent behavior. Further, the growth of conservative churches (Bibby 1978; Kelley 1978), although partly affected by differential retention of members and birthrates, has been cogently argued to reflect their serious and primary attention to issues of profound or ultimate importance.

Argyle and Beit-Hallahmi (1975) correctly observed that the theories they surveyed are reductionistic and, therefore, may not be the entire story. Although they set the limits of psychological investigation at the limits of empirical investigation, they recognized that these limits are not necessarily unchangeable. The theories and data surveyed here indicate a range of concepts and results, as well as an overall lack of agreement.

Indeterminacy in the Psychological
Functions of Religion

Bertocci (1971) reviewed several theorists on the psychology of religion and noted that most of those reviewed (such as James, Freud, Erikson, Fromm, and Maslow) used an empirical approach that saw religion as a completely human reaction to the problems of life. Bertocci introduced an interesting stipulation. If the psychologist assumes a psychology of religion that leaves room for the idea of a religious experience as a "joint product of God's interaction with man" (p. 32), then what, for the empirically oriented psychologist of religion, is an "overbelief"[1] is for the religiously oriented psychologist of religion—a structure or process? To express Bertocci's point differently, empirically and religiously oriented psychologists approach their subject matter with a somewhat different set of axioms, which are likely to affect the interpretation of some data significantly. Myrdal's (1944) position on values in the social sciences and the necessity for making them explicit to avoid contamination is especially relevant here.

Marty (1971) has pointed out that we no longer define religion in single, objective terms only, but rather are aware of alternative meanings and definitions. Religions meet powerful psychological needs and motives, which even a cursory examination of the terminology makes clear. "Turning to God (or Jesus) with your problems," "Jesus loves you," "the family that prays together stays together," all speak to important human needs. Further, religion is a human process mediated through the personality.

---

[1]A belief that does not have an external referent; James' term.

McFadden (1969), who is both a Jesuit and a psychoanalyst, rather optimistically, but I think correctly declared "religion has learned to accept the fact that a man's religious acts are carried out through psychic mechanisms . . . and are subject to all the distortions and barriers that every other human act is" (p. 498).

Let us follow McFadden's suggestion a bit further. For the traditionally religious person, the concept that human formulations about God arise from internal sources may be disturbing, if not blasphemous. For the rationally empirical person, however, the notion of an external, largely unknowable supernatural power that is personally concerned with the world's doings is offensive, if not ridiculous. Let us suppose for the moment that some supernatural power labeled God actually exists and that our representation of God as the creator of the universe is in accord with reality. Further, let us suppose that God is concerned with the world and with people in an individual way. What would be the nature of the human experience of an encounter with such a power? An ancient awareness of this question is described in Exodus 33:18–23, when Moses asks to see God's face and is told "you cannot see My face, for man may not see Me and live" (JPS 1967, p. 161). Any human representation of God would be limited both by our capacity for perception and knowing, on the one hand, and shaped by the modes of representation and expression available to the individual, on the other. Given the importance of the issues religious experience deals with, we would express this experience in a particular language, imagery, and conceptual form modified and shaped by personal, dynamic factors.

Now let us suppose for the moment that God does not exist and that the multiplicity of forms of religious expression are exteriorizations of various emotional, developmental, and existential needs, given a cosmic, universal idiom, but only arise out of the individual and general human condition. When a therapist is presented with a specific religious concept (doctrine) or experience (revelation) by a patient, and it is possible to connect the particular formulation with formative events in the life of the person, *is it possible to determine whether the final expression reflects only the personal dynamics of the person without contact with God, or whether it reflects such a contact filtered through the personal life of the individual?* Psychological interpretations are indeterminate in that one cannot be sure of accounting for all the factors or influences in the clinical situation. At best, an interpretation deals with enough of the factors to bring about change.

The position taken here is that we cannot make such a differentiation and that it does not matter to therapy if we could. Therapy can proceed if we are able to understand the personal meanings implicit in the particular form of religious expression. However, the twin propositions that religions meet important human needs and that religions are mediated through and modified by the personality lead to the quite common conclusion that these twin concepts disprove the truth(s) claimed by various religions. This is an expression of the "nothing but" equation: Religion is *nothing but* a projection of human needs and personality and therefore is false. It is here that we enter into careless reasoning. That religions involve projections of needs and personality is accepted. This can be desirable and useful for therapy with religious patients, but that does not in itself prove that religions are false. It is less comfortable to accept that this is not subject to proof one way or another and leave the matter there. For therapy, it should not make a difference.

OBJECT-RELATIONS AND RELIGION

The central conceptual framework that contains the approach to psychotherapy is presented here. The patient's religious imagery is a set of ideas, experiences, attitudes, and expectations, with important meanings and utility for the therapeutic enterprise. It would be very convenient if the various religious images, symbols, and concepts patients use translated directly to psychotherapeutic operations, but such a hope is vain. Rather, it helps if one looks at these images somewhat like manifest dream images that need to be associated to. Consider, for example, the Virgin Mary. She is easily seen as simply a mother image, but I doubt that it is that simple. The Virgin can have both an unavailable quality, perhaps indicative of an absent or abandoning mother, a sexually teasing and exciting female image, suggestive of a seductive mother, and as Jesus's mourning mother, a depressed and somber quality. Although a male quality seems relatively less likely, if a patient had a very significant relationship with a more nurturant father, then the Virgin Mary may have associated images related to the father. Finally, a word about terminology. What follows has been expressed mostly in current psychoanalytic terminology and such concepts as object-relations and representations. What is referred to here are interpersonal relations (human experiences, memories, and expectations based on interactions between the patient and significant others), internally motivated states (cognitive strengths and weaknesses, aesthetic preferences, affective drives), and characteristic modes of adaptation and response (vigilance, avoidance, defense, and coping). This approach seems basically compatible with other psychodynamic theories, although there are differences in terminology and outlook as well. Guntrip's (1971) discussion on this is much to the point.

Object-relations theory is actually a number of intersecting and diverging concepts that essentially aim at understanding human relations in terms of

1. The effects of early mother–infant relations
2. The development of records within the infant of these relations (representations)
3. The interaction of these representations with the infant's burgeoning perceptual, cognitive, affective, and motor capacities
4. The eventual expression of these complex and obscure early events in consistent, stable patterns of object- (human) relations

In the interests of brevity, a synopsis of concepts derived from several major positions will be presented (Blanck and Blanck 1974; Fairbairn 1952; Guntrip 1971; Kernberg 1975; Kohut 1968; Winnicott 1975) without considering the conflicts and convergences among these positions in detail.

Early Development

At birth, the infant is exposed to much more intense and varied stimulation from the physical and social environment and to much more intense and varied internal stimulation from the cyclical ebb and flow of nutritional requirements, waste disposal, and heat maintenance. As far as we can tell, although the infant may be disposed to orient to the mother (e.g., Fantz 1961), the sense of recognition and continuity of the mother in the infant's experience emerges slowly after the first month of life. The baby's very limited capacity to care for itself, coupled with the extensive capacity for sensual pleasure inherent in the eyes, ears, skin, and other regions implicated in child care (mouth, anus, genitals), makes the mother the provider of care, protection, and pleasure. If the mother is "good-enough" (Winnicott 1975), she will provide the necessary physical care, emotional stimulation and soothing, and stable and reliable setting so that the infant begins the representation of a baby–mother union called symbiosis.

The "good-enough" mother is, of course, not perfect in meeting the child's needs (Kohut 1968), and the inevitable delays, failures to understand, and inherent inability to promptly and fully relieve colic and teething pains leads to the baby's basic satisfying experience of her as a "good" object being supplemented by painful and unpleasant experiences as a "bad" object. These bad object qualities are further divided into what Fairbairn (1952) characterized as the exciting object (the mother who tempts) and the rejecting object (the mother who frustrates). The exciting quality comes, I think, from some recognition by the baby that this is the person who has satisfied in the past, but is not doing so now, whereas the frustration is at least minimally inherent in preventing the infant from doing something alluring but dangerous. Fairbairn proposed that the good object was assimilated to a "central ego," whereas the exciting bad object was internalized as a "libidinal ego" and the rejecting bad object was internalized as the "anti-libidinal ego," and both were repressed. These three ego states were recognized as being similar to the ego, id, and superego, respectively, although with theoretical differences, most of which are not important for our purposes. One of the main differences, however, is that Fairbairn considered the libido not as an energy-seeking pleasurable discharge through some specific zone of the body, but rather as an attitude of the person toward good and bad objects. In other words, libido appears to be a metaphor for structural patterns of relationships. The good-idealized, bad-exciting, and bad-rejecting objects as concepts have implications for our concerns here. The good object can readily be seen as the foundation for some common modes of expression about divine personages, whereas the combined bad-rejecting and bad-exciting objects fit the descriptions of the devil as both evil and tempting rather well. This characterization of the devil as evil is derived from critical aspects of the superego (or anti-libidinal ego). McFadden's (1969) suggestion that religious behaviors are expressed through psychic mechanisms can be more explicitly formulated through Fairbairn's proposals.

Although, conceptually, Fairbairn's scheme predates the development of religion in the life of the child, it is not uncommon in older children and adults for the question to be raised whether images of God help determine the self-image or vice versa. In a sophisticated study, Benson and Spilka (1973) studied 128 Catholic male high school students who were selected for homogeneity of background, attitude, and religious commitment. They found fairly substantial correlations between self-esteem and semantic differential images of God. Self-esteem was positively correlated with loving and kindly images and negatively correlated with controlling and vindictive images. The correlations were not affected by parceling out various control variables, and there was some evidence that self-esteem scores tended to determine God-images, rather than vice versa.

Good and bad here are the equivalent of pleasant and painful or satisfying and frustrating. It seems that the infant forms a record of this bad object, which, because of the lack of sufficient differentiation between itself and the mother, is experienced within. Fairbairn saw this internalization of the bad object as a way to maintain a picture of the mother as a good object; that is, this was an adaptive response on the part of the infant. It is useful to distinguish between objects (i.e., people) external to the individual and object-representations that are internal patterns of experience and expectation regarding other people. These object-representations are not merely memories, but also organizing patterns that orient the person's needs and relationships in seeking satisfaction and accomplishing purposes. In this early symbiotic phase, the infant's object-representations are not distinguished from representations of self; that is to say, the self-object representations are merged, but the good and bad representations are not. As the baby matures physically and neurologically, and as its fund of experiences grows, it can increasingly retain memory images in the absence of the mother, that is, object-permanence grows.

Since a consistently stable representation of the world is beyond the infant's competence, experiences are initially registered as discrete events, so good and bad object-representations are separate. A too-early realization of the mother's positive and negative aspects would frighten the infant, but in further growth, these representations blend. If the early environment has been too damaging, then blending of these images is prevented, and splitting becomes an eventual defense, much to the confusion of others in the person's environment who find themselves perceived very inconsistently. Melanie Klein (1975) quite early proposed a two-step development in the infant, beginning with the paranoid position in which the bad object-representations were experienced as aggressive and persecutory. If development proceeded adequately, this led to the depressive position, wherein the splitting of object-representations was diminished and the infant became anxious about the safety of a more wholly perceived object because of the infant's need for the mother. Fairbairn proposed a phase before the paranoid position that he called the schizoid position, when the infant gets so little gratification that it sees no hope of getting its needs met and a basic sense of distance and distrust is engendered. Although many writers have not followed Klein's thoughts on this, perhaps put off, in part, by her flamboyant terminology, essentially similar concepts have been described by Mahler (Blanck and Blanck 1974). The Blancks' developmental scheme indicates a sequence of defenses, identity-formation, and object-relations that seems compatible with that of the "English" school.

The qualities of these self- and object-representations have been expanded by a set of concepts put forth by Kohut (1968). The very young child, now somewhere in the second half of the first year of life, has begun to separate from the mother emotionally and to develop a sense of individuality or separation-individuation, to use Mahler's term (Blanck and Blanck 1974). The merged self-object–representations begin to separate, and the increasing motor maturity allows the child to explore the world, which is much facilitated if the mother is readily available when the child needs her. Kohut described two lines of development within the child at this time: an image of the idealized parent that can eventuate into the kernel of the superego and an exhibitionistic image of a grandiose self that can eventuate into a sense of self-esteem and that can energize effective life accomplishments. Serious impairment in the mother–child relationship at this time hinders or prevents the gradual integration of the idealized parent image and of the grandiose self into the personality and into accord with reality, leading to a line of development referred to as the narcissistic personality. This has profound implications for personal development, including serious difficulties in the capacity for empathy with others and the inclination to structure relationships in exploitive patterns (either of the other person or of oneself).

Kohut (1968) went on to describe three transferencelike conditions that are relevant to our concerns here. What he called mirror transference occurred in three forms: merger with the powerful other, alter-ego or twinship, and mirroring. In merger, there is the least differentiation of the person from the other, which approaches a psychotic or near-psychotic state. In twinship, the other person's existence is acknowledged, but as if it were part of the self. In mirroring, the person seeks validation of his or her existence from the other person.

Lest it sound as though the child is at dreadful risk in case of the slightest failure on the part of the mother, it should be noted that Kohut is referring to serious, long-standing, early failures on the part of the mothering person to empathize and respond to the infant's needs and to provide soothing, adequate stimulation and the necessary admiration and pleasure in the infant's activities and accomplishments. A mother has other concerns in the course of living, such as other children, her husband, household tasks, work outside the home, schooling, rest, and recreation. The developing child has received various objects from the adults in his or her environment, such as toys or blankets, and these may substitute for the temporarily missing mother. Winnicott (1975) described this and labeled this the transitional object when he talked of "the use made of objects that are not part of the infant's body yet are not fully recognized as belonging to external reality" (p. 230). Winnicott distinguished between this first possession he called not-me (although without Sullivan's meaning for the same term) and either external objects or internalized object representations.

The Transitional Sphere

Play and fantasy are often accorded little respect in our society, but psychodynamically, fantasy became very important when Freud discovered that some of his patients' reported seductions were wishes and that fantasy had a power similar to external reality. The transitional object is set within the transitional sphere, *Between Reality and Fantasy* (Grolnick, Barkin, and Muensterberger 1978), or the sphere of illusion. Winnicott saw the transitional sphere as accommodating play, art, and religion, or in other words, being neither solely subjective nor objective, but rather forming a bridge between needs, impulses, and drives, on the one hand, and object-relations, on the other. Because of this intermediate quality, people and things become invested with feelings likely to be experienced in ways that are eventually described as ideal, mysterious, awesome, or sacred. Pruyser (1974) elaborated Winnicott's discussion of the transitional sphere to include "the illusory intermediate reality of religion and art and the hallucinatory projections and delusional ideas which indicate madness" (p. 112). Reality-testing, Pruyser stipulated, was needed to contain the transitional sphere adequately. Finally, Winnicott distinguished between symbolism, in which one thing is a sign for another, and the transitional phenomenon, seen as a process of developing toward symbolism. He stated "it is assumed here that the task of reality-acceptance is never completed, that no human being is free from the strain of relating inner and outer reality, and that relief from this strain is provided by an intermediate area of experience which is not challenged (arts, religion, etc.)" (Winnicott 1975, p. 240).

As the child matures, his or her capacity for symbolism increases, depending upon both personal and cultural sources (Elkind 1970). This increased capacity for symbolism, particularly in the cultural sphere, plus the child's inherent orientation toward control of the environment through cognitive functions (e.g., explanation of "why"), can facilitate acceptance of religious symbolism and imagery. This is even more the case if such symbolism is offered or imposed by the environment. In inspecting the final product in an adult, it is easy to be misled as to the sources of imagery. For example Freud, in *The Future of an Illusion*, saw God as an oedipal resolution with the person's father transformed into a cosmic Father. "Our Father, who art in heaven" is a simple conversion. But some fathers are demonic and persecutory, distant or unreliable, sadistic or sexual (see, for example, Freud 1923). Two points can be made. First, cultural imagery is available for personal use, so the person tends to utilize what is available. If the mother was sadistic and the patient is Protestant, then the Virgin Mary is usually not an easily available image,

father and mother images

and God (or Jesus) will likely reflect experiences related to the patient's mother, to some degree, if religious issues are prominent for the patient. There is even a defensive advantage to this gender shift. Second, if the early defenses of splitting and denial are prominent, then one may readily see aggressive, sexual, or dependent impulses contaminating all-good, idealized, divine images. Presumably, the reverse is also true, so that all-bad, demonic images are experienced with abhorrent cravings. Sullivan's (1953) discussion of these cravings in uncanny emotions is very relevant to these issues.

> To give a clinical example, Mr. D. had had several hospitalizations and a good deal of unsuccessful psychotropic medication before he tried psychotherapy to rid himself of persistent hallucinations. He came from a large, strongly Lutheran family. His father was a very domineering and critical professional whose sexual and alcoholic acting-out caused considerable family stress. Two hallucinatory experiences were prominent during part of the treatment: a devilish-looking face on an orange background, who called him critical names or ridiculed him, and a row of stars, which entered a rainbow-covered aperture in the heavens. The demonic face was eventually connected to his father's sadistic criticisms, which he had internalized as part of his effort to do anything to win his father's love; the row of stars seemed to symbolize his siblings, also under his father's domination. The father, in turn, was utilized by his mother to punish the children. This heavenly aperture was also experienced as evil. Although God was a recurrent theme in the content of many sessions, he experienced God as distant and pain-producing and there was a malicious quality to his image of God. Mr. D. repeatedly puzzled over the meaning of God's plans for him and why God caused him so much pain. His sense of distance and alienation from God paralleled his distrust of his therapist. This is one of many ways that religious imagery may appear in the therapeutic process.

I am not going to follow the child's development into the oedipal phase, since this is quite generally available in standard sources, but as subsequent examples will show, a client's religious imagery can reflect issues from different, and sometimes multiple levels of development. Although there is not space to connect all the levels of development with their multiplicity of forms of expression in a religious idiom, some significant themes are briefly presented here.

Religious Imagery and Object-Relations

Freud's equation of God with the oedipal father was a very important step in deciphering the psychodynamic content of religious symbolism and imagery, but it stopped far short of what is needed. Rizzuto (1979) presented case histories of four patients, three of whom were Catholic, who connected their images of God to decisive formative events in their lives. The first patient's conception of God was clearly in line with Freud's oedipal formulation; the second patient saw God as a mirror image consistent with Kohut's presentation of the narcissistic personality; and the third patient's image of God shifted from oral to oedipal images, depending on which aspect of the image was focused on, and this was consonant with a borderline personality (Kernberg 1975). Rizzuto concluded that the sources for "God as a representational object" (1979, p. 8) can come from any level of development and more than one level, too. Unfortunately, the lack (indeed the rejection) of empirical treatment of the 40 cases Rizzuto collected data on makes it unnecessarily difficult to evaluate her findings.

Winnicott's (1975) suggestion, elaborated on by Pruyser (1974), that the transitional sphere is a source of play, art, illusion, and religion is a useful way to conceptualize these phenomena. Specifically, religious symbolism, imagery, and ideation can be understood as partly rooted in the transitional sphere. That is, it involves interfaces between the early internal world of needs; partly differentiated self-objects; burgeoning motor, language, and cognitive skills; and the external world, exciting and dreadful in its opportunities and dangers. Thus a person's religious imagery not only serves as a repository of significant life experiences and adaptations to life, but also as a truly transitional object in providing reassurance and comfort in the face of abandonment, loneliness, and fear.

At this point in our discussion, connections between religious imagery and developmental issues will inevitably be truncated because specific denominational beliefs, images, theology, and practices are not considered in detail until Chapter 5. Thus, the quality and patterning of a patient's imagery must be evaluated in the context of his denomination's standard idiom. An emphasis on the Devil is more normative in a Pentecostal church than in an Episcopal one, but the degree to which a person chooses a church because of specific doctrinal implications for his or her personality, as opposed to the degree to which a specific doctrinal pattern affects personality, is an open question.

The nature of the image of God is often a useful place to begin to survey the nature of a patient's object-representations. Although the common image of God as all good is prevalent, it is not that simple. The question of evil in the world, the failure for good behavior to be rewarded (e.g., Job), the pain of sickness, disaster, and death all modify this image of God. How does the patient construct his or her image? Is it sharply divided with a duality implied between God as Good and Satan as Evil? Are they of equal or nearly equal stature and power or is God more powerful? Both stances suggest a propensity to split object-representations, but the former suggests that rage and other unacceptable impulses are nearer to expression. To what degree is the image of God abstract or concrete, and how near or distant is it? A concrete image of a kindly old (white?) gentleman with a long beard and white robe in an adult suggests a failure to develop an appropriate degree of abstractness, i.e., a form of idolatry, in theological terms. It also suggests an orientation to significant relationships based essentially on need-satisfaction (Blanck and Blanck 1974), without much capacity to see the other person in any other terms. A near and relatively benign image indicates the presence of some potentially available good objects in the person's experiences; a distant image, the presence less available, or bad objects.

Images of God or of other divine or demonic figures in which the person sees a merging or duality that mirrors the person points in the direction of narcissism or even an overall narcissistic orientation to the personality. Although the usually available cultural patterns defining the images of God, Jesus, and other such figures tend toward idealization, a distinction should be made between normal idealization without any especial force behind it and idealizations that have an individual meaning and great force.

Images of divine or demonic figures that vary in quality, at times having prominent oral nurturant or aggressive aspects, and at other times anal or oedipal aspects suggest the presence of borderline features in the personality. On the other hand, variations in images related more to distance than developmental level are more likely to suggest problems having to do with the separation-individuation phase, most likely related to the rapprochement subphase (Blanck and Blanck 1974).

Devilish or demonic images should be considered carefully, especially in reference to the patient's religious affiliation. Although Satan, or the Devil, is a common figure, it is more or less prominent in different denominations. If it is not a significant figure in the patient's religious group, but the patient gives it a central place, one has to suspect the presence of splitting as an important defense, or perhaps the use of displacement or projection. The reverse, when Satan (in Hebrew *satan* and literally the "adversary, accuser," 1 Chron. 21) is a readily available figure, but is not used, suggests a capacity to see both positive and negative aspects of the significant people in the patient's life.

Strong feelings of defiance toward the rules of divine figures or excessive submissiveness may arise at a number of different levels of the personality, but autonomy or anal stage issues are the most likely origins of difficulty. One would expect the patient, at this level, to hold a more unified view of object representations, with both positive and negative aspects appropriately present. Last, divine images of a clearly parental quality would point to the attainment of oedipal levels of development or even more mature functions. Rizzuto (1979) attempted to reconcile the Eriksonian stages (e.g., trust versus mistrust), Freudian psychosexual stages, self-image and object-relations theories, and various aspects of religious experiences and images of God. Figure 8 in her book can be used in a diagnostic assessment when religious imagery is prominent.

EXISTENTIAL PROBLEMS AND VALUE ORIENTATIONS

The developmental psychodynamic issues dealt with in the preceding section are an important dimension in our consideration of religion in the lives of our patients. Another, important, but more minor dimension should also be considered, however. The term *values*, or *value orientations*, as used here, is likely to be confusing in light of the discussion of values in Chapter 2. The "stiff upper lip" of the English, the volatility of the Italian, or the eager-beaver of the American are stereotypes of what is often called national character. Sociologically, these dimensions refer to value orientations, although Kluckhohn and Strodtbeck (1961) sharply criticized overly facile and simplistic characterizations of national character. Building on the prior work of Florence Kluckhohn and her associates (Clyde Kluckhohn 1951; Parsons and Shils 1951, Florence Kluckhohn 1956; Spiegel 1959), Kluckhohn and Strodtbeck, in *Variations in Value Orientations* (1961), argued that although dominant value orientations may typify a group, there are significant variant orientations as well. These variant orientations are not deviant and thus not likely to call forth disapproval or sanctions (Kluckhohn 1956), but rather reflect a more or less different patterning of values. Values, in this context, appear to refer not to moral or ethical values in their usual sense, but rather to modes of patterning the social aspect of one's life and culture. Kluckhohn and Strodtbeck (1961) argued that a society encompasses different social institutions or behavior spheres, such as the economic-occupational (or industrial-commercial), recreational, religious, intellectual-aesthetic, political, and familial, and that these different institutions tend both to require and to be congruent with people who have differing patterns of value orientation. Thus, the dominant middle-class American emphasis on an active, future-oriented, individualistic pattern fits the economic-occupational pattern, but a psychotherapist or a musician, for example, is likely to have value orientation patterns that differ from the dominant pattern, and each one would have a pattern at least partly different from the other. Further, although these patterns would be variant within the society, they would not only be permitted, but required, since different social institutions each supply necessary goods or services.

Although cultures do differ from one another, cultural relativism has limits and Kluckhohn and Strodtbeck (1961) set these limits rather boldly in the form of five questions:

1. What is the character of innate human nature? (*human nature* orientation)
2. What is the relation of man to nature (and supernature)? (*man-nature* orientation)
3. What is the temporal focus of human life? (*time* orientation)
4. What is the modality of human activity? (*activity* orientation)
5. What is the modality of man's relationship to other men? (*relational* orientation) (p. 11)

A sixth question was proposed as "man's conception of *space* and his place in it" (p. 10), but it was not worked out in their scheme. The value orientation was based on four assumptions (Spiegel 1959).

1. There are a limited number of common human problems which all groups of people have to face and solve
2. Solutions to problems can vary but not randomly or without limit
3. All societies contain the variant solutions to different degrees
4. There is a preferred sequence of value orientations to problems rather than only one emphasis

Each value orientation had three alternatives, as outlined below:

The *human nature* orientation saw people either as basically *evil*, a mixture of *good-and-evil*, or basically *good*. Under each alternative, human nature was seen as mutable or immutable. Thus people could be basically evil and unalterable, or evil, but improvable. Calvinists saw humanity as totally depraved (Whalen 1972), with no hope of becoming free of sin, whereas Roman Catholics saw humanity as either evil or a mixture of good-and-evil (depending on the ethnic group), but improvable.[2] These three categories did not fully cover all possibilities, so Kluckhohn and Strodtbeck added a neutral category. Similar to good-and-evil, the neutral category was more flexible and rather specific to the stance of many social scientists.

In the *man-nature* orientation, they distinguished *subjugation-to-nature*, *harmony-with-nature*, and *mastery-over-nature*. The first was marked by a resigned or fatalistic attitude as in; "if it is the Lord's will that this happen, then it will happen." In the second alternative, man, nature, and supernature were seen as a whole, one being an extension of the others. A commune oriented around organically grown foods might exemplify this. The last alternative could be expressed as, "the Lord helps those who help themselves."

The *time* orientation involved the temporal focus or emphasis of the society: *past*, *present*, or *future*. Thus, a fatalistic view was likely to have a present focus, since the past was not important and the future was vague or could not be planned for. A future focus has been the dominant one in American society, but it was not the only one. A past focus was seen in societies that emphasize tradition, and most extremely, ancestor worship.

The *modality* of activity orientation was represented by *being*, *being-in-becoming*, and *doing*. Being did not mean the unrestricted discharge of impulse, but rather an acceptance of the relatively spontaneous expression of whatever a society saw as typical of "human nature." Being-in-becoming also involved the concept of spontaneous expression, but with a view toward creativity and the development of the person in a whole fashion, as in self-actualization. Doing was characterized by a valuing of the activity in itself, external to the person performing it. Doing was construed as characteristic of the dominant American economic value pattern.

The *relational* orientation dealt with three main forms of social organization: *lineal, collateral,* and *individual*. In the lineal alternative, the group had a temporal continuity and a hierarchical structure, as in the Roman Catholic Church where the hierarchy is clear and the priesthood is based on continuity back to the original apostles. The collateral alternative was a group rather like an extended family. As with the lineal organization, there was adherence to the group's goals, but the time continuity was weaker. Authority tended to be diffused, but could be compelling,

---

[2]As discussed before, total depravity does not mean total evil (see p. 120). In theory, people are good in Catholic theology. On the preaching and teaching level, the good-and-evil mixture enters.

nevertheless. For example, a Baptist congregation has relative independence from whatever central body it is a member of, although the congregation or the minister (Ingram 1981) may exert considerable pressure toward conformity to group norms. Individualism did not mean that there is no group, but only that, within the group, autonomous activity was expected. Thus, in the United States, changing jobs to improve oneself is expected, whereas in Japan, this would be much less likely.

This scheme was a bold one in its conceptual sweep and claim to universality. Further, it was uniquely flexible in proposing that the three alternatives within each of the five value orientations existed in all societies, but with a different ordering. Within each society, there was held to be a potential for a different ordering of the alternatives for different subgroups. In Chapter 3, a religion was seen as bringing order and meaning to the physical, social, and interpersonal world. Similarly, this scheme by Kluckhohn and her associates categorizes the ways in which societies (and subgroups within societies) do just that. The five value orientations and the three alternatives within each orientation readily lend themselves to the construction of a 5×3 table (see Kluckhohn and Strodtbeck 1961). Further, they tested this scheme with five different communities (Zuni, Navaho, Mormon, Spanish-American, and Texan) all in the same geographical area in the Southwest. Using a set of life situation items with questions derived from the theory, they found very good agreement between predictions and their data in spite of the small number of people studied (20 to 25) in each community.

Of the five communities studied, two are relevant to our interests here; the Mormon and the Spanish-American (the latter presumably all or nearly all Catholic). Although Kluckhohn and Strodtbeck omitted the human nature orientation in their study, in the four remaining orientations there were notable differences between the two groups. For the man-nature orientation, Mormon group values held mastery-over-nature equal to or above harmony-with nature, with subjugation-to-nature last, whereas the Spanish-Americans placed subjugation in first place, mastery in second, and harmony in third. For time orientation, the Mormons held future equal to or greater than present, whereas the sequence was reversed for the Spanish-American group. For activity orientation, the Mormons emphasized doing over being, the Spanish-American group being over doing. Thus, the dominant value orientation in the Mormon community was an active, future-oriented stance that valued individual mastery and accomplishment; in the Spanish-American community, the dominant orientation was a more expressive, present-oriented, environmentally accepting position. The Spanish-American group is closer to a "traditional" society than the Mormon group, yet both have traditions that are very important to them, so such a differentiation may be misleading. Further, when the second-place rankings are examined, one sees that the Spanish-American group has a pattern of value orientations similar to the dominant Mormon rankings. Thus, there is a place in the Spanish-American community for the entrepreneurial "go-getter," and there is a place in the Mormon community for the placid or resigned pastoralist, or farmer.

In the same vein, Spiegel (1959) compared groups of middle-class Americans, lower-class Italian-Americans, and lower-class Irish-Americans from the Boston area. The middle-class group had a dominant active (doing), achievement-oriented (mastery-over-nature), future-oriented (future), autonomous (individual) stance. The Italian-Americans and Irish-Americans shared an accepting (being), present-oriented (present) stance, but the Italian-Americans were more family oriented (collateral), more resigned (subjugation-to-nature), and more inclined to see people as a mixture of good and bad (good-and-evil). The Irish-Americans were more hierarchical (lineal) and very strongly inclined to see people as bad (evil), with improvement doubtful. Their view of the man–nature dimension was unclear.

Comparing the middle-class American value orientations with those of lower-class Irish-Americans, Spiegel (a psychiatrist) related the cultural background of the Irish-American group to manifestations of apparent resistance and transference. We will return to the specifics of his findings when therapy is considered, but for our purposes here, the lineal or hierarchical value orientation was reflected in a stance in which authority (father, boss, priest) is powerful and may be obeyed, evaded, or rebelled against, but useful collaboration (the usual therapeutic approach) is not expected. To confess, except to a priest, is not done, so the authority to hear confession (free associations) must be developed before therapy can effectively proceed. Sin (evil) is the natural condition of mankind, so to relate this attitude to the self in therapy is likely to be experienced as an attack on the client's identifications with his or her parents. The therapist will not usually become a readily available object for identification because he or she is outside the line of authority in the hierarchy, making the difficulty in accepting alternative viewpoints seem like greater individual resistance, whereas it is really embedded in the culture to a greater-than-expected degree.

A search of the literature does not indicate that this very promising line of inquiry, exemplified in the work of Kluckhohn and Strodtbeck (1961) and Spiegel (1959), has been pursued further. The relevance to the impact of specific religious denominations, which form cultures of their own, is quite straightforward, although Spiegel did not make this the focus of his inquiry. In Chapter 5, we will be considering about two dozen specific denominations, and speculations on value orientations will be made when some clear estimate can be offered.

5

Religious Denominations and Some Implications for Personality

The number of Protestant denominations is staggering, even if one only considers those that report to the *Yearbook of American and Canadian Churches*. Some groups, such as Christian Science, do not report, and others, such as Baptists and Pentecostals, have a large number of subgroups. The various Catholic groups, other than Roman Catholic, Greek Orthodox, and Russian Orthodox, as well as the various divisions among Judaism, make a systematic survey of this diversity an overwhelming task, even if one leaves out the major so-called cults ("Moonies," Hare Krishna, etc.) and the innumerable small churches one finds in homes, storefronts, and other settings. On the other hand, a discussion of religious groups only in general terms is not sufficiently detailed for the therapist to appraise material presented by the patient and to find his or her bearings. Thus, in this chapter, thumbnail sketches of some two dozen denominations, as well as the core aspects as they are likely to relate to therapy, are provided. These sketches are very brief, and more descriptive material is included in Appendix 3. Bibliographic sources are at the end of the book.

Implicit in all this is the assumption that religions do make a difference in the lives and personalities of their adherents, but do they? One very knotty methodological problem is a directional one. When religious affiliation and some other characteristic are compared, can one tell which caused the other or are both related to a third variable? Not easily (Benson and Spilka 1973). The common assertion relating religious interest and mental disorder has been repeatedly studied, and several reviews of the literature (Dittes 1969; Spilka and Werme 1971; Sanua 1969) indicate that there is no consistent relation. The long-standing assertion of a correlation between religious conservatism and prejudice and/or dogmatism has been the object of a running argument in the literature. One useful thing to emerge has been that much more careful attention has been given to empirical definitions of religiousness, and the awareness of stable multi-dimensionality in the definitions. Further, socioeconomic status and prior socialization (Davidson 1977, Greeley 1963, Parenti 1967) are contributing factors in attitudes toward a wide variety of social issues. Still, with all these factors parceled out, there seems to be something left. Parenti (1967) noted that political attitudes tended to be less tied to socioeconomic factors than to religious orientation. This study compared Jews, Catholics, and Protestants, groupings too broad to be very informative. Davidson (1977) studied Methodists and Baptists divided by socioeconomic status along five religious dimensions and found that group membership contributed more to differences than socioeconomic status. Other studies to be considered later indicate clear differences in attitudes more closely related to religious issues, such as liberalism–conservatism (in a religious, not a political sense). Part of the problem with inconsistent results relates to problems in definition of religiousness. Again, too broad a grouping tells little specific detail. Further, from an object-relations perspective, one would not expect all people in a specific denomination to use their religion in the same way, so that observed group differences occur in the face of wide variations among disparate individuals.

Three main groupings in American religion, in its institutional sense, will be considered: Judaism, Catholicism, and Protestantism. Each will be discussed in more detail: the several divisions in Judaism and Catholicism and 19 of the more important Protestant denominations. We will also discuss the American Moslem Mission, commonly called Black Muslim. Roughly, they will be discussed as they appeared, historically.

JUDAISM

Commonly regarded as a religion, Judaism may better be understood as a culture bound together by a common history, literature, and worldview. Religious rituals, detailed modes of observance of the dietary laws (*kashrut*), and country of origin of one's ancestors (e.g., Lithuania versus Galicia) are often the source of diversity, disagreement, and conflict, but this more nearly resembles a family quarrel than religious warfare. Paradox and contradictory tension might well characterize the Jewish experience; the world is good, yet evil exists; Jewish life needs a community to exist, yet the individual communicates directly with God; the family is of great importance, yet individuality is prized. Because Judaism does not depend on belief, there are no core doctrines, creedal statements, or confessions of faith, although certain basic concepts obtain. All religions discussed here hold a monotheistic view, but Judaism's position is stark and austere. Definitions of God really state what God is not rather than what God is, and visual symbolic representations are sharply avoided. Although Hebrew is a very earthy and concrete language, the representation of the concept of God is most abstract. It is held that the world is God's gift and therefore is good and should be legitimately enjoyed. Moderation is generally the key; work is valued; and education and study are religious acts, being both ends in themselves and practical. Any good person will receive whatever is given in the afterlife. Judaism provides *a* way, but is not *the* way. How one deals with others is an expression of one's attitude toward God, yet people need detailed guidance and the *Torah* outlines this, which was later expanded in such commentaries as the *Talmud*. A person's capacity for evil is recognized and repentance (in Hebrew, *shuvah* or return) and atonement are desirable. Since there is a this-world emphasis, healing (medicine) and education are important, whereas social welfare[1] is of both practical and religious value.

The fall of Judea in 586 B.C.E., and the consequent Babylonian captivity, led to the establishment of a national culture not bound to a national homeland; and although Jews did return to reestablish a Jewish state, the Exile (*galut*) became permanent as a dispersion (*Diaspora*). Whether because of this or not, the family is of major importance in Jewish life.

Elkind (1964), in a Piaget-type interview with a large sample of Jewish, Protestant, and Catholic ($N = 790$) children, found three stages of development in their religious identity. In the first stage (age 5–7), the children confused religious and ethnic designations; in the second stage (age 7–9), religious identity was based on concrete behaviors; in the third stage (age 10–12), there was an abstraction of religious identity based on belief or faith. Both Jewish and Catholic children had a clearer sense of identity in the first stage, whereas in the second stage, Christian children based their identity on church activities, but Jewish children based their identity more on home and family activities.

The Diaspora led to two main divisions among Jews; the European Jews are called Ashkenazic, whereas the Spanish and the Middle Eastern Jews are called Sephardic. Although Sephardic Jews had a high and

---

[1]Charity is a very strong religious value. The giver of charity is to feel grateful at having the opportunity to do a good deed, a precept not always manageable. One translation of the Hebrew for charity is justice.

brilliant culture in Spain, after their disastrous expulsion by Ferdinand and Isabella and their dispersal throughout the Middle East, the cultural emphasis shifted to Europe and, particularly, to Northern and Eastern Europe. The differences in outlook and culture are important and complex, but most Jews in the United States are of Ashkenazic background. For both groups, however, the family is very important and although the "Jewish mother" is something of a figure of fun, the stereotype reflects an intense emotional impact and bond between mother and child that leads both to strong achievement motivation and common problems in separation and autonomy. The father is often a strong figure in the family, but tends to set standards and roles somewhat later in the child's development. As a crucible for socialization, the effects of the Jewish family cannot be minimized. Thus, Skolnick (1958) studied samples of college students of Jewish, Methodist, and Episcopalian background and found that although nearly all Jews (92 percent) used alcohol before age 11 as compared to 58 percent of the Episcopalians and 28 percent of the Methodists, only 10 percent of the Jews had their first drink outside the home as compared to 29 percent of the Episcopalians and 53 percent of the Methodists. The Jewish group was inclined toward lighter consumption of alcohol, with few social consequences, such as failed obligations, damaged friendships, or accidents and injuries. With regard to social consequences, the incidence among Jews was 4 percent; Episcopalians, 39 percent; and Methodists, 57 percent. In general, Skolnick's data indicated that abstinence does occur, but that when there is a regulation regarding alcohol use that incorporates it into the family, abstinence is unlikely, but so is abuse. For those without this family regulatory system, involvement with alcohol is more likely to lead to abuse; hence, alcoholism among Jews is relatively low. The cultural aspects of Jewish life also tend to perpetuate moderation in alcohol use independent, to a considerable degree, of the person's formal religious orientation. Both alcohol and food are strongly implicated in family activity, but moderation in the use of alcohol is not always matched by moderation in food consumption.

The emphasis on community in Jewish life is particularly opposed to intermarriage, and although there is a good deal of alarm over this, the incidence of intermarriage is reported to be rising. Some figures are as high as 40 percent, although conversion of the spouse is not uncommon. Conversion to Judaism is not encouraged and occurs primarily around intermarriage, even though conversion in order to marry will technically invalidate the conversion. I once participated in a conversion (in a Reform synagogue) and it had more of the character of an oral examination than of anything else. The candidate was examined in terms of knowledge of

Judaism and was asked if the conversion was undertaken freely and without reservation. Not once was an inquiry made as to the belief structure, although there were three examiners, including the congregation's rabbi. Given the intense nature of the family life and the relationship between parents and children, intermarriage should first raise questions of oedipal issues in the therapist's mind, unless preoedipal issues are prominent.

There are three main divisions within American Judaism—Orthodox, Conservative, and Reform—but the spectrum is actually wider, ranging from the ultra-Orthodox Hasidim through several Orthodox groups (Hoffnung 1973) to very assimilated Reform. Although no longer common, some Reform congregations held services on Sunday, but among these groups there is a move toward greater traditionalism. In general, a person is a Jew to other Jews if the mother is Jewish. Degree of observance of the detailed prescriptions is often admired (and sometimes ridiculed), but does not determine whether or not one is considered Jewish.

The relations between Jews and Christians have been marked by a long-standing series of persecutions and massacres (*pogroms*), detailed by Flannery (1965), so Jews are inclined to be cautious with Christians, although a basic sense of optimism minimizes a generalized embittered feeling. Still, a Christian therapist with a Jewish client should be alert for negative feelings, and it would be an error to see them as transferential without sensitivity to their cultural foundation as well. Both Jewish and Christian therapists need to be aware of the phenomenon of Jewish self-hate, particularly in older clients who grew up before the establishment of the state of Israel had its effect on the self-image of Jews as submissive to abuse and aggression.

Although the Jewish experience in the United States has been quite favorable, many Jews would like to feel more accepted and others experience a sense of marginality. This uncomfortable sense of not being in the mainstream, coupled with a propensity for both study and debate, has led to relative freedom with regard to the intellectual boundaries of society and a somewhat greater readiness to develop new concepts and views of the world. For the patient whose Jewish identification is shaky, discomfort, rejection, and hostility toward stereotypically Jewish characteristics may be common. Excess emphasis on the same characteristics may operate in reverse to shore up an uncertain identification. In general, Jews are more likely to respond to the therapeutic situation in free association and introspection. In one study, as many Jews as Protestants were clients, in spite of the fact that Jews are a relatively smaller proportion of the population (Weintraub and Aronson 1974).

CATHOLICISM

The Early Church spread over the Mediterranean into Asia Minor, Eastern and Western Europe, and Britain. The Great Schism in 1054 C.E. led to the Eastern Orthodox Church and the Roman Catholic Church. Because these churches both converge and diverge, they will be described together in terms of key doctrines. With the exception of the Non-Trinitarian Protestant churches and the "Oneness" Pentecostal churches, to be discussed later, all the other Christian churches generally accept that Jesus Christ is the second person of the Trinity, composed of God (the Father), Jesus[2] (the Son), and the Holy Spirit (the Holy Ghost). With the exception of the New Scripture group (Christian Science, Mormon) and the Seventh-Day Adventists, to some degree, all the other churches see the Bible as either the literal or revealed or divinely inspired record of God's communication to humanity. These latter churches add additional writings to the body of Scripture.

The Roman Church and the Eastern Orthodox Church believe that they have received God's Word and have the duty to provide authoritative teaching; the Orthodox Church staying with the Scripture and traditions, the Roman Church adding Papal infallible statements. Both accept the actions of the first seven church-wide councils (up to 787 C.E.), but the Roman Church accepts the Bishop of Rome as its supreme head. The Orthodox Church is organized under several relatively independent Patriarchs, with the Patriarch of Constantinople the Ecumenical Patriarch. The Orthodox Church sees people more as incomplete than as sinful, and one is saved *for* service to God rather than *from* sin, whereas the Roman Church emphasizes a person's sinful nature and need for salvation, although a capacity for goodness is also postulated. The Roman Church sees the Holy Spirit as coming from the Father *and* the Son; for the Orthodox Church, it comes from the Father *through* the Son. It was this difference in doctrine that nominally precipitated the Great Schism. Both churches claim apostolic succession, i.e., the priesthood is traced back to the Apostles and the Church has both visible and invisible aspects. For Protestants, the Church is considered an invisible body only, part of the mystical Body of Christ. The Orthodox priesthood is allowed to marry once, but higher orders cannot be married, whereas celibacy has been the rule in the Roman Church since the eleventh century. The sacraments are

[2]More accurately, the humanness of Jesus is lost when he is equated with God, and this equation is theologically incorrect.

referred to as mysteries in the Orthodox Church and resemble those of the Roman Church. They were described in Chapter 3.

The federated character of the Orthodox Church, along with its predominant Mediterranean and Asian siting, has perhaps contributed to its somewhat greater acceptance of sensual enjoyment and a somewhat more benign view of human nature than is true of the Roman Church. With both churches, there is ample liturgy and ritual, but the Orthodox Church seems to have a more mystic bent than the Roman Church.

Speaking in tongues, interpretation of tongues, spiritual healing; these are all spectacular parts of Pentecostal practice. Catholic pentecostalism, or charismatic renewal, began in 1967 in the wake of Vatican II (McGuire 1977), but has tended to attract more middle-class, better-educated people. From the outside, glossolalia and healing seem strange if not frankly bizarre, and healing is sometimes misused through preferring faith or spiritual healing to medicine (MacNutt 1974). Although physical ailments are often involved, reports indicate that healing is experienced as an emotional reintegration, too. This relatively recent development represents a return to very early practices in the Roman Church and is a source of considerable excitement in current Catholic thought and practice. It also represents a resurgence of mysticism in the Roman Church, which was much muted in the past.

There appears to be little available in the psychological or sociological literature on Russian Orthodoxy. Tashurizina (1974) discussed superstition in the Russian Orthodox Church and noted that although the Church opposed these beliefs, many church members and some clergy subscribe to them. It was also suggested that, in rural areas, superstition was more likely to be associated with the devil than with Christianity, whereas in more urban areas, superstitions were more likely to be integrated with images of God.

The Roman and Orthodox churches are affected by national trends: Italian Roman Catholics appear rather like the Greek Orthodox; Irish Catholics are often described in a mixed fashion. The literature (Chafetz and DeMone 1962, Opler 1957, Spiegel 1959) has ascribed to the Irish a dour, repressed stance similar to that reported for Scandinavian Protestants of the last century or perhaps Russian Orthodox. More popular reports typify people of Irish background as cheerful and happy-go-lucky. Perhaps the observed differences have to do with how alcohol is used in various cultures. Chafetz and DeMone (1962) reviewed alcohol use in several cultures. Among people of Irish or Irish-American background, alcohol served to relieve tension among males who could not marry until late and it formed a basis for male companionship at local pubs. Drunkenness tended not to be disapproved of. Among Italians and Italian-Americans, nearly all drink, but wine is the primary alcoholic beverage and is served regularly at meals.[3] The dominant value orientations described seem to constitute the main trends, but one must be alert to the regular variant trends as well.

Both churches see themselves as authoritative interpreters of the Bible, and in the past, individual reading of the Bible used to be forbidden or discouraged. The Lutheran revolt held individual reading of the Bible to be a main tenet—initially. For Roman Catholics, this has changed considerably and involvement of the laity (parishioners) in a variety of study and action groups has steadily increased. Roman Catholicism appears to many outsiders as a massive, monolithic structure, saturated with ritual, liturgy, and even "magic." The systematic sacramental apparatus is most striking and tends to obscure matters important for the psychotherapist. First, although the Orthodox Church appears to vary more on initial inspection, both churches saturate the lives of their members in what would be called religious practices and also in most other areas of living. Permissible foods and fasts, permissible birth control practices and conjugal relations, an extensive educational system (especially the Roman Church), acceptable dress,[4] hygiene,[5] and detailed and extensive outlines of religious observance are all examples of the degree the Catholic religious culture permeates the lives of its members. Sunday Mass is the tip of the iceberg of Catholic religious experience. In this, Catholicism is much akin to the Judaism from which it arose. The impact on the lives of Catholic patients is typically very substantial, even if the adult patient has apparently fully rejected his or her Catholic background. Confession, which free association superficially resembles, requires a full declaration to be valid. Such an attitude increases a Catholic patient's guilt over resistance in the therapeutic process, even though, from a therapist's point of view, resistance is the bread-and-butter of therapy. Similarly, the examination of conscience expected to precede confession would seem to prepare the Catholic patient for a

[3]It is, of course, an error to fully equate Italian or Irish ethnic membership with Catholicism, although the relative proportion is high enough to provide a rough and serviceable estimate.

[4]Catholic girls have, in the past, been commonly, although not universally cautioned against wearing patent leather or highly polished shoes so as to avoid reflecting their underwear in the polished leather.

[5]I have heard reports from male Catholics regarding instruction as to the permissible number of times the penile shaft could be squeezed toward the tip to expel the urine remaining after urination, obviously to prevent masturbation.

therapeutic session, but is more likely to serve his or her resistance by indirectly impeding the associative process.[6]

Parochial school education is commonly seem among four groups. There are increasing numbers of Christian schools, most of which appear conservative or fundamentalist. Catholic parochial education, a defensive reaction to severe discrimination experienced in the last century, is widespread and covers the entire system through graduate school. There are quite a few Lutheran schools, up through high school, several Lutheran colleges, and a range of Jewish day schools, high schools (*yeshivot*), and colleges. Other denominations also maintain private schools, so this list is not comprehensive. In reviewing the effects of parochial education, Greeley and Gockel (1971) noted that if the student's family is not religiously active, the school has only a short-term effect. When the family supports the values and practices of the school, there is more likely to be a long-term effect, but the quality of family relations is very important. A close, warm family relation is more likely to perpetuate school and family values. Thus, when a Catholic patient was exposed to religiously based education and there has been little consequence in adulthood, one may suspect either a lack of warmth in the family of origin or perhaps a defensive withdrawal on the patient's part to overintrusiveness by someone in the family or school environment.

Second, although the Roman Church is the largest religious group in this country, approaching some 50 million people (including children), there has been considerable antagonism toward it. The Roman Church, in particular, has been the object of considerable Protestant and secular hostility, some of it very crude, which arises from a long and often bloody history and is further contributed to by the sweep and scope of the claims of both Catholic churches. The competitive religious marketplace of most communities has led to a need for explanatory material for Catholics, such as Miller's (1959) *How to Explain What You Do as a Catholic.* Although outdated by Vatican II, it exemplified a long-standing defensiveness, which has modified considerably. Even though Catholic patients may have relinquished much or all of their adherence to the Catholic aspects of their upbringing, they may be quite sensitive to remarks by the therapist that sound critical or disparaging. In Catholic patients, also, there is often considerable anger (with guilt about the anger) about experiences as a youngster or adult that were felt as invasive. Sometimes this anger may be a defense, warding off residual yearnings for reunion,

---

[6]The process of confession is changing rapidly and drastically. If this is a particular problem, the local priest should be consulted.

reconciliation, or some restitution of an acceptable (although not necessarily Catholic) religious experience. In Protestant patients, a special interest in Catholicism might reflect a wish for an affectively more intense contact with their parents.

Third, Catholic ritual and thought provides a detailed and extensive framework for viewing the universe, and a similar plan to correct for errors (sins), yielding more security and confidence for the observant Catholic than most Protestant denominations provide. However, because of the intense concern for proper belief, Catholic education, which is extensive, competent, and scholarly, is often stultifying in its effects on creativity. Catholics are underrepresented among Nobel Laureates, and Catholic educational institutions have produced fewer scientists and scholars (Hardy 1974), although there appears to be a change in the direction of more doctorates in the natural and the social sciences (McNamara 1967). Catholics tend to be much better represented in the literary arts.

One corollary is what might be called the "good Catholic" syndrome, a term with an unintended pejorative connotation. These people appear really *nice*, nor is this a cover for some not too well concealed hostility. Really very pleasant, sweet people, they generally have difficulty in thinking negatively about people even when there is ample justification. They also tend not to be very psychologically minded, although they are not tactless and sometimes are capable of sharp perceptions even if they are not readily available. From limited experience, treatment tends to be slow, although these good Catholics are cooperative patients.

PROTESTANTISM

Neither Judaism nor Catholicism represents a single mode of practice, but overall, there is much greater unity within these two groups than with Protestant groups in this country. For this reason, a taxonomy will be offered, modified from Mayer's (1961) in *The Religious Bodies of America*, since the proliferation of Protestant churches during and after the Reformation has reflected both a development along the main Christian–Catholic line as well as branch lines that are more or less implicit in the Hebraic–biblical core with a Christian admixture. For the therapist, this taxonomy will help him or her understand the relationships among various families of churches and help locate the religious background of a patient, especially if it is of a church not specifically mentioned here. There are seven groupings in this taxonomy:

Reformed. These include the Lutheran, Presbyterian, Reformed, and Episcopal churches. They arose around the time of the Reformation, are rather structured in theology and organization, compared to many other churches, and retain a relatively larger amount of Catholic practice (with variations) and theology (also with variations).[7]

Free Will and Salvation. These include the Baptist, Methodist, Holiness (Perfectionist and Pentecostal), and Salvation Army churches. Diverging from the Reformed churches, they emphasize a person's active effort and free choice in accepting salvation. They foster strong emotional involvement and expression, in contrast to the more restrained, intellectual quality of the Reformed churches. Both accept the Bible as authoritative, although in some denominations the supplementary writings of their founders have secondary authority as a form of scripture.

Inner Light. These include the Mennonite, Brethren, Quaker, Amish, and Amana churches. They are somewhat similar to the immediately preceding group in emphasizing the immediacy of the experience of the Holy Spirit, but there seems to be an intensified mystical or enthusiastic element,[8] which is variously expressed. These churches stress simplicity of living, oppose military service and oaths, and are not evangelical in seeking new members.

Millennialist. These include the Seventh-Day Adventist and Jehovah's Witness churches. Rooted in cataclysmic imagery that pivots around the Book of Revelations, they emphasize the conflict between good and evil, wherein evil will be destroyed and a new world order will be established. Because churches of this sort have often predicted a specific date for the return of Christ, there is a tendency for them to self-destruct when the prediction fails to come true. Those millennialist churches that have survived have been able to make the transition to an ongoing state in various ingenious ways, as did the Early Church when Christ did not return according to expectations.

New Scripture. These include Christian Science and the Church of Jesus Christ of Latter-Day Saints, although Mayer (1961) included the latter in the Millennialist grouping. Although perhaps a bit closer to normative Christian doctrine regarding Jesus Christ than the Non-Trinitarian group,

[7]Lutherans tend to regard themselves as separate from the rest of the Reformed group for reasons that have escaped me.

[8]In this context, mysticism means the person's "upward" movement toward God; enthusiasm means God's "downward" movement toward the person.

they are distinctive in having additional scripture that is substantially equivalent to the Bible in authority. Incidentally, the Seventh-Day Adventist Church could have been included here because of the writings of Ellen White, an early founder.

Non-Trinitarian. These include the Unitarian Universalist Association and the Ethical Culture Society, although only the former will be discussed. In different ways, this and the previous group are probably the most extreme in terms of normative Christian views of the Trinity, the Resurrection of Jesus, and the authority of the Bible. In this group, the size of the membership of the denominations is small, but they have had a disproportionate impact on American society. They accept diversity and are non-creedal. Not included here are the "Oneness" Pentecostal churches, which also discount the Trinity and see Jesus as God, but which differ in fervor, fundamentalism, and tolerance of diversity.

Unionist. These include the Moravian, Disciples of Christ, United Church of Christ, and Churches of Christ churches. Based on a desire to restore Christian unity as much as possible through a return to biblical principles, these churches do not require creedal assent for membership, although doctrinal principles are often proposed. Diversity seems to be the price of unity, but this generally fits well with the prevailing American ideology on self-determination and pragmatism.

This is not the only possible scheme and it has the drawback of being based on theological rather than psychological factors. Barkman (1977) proposed a psychologically oriented plan based on three of Guilford's temperament traits, *verbal, affective,* and *social-relational,* to which he added a fourth, *transcendental.* This was transformed into churches with a doctrinal emphasis he called the *Believers,* largely equivalent to the first group or Reformed. The second group emphasized affective experiences through communion with God and he labeled them *Pietistic;* they were equivalent to the second group or Free Will and Salvation. Barkman's third group emphasized relations with others; called the *Brethren,* they were equivalent to the Inner Light grouping. The final group emphasized both ritual and mystic experiences and were called *Communicants.* The Episcopal Church exemplified this group, which is not really equivalent to any of the seven groups sketched here. In spite of the potential inherent in Barkman's scheme, the seven groupings outlined above have the advantage of having a finer structure and being more descriptive of the distinctive surface features seen in these churches.

Taxonomic Dimensions

In addition to the seven groupings described above, which are substantive or content-based, a number of other dimensions of a more process nature characterize nearly all Christian denominations. Although several of these dimensions have been proposed (Snook 1974, Stark 1965), the four given below seem to deal with a number of the major factors of most denominations. They also seem to be relevant to the experiences of many patients relative to one or another aspect of their involvement with a particular religion. Thus, these four dimensions are ad hoc, to some degree, but they appear repetitively in a variety of contexts (Jeffries and Tygart 1974, Russell 1975). These are the

Liberalism–conservatism–fundamentalism dimension
Informalism–sacramentalism dimension
Ecumenicalist–exclusivist dimension
Individualism–creedalism dimension.

Liberalism-Conservativism-Fundamentalism

The similarity of these terms to political epithets makes it necessary to define them in the religious arena, although to confound matters, there does appear to be a considerable similarity between these terms as theological and political stances in terms of the attitudes of the holders of these positions. Liberalism or modernism was described by Mayer (1961) as a method whereby Christian thinking is modernized through empirical methods to give current meaning to classic doctrines, such as grace and revelation. Fundamentalism was a reaction to liberalism, to conserve and restore traditional Christian beliefs and values eroded by (1) the variety of Christian reinterpretations of the Bible, (2) an increasing number of archaeological and anthropological studies of religions and cultures, and (3) psychological analyses of religion. If a function of religion is to give order and meaning to the world, then protecting that function is not an insignificant matter. Although perhaps not the driving issue originally, the literal inerrancy of the Bible has become a sort of litmus test for fundamentalism. Literalness has many shades of meaning and application. The Creation story is more likely to be taken literally than are Jesus's parables. For some, inerrancy means the original text; for others, inerrancy means a particular translation of a received (original) text.

The liberal pole of this dimension is more likely to prove attractive to most therapists, since it is more nearly synonymous with freeing up or liberation, creativity, and progress. But it can also have a directionless, flaccid quality, with progress having no direction or aim and creativity lacking disciplined craftsmanship and effort. The fundamentalist pole is similarly aversive, representing narrowness, prejudice, intrusive control over behavior and thought, and concrete literalness in understanding others. However, fundamentalism can also provide firm and confident directional aims in living and strong integrative assurances of divine love. These alternatives are mentioned to illustrate the caution needed in evaluating the impact and effect of a specific church in the life of a specific patient. The "good guys" and the "bad guys" don't wear hats, so the therapist's task is far from easy.

Informalism–Sacramentalism

Sacraments are formal procedures or rites that express religious processes. They can be construed as literally efficacious, conferring actual spiritual properties to the communicant, or they can be symbolic or memorial activities. Their presence and use adds a degree of structure to the worship service, whereas their progressive diminution either in importance or efficacy leads to increased informality, with the potential for increased creativity and affectivity of expression. Since sacraments have mystical properties, however, their strong presence does not rule out strong affective experience. Thus, the Roman Church might be considered the most formal end of the sacramental continuum, with both Pentecostals and Unitarians the least formal, although these two latter groups differ very markedly from each other.

Ecumenicalist–Exclusivist

These are relative terms referring to the degree to which salvation is seen as being available outside a particular denomination. In general, Christianity has a greater or lesser exclusivist bent, whereas Judaism does not; nevertheless, Christianity differs widely on this issue. Mainline Protestant denominations generally see salvation as being possible in another, more or less adjacent Christian denomination. Thus, from a Presbyterian viewpoint, a good Methodist should be able to attain salvation and grace. As one moves toward the Millennialist and New Scripture churches, starting perhaps with the Holiness churches, however, there is increased exclusivity. Salvation is considered either unobtainable or of a lower order or quality if one is outside the specific denomination or even the specific church. Some Baptist churches do not recognize "alien" immersion; that is, baptism performed in another Baptist church. The Roman Church had a very strong exclusivist direction, as a perusal of the Miller (1959) booklet shows. Since Vatican II, this has been modified considerably, and older images of the Roman Church's stance should be updated.

Individualism-Creedalism

The Catholic churches and most of the mainline Protestant churches have creeds—formal statements of belief or position to which greater or lesser assent is required. For some Protestant churches, these creeds are the same as for the Catholic churches; for other denominations, there is considerable variety and divergence. Some churches eschew creeds entirely and yet are very strict on many matters of belief and/or behavior. It would be an error, I think, to equate creedalism with conservatism and individualism with liberalism. In Judaism, there are no formal creeds or confessions of faith, although Maimonides's Thirteen Principles come close. However, when formal bodies capable of formulating and imposing a creed existed, they never did so, and no such formulation, including that of Maimonides, ever won complete acceptance.

The informalism, ecumenicalist, and individualism poles of the preceding three dimensions are likely to be more comfortable for and congenial to most therapists than are the sacramentalism, exclusivist, and creedalism poles. Sacramentalism has a magic-like quality; the exclusivist stance appears prejudiced and unempathic; and creedalism smacks of thought control. At times, these dimensions may well be used in just these ways, but there are alternatives. Sacramentalism provides a concrete and tangible symbol of an important event and relieves the strain of functioning in an abstract mode. For a person with a low level of trust and a strong need for restitutive assurance, an exclusivist promise can be strongly integrative. Creedalism, with its risk of thought control, also promises a clear statement of a church's position on important matters. A creed, like a written constitution, protects the congregant from temporary tides of trend, fad, or opinion in a church and a brake on the excesses of majority rule.

The Reformed Churches

Lutheran. In Europe, Lutheranism is the official state religion in a few countries and, worldwide, Lutheranism is one of the largest Protestant denominations. In this country, over 8 million Lutherans are divided among four main groups, making it second only to the Southern Baptist Convention in size among Protestant groups. With the exception of the Episcopal Church, which varies widely in this country between almost Catholic to Broad or modernist, Lutheranism is probably closest to Catholicism in having retained the largest amount of Catholic ritual, liturgy, and sacraments.[9] A significant, widespread educational system exists as well. The Lutheran Church has four main divisions in the United States, of which two, currently in the process of uniting (the Lutheran Church of America and the American Lutheran Church) are relatively more liberal; the Missouri Synod is quite conservative. The smallest group is the Wisconsin Synod, which split from the Missouri Synod because the latter was too liberal, a measure of the Wisconsin Synod's fundamentalist, exclusivist stance.

Membership in a church in one of these four divisions is not a certain indicator of the person's attitudes, but the more conservative and stricter the church, the more likely it is that members will fall within a narrower range. The more liberal the church, the greater the probability that the range will be wider. As is seen with many denominations, there are varying degrees of insistence that outside of Jesus there is no salvation. Some Lutheran hymnals express the hope for the conversion of the Jews, but this issue does not appear to have much general vitality. When concern for the therapist's salvation is expressed ("Have you been saved?") by the patient, it is easy to hear a hostile or rejecting tone. Such a question may also reflect a defense against a developing intimacy with the therapist or perhaps a move toward making a "gift" to the therapist. Careful inquiry is needed to differentiate the two.

The value orientations discussed in Chapter 4 have apparently not been investigated for Lutherans. In general, it seems reasonable to assume that many Lutherans have a dominant value orientation typical of those of most Americans. Human Nature is seen as Evil, with a Good-and-Evil view holding equal or nearly equal status. The Man-Nature orientation probably places Mastery-over-Nature ahead of Harmony-with-Nature, with Subjugation-to-Nature last. The Time orientation is most likely Future ahead of Present, with Past in third place, whereas the Activity

[9]The 19 Protestant denominations discussed here have additional historical and descriptive detail given in Appendix 3.

orientation is likely sequenced as Doing ahead of Being-in-Becoming, with Being in last place. Finally, the Relational orientation is most probably Individual, then Collateral, with Lineal equal to or slightly behind it. Since Lutheranism had its primary roots in a fairly stern, structured, lower- and middle-class German society, these patterns may differ for the last four orientations if the patient's background is very close to these roots. Thus, comments about the sequencing of value orientations will only be made if there is some reason to suspect that they differ from what seems to be the dominant American pattern.

Reformed and Presbyterian. Developing shortly after Luther's ideas began to spread, this movement began in Switzerland from the impetus of Ulrich Zwingli, in Zurich, and John Calvin, in Geneva. The various Presbyterian and Reformed churches number somewhat less than 4 million members, making them about fourth in size among the Protestant denominations after the Baptist, Methodist, and Lutheran churches. Coming slightly later than the Lutheran movement and being somewhat closer to the Radical Reformation (from which the Baptists, among others, descended), they have diverged somewhat further in conception and practice from the Roman Catholicism of the early sixteenth century.

Although primarily descended theologically from the teachings of John Calvin, the churches in this group span a wide range from quite strict and conservative to very liberal, theologically. Calvin opposed schism over extreme efforts at doctrinal purity, so there is more elasticity than people commonly suppose. Since Calvin saw economic prosperity as a mark of God's favor, even though he held that this favor was not affected by one's behavior, the theology of the Church could lead to smugness. It would be an error, however, to suppose that Calvin's doctrines truly characterize these churches as they are now. Hoge, Perry, and Klever (1978) studied priorities in the United Presbyterian Church and found that, although there was general agreement over such church goals as preaching the Gospels, religious education, fellowship, and spiritual growth among members, there were strong differences of opinion over the form and nature of outreach programs. Evangelism was pitted against social action, and these differences were evinced in sharp and specific theological differences within the denomination. Age differences tended to be a lesser factor in their study, whereas minister–laity conflicts were not seen as systematic factors.

Protestant Episcopal. The Protestant Episcopal Church is the United States equivalent of the Anglican or English Catholic Church. If Henry VIII had not wanted to annul his first marriage, the break with Rome would not have occurred at that time, but other contributory forces sustained the break with Rome after Henry's initial break. As the established Church of England, it had many variations in its standing and impact in England, but in the more open and competitive society of America after the Revolution, the Church has changed. In the last 20 years, many of the more conservative churches in America have grown considerably, but the churches in this grouping have generally not done well. From 1960 to 1977 (Jacquet 1979), Lutherans have grown slightly (about 5 percent), but the Presbyterian and Reformed and the Protestant Episcopal Churches have each declined about 15 percent.

Diversity is very characteristic of this denomination, and practices range from Catholic to starkly informal, in sacramental terms. As with the previous denomination, parishioner involvement ranges from genteel and reserved to passionate and enthusiastic. In general, there is not as prudish an attitude toward tobacco, alcohol, and other such pleasures, and considerable diversity has been tolerated among clergy. In other words, it is particularly difficult to generalize about this denomination.

Free Will and Salvation Churches

Historically, it would be much simpler if it turned out that the later a denomination developed after the Reformation, the more it diverged from Catholic concepts and practice, but this is only approximately the case. Even in advance of the development of Lutheranism, some "radical" theological developments pivoted around the issue of infant baptism. The main tenets initially (Piepkorn 1978) were (1) adult baptism of the repentant adult, (2) use of the ban, not force, to keep the community pure, (3) the Lord's Supper as a memorial (rather than a sacrament), (4) avoidance of drinking houses, (5) avoidance of Roman and Protestant worship, (6) the requirement that the pastor qualify spiritually to be a leader, (7) strict separation of church and state, (8) pacifism, and (9) avoidance of oaths. The term "radical," in the early 1500s, was well deserved.

Baptist. Piepkorn's (1978) monumental study listed 42 separate Baptist groups in the United States, although the largest is the Southern Baptist Convention that contains about one-half of the 25,000,000 or so Baptists listed in 1977 (Jacquet 1979) and is the largest Protestant denomination in the United States. In the 1960–1977 period, the Southern Baptist Convention experienced an overall growth of 42 percent, while the other

Baptist groups experienced an 11 percent growth rate. Church statistics are often only approximate, but the trend is quite clear.

The basic unit is the individual church, which provides much more flexibility and freedom of choice in governance and doctrine (Ingram 1981) than in the churches covered so far. There is much emphasis on behavioral controls over a variety of disapproved pleasures (alcohol, gambling, and movies, in some instances), which many therapists find most offensive as it collides with their emphasis on internalized and flexible control. What is less obvious is that there are many avenues for satisfaction of emotional needs in intense, expressive religious activities, for gratification of dependency and intimacy needs in the close circle of the church "family," and for opportunities to discharge aggressive impulses in combating disapproved-of activities in the larger society. The emphasis on behavioral standards and controls, without a concomitant awareness of the imperatives of inner experience, can leave the naive patient unprepared for and horrified by typical erotic or aggressive transferences, particularly the former. One poignant statement illustrates this well: "I know Christian clients who have terminated therapy at this point of emotional involvement—it becomes too sinful, too hard to handle. Guilt enters. It is one of the first places in self-disclosure that can become a stumbling block" (Anon 1977, p. 31).

Methodist.   The People Called Methodist was a religious society within the Church of England until after the death of the founder John Wesley, in 1791. Only then did these congregations split off and form an independent church. Wesley, an Anglican clergyman, did not intend to found a new church, but rather he was trying to revitalize the stale, politicized Church of England. His methodical efforts at holiness gave the name. Holiness is not a vague state, but rather a technical term of considerable importance. Wesley held that the grace to bring about salvation and justification was readily available, but that a person could choose to accept it or not. The sinner who accepted grace was then justified, but should then go on to seek perfection (freedom from deliberate sin) or holiness through specific personal encounters with God, probably through the Holy Spirit. Although Methodism in this country has the reputation of opposing a variety of pleasures (notably alcohol), it is basically genial and optimistic, and Methodist churches are well liked and well regarded by people outside the denomination. Serious Methodists are likely to take an intense interest in spiritual activities, with much more emphasis on experience and encounter than scholarly study and debate. Although education and learning are much more highly regarded among Methodists than among Baptists, they are not central issues. In terms of therapy, Methodism tends to be a mixture of trends, which, if unevenly emphasized, can give a dour and restricted or a relaxed and indecisive quality to the client's life. A normative trend would be cheerful good sense about religious matters without theological hair-splitting.

Holiness or Perfectionist and Pentecostal. These two movements (denomination suggests more coherence than may obtain) descend from Methodism and Wesley's ideas about perfection or entire sanctification. The Holiness or Perfectionist movement then gave rise to the Pentecostal churches, which went a step further through Baptism in the Holy Spirit, and they all trace their roots back to Anglican and Catholic mystical thought and experience. Ironically, the Holiness movement grew up within Methodism, and for a long time it was a religious society or movement rather than a separate church. Holiness was seen as an immediate possibility, rather than an ongoing process, as Wesley had viewed it. Further, holiness or sanctification was seen as the "second blessing" of grace, whereas baptism in the Holy Spirit or speaking in tongues (glossolalia), among other "gifts of the Spirit," became, for the Pentecostal movement, the "third blessing" after one's conversion. Schism and fragmentation characterize Pentecostal churches to a much greater degree than Holiness churches (Warburton 1969). The latter tend to reject glossolalia and other such marked manifestations. The Pentecostal churches further divide into trinitarian churches, which accept the Trinity in more or less traditional terms, and "Oneness" churches, which see Jesus as God, although they resent the label of Unitarian.

Overall, strong behavioral controls are emphasized against a wide, but varied list of prohibited activities in most Pentecostal churches. Some, however, are a good deal less specific, and different churches vary greatly. Schwartz (1970), in an urban anthropological study, compared two Pentecostal churches with a Seventh-Day Adventist church, and his descriptions vary considerably from the group studied by Dearman (1974). The Bible is held to be inerrant (in the original), so room can be made for new studies to modify translations.

There appears to be wide variations in standards of behavior as to specific details (Schwartz 1970), but these churches are not monastic in withdrawal from a sinful world. Rather, they encourage and expect people to work for a living, and securing an adequate and comfortable living is not despised. Diligent work, delay of gratification, and efficiency are admired (Dearman 1974), although outstanding accomplishment is not really expected. Generally, people in these churches see their behavior in the outside world as reflecting their beliefs; to set a good example brings honor to the name of Christ.

A therapeutically relevant theme that runs through the Holiness and Pentecostal groups is that of "Christian love." Many of these people seem to have experienced considerable early deprivation of love and affection. Although perhaps not severely abusive, their early environments were often cold, if not actually cruel. Typically, under such conditions of development, a person preserves a good image of one's parents by internalizing their own hostile impulses and by incorporating into one's self-image an overall "bad" self-representation. This process is considerably reinforced and aided by their religious training, which supports the repression of negative feelings toward one's parents. As children, many of these people now seen in therapy experienced a good deal of parental (and sometimes ministerial) communication about Christian love that lacked affective genuineness and may have screened out parental hostility and rejection.

Thus, coming out of a nonreligious, but deficient home, or a religious home of some other denomination that was not nourishing, such children, as they moved toward adolescence or adulthood, may well have begun to act out their self-image through sexual or drug activity and petty or not so petty crime. If they have not acted-out, they may experience ongoing neurotic distress. When surrounded by intense affective expressions of interest and warmth in the setting of a church of this type, the common response is to "accept Jesus as their personal savior" or "baptism in the Holy Spirit." The therapist who fails to listen carefully and openly will miss the profoundly significant processes at work, in which, perhaps for the first time in their adult life, patients begin to reach out for and experience significant and positive object-relationships that have the obvious consequence of markedly and positively altering self-representation. That their first choice is the Holy Spirit or Jesus indicates the tentative nature of the selection of a "person" who will not hurt or reject them. The therapist needs to recognize that their treatment has probably prepared the way because the patient's recognition will be slow in coming, if not absent. An insensitive or ridiculing response on the therapist's part will reinforce the expectation that real people are indeed hurtful and that it is better to stay with "people" who will not be hurtful.

A therapist will probably have to deal with the distinct feeling that such behavior is bizarre and that the patient is sicker than before. By and large, careful study of these two movements does not support such assumptions (Gilmore 1969, Hine 1969, Hood 1974, Pattison, Lapins, and Doerr 1973, Richardson 1973, Sanua 1969). The reverse supposition—

that religious membership relieves emotional problems—is not clearly supported, either. Another, related issue seen very clearly in Pentecostal churches, but that also spans the range of Christian denominations (with gaps), has to do with another gift of the Spirit—healing. The rational orientation of most therapists is a very useful anchor in the face of a flood of intense, often primitive feelings encountered in intensive, dynamically oriented therapy. This, coupled with the onward march of medical advances of the past half-century, can make such healing seem ludicrous, regressive, and bizarre. It also makes it that much harder to understand. Hegy (1978) has pointed out that the Greek word for salvation also means healing (from illness), and this was the primary New Testament meaning. Healing (sometimes called faith healing) does not normally involve fraud or gimmickry, but rather relates to both physical relief from symptomatology as well as psychological reintegration (MacNutt 1974, Pattison et al. 1973). In groups in which it is practiced, and these now include Episcopal and Roman Catholic subgroups, it is not bizarre, nor does it preclude medical treatment. To set medical treatment against spiritual healing is not usual in the healing approach. In the patient, it may reflect a rejection of societal mistreatment and a reaction to parental "care," and it requires exploration. If in a minister, this is idiosyncratic practice and the patient can be encouraged to find a new minister.

Baptist and Methodist churches typically share the dominant American value orientations, although in some Baptist churches, the Human Nature orientation might have Evil placed ahead of Good-and-Evil and in the Time orientation, a Present orientation and a Future orientation might be seen to be equal. Regional differences may be very important. Holiness and Pentecostal churches vary greatly, particularly the latter, and study of a particular church is necessary.

Salvation Army.   Although the Holiness movement arose primarily in the United States, it had effects in other countries as well, and one of its more significant impacts was upon William Booth. His origins in English Methodism led him to preach to the impoverished inhabitants of the worst, most chaotic, distressed slums of London. His members could not handle a self-governing church organization, which led him to develop a highly structured, army-type format to provide coherence, direction and clear demands, expectations, and rewards for the members, as well as visible signs of status and worth, with appropriate and attractive rank and garb. Originally aimed at very disadvantaged and distressed people, Booth saw that a theology in the worship service would interfere with his message. The sizable growth of the Army (56 percent from 1960 to 1977) reflects the desire for the kind of concrete and spiritual help they offer.

Inner Light Churches

The churches discussed here are all small. They are included not because of numerical size, but rather because they represent a distinct line of thought and experience, and in the case of the Quakers, their impact is quite disproportionate to their numbers. The Mennonite and Brethren churches are fairly similar in doctrine and practice; the Quakers or Friends are rather different. The underlying theme binding them together is a restrained mysticism called enthusiasm, expressed in a body of practice that enables them to experience closeness to God or to have the sense of hearing God's messages. This must be distinguished from hallucinatory experiences, which these are not.

Mennonite. Derived from a man named Menno Simon, who was involved with the beginnings of the Radical Reformation, the Mennonite churches (as well as Amish) emphasize separation from the world to maintain purity of the group and a mystical piety that leads to an inner light that illuminates the Bible. A great deal of emphasis is placed on rules and avoidances, so they may appear puritanical, but although they differ in many specifics, descriptions of these groups (Mayer 1961, Piepkorn 1978, Vol. 2) are reminiscent of the inner experiences of the Hasidic movement in Judaism.

Brethren. Although the Brethren are similar to the Mennonites in a variety of practices, they are anti-creedal and value detailed and extensive adherence to the behavioral rules set down in the New Testament. The style of life of these two groups is unlikely to appeal to most therapists, either because of the creedal emphasis of the Mennonites or because of the behavioral strictures of both groups. These two denominations provide a highly structured and supportive environment for their adherents, and although avoidance of some usual pleasures is required, members have a very strong sense of community and they tend to be honest and prosperous and to have the regard of their neighbors. It is probable that both denominations give their adherents a sense of high and select purpose, a mystical sense of union (perhaps related to an early mother–child symbiosis), as well as a clear sense of how to deal with the vagaries and confusions of life. People who leave the church are like emigrants and may have life-long yearnings to return or feelings of betrayal.

Quakers or Friends. Although the Quakers are grouped with the two previous denominations, they are, in practice, quite different. They emphasize an openness to the "inner light," exemplified by the quiet in the services of many, but not all churches. If the congregants are quiet, they then will be better able to hear God's whisper. The "inner light," with the implication of self-awareness and self-understanding, as an approach to the world is very compatible with the general dynamic approach to psychotherapy.

Millennialist

Millennialism, and its variants, is derived first from the Latin *mille* for thousand and *annus* for years, hence, a thousand years. There are several biblical bases, but the most vivid imagery is in the Revelation of John, in which a cataclysmic battle between Jesus and Satan is described in great detail. The practice of using both the language and the imagery in the Bible to discern secret meanings is ancient and the material in the Revelation of John particularly lends itself to this practice, since a plain reading of the text is very difficult. The three subtypes, *premillennialism, dispensationalism*, and *post-millennialism*, are described in Appendix 3.

The eschatological, apocalyptic visions of this position are consistent with the accelerating social change that has accompanied the Industrial Revolution, World War I and II, and the threat of nuclear holocaust. World-destroying fantasies have an individual meaning, as well, so such a position is especially attractive to some patients. Although having the quality of restoring a perfect, blissful relationship with God (and/or Jesus) reminiscent of infancy (Mahler 1979), these millennial images are also contaminated with considerable aggressivity of a cosmic nature. When these concepts are particularly important, intense difficulties with poorly regulated aggression and perhaps loss of reality-testing may be involved.

Seventh-Day Adventist. This group derived from the prediction by a William Miller, a former army officer, farmer, and licensed Baptist preacher, that Jesus would return in March 1844. When this did not happen, a recalculation to October 1844 led to even greater enthusiasm and further disappointment. A group of Miller's followers rethought their position and concluded that the events predicted had happened in heaven, not on Earth. Although the Adventists are non-creedal, in seeing the Bible as containing a sufficient rule for their faith, they have a well-defined set of views and beliefs. Often literal with regard to the Bible, they strongly oppose the Papacy, which is represented as the Beast (Rev. 13:1) that led people astray as to the Sabbath. They have returned Sabbath observance to Saturday. Basic dogma cannot be questioned, but there is room for honest dissent and biblical interpretation (Schwartz 1970).

Toward the external world, their expectation is that hard work and right living will be rewarded by success. Their theology is forboding and aggressive, but there are very strong bars to overt aggression through prohibition of military service and promotion of active work to alleviate war's damage (Mayer 1961). There can also be a sense of considerable individual and group importance in completing the work of the Protestant Reformation, which is regarded as incomplete.

Evil (and the Devil) are seen as independent competitors with Christ for the person's soul. This Zoroastrian quality to the good-evil, light-dark quality of their imagery seems likely to foster splitting, as well as projection, particularly since the world is presented as a constant battle against Evil and one slip can lead to death. On the other hand, Evil is a choice, not an accident, and temptation is not a sin per se without the person's consent. That is, to think it is not the same as to do it.

Jehovah's Witnesses.   This group was founded by Charles Russell in 1872. Troubled by doubts as to certain biblical concepts, he found that Adventism renewed his confidence in the Bible. Similar to the Adventists in a number of ways, there are also some real and important differences. Both are eschatological groups with a cataclysmic idiom and see the world in conflict between good and evil, but the satanic forces are more pervasive for the Witnesses. Although both groups draw very heavily from the Books of Daniel and Revelation, the Witnesses seem more prone to treat the material allegorically or to ignore the context (Mayer 1961).

The Witnesses hold that the Bible has been wickedly mistranslated or that ancient manuscripts have been tampered with. The Papacy is blamed for this; the three main evil forces in modern life are religion, commerce or finance, and government. The Witnesses also have a history of martyrdom because of their aggressive missionary activity, but this is largely over now. Persecution does enhance, however, the validity of one's message to prospective converts in a way that massive indifference in the general population does not. The Witnesses do not appear to be a popular denomination in the eyes of others, and it appears that occupational success beyond a certain level may not be fostered. At least one report (Montague 1977) suggested more than the usual severity of pathology among the Witnesses, but presented little empirical data. Montague did indicate that the Elders of a church are unlikely to look favorably upon psychotherapy.

The psychological implications of the Adventists' doctrines seem to apply to the Witnesses as well. Their imagery seems more vivid, with an even more dramatic, concrete, aggressive coloration. Both systems are relatively all-embracing of the lives of their members and provide a strong sense of special identity and worth in being one of a relatively small group with a special message and purpose. Jesus's status is diminished in Witness theology, which may serve to bring members closer to God whose terrifying power is ameliorated by strong assurances of God's love for his chosen ones.

New Scripture

Many of the denominations described so far have a body of literature that supplements the Bible and many also revise or reject parts of Catholic doctrine or practices. This supplemental literature is generally inferior in status to the Bible, but this varies widely, and there are varying emphases on different parts of the Old and New Testaments. The denominations to be considered now have a divinely revealed set of Scriptural writings that are about equal in status to the Bible. The churches in this category, as the ones in the preceding group, had their origins in nineteenth-century America, a time of much religious ferment.

Church of Jesus Christ of Latter-Day Saints.   A simple narrative of the founding of this denomination is likely to evoke puzzlement, laughter, or even ridicule from outsiders. The account of the origins of any church may seem incredible to outsiders, but when it is considered, like the manifest content of a dream, as the starting point in the direction of understanding meanings, then it is no longer laughable, but only obscure.

In the mid-1820s, the angel Moroni appeared to Joseph Smith and told him that he was to translate *The Book of Mormon*, which he and Oliver Cowdery then did. After publication, they organized their church in 1830 and established a number of social–religious settlements. Hostility from the surrounding community, especially over the doctrine of polygamy, led to the murder of Smith and his brother. Much of the church, under the leadership of Brigham Young, then moved to Utah where they founded an autonomous society at Salt Lake City. Mormon is a nickname, but for brevity here, they will be referred to as Latter-Day Saints. Although usually grouped with other Protestant denominations, they do not consider themselves as being of that tradition (Rosten 1975). The Latter-Day Saints need to be distinguished from the Reorganized Church of Jesus Christ of Latter-Day Saints, which is about one-fourteenth the size and which split off after the death of Joseph Smith under the leadership of his son.

Although Mayer (1961) classified the Latter-Day Saints as Millennialist, their scriptural additions seem to make them fit here. Compared with the Adventists and Witnesses, the Latter-Day Saints' theology and imagery is now much less aggressive. The general tenor sees people as moving through their work and experiences in the direction of material perfection. Humanity "is of the same race as God and, moreover, was made that he might have joy" (O'Dea, as cited in Kluckhohn 1951, p. 411). Family relations and loving bonds are emphasized; celibacy is frowned upon; and the unmarried person will not enter heaven. The strong expectation of service to others in the course of one's life through missionary and social welfare work, the promise of a material continuation of certain aspects of life after death, the image of a loving God who makes His benefits available to a variety of peoples, and the emphasis on ordered and productive work and on family activities provide a gratifying and structured environment for the congregant. As with Orthodox Judaism, traditional Catholicism, and the Mennonite, Brethren, and Adventist churches, a member of the Latter-Day Saints with emotional difficulties seems more likely to experience them in the areas of conflicts over controls or invasiveness by others. Former members may well feel a sense of apostasy and treason to their Church.

Part of the general food practices of the Latter-Day Saints include the prohibition of tobacco, alcohol, and hot drinks (coffee, tea, and chocolate). Chafetz and DeMone (1962) reported that, among Latter-Day Saint high school and college students, one-third to one-half report alcohol use. Although use of alcohol is lower among Latter-Day Saints than among most other religious groups, alcohol use is more likely to lead to social complications, since there is no regulatory system other than abstinence. Its unregulated use may well be a vehicle for expressing anger and rebellion.

Christian Science. Very few significant religious movements have been founded by women. The Shakers, founded by Ann Lee in this country after their start in England, and the Adventists, under Ellen White's inspiration and writings and her husband James' leadership, are partial exceptions. The Church of Christ, Scientist, founded by Mary Baker Eddy around 1870, is the most striking exception, since it has fewer antecedents than the other two mentioned and was totally under her control at her death in 1910.

Non-medical healing, which Christian Science is most readily associated with in the minds of many, was more or less commonly practiced in the eighteenth and nineteenth centuries and was not an unreasonable procedure, since the avoidance of medical treatment in that time was more likely to prolong your life than to shorten it. Sterile operating procedures, and anesthesia in general surgery, are perhaps a century old; and antibiotics were discovered less than a half-century ago. Sometime around 1862, Mrs. Eddy met a Phineas Quimby who held that illness was due to incorrect thinking. Influenced by this, she used this idea after she was injured in a fall on the ice in the late 1860s. She gained several followers and in 1875 published *Science and Health with Key to the Scriptures*, followed by the establishment of the Church of Christ, Scientist in Boston in 1879. From the outsider's perspective, prayer or faith healing and the avoidance of medicine are the most prominent features of Christian Science, but this is a vulgarization for the Christian Scientist who sees this as a whole way of existing, relating, and healing.

Pruyser (1974) stated that a basic tenet of Christian Science denies the reality of evil by seeing it as a false perception. In addition to denial, bad events in a person's life can be attributed to what Mrs. Eddy termed Malicious Animal Magnetism, which appears to involve projection. Denial and projection preserve a good-mother object-representation, whereas the concept of thought transfer and healing at a distance, which are two other elements in the Christian Science formulation (Wardwell 1965), is consistent with very early experiences related to the symbiotic phase (Mahler 1979). The rather explicit imagery used (e.g., Mother Church) makes Christian Science well suited to deal with issues related to the mother. The theological formulations also foster idealization of relationships and an emphasis on abstractions. I supervised treatment of one patient whose parents were Christian Scientists, and the main difficulties involved withdrawal and unattunedness by the mother and the patient's confusion and vagueness as to what was actually occurring in this primary relationship. The patterns in this one case are consistent with what might be expected from the Christian Science theology.

It is easy to see this very extreme group as bizarre, which may be a serious error. The theology of nearly any denomination, particularly as developed by its founder, may well be both stark and striking. As currently expressed, it may be a good deal nearer center than one might expect. Nudelman (1971) compared the factor structure of religiousness of Catholics and Protestants with the results from interviews with Christian Science college students. Overall, his findings indicated the Christian Science students had a largely similar factor structure.

Non-Trinitarian

To a greater or lesser degree, both Latter-Day Saints and Christian Science depart considerably from the standard view of the Trinity, although superficially they appear to accept this concept. Churches in this group reject the concept, but would otherwise not be considered extreme in their conceptions.

Unitarian Universalist Association. The rejection of the Trinity and the divine nature of Jesus is not a modern development. Debates over the nature of the Trinity are ancient, and Unitarian views had actively surfaced again at the time of the Reformation. The Universalists began by accepting the Trinity; the name, however, indicates that salvation was not reserved for an elect, but rather was available to all. In this country, the two groups gradually drew together and joined formally in 1961. A creedal statement is avoided, and there is a much wider freedom of belief than is characteristic of the Christian groups discussed so far. Many Christian churches do not see the Unitarian Universalist Association as Christian; thus, the Association was denied membership in the National Council of Churches.

The diversity and open-endedness of the Association would lead one to expect that they have somewhat less of an impact on the personality organization of their members than do many of the denominations already discussed. Further, their approach is likely to be congenial with that of many therapists, leading to less sensitivity to the influence of the Association on the lives of patients. However, the accepting, laissez-faire approach of the Association may become an excuse for parental disinterest or lack of involvement and be disguised as "freedom" or "personal growth."

A study of a small sample of Unitarian Universalists (Rice 1971) indicated that, compared with such traditional Christian groups as Lutherans, Congregationalists, and Roman Catholics, they differed considerably in their religious values. A much larger study (Miller 1976) examined members of the Association on Rokeach's instrumental and terminal values (1969) and found that of the 18 terminal values, Protestants rated Salvation fourth, whereas Unitarians rated this traditional Christian value eighteenth. Of the 18 instrumental values, Protestants rated Ambition second and Forgiving fourth, whereas Unitarians rated them fifteenth and eleventh, respectively. Generally, the Unitarians tended to resemble Jews and religious "Nones" in a number of respects, and their values were less affected by economic level than was true for the nine other groups studied. Frequency of church attendance, size of church, geographic location, and rural or urban siting had little effect, although these factors are normally correlated for other churches. This indicates that the apparently low-key, non-demand quality of the Association nevertheless has a powerful impact on its members, most of whom

(85 to 90 percent) are converts. It may be that the impact occurs in the self-selection process inherent in converting to and joining the Association.

Unionist

These churches might well have been considered earlier, since they are considerably more traditional, but it seemed reasonable to close this review of Protestant denominations with their attempts at reunification. The early beginnings can be traced to Jan Huss (Mayer 1961), a century before the Reformation. In the United States, these churches developed on the frontier and represented efforts to have a Christian church without the divisive, exclusionary effects of creeds, hierarchies, and other non-democratic factors. Three churches are considered here, and although there are some differences, their similarities are quite real. These are the Churches of Christ, the Disciples of Christ (or Christian Church), and the United Church of Christ (formed in 1957 by the union of the Congregational Christian and the Evangelical and Reformed churches), in about that order of increasing liberalism (DeJong and Ford 1965, Glock and Stark 1966, Jeffries and Tygart 1974, Stark, Foster, Glock, and Quinby 1971). The Churches of Christ split off from the Disciples of Christ at about the turn of the century. Although democratic in many ways, these churches are also serious and fairly traditional, with a definite liturgy or worship service (varying from church to church) and the use of sacraments.

The Disciples of Christ and the United Church of Christ might be good examples of the difference between theological and political liberalism. Theologically, these churches tend to be on the conservative side, although we are only talking of an average, yet their non-creedal status encourages independent thought. Rigidity in a parishioner indicates a personal emphasis.

AMERICAN MOSLEM MISSION

"Black Muslim" seems to be a media label for this denomination, which formerly called itself the Nation of Islam. Most members refer to themselves as Muslims or Moslems. Mayer (1961) noted one other Islamic group restricted to Blacks, but the movement, founded by W.D. Fard in the early 1930s and subsequently developed by Elijah Muhammad, the son of a Baptist minister, has attracted most attention because of its rhetoric. The Black separateness once emphasized conflicts with orthodox Islam, but since the death of Elijah Muhammad, in 1976, the direction of the denomination has changed under the leadership of his son, Wallace D. Muhammad. Now anyone can join and some whites have done so, at times to the discomfort of some of the older members. There has also been a general shift to more orthodox Islamic theology. These changes were rapid, which led to some stress within the group. Currently, membership is estimated at about a million. Contributions by members and sympathizers have been reported to be substantial, and enterprises that employ members have been purchased.

Theologically, this denomination originally appeared similar to the Jehovah's Witnesses (Maesen 1970), with the expectation of a cataclysmic Armageddon with only 144,000 Blacks being saved. A new world on Earth was expected, with the millennium having commenced in 1914. Currently, the theology is much more in the direction of normative Islamic thought. The soul is considered immortal (a change from the older position) and Friday is roughly equivalent to the Saturday Sabbath (for Jews) or to the Sunday Lord's Day (for most Christians). Since the ethical principles of Islam are not really different from Judaism and Christianity, which are valid, if limited revelations (Smith 1958), some specific practices will be noted here. Thrift, self-control, and strict morality are highly valued, whereas liquor, tobacco, drugs, gambling, and pork are prohibited. Steady work, honesty, cleanliness, and a strong family are major values (Rosten 1975, Whalen 1972, Williams 1969), but the use of sanctions to enforce behavioral conformance has declined, with more responsibility for control being given over to the individual.

Hatred of whites has been played up in the public press rather flamboyantly, and although this formed part of the message of Elijah Muhammad (1965), the general thrust has been to conserve and restore the functioning of the family and community in a largely peaceful context and to instill self-esteem, self-reliance, and the attitudinal bases for material and educational achievement. The extensive, severe, and longstanding oppression and abuse that Blacks have suffered does not make the reaction of Elijah Muhammad difficult to understand. The sharpness and anger in his statements have been unsettling to many people, and secondary materials about the American Moslem Mission should be viewed with caution. Further, as was previously noted, there has been a considerable shift in attitude under the leadership of Wallace Muhammad (1980).

Most of the members were probably once in Baptist or Methodist Black churches, if they had had any religious exposure in their youth, although by now some adults may have grown up as Muslims. The original theology seems restitutive of the many injuries Blacks have received in this country. By moving toward a more orthodox Islamic stance, the movement is now allied with a major, significant religion. The behavioral and attitudinal components encouraged in individual members serve integrative requirements in the personality. In treatment, strong hatred toward whites, if not supported by significant injurious experiences, may also serve to defend against the awareness of deficiencies in the patient's parents. For lower-class Black patients whose parents were seriously deficient, however, this is extremely difficult and painful material and premature interpretation should be avoided. The patient's attitudes toward prior religious training or feelings about adopting a new name may be very useful to explore in therapy.

Taxonomy Revisited

It may be useful to rate the four taxonomic dimensions mentioned earlier for the various denominations discussed here. These ratings come from impressions formed in reading various sources, although some empirical data exist as to the place of different denominations on the liberal–fundamental dimension (DeJong and Ford 1965, Jeffries and Tygart 1974). The descriptive material in Appendix 3 should also be reviewed when these ratings are considered. Table 5-1 lists ratings, insofar as they could be determined, on the 25 denominations previously discussed. The Liberal–Fundamental dimension is structured so the most liberal group is rated 1 and the most fundamental, 7. Similarly on the next three scales, the first item is 1 and the other pole, 7. Just considering the Christian groups on the Liberal–Fundamental dimension, it begins with a mid-point rating for Catholicism and steadily increases to a more fundamentalist stance with the Adventist and Witness churches and then declines again. On the Informal–Sacramental dimension, the most sacramental groups are Catholic, and the decline is more or less steadily in the informal direction. Mainline Protestant groups are more or less ecumenical, although salvation outside the Christian realm is doubted by some. Some denominations see little if any chance of salvation outside the denomination. The Creedal dimension resembles the Sacramental dimension. These ratings are sometimes problematic with certain Christian denominations. With Jews and the American Moslem Mission, these have been estimated as best as possible, but they could be ignored or

Table 5-1
Ratings of Twenty-Five Denominations on Four Taxonomic Dimensions

Denomination	Liberal versus Fundamental	Informal versus Sacramental	Ecumenical versus Exclusive	Individual versus Creedal
Jewish:				
Orthodox	4	3*	2	7*
Conservative	3	4*	2	5*
Reform	2	4*	2	3*
Catholic:				
Eastern	4	7	6–7	7
Roman	3–4	7	7→5	7
Protestant:				
Lutheran	4	6	3–4	6
Presbyterian/ Reform	3–6	5	3–4	5
Protestant Episcopal	2–6	3–6	3–4	3–5
Baptist	5–6	3	3–4	2–3
Methodist	4–5	3	3	3
Holiness	5–7	2–3	4–6	2–3
Pentecostal	6–7	1–2	6–7	2
Salvation Army	5	2	3	2–3
Mennonite	6	5	6	5–6
Brethren	5–6	5	6	2–3
Quaker	2–5	2–3	2–3	2–5
Seventh-Day Adventist	6–7	4	6–7	3
Jehovah's Witness	6–7	4	7	3
Latter-Day Saints	5	4	7	6
Christian Science	N/A	2	7	5–6
Disciples of Christ	4–5	3	3	2
Churches of Christ	5–6	3	3	2
United Church of Christ	3–4	3	3	2
Unitarian-Universalist	1–2	1–2	1	1–2
American Moslem Mission	N/A	2–3	7	5–6

*Does not really apply; ratings refer to behavior. See discussion in Chapters 1 and 3.

taken with great caution. When such caution seems especially needed, this has been indicated.

There is another dimension not fully addressed in this chapter in many if not most Christian denominations. This arises from the Pentecostal, or charismatic renewal (among Catholics) movement, which is not confined to the Pentecostal or fundamentalist churches. One sees it in many established mainline churches, such as Presbyterian, Lutheran, and Episcopal, and it appears to be an increasingly divisive factor (Hoge et al. 1978, Kelley 1978, McGaw 1979, McGuire 1977). In brief, and at the risk of oversimplifying a complex phenomenon, it appears that the Pentecostal experience provides a strong sense of belonging, commitment, clarity of standards and expectations, and intense affective contact with restorative and reintegrative good object- and self-representations. I would venture to compare such experiences with the quite secularized encounter and EST group experiences, and it is not surprising that many churches are promoting encounter groups, marriage enrichment, and so on.

Outside of Christianity, there are comparable-appearing developments, such as the outreach activities of the Lubavitcher Hasidim and the Chabad movement. These do not have the same implications for divisiveness, since they are not evangelical, in a Christian sense, and since Judaism is a good deal more elastic regarding diversity in thought. Further, mysticism in Judaism and concomitant Gnostic and theosophic trends appear heretical to Christians with theological training, but have no such implications for Jews (Rexroth, in Waite).

6

Dealing with Religious Issues over the Course of Psychotherapy

The general approach to psychotherapy taken here is a dynamic, ego-psychological one. This means that the patient is understood as a person attempting to deal with life in terms of motives, meanings, intentions, symbols, time (past, present, and future), relationships, fears, and satisfactions. Because psychotherapy, as understood here, is not psychoanalysis, a good deal more flexibility and range of therapeutic repertoire is needed (Blanck and Blanck 1974). Interpretation is one tool, but many others are needed; thus, psychotherapy as a general technique will not be dealt with here.

Before the therapist ever hears from a patient, the patient has been in contact with the therapist. Whether having received a referral from someone, having been assigned to the therapist in a mental health center, or having heard of the therapist in some other way, the patient has "talked" with the therapist in a one-sided, imaginary conversation. With a religious patient, this basic process often has additional overtones to which the therapist should be sensitive. In addition to the varied, but typical fears most patients will have about therapy and the therapist, the religious patient may well anticipate danger to their religious beliefs or fear that you will resemble certain ministers or preachers they have not liked. Quite possibly, they have been warned about the dangers of secular therapists and may be very wary. The reverse may also be true if the therapist is also clergy or associated with an agency that is run under religious auspices. Since there will often not be much information available about these anticipatory "conversations," the therapist must be alert to small cues as to the patient's probable orientation and may have to intervene on the basis of very limited information. Of course, if the referral is from someone (physician, clergy, probation officer, school official, etc.) who has contacted the therapist first, then the therapist may be better oriented.

> Without prior contact, I was called by Mrs. F., a woman in her thirties, who was concerned about the potential breakdown of her third marriage. As she talked of her problems in the first session, Mrs. F. referred to her father, a strict, fundamentalist Baptist preacher. Later in the session, I inquired as to how she happened to seek therapy and she informed me that she had taken some psychology courses that intrigued her. Mrs. F. had found the behavior modification course interesting, but a theories of personality course she was currently enrolled in seemed to fit her problems better. However, she continued, that Freudian stuff about children lusting after their parents, well she didn't really buy that. Expecting that her religious training heavily emphasized belief in doctrines, I replied that there was nothing here (in therapy) that she had to believe except what she was convinced of by her own experience. She looked relieved and therapy continued for quite a period and dealt with some quite painful material. This illustrates the uncertainty the patient may feel during the initial phase of therapy when special fears, concerns, and resistances of the religious patient may not be voiced. Late in therapy, we came to understand that strong demands had been made on Mrs. F. by her parents to accept Jesus as her personal savior, that is, to undergo conversion. Therapy was feared in the same way as demanding belief and faith, and entailing a loss of freedom. Although I did not know this specifically, my remark about not having to believe anything was based on general expectations along these lines.

THE INITIAL PHASE OF THERAPY

Preparation for Therapy

Certain therapeutic approaches, such as rational-emotive therapy or behavior therapy, are relatively active and provide a structure for the patient. In general, however, most therapists tend to avoid explanations as perhaps smacking of propaganda or as contaminating transferences.

This is unfortunate because many people can profit from some straight-forward explanations about what the therapist is going to try to do and why. This is particularly the case in therapy with lower-class (Heitler 1973) or poor people (Karon and VandenBos 1977), many of whom are not used to receiving reasonable explanations from the bureaucracy and do not find verbal interactions useful in solving problems. Further, the lives of these people are often so hard that there is a real temptation to assume that social factors are all that are the problem (Karon and VandenBos 1977). When a strong religious orientation is added, especially if it is conservative, the therapist has some serious preparation to do with the patient.

Even if some background material has already been received on the patient, I find it useful to begin by asking the patient "What seems to be the problem?" or "What seems to be the trouble?" If I have a referral from some other professional, I will share what I have been told with the patient, conveying the idea that this is what I have heard, but expressing interest in the patient's perception of the problem. If there has been prior counseling or therapy, I will inquire about that, if it is opportune. An early request by the patient for an answer can be met with the statement "I need to know more about you before I can tell you much," but I would rather use this request to begin to explain what therapy is about. In general, confidentiality should be explained (although many patients do not really believe this), and the therapist's policy about reports. If the patient is court-ordered, I tell them what the probation officer and I have agreed to (usually attendance reports). If the person has come voluntarily, I tell them that any reports I send to anyone, such as their insurance company, will be shown to them first and will be sent only with their permission. Then I go on to say that we will be talking about their problems so I can help them figure out what they are about and what the best course of action is. I may give a simple explanation of the unconscious and its potential for effect on behavior if this seems to be needed, although this is a concept that has permeated society generally. I will say, "What we will do may seem kind of roundabout. I am interested in anything that you want to tell me, even if it seems trivial. People had ways of dealing with their problems long before there were psychotherapists and they used their minds to figure out problems. The person's mind solved problems of all sorts, including emotional problems, but the way their mind solved these problems was to set up some automatic protections. So if a person tries to figure out their emotional problems in the same way, the mind's automatic protections will prevent any changes in the system. It's like setting the fox to watch the henhouse. So in order to slip past these automatic protections, I will ask you to talk about whatever comes into your mind." This sort of explanation of ego defense mechanisms is usually accepted. Appointment times, fees, and cancellations can be dealt with now, or later. If the patient indicates that he or she is having hallucinations or delusions (with or without a religious content), I tell them that that's OK, we will try to understand what that is all about. I also ask them if they have any questions or if anything is unclear. Sometimes, of course, this all has to be deferred until a later session, if the patient is in an immediate crisis of major proportions.

Many agencies require that an initial history be gathered as soon as possible, and some insist on this being done in the first session, without regard for what the patient may need. The insensitivity of requiring an initial history is commonly experienced by a lower-class person as another example of being used to meet other people's needs. If an initial history is insisted upon, at some point therapists may introduce the need for a history as an agency requirement, while dissociating themselves from approval of this process. Even in a crisis, most patients will accept this if they have been first heard out for 25 or 30 minutes. If the patient introduces religious issues or doctrine, the overall stance should be one of interest (Stamey 1971), but the therapist should be alert to the patient's fears and may need to stop to discuss them. Otherwise, resistance may be unwittingly fostered.

Self-Disclosure in the Initial Phase

The subject of patient–therapist "fit" is complex and the issues are far from clear. The argument is readily made that a therapist who comes from the same background as the patient is best suited to understand that person (Peteet 1981). This may well be true to begin with, but such arguments tend to slide past the issue of competence. The reverse argument that someone from a different background may pick up on important issues that may be overlooked if both parties have a similar background is not often made, but may miss the point as well. The specific demographic qualities of the therapist may be crucial in certain instances, but these are rarer than one would expect. Competence seems preferable to demography. If the therapist does not have cultural information relevant to the patient's background, then it must be acquired. Often the patient is well able to provide this, and therapy is not usually impeded by the frank statement that the therapist needs some education in this or that in the patient's background. Early in my experience, I worked with a number of Catholic patients and they were more than willing to educate me. They seemed both flattered and surprised that I was interested enough to read things like *The New Baltimore Catechism*.

The question of the therapist's religious orientation is likely to arise with the religious patient, and the therapist may feel that it is necessary to introduce the matter. It is easy to see a frank self-disclosure in such terms as truth-in-advertising or "non-mystical sharing of power" (Coyne 1978), without asking for whose benefit a self-disclosure is made. Beit-Hallahmi (1975a) discussed two cases in which religious affiliation was a notable issue. In one case, the patient, an orthodox Jew, was treated in Israel. The patient wore the traditional skullcap (*yarmulkah* or *kippah*), whereas the therapist did not. This made their nominal stances immediately clear (consistent with the division of Jewish Israeli society into religious and secular subcultures), and Beit-Hallahmi and his patient had the option to discuss the matter directly and immediately. The patient chose to do just that. In the other case he reported, in the United States, the patient was a devout member of the Latter-Day Saints. Eventually, according to the case report, the patient who had been discussing his view of God, the Bible, and the world demanded to know what Beit-Hallahmi's stance was. Seeing this as a test of boundaries by the patient as well as a test of his honesty, Beit-Hallahmi made it clear that his views were quite different, but that he felt they could work together. This was accepted by the patient. Beit-Hallahmi concluded that religious differences between patient and therapist should be handled openly and directly because it aids the therapeutic alliance.

An important qualification to this position can be seen in a case, reported by Kohut (1968), on which he had been consulted.

> The patient was a narcissistic woman of Catholic background with a very traumatic childhood. At the point Kohut was consulted, treatment was stalled, but early in treatment, there had been dreams in which the idealized image of a priest appeared. The analyst informed the patient in this early phase that he was not Catholic, which was intended to shore up the patient's tenuous hold on reality. In this consultation, however, this was understood as a narcissistic rebuff. Kohut concluded that with narcissistic personalities one must accept the development of an idealizing transference and not hasten to deflate it through premature interventions.

It should be noted here that the patient was given information that had not been requested.

Although it is possible to argue that the therapist should maintain anonymity to encourage transferences, a refusal to answer basic questions about factors a patient may reasonably be expected to inquire about (training, length of prior experience, theoretical stance) will be seen as evasive at best. Religious orientation appears to be in much the same category—when it is asked about. The questions of when the therapist discloses and what the therapist says cannot be answered simply. In general, I will not bring up the subject if the patient does not, at least until some time has gone past.

> In the second session, a patient (Mr. D.) raised the matter of religion and I gave him the general assurance that I regarded it as important. Two months later, he expressed the feeling that I would not be able to understand something because I was an atheist. I replied that I was Jewish, and he felt relieved. He was able to discuss the material troubling him, but also said that he had experienced my initial answer as professional evasiveness.

If the matter of religious orientation seems likely to contribute to resistance or other problems early in therapy, I will introduce it, as I did with Mrs. F. Later, I will introduce the topic if it seems relevant and useful to therapy then.

> Thus, J., a 16-year-old adolescent I had seen for 11 months, was a member of the Church of the Nazarene (a Pentecostal church). He was having difficulty with schoolmates partly because he deliberately dressed in a "Mod" style, which, although consistent with his small group of school chums, set him apart from the majority of his peers at school. His dress was also regarded askance in his church. Some of the older students had planned to rough him and a couple of friends up. In discussing his feelings of being different and his need to be different, I remarked on his need for others to recognize his difference. He seemed to have difficulty with this distinction, so I made a reference to what it was like to be Jewish in a small town and how my being Jewish was mostly how I felt about myself, not how others defined me. This sharing seemed to help him to understand his self-identity as different from the attributions of others.

Dealing with Religious Differences

For the therapist to express the attitude to a patient that he or she differs from them regarding religion, but is able to work with that patient, may not resolve the issues. For one thing, therapists may be perceived as anti-religious if they are not pro-religious. Further, if the therapist belongs to a different denomination, the religious patient may expect a conversion attempt, especially if the patient is from an actively proselytizing conservative or evangelical church. If the patient does not immediately challenge the therapist, and if the therapist is apparently knowledgeable about the patient's church, then the question of the therapist's denomination will likely be put off for a while. But the therapist may not be knowledgeable about the particular denomination, or the patient may ask anyway. I try to answer concisely without withholding information. If the patient asks if I am a Christian, I say "No, I'm Jewish. How do you feel about that?" Being something distinctly different may have certain advantages if the patient fears merger, as may have been the case with Mr. D. who was relieved that I was Jewish, taking that to mean that I was *something*.

Many therapists are not Jewish, but rather "Christian." This is said advisedly, because for many people in a conservative or fundamentalist church, being Christian does not mean being born of Christian parents or having been baptized, but rather having "accepted Christ as your personal savior." It is probably better to acknowledge that your parents are Christian and you consider yourself a Christian (if that is so), but that the patient may not. Even if the therapist and patient share the same denominational membership, the therapist's "orthodoxy" may be questioned if the patient interprets some dogma differently. If the therapist is saved or born-again, this too can be shared, if appropriate. With all these complications, the therapist should be alert to the possibility of a common group membership being used as a reason not to explore motivations. Conversely, the therapist may feel that he or she is an agnostic or atheist— simple words for complex attitudes. These are code words, and a simple statement of belief or unbelief is probably better, for example, "This is a very complex thing and I am not sure just how I feel, but I know that religion is very important to other people." Schwartz (1970), in reporting a sociological study of an Adventist church and a Pentecostal church in an urban area, commented that "religious sects . . . have their own distinctive cultural idioms, and the outside observer must learn the language of religious discourse before he can communicate effectively with the members of the group" (p. 234). He went on to note that to do this he had "to talk about sect doctrines in a serious and almost accepting way" (p. 235).

But do differences in religion between patient and therapist make a difference? Certainly a therapist who has encountered this in practice and had difficulty in resolving it would think so. For example, some (Ferreira and Ferreira 1978, Greene 1978) have noted that differences in background between therapist and patient (Hispanic or hard science, respectively) made it more difficult to work with a patient or family. Gersten (1979) made a similar point about working with very Orthodox Jews who will accept medical help, but not psychological services unless such services are an accepted part of the community. The little research in this area (Beutler, Jobe, and Elkins 1974, Beutler, Pollack, and Jobe 1978, Haugen and Edwards 1976) suggests that the therapist's label, as such, does not seem to make much difference. The Beutler studies even suggested that greater attitude change occurred if the therapist and patient came from different positions.

> About halfway through therapy, Mrs. G. was dealing with issues of sexuality, dependence, and assertiveness. She expressed her feeling of being very different from me—she was a woman and I was a man; she was Catholic and I was Jewish. Her home had been repressive of feelings, and she had been denigrated for her mild efforts toward assertiveness or garnering support for self-esteem. In these same sessions, she expressed a fear (which was realistic) about losing her job and wondered if I would see her without charge. Although this was interpreted in terms of her family's tendency to stifle feelings and depreciate children, it eventually came to be understood as related to an early maternal abandonment, uncovered much later in treatment. Her sense of being different and longing for unconditional care reflected this early loss, expressed in gender and religious differences. Similarly rather late in therapy, Ms. H., who was a religion major, gave me a copy of a term paper written for a religion class. She felt uncomfortable doing this because, as a Christian, she felt she should try to convert me, but felt too much respect for me to do that. As we explored the matter, it emerged that Ms. H. was afraid of my reaction to Christianity and feared she might be drawn to Judaism. The former fear was related to changes that had already occurred in her theology during the course of therapy, which, unconsciously, were related to changes in her perceptions of her parents.

Beginning Therapy

In addition to the usual problems encountered at the start of psychotherapy (assessing the problem; developing an initial working relationship; agreeing to times, fees, and other policies; etc.), the religious patient *attitude of the patient* /

is likely to have another problem. This is the common attitude that "if I am sufficiently religious (believe enough, pray enough, have enough faith), then therapy won't be necessary." In the same way that hard science professionals (Greene 1978) will bring their scientific problem-solving methods into their lives, so devoutly religious people will see their religion as a powerful aid in other problems in life. Since it often has been such an aid, and since their failure to solve the problems that brought them to therapy is obvious, this casts doubt on their religion in general. At least this is how it will be seen, and these feelings need to be dealt with early in therapy because they contribute greatly to resistance.

To see these feelings just as resistance, however, is an error. Most people do not give up a valued object easily; doing so, in this case, would not be a favorable indicator of the patient's capacity for constancy in relationships. Merely acknowledging that this is a problem may be enough, since it says that the therapist does not reject religion automatically. It may also be useful to draw a parallel between seeking medical help and seeking psychological help. Such an analogy may cause later difficulties, so the need for the patient's participation must be mentioned, but with people of limited sophistication, it may do temporarily until they better understand what therapy is about. Stamey (1971) has described such methods with older, conservative, and unsophisticated patients. As an alternative, the therapist may wish to undertake a longer initial explanation. "Religion," it may be said, "deals with how to live, spiritual values, and one's relationship with God and other people. Healing comes in many ways and who is to say how God will choose to make help available." To adopt the patient's idiom to enhance communication is useful (Schwartz 1970), if one can be comfortable doing that. Even if the patient emphasizes spiritual healing, this type of answer may help the patient to at least investigate the services the therapist has to offer.

The above comments would probably apply mainly to conservative Protestant patients and, perhaps, Catholic patients in the Charismatic Movement. For Catholic patients with a conservative upbringing, which has not been updated in response to modern practice, the typical therapeutic conversation will look rather like confession. Even moderately sophisticated patients will probably know that this is not confession, yet the similarities are apparent. Thomas (1965) listed six characteristics of the confession, as given below. How therapy will likely differ follows each characteristic.

1. *Examination of conscience*—a directed act not consistent with free association
2. *Confession of sins*—these or anything else may be spoken of

✕ 3. *Confession involves repentance and amendment*—although patients may wish to make amends, they need to "own" their feelings and behaviors first

✕ 4. *Confession to a priest is usually not detailed or affect-laden*—affect and detail are important to therapy

✕ 5. *Confession must be made at least once a year*—therapy is much more frequent

✕ 6. *Penance and absolution are given*—although self-acceptance is important, this is not usually "given" in therapy

In a study of value orientations mentioned earlier, Spiegel (1959) discussed the specific problems seen in therapy with lower-class Irish–American Catholics in Boston. According to Spiegel, the therapist does not have the authority to "hear confession" and this fact needs to be developed in the face of some cultural impedance. Probably the therapist does not have this authority as a formal role, but may acquire a proto-acceptance. Authority is generally seen as something to be obeyed, evaded, or rebelled against, but not something that offers collaborative help. Neutrality is perceived as hypocrisy and to relinquish a sense of sinfulness is to lose one's identification with one's parents. Not all lower-class Catholics will hold these attitudes, since ethnic background is a very important qualifier; Spiegel, in his report, details the complexity of the problems he encountered.

Different in form and content, but analogous in process are the problems encountered in work with Orthodox and Hasidic Jews (Gersten 1979). *Halachah*, which is roughly translated as "the law," although "path" may be a better term, is a predominant theme. Gersten gave one example of a husband who, when he married, bought second-hand furniture. The money saved was given for *tzedekah* (charity, but also justice). The diagnostic question here was whether this was a very high level of genuine piety or whether it was neurotic. Such a question is far from easy to answer and will involve exploring the patient's less conscious motives and perhaps consulting a person who knows the culture and its practices.

THE DELICATE ASSESSMENT

When faced with a religious patient in therapy when the topic of religion is an active issue in some way, most therapists will want to know how to appraise this material, as they would with any other sort of material. Since a religious idiom lends itself to all sorts of expressions of internal states, the therapist will likely want to know if what the patient is saying is something idiosyncratic or is rather an expression of group attitudes, ideas, or practices.

> I had seen Ms. H. for about a year in late adolescence. She returned to therapy the year before graduating from college to continue the work that had not been completed earlier. A member of a broad-gauged, mainline Protestant denomination, she began the first session by stating how her concerns set her apart from her peers and contemporaries. They were concerned with the inerrancy of the Bible and the gifts of the spirit. She was interested in political and social action to alleviate hunger and misery and to extend the Church's missionary scope and effectiveness. She wondered if there was something wrong with her, religiously. If she had been a member of a Pentecostal church or some similar denomination, then her concerns would indeed be at variance with what was typical of her denomination. However her church had a heritage of social concerns, wedded to faith, so her "theological" concerns reflected her own self-doubts.

This example is relatively unusual in a general psychotherapy practice and perhaps would not have emerged so clearly and so early if she had not already been in therapy with me and knew that I was interested in the religious side of her life. Further, it represented a sort of "false positive," since religion was not then a therapeutic issue, although it appeared to be. However, if a patient reports delusions or hallucinations with a religious content, there is not much doubt as to the presence of pathology. The more problematic aspect is when such a patient asks if you believe them or spontaneously expresses doubt that you would believe them. Often, they have been told that they are crazy. If asked by patients whether I believe them or not, I reply that I don't know what they have experienced, but I am certainly interested in understanding what they think, feel, or perceive. Hallucinations are similar to dreams in structure and can be treated the same way. Furthermore, functionally based hallucinations are usually auditory, whereas organically based hallucinations are visual (Karon and VandenBos 1981).

Between these two extremes, how does the therapist assess the nature of religious material in therapy, particularly in the early phase? As indicated earlier, speaking in tongues (glossolalia) cannot be assumed to reflect pathology (Hine 1969, Richardson 1973), especially if the patient is associated with a Pentecostal or Fundamentalist church or a Catholic

Church with a charismatic community. Similarly, receiving the "gifts of the Spirit" or the "Baptism of the Holy Spirit" is normative in some, but not all churches. Mainline Protestant churches, Holiness (but not Pentecostal) churches, and Inner Light, Millennialist, New Scripture, and Unionist churches are unlikely to sanction these forms of religious expression. The presence of such phenomena suggests more intense, individual meanings and, perhaps, pathology.

Assessing the Quality of Religious Orientation

Although Freud's various comments about religion are of historical interest, his critiques of religion, his parallels between obsessional and religious rituals, and his speculations on the origins of religion in primitive humanity are of little help in dealing with the religious patient. Rubins (1955) acknowledged that religious organization is a function of personality organization and suggested five characteristics or criteria that he thought typified neurotic attitudes toward religion. These were

1. Shallowness
2. Narcissistic display of oneself, one's piety, or one's good deeds
3. The inappropriate effort to keep parental approval (this may be introjected)
4. Bargaining with God or the expectation of reward
5. Dependence on an outside authority

In a similar vein, Salzman (1953) examined conversion and proposed three types: a sham or expedient conversion for ulterior ends, a maturing conversion (usually slow), and a regressive conversion (typically rapid). His case material suggested that what he called regressive conversions reflected a defensive reorganization within the person. The term regressive seems ill-chosen, although such defensive realignments may well be expensive for the person and those around him. Salzman also indicated that people do not come to therapy because of their conversions and may be quite protective of these experiences. He thought that problems with anger or hatred in a conflict with authority figures were the major issue in a defensive resolution, which suppressed or displaced the hatred. Although this may be a common motivator, he appears to have overlooked the needs for dependency, self-abnegation, reassurance, support for ego-identity, and a reorganization of one's *weltanschauung* a conversion may also provide.

Both Salzman and Rubins have approached this problem of assessment from a therapeutic point of view by suggesting criteria or characteristics that evaluate the quality of the patient's relation to his or her religion. Pruyser (1971) approached the matter from the perspective of specific aspects of religious behavior and listed eight religious pathological syndromes.

1. *Demonic possession.* In spite of the current spate of movies, this is relatively rare in this country and may depend on the religious forms available. Although I have never seen such possession myself, if it is encountered, the therapist might consider the possibility of multiple personalities or some sort of encapsulated introject.

2. *Scrupulosity.* This is an obsessional overconcern for one's sinfulness. Beneath the depression of being a terrible sinner, repressed anger may be found, or the patient may be concealing the narcissistic conceit of being the worst (biggest) of all sinners.

3. *Ecstasy or frenzy.* Seen as a regressive, oral state, with the superego largely non-functional, Pruyser did not note that some frenzied or ecstatic behavior may be common in certain churches.

4. *Repetitive denominational shifting.* Here the trend is usually toward a more simplistic, affective, and clearly structured faith, ritual, or community. Often the church will have a strong, charismatic leader.

5. *Acedia.* A spiritual languor or depression, mentioned by Chaucer in the Canterbury Tales, it may be countered by mysticism, Eastern religions, or drugs.

6. *Glossolalia.* This is included here when the personal milieu does not esteem this activity.

7. *Sudden conversion.* Included when this is not part of the person's particular cultural pattern.

8. *Crisis.* Sometimes referred to as the "dark night of the soul," this may be experienced as panic, catastrophe, or death and rebirth. Although there may be schizophrenic implications, the crisis may well have religious associations.

With these last three points, Pruyser recommended that one watch the outcomes, which can be regressive or reintegrative.

Pruyser's implicit frame of reference seems to be the overall quality of the patient's internal structure, as well as the nature of the object-relations. Although this is a feasible approach for someone as knowledgeable about religions as Pruyser is, the approach taken in this book is to view the individual in the frame of reference of the church affiliation or denomination. Such an approach does not help appraise an individual religious expression that is not anchored in a specific denomination, but it is serviceable for work with most patients.

Pruyser followed up this 1971 paper with a more general (1977), thoroughgoing critique of what he called the "seamy side" of religious beliefs. Very interesting in its own right and worth further study, only a few points will be noted here, to extend the criteria listed above.

1. *Sacrifice of the intellect.* Although demanded by some religious movements, this is considered a warning sign. Related to this are various forms of thought control that may be imposed by the group.

2. *Surrender of agency.* Statements like "the Devil made me do it" are, in reality, a loss of ego-control.

3. *Love and aggression.* Here the themes of love, charity, and peace are emphasized, yet the person's functioning indicates that aggression is poorly neutralized.

4. *Aggressive "love."* This is related to the item above, in which love or service are used to express hostility, dependency, demandingness, or immaturity. Often this is done in such a way as to leave others unable to respond in the face of such "sweetness" or "helplessness" (Stamey 1971).

As an example of the latter, Mrs. I. was married to the son of a minister of a very conservative denomination. Her father-in-law had been a very dominant and powerful figure, but her mother-in-law seemed to sail passively through life, oblivious to everything around her. Now that the father-in-law was dead, the mother-in-law continued this pattern. In the incident related by Mrs. I., her mother-in-law leased her house to a quite unsuitable family likely to be destructive to the property because she could not say "no" to them. She then went South on a winter vacation, leaving her children and Mrs. I. the task of stopping mail, milk, and newspaper deliveries; shutting off the telephone; changing over the utilities; etc. Had not the family to whom the house was leased decided not to go through with it, Mrs. I. and her husband would have either had to break the lease or supervise the rental very closely. Mrs. I. was quite annoyed (expression of anger was a problem for her, too), but felt helpless even though this pattern was repetitive. All she could see was how helpless and foolish her mother-in-law was, not how precise and efficient was her mother-in-law's hostility. Pointing this out to her in therapy was not easy, and it was some time before confirmatory associations and more focal anger began to emerge.

Some patients may bring biblical statements into therapy. It is easy to see this as a resistance to the treatment process or a way of testing the therapist to invalidate his or her expertise or to change the terms of the therapeutic situation. Perhaps so. However this is no reason to relinquish the diagnostic value of such material (Bowers 1963, Oates 1950). Oates cited Oskar Pfister, who, in his book *Christianity and Fear*, stated "Tell me what you find in the Bible, and I will tell you what you are" (p. 43, in Oates). Oates suggested that the Bible is sort of a "royal road" or projective test. He gave a clinical example of a woman who felt she had committed an unpardonable sin by calling God a goddamn son-of-a-bitch. This patient, a Presbyterian, had become a Baptist (her husband's church) and felt inadequate in competition with her mother-in-law for her husband's attention and loyalty. The husband then was idealized and became her "god." In reality, the anger was aimed at the husband.

In part, the material considered so far will have some application to Jews, but it will mainly apply to Christians. Although Jews are generally willing to accept psychotherapy because of their strong verbal orientation, greater readiness to accept the reality of feelings, emphasis on the importance of family relationships, and positive attitude toward problem-solving (Zuk 1978), Gersten (1979), in his discussion of very Orthodox and Hasidic Jews, noted an important exception. Jews can also pose a somewhat different set of problems in therapy, which Zuk (1978) described in some detail. The family is very important both in child-rearing and in maintaining later ties after the children have grown and left home, a characteristic common to many families of Mediterranean origin. With Jews, however, there is a strain of egalitarianism between spouses and between parents and children that is not frequently seen in other groups that emphasize the family to the same degree. This is accompanied by a higher level of competitiveness, bickering, and verbal aggressiveness, which is also normative. The traditional synagogue, with congregants praying at their own rates, chatting with neighbors when they are done, young children running around, and the general noise and a lack of expected decorum are consistent with this familial description.

Although the term "Jewish mother" has penetrated many areas of popular culture, it is a real phenomenon, representing a high level of maternal activity and even intrusiveness, which can occur throughout the child's life. There are suggestions that the same phenomenon may be an important factor in enhancing or stimulating later intellectual development, but it also contributes to a variety of emotional difficulties. Attachments to the therapist may be very strong, but there may also be considerable conscious or unconscious wariness. The therapist may be surprised to be the target of not a small amount of verbal teasing/aggression. Whereas the usual exploration of hostility may be appropriate, some of this is both a way of expressing positive feelings (while building in a safe distance) and testing the therapist. One patient asked his analyst if he was really an analyst, since he wasn't Jewish. Another patient, whose therapist suggested twice-weekly sessions, resisted in part, because of the long distance the patient had to drive. The patient (a therapist, too) suggested having a double session on the same day and when the therapist expressed doubts about the procedure, the patient replied, "Stick with me, kid, I'll teach you something."

Finally, Zuk pointed out that the scapegoat theme is of no small importance. Although overt prejudice against Jews in this country is currently low, and has never been as virulent and vicious as in Europe, it does occur. It also is a convenient way to avoid considering one's own contribution to various sorts of interpersonal and vocational difficulties, but handling this takes tact and patience if the therapist is not Jewish. In addition, the theme of being special, or wanting to be special, is not an uncommon theme among all people. With Jews, the theme of "special election" or a special relation with God is readily distorted to serve narcissistic ends.

All these factors can predispose to a certain degree of emotional difficulty, but there is evidence to suggest that there are self-limiting factors in the Jewish family, as well (Srole et al. 1962). Thus, neurosis is a more likely development (not infrequently with paranoid overtones), but psychosis is less likely. Nevertheless, psychoses do occur and may have specific content characteristics (Clark 1980). Clark noted that those Jews embedded in a largely Jewish matrix will, if delusional, present materials related to Jewish culture, whereas those from a mixed or largely Christian matrix are more likely to present Christian or combined Jewish-Christian themes. Clark also noted that the messiah is a very important concept in Jewish life, but that it does not have quite the God-like status in normative Jewish thought that is seen in Christian theology; hence, there are somewhat less grandiose implications. If delusional messiah contents are seen in a woman, there may be confusion over sexual identity.

Religious versus Therapeutic Values

Not only in this early phase, but later on as well, there is the potential for a collision between religious values and psychotherapeutic values. Some (Bowers 1963, Jackson 1975, Wise 1980) see little if any basic conflict between value sets. Others see partial (Vitz 1977, Vayhinger 1973) or almost total conflict (Adams 1970). The issue, to a real degree, depends on the values inculcated by the patient's denomination or church. Nevertheless, if value conflicts occur, they will not go away by being ignored, and the potential for their occurrence is inherent in overall Christian or Jewish doctrine or thought. As noted previously, the need for therapeutic help is taken by some people to mean that they have failed in their religiousness. Christianity emphasizes the importance of obedience (to God), self-sacrifice, service to others, humility, and the value of suffering (Bergin 1980a, Vitz 1978). Although these values are more pervasive among conservative denominations, they are clearly present among sophisticated Christian theologians (Küng 1976), as well. Of course, Christianity is not monolithic on this topic, and although these are major trends, there are much more flexible alternatives that are consistent with Christianity and yet yield quite different outcomes (Hooker 1978). These concepts (obedience, self-sacrifice, humility, suffering) are interpreted quite diversely, ranging from self-abnegation of the doormat sort to considerable activity and concern for others, without personal narcissism, but with adequate self-respect. One must inquire into the content, for these terms can be misleading. Psychotherapy, however, will likely value self-direction, firmly seek appropriate satisfactions, and realistically positive views of oneself, and avoid masochistic pain. It can well be argued that there really is no value clash here if the terms on both sides are clearly and thoughtfully defined, but such optimism does not seem fully warranted to me. The article by Bergin (1980a) on some of the clashes between therapeutic and religious values and the various replies and comments accompanying it (Bergin 1980b, Ellis 1980, Walls 1980) discuss this fully. For the purposes of this book, religious and therapeutic values (and not all have been listed) have a potential for collision in the practical and real therapeutic encounter and the therapist should be prepared.

At the end of the chapter, working collaboratively with the clergy will be discussed, but in the initial phase of therapy, this collaboration may not be available. If the patient confronts the therapist with questions or a challenge, such as "Do you (or does therapy) advocate 'free love'?" or

"Am I supposed to hate my parents?" or "I hear you are supposed to fall in love with your therapist" this has to be met directly. Asking for more detail on the ideas or assumptions the patient has brought into the situation is often useful, but the patient's insistence on an answer should be met in a candid, forthright manner. The answer given should reflect something genuine in the therapist's own values, although the patient rarely needs a full tour of the therapist's thoughts on such matters. I might say that "sex in the absence of a relationship seems sterile to me, but in any case, I don't tell people how to live their lives." If I feel particularly tart, I may add that "in my experience, most of the people that I see already have a lifetime's supply of advice and I don't see any need to add to that." Similarly, the therapist can say that "you need only have the feelings that you have and there is nothing programmed here" or that "while I am certainly interested in any feelings you have, you can feel whatever you like." Although the therapist will appropriately take note of the diagnostic significance of the question or issue chosen, it does not seem to be useful to pursue this in the initial phase, unless the patient is very persistent, which then indicates intense, focal concerns.

SPECIFIC THERAPEUTIC TECHNIQUES

Having gotten past the problems inherent in the initial therapeutic engagement and having started treatment, at least two further problems related to religious issues lay in wait. The first stems from a problem that has a religious underpinning, without the therapist and/or the patient being aware of it. One example was given earlier in which a patient of Catholic background conscientiously prepared for the session by reviewing the material he planned to discuss, which paralleled the "examination of conscience" prior to confession. This event was looked at only in terms of the therapist's own resistance because he, too, was of Catholic background. Now it can also be seen as a problem of religious roots being detached from their origin. Similarly, another Catholic patient expressed her dissatisfaction with my accepting attitude toward her communications because she had not told me "everything" and I seemed to accept her resistance. She, however, felt that her resistance invalidated therapy, an ironic reversal of patient–therapist stances. Finally, after some confused exploration on my part, she informed me that in confession the failure to confess everything (actually, this applies only to mortal sins) made the confession invalid. Once this had surfaced, the difference between confession and free association was clarified and she could better accept the statement that "resistance is the bread-and-butter of therapy."

The second problem has been repeatedly considered in various ways up to this point and relates to attitudes, relationships, and behaviors that have an explicit religious coloration or rationale. A problem the therapist is unaware of is, of course, much harder to deal with effectively, so therapy involving religious issues will be approached from this second position. Once an issue in therapy is discovered to have a religious quality, therapy would proceed from this second position, in any case. Further, it may bear repetition that the therapeutic goal is not to "cure" the patient's religious understandings or misunderstandings, but rather to help the patient encounter, experience, and resolve the "hurts, needs, angers, impulses, thoughts and feelings that arose from the patient's interactions with significant people" (Lovinger 1979, p. 425) in the patient's past or present.

Using Religious Imagery

Personal issues in treatment may be expressed through a variety of religious images, sometimes of a fortuitous nature. One patient had a dream of securing art lessons for her children from a man whose last name was Priest. This led to significant issues related to a very significant man in her life, who had left the seminary shortly before ordination. The religious content of the dream seemed of minor importance, other than conveying to the patient that the therapist was able to hear things worth paying attention to. Another patient who planned to enter the ministry dreamt of being in a musical ("Annie Get Your Gun"). Standing next to a big wooden wheel during the number "Anything You Can Do I Can Do Better" related to his ministerial ambitions for advancement (becoming a "big wheel"), in conflict with more mundane interests related to certain of his problems.

Similarly, Ms. H. (mentioned previously) used a form of religious imagery to initially describe her difficulties as being different from her peers in theological matters, when personal doubts were really what was at issue. The therapist, too, can utilize such imagery in framing interpretations or other interventions. J., the adolescent mentioned previously, was troubled by conflicts with his peers, who, as a group, would harass him, but who, individually, were more pleasant. It was suggested that, as a

Christian, he might try to "love his enemies" by making contact with them at such times so as to appear less strange. Such interventions are risky, however, and need to be set in the context of an adequate relationship, or they may border on being overtly manipulative.

Using Alternative Translations

The various problems with translating the Hebrew, Aramaic, and Greek of the Bible, written at different times and places and representing different views of the universe, humanity, and God's action in history and its meaning for people, are dealt with more fully in Chapter 7. Here the focus will be on therapy and how it may be useful to employ these materials. If a patient presents a particular issue in therapy, which is buttressed by a specific quote or quotes from the Bible, the useful beginning stance is to try to understand the meaning(s) from within the faith position of the patient. This does *not* mean adopting the faith position, but rather trying to empathize with its meanings. A detailed scrutiny of the meanings in such materials at the start of therapy may not be effective, but expressing interest in what the patient is saying establishes that the therapist is receptive, but will inquire as to meanings.

One of the more problematic encounters is with the patient of conservative or fundamentalist background who justifies behaviors by regular or even extensive citations from the Bible. If the therapist is also knowledgeable, this can be communicated by responses that show such a background without being either competitive or adversarial. Such patients may then relax a bit, knowing that they are being heard, or they may ask about the therapist's position, which may then need to be addressed. If the therapist is not so knowledgeable, then it is useful to admit this, recognize the patient's expertise, and ask for the citations (if they seem important to the issue at hand) so the therapist can read up on these materials.

Asking which Bible translation (and there are many) the patient uses will also be useful. The Jerusalem Bible or the New American Bible are modern Catholic editions, whereas the Douay Version is no longer commonly used among Catholics, and its use may reflect a very conservative stance. The King James Version, which is preferred by many conservative Protestant churches, is also popular with (and even revered by) many other church groups because of its sonorous and majestic English. The King James Version has recently been revised again while retaining equivalence to the earlier edition, which testifies to its importance and vitality. Also popular with conservative churches is the New American

Standard Bible, which is a revision of both the King James Version and the American Standard Version. The New English Bible is largely used by mainline Protestant churches, which may also use the Jerusalem Bible. If a patient uses the Anchor Bible, then they are quite scholarly in their approach and they may have access to a library that contains the 40 or so volumes published so far. One may encounter a Jewish edition of the Bible (only the Old Testament) that appeared in 1917, based on the Masoretic or traditional text; it largely follows the style of the King James Version, but also utilizes rabbinic commentary and Jewish scholarship. A new Jewish translation has appeared over the last 20 years in modern, readable English, which has won some favor among mainline Protestants as well. Although the Bible preferred may not exactly indicate the patient's attitude, it is a relatively informative and easily obtained indicator.

Within the patient's preferred Bible translation there will likely be many parts that would bear on and modify the position taken by the patient on any specific point. What is more difficult to deal with is a fairly common conservative or fundamentalist stance on inerrancy. Even here, one faces a spectrum. For some, the Bible as God's word is without error—in the original manuscripts. Since these are now lost, of course, room is left for revised and improved translations. Word usage has been altered even in the new King James Version. "Showeth" is now "show," "thee" and "thou" are now "you," and a word like "naughtiness" (James 1:21) is now "wickedness." The patient who takes inerrancy to mean that the particular translation is without error is extremely rigid. Occasionally, one will find someone who refers to the King James Version as the "Saint" James Version. Handling such a patient requires both tact and firmness.

If it is necessary to deal with a particular passage, then several tactics are possible. First, one may look at the context in which the passage is set. The statement to "love your neighbor as your self," which Jesus quotes (Matt. 19:19, 22:39, Mark 12:31) originates in Leviticus (19:18) and *in context* refers to firm and vigorous action with regard to the misbehavior of others.

> Ms. H. showed me a note she received from a young woman a few years younger than she was, which contained a good deal of idealization, but with homosexual undertones. She felt she had to respond, but did not want to be brutal. In the course of the discussion, she commented that her Church's teachings on love seemed incomplete. I raised the statement in Leviticus on "love your neighbor" in the context of associated statements, which

seemed to help free her to make clear to the writer of the note what her limits were.

Similarly, Jesus (Matt. 5:27-28) equated lustful feelings with adultery, which has been developed into "to think is the same as to do." As even a cursory examination of the text will show, Jesus was calling people to change attitudes, not just behaviors. Otherwise, one might conclude that if the thought is the same as the act, you might as well have the pleasure of the act, since you have already incurred the penalty just by having the thought.

A second tactic is to consider whether a person is simply misusing a word.

Many years ago, I did educational and vocational counseling. One client was a very disturbed adolescent boy, who was probably a borderline schizophrenic with relatively limited abilities except for very high clerical speed and accuracy. His motivation was also low, and his mother, in exhorting him to use his abilities to a greater degree, recalled the parable by Jesus of the five talents (Matt. 25:14-30). The parable does refer to three people who are given talents (a fixed measure of money) according to their ability, facilitating the misreading of "talents" as referring to potentials rather than money. At the time, I thought talents had to do with money, but I wasn't sure and did not know enough to intervene.

A third tactic that can be used when a person is misreading a text meant figuratively or allegorically is to remind the patient of Jesus's explanations of the meaning of parables (Matt. 13:10-15, 34-35; Mark 4:10-12, 21-25, 33-34; Luke 8:9-10, 16-18). Further, not all the stories in the New Testament are labeled as parables, even though many are. Similarly in the Old Testament, many of the books or parts of them are meant allegorically or symbolically. Job was probably a philosophical discussion in the form of a story, and the Song of Songs was erotic wedding poetry, preserved as a statement of God's relation to Israel. Further, this literary style was recognized in common discourse and can be seen in Nathan's accusation against King David for having taken Bathsheba and causing her husband's death (2 Sam. 12:1-15). A much more risky and confrontive variation is to ask the person what he or she thinks are the most important words of the Bible. The answers vary, but the therapist may then say that perhaps the most important words are "And God said to Moses" (actually a very common phrase). In response to the patient's expressed surprise, the therapist may explain that "it is important because if God spoke to Moses, if you are very quiet, God may speak to you and you may be able to hear. Are you sure you are hearing what God wants you to hear?" The therapist should not, however, be surprised if the patient still maintains absolute confidence in the correctness of his or her understanding.

Using Contradictory Imperatives

One of the goals of therapy is a condition of "wholeness" in the patient, that the person's competing impulses, thoughts, needs, and feelings will be reasonably harmonious: aggression will be tempered by and in the service of love, autonomy will have room for dependency, and activity and passivity will both be available stances according to the needs of the person and the situation. Whether one thinks that wholeness is fully attainable or that no more than a reasonable balance is possible, therapists are more likely to see themselves more as healers than as troublemakers. Nevertheless, there are times when it is useful to create tension, as, for instance, when dealing with destructive but ego-syntonic behavior, entrenched characterological problems, or inadequate superego functioning. Patients who rely on the Bible or some other authoritative source of direction for patterning their life will always make selections from these materials and will prioritize their importance. Selections involve choices and what is downplayed or left out can be quite illuminating and may be useful in the therapy.

A number of straightforward examples have been given (Coyle and Erdberg 1969) in which religious values are pitted against specific biblical statements, which can serve as countervailing effects in such areas as feelings of sinfulness, enjoyment, anger, drunkenness, and sexual inhibition. More such are given in Chapter 7, which discusses translations. These are general-purpose kinds of statements that may help with a specific problem, although if the therapist can individualize the response, more of an impact is likely. For example, one woman who rationalized her mistreatment by others was told by her therapist, "There's a difference between Christian charity and being a Christian doormat." Such a comment has the advantages of vividness of imagery and connects with the patient's own words. Similarly, with one male patient who was troubled by his tendency to look at attractive women, I asked who had created these women. "God, of course." "And does looking at them harm them?" He conceded that it did not, since he did not stare at them. "Well, then" I asked "how will you account to God for your ingratitude in failing to properly appreciate His creations?" He was able to laugh and relax to some degree on the issue. Incidentally, this is a variant on an ancient position, probably of Talmudic origin.

These examples can be supplemented by another from Frankl (1968), which he characterized as "persuasion," in preparation for applying paradoxical intention, and is worth repeating. In dealing with blasphemous obsessions in priests and ministers, he states

> This is obviously a full-fledged case of obsessive neurosis. Do you agree?" When they answer "Yes," I go on to ask: "Are you convinced that my diagnosis is right?" When they say they are, I then ask: "Then what about God? Will not his diagnostic skills infinitely exceed my own?" "Of course," they answer. So I go on: "Now, if God knows that all these blasphemous ideas are of an obsessive–neurotic nature, he certainly will not make you accountable or hold you responsible for these ideas. By the same token, however, there is no need to fight them; on the contrary, your fighting them would rather be the only real blasphemy you run the risk of committing, inasmuch as thereby you would implicitly declare that God cannot differentiate between what is only an obsession and, on the other hand, a real blasphemy. So stop fighting your obsession if you don't want to offend God. (p. 239)

The technique here is to bring into conjunction contradictory aspects of the patient's system of thought that strain the system. The aim is not to destroy or ridicule, but rather to loosen a system that is defensively too tight, so that the dynamics of the patient's stance can be explored. There is the risk of offending the patient, however. Although Frankl described his approach as being early in his contact with the patient, such an approach should be used cautiously and only when an adequate rapport has been established. Argumentativeness is not often useful in therapy.

Using contradictory imperatives is a relatively confrontational technique, which may intensify resistance to rather than forward movement in therapy. As an alternative, the therapist may try to support or encourage the resistance as a way of loosening it. For example, the patient who expresses caution or distrust of the therapist may be told "Good. You have no reason to trust me yet. You should watch me carefully and if you think I've done something, you should tell me." Similarly, religious doubt, which was considered in Chapter 3, can be highly significant. When exploring the meanings of the patient's doubts is either not productive or not a suitable move at that point and when the issue of doubt has to be dealt with, the therapist may comment that doubt is important, since it helps one distinguish between believing what is false and what is true.

Corrective Experiences and After-Education

Corrective emotional experiences as a therapeutic procedure have long been associated with Franz Alexander. As understood and misunderstood, this technique has had rather a "bad press" in American psychoanalysis and psychoanalytically oriented psychotherapy. Psychotherapy, in which one person attempts to listen nonjudgmentally and empathically to another, is, in itself, a corrective emotional experience. It is just not labeled as such. Since many patients, who are now quite religious, have been exposed to more or less intrusive, painful, or just clumsy indoctrination experiences, the repeated experience of a therapist just trying to understand the patient's religious issues objectively may in itself be a corrective emotional experience.

It is unfortunate that a person's cognitive and emotional processes tend to be considered separate, a distinction that biblical writers avoided. Thus, the therapist who attempts to understand what the patient is saying about his or her religion and what dynamic significances may be contained therein is exploring intellectual structure as well. Although the idea that religion, in general, or specific religions, in particular, are silly, infantile, or just emotional is not at all uncommon among many secularly trained therapists, most religious denominations take some care that their conceptual (i.e., doctrinal) organization not be illogical, even though mysteries exist to a greater or lesser degree. Theologians are generally subtle, capable thinkers, even if one disagrees with their ideas. If during treatment, the therapist discusses (1) alternative translations or meanings, (2) whether the patient has taken a point out of context, or (3) if a particular statement in the Bible is perhaps modified by another statement, then the patient is implicitly undergoing a *corrective intellectual experience*. This is not to suggest that the therapist should undertake to provide a course in logic or engage in theological debate, but rather that the process of therapeutic inquiry indirectly helps patients to structure and clarify their thoughts and their logical connections.

In *An Outline of Psychoanalysis*, Freud referred to after-education, a process whereby the patient's identification with the analyst modifies the superego, leading to further changes within both the ego and superego. Chessick's (1969) discussion of this is a useful elaboration of Freud's suggestion. He focused more on unconscious changes as a result of treatment that permit or aid personality change by the use of the therapist as a role model. Chessick also noted that after-education can entail more conscious operations, such as giving information to the patient. Although interpretation and concomitant insight have been idealized as the sine qua non of psychoanalysis, a good deal more actually goes on. Patients acquire a form of problem-solving skill for interpersonal and intrapersonal difficulties. They learn to grasp symbolism and body language and may learn to value different tastes in art or hobbies by observing the furnishings of the office. Further, analysis and dynamically based therapies deal largely with difficulties caused by conflicts, damaging character traits, motivated misperceptions, and so on. Such treatment is not efficient when problems caused by lack of information emerge. Although a patient's problems may often be rooted in the failure or inability to utilize acquired knowledge or to learn from experience, sometimes the difficulty may just be ignorance. In essence, much of the material in Chapter 7 (translations and their uses in therapy) may function as a form of after-education. The use of library resources as bibliotherapy is a system of conscious after-education.

Use of Literary Resources

The use of written materials, detailed explanations of psychoanalysis, and other such aids was rejected by Freud. Many therapists have largely followed his recommendations, often without trying alternatives, but this stance is not unreasonable since intellectual activity quite easily becomes the "enemy" of the therapeutic work of uncovering repressed experiences and blocked emotions. Rogerian approaches (Strunk 1972) have similarly avoided methods that would utilize nonaffective factors, although such methods might be more compatible with the behavior therapies, rational-emotive therapy, reality therapy, and perhaps transactional analysis. However, religious patients are exposed to religious education, training, and indoctrination outside their church through the media and through written material. It was not for nothing that Mohammed referred to Jews as "the people of the Book."

Relatively little has been written on the use of literary resources, however, and little of this is in the psychotherapy literature (Sclabassi 1973). Strunk (1972) recommended four points if such material is to be used.

1. The therapist should be a reader personally and should be well acquainted with the materials being recommended, or the suggestion will seem superficial

2. Any material suggested should be significantly related to the context of ongoing therapeutic work

3. The method or materials should be congruent with the style of both the patient and the therapist. For example poetry is suitable for some patients but not others

4. Some explanation or guidance may be given to provide a framework for the reading suggested

One could argue with these suggestions, although they provide a framework within which an approach to the matter can be considered. I once found it useful to suggest to a patient that he go to the library and investigate some relevant topic because he was now troubled by his youthful learnings, but wanted some sort of rapprochement with his religion. This was late in therapy, and guiding him would have been inappropriate. Similarly, another patient's experience of her religion was of a rigid, mind-controlling dogma and she generalized this to all religions. Since there was some longing for a religious affiliation, I lent her a copy of a Bible with fairly extensive commentaries and discussions of alternative meanings and translations. This helped her to see that her early experience was not characteristic of all religions.

The consideration of religious literature has been deliberately limited to the Bible, although there are denominations that have extra-biblical literature and traditions that are of equivalent or nearly equivalent authority. If a particular issue in therapy devolves on some of these sorts of materials, the therapist has little choice other than to acquire some expertise or admit defeat.

Specific Denominational Resources

From time to time, a member of the *Jehovah's Witnesses* or the child of a member is injured or ill and requires surgery. Not infrequently, members will refuse surgery or deny it to their child rather than risk having blood transfusions. Where a child is involved, surgeons will not infrequently seek a court order to permit a life-saving operation in violation of the parent's religious beliefs. Jehovah's Witnesses prohibit blood transfusions, apparently because the Old Testament forbids eating blood. That the Bible never intended such a meaning does not convince a confirmed adherent to the Witnesses' beliefs. Further, the Witnesses believe that their blood should remain in constant contact with their body. Using this information, in 1981, two physicians in the M.D. Anderson Cancer Institute at the University of Texas came up with the idea of drawing off the patient's blood during an operation and processing it through a blood separator and then returning the appropriate parts to the patient as needed during the operation. Connected to the machine, the patient was not out of contact with her own blood and hence could receive it. This procedure illustrates the principle that the practices or ideas of various denominations may pose obstacles or difficulties that can be gotten around, to help the patient. Although this section is not a comprehensive survey, it does note some possibilities and may suggest others.

Among *Jews*, a number of well-structured rituals surround the major events in life. Birth, adulthood, marriage, aging, and death are major transition points, and death is perhaps the most grievous. At death, the close relatives of the deceased will typically observe seven days of intense mourning (*shiva*, or seven), followed by mourning periods of decreasing intensity. *Shiva* has been characterized (Kidorf 1966) as a form of group psychotherapy. Although *shiva* may function as a leaderless group or a psychodrama, its purpose is to discharge intense painful feelings and to help people accept the reality of the death without denial. The eventual thrust is for the survivors to go on with life. In therapy, this may not become a religiously related issue if a death occurs in a Jewish patient's family, but for Jews who have lost contact with their religious practices and who are unable to process out the feelings associated with the loss, it may be useful to suggest that *shiva* be observed. Of course, such a suggestion has to be considered in the total context of the therapy.

The *Seventh-Day Adventist Church* is commonly seen as conservative. Although many conservative denominations do not look favorably on psychotherapy, the Adventists emphasize a holistic view of the person according to Evans (1973), who is both a psychotherapist and an Adventist. The Adventists are active in medical, educational, and nutritional activities, and they see the Bible as holding out an orderly, lawful, and responsible pattern of life. Evans saw Christ as offering a corrective emotional experience by demonstrating that God was available to people, offering understanding, acceptance, and forgiveness. The parallel to therapy is fairly direct on an emotional level, although one may not also agree with Evans who saw the therapist as implicitly encouraging a religious component. I have observed similar attitudes among both patients and other professionals with a very strong conservative religious orientation, who found no difficulty accepting both sophisticated psychodynamic and strict religious concepts.

Christian Science is another denomination that emphasizes health and healing, although the focus is entirely spiritual. Wardwell (1973) has suggested that there is "little specific concern with mental illness as a distinctive malady" (p. 75), nor does he think that Christian Science has much concern for other people. He also stated that socialization and the formation of relationships tends to be discouraged, whereas there is more concern for material possessions called "supply." The parallel to the common psychoanalytic term "supplies," referring to both material and emotional inputs, is remarkable. Wardwell's articles (1965, 1973) are quite critical of Christian Science, and my limited experience, including supervising the therapy on one case of a woman raised in a Christian Science home, was consistent with his characterizations. However, some potentially positive aspects may facilitate therapy.

Certain Christian Science doctrines (the denial of evil and aggression, the projection of hostility through Malicious Animal Magnetism, thought transfer, and healing at a distance) may make Christian Science seem strange if not pathological to psychotherapists, but the emphasis on the mental source of physical illness and the use of meditation are possible starting points for therapy. In Christian Science, the mental source of physical illness tends to be mainly in the conscious sphere, but the problem of demonstrating unconscious motivation is ubiquitous.

Specific Problem Areas

Suicide

The possibility or the threat of suicide, or the appearance of life-endangering behavior without an awareness of suicidal ideation, is an especially anxiety-provoking event for the therapist. The denominations reviewed in this book all oppose suicide, although the structured response to suicide varies. Catholicism used to consider suicide a mortal sin, which, in theory, deprived the soul of eternal salvation and condemned it to eternal punishment. Since suicide is often a hostile act, only partly against the self, the latter threat may actually increase the motivation to commit suicide. Currently, it is often recognized that for suicide to be officially condemned by the Roman Church, the person must be assumed to have free will. Most suicides are now considered to have been performed under great stress and thus free will was not available to the person. The older view, however, is still quite common.

In Judaism, suicide is also condemned (without the sanction of being a mortal sin) and this is supported by a number of Midrashic stories. As a practical matter, condemning the deceased as a suicide in orthodox Judaism is so serious a matter that every possible extenuation is considered.

Among Protestant denominations, there seems to be more variability, but none regard the matter lightly. For a religious patient in psychotherapy, the assessment of suicidal potential has to consider the weight of religious motivation, in addition to the usual factors. Beit-Hallahmi's (1975b) review of both the historical and current standing of religious factors in suicide suggested that although it was once true that Jews had the lowest suicide rate, followed rather closely by Catholics, and that Protestants had a notably higher rate, on the average, this has now weakened considerably. Nevertheless, Beit-Hallahmi's review indicated that although the intensity of one's religious affiliation is somewhat associated with suicidal behavior, the size of the effect may not be useful in predicting the outcome in individual cases. Thus, relying upon a strong religious attachment, without assessing suicidal potential, is risky.

Overly Severe Conscience

An overly severe superego is a common therapeutic problem, but this is one area in which the religious patient is likely to find strong support in religious doctrine. Such overconcern for proper thought or action has been distinguished in Catholic theology as *scrupulosity* and Luther, among others, suffered from it. His "therapy" was based on the New Testament (Rom. 1:17), which stated that the just person shall live (or find life) through faith, that is, he was able to find a good sense of himself by accepting "God's spirit of justice" (Johnson 1973, p. 47). Luther modified his superego without the aid of a psychotherapist, and several writers (Coyle and Erdberg 1969, Evans 1973, Frankl 1968, Johnson 1973, Sexton and Maddock 1978, Vayhinger 1973) have dealt with the problem within a largely religious framework.

Sexton and Maddock's (1978) report of three such cases is typical of many that have appeared in the literature. In one, a woman, aged 29, was hospitalized for suicidal depression and her history showed that at age 11, in an altercation with her mother, she had wished her mother dead. Shortly thereafter, her mother developed cancer and died two years later. In the second case, a 34-year-old woman in therapy felt overwhelming guilt because of two extramarital affairs. These cases were seen as examples of self-punishment to avoid more severe divine punishment and an inability to understand the "New Testament concept of forgiveness" (Sexton and Maddock 1978, p. 165). The problem in understanding the severity of the reactions seen in these two cases is highlighted by their third case of a woman, aged 28, with compulsive handwashing and dirt phobias. This was traced to two incestuous events at ages five and twelve with her cousins. Although she understood that these events were not unusual, her symptoms remained. This eventually led her therapist to do hypnotic age regression to age two, when she had been briefly trapped in a house fire in which her older brother had burned to death. Sexton and Maddock connected her fear of a literal hellfire to the original traumatic event, which was then displaced forward to the sexual events, but there is no mention of her probable competition with and anger toward her older brother, which then makes her dynamics, and the severity of her superego, more comprehensible.

In all three cases, it seems plausible that projective identification or similar early defenses and experiences were at work, although the history given in the first two does not permit one to judge. Rather, it seems that in the first two cases, the therapists were able to effect modifications in the patients' superegos through an adequate therapeutic relationship, and these interventions were organized around both therapeutic and theological interpretations. In the third case, the same kind of intervention did not work, and it was necessary to look further, which led to the discovery of the earlier traumatic fire. A few points may be made here. First, therapeutic effort is pursued, in most instances, until a desired result is obtained, although theory may direct or limit the therapist's degree or range of activity. Second, a variety of interventions (with their attendant explanations) are likely to be effective, so one must recognize that most interpretations and explanations are tentative. A psychodynamic construction of these cases is useful in more fully evaluating symptom severity and probable locus of difficulty, as well as suggesting alternative therapeutic strategies. Overall, it seems that with an overly severe superego in a religious patient, a direct attempt to modify the introjects and identifications that form the superego through the use of alternative readings of relevant biblical texts may not be too productive without a solid therapeutic relationship. It should be noted that Maddock was an Episcopal priest, as well as a psychologist, and this may have lent weight to his use of biblical texts and their interpretation. One of my cases follows.

Mrs. G.'s guilt feelings were a persistent issue during much of her therapy. About halfway through her treatment, she had begun to acquire some perspective on them and was beginning to differentiate between those that were reasonably related to concrete events and those that inhered to ordinary events, which, by themselves, should not have triggered such feelings. In a session at this time, she expressed passive wishes for care, which were related to her feelings about her mother not being available to her when she wanted her to be. This led to the recollection of her mother saying to her "Just who do you think you are?" in response to modest assertions. In the next month, I was able to uncover a particularly traumatic loss in the life of Mrs. G.'s mother when Mrs. G. was little more than one year old. In continuing to deal with both her past and present relation with her mother, Mrs. G. was slowly able to establish some increased sense of competence and self-esteem. She recounted her experience with a coworker who was very rigid and religious, and this led her to an awareness of suppressing fantasy because it might lead to impure thoughts and hellfire. The latter was connected to her mother's traumatic loss of a relative in a fire. Although her severe conscience was not then fully resolved, my being able to recover this event was experienced as caring and seemed to help modify Mrs. G.'s superego.

Intermarriage

Unlike suicide, which directly bears upon therapy and the therapist, marriage is usually approached from the general therapeutic stance of the therapist. Typically, it calls for inquiry and we will not proceed with that aspect here except as it bears upon the issue of intermarriage. Intermarriage here refers to a marriage between any two people when there are differences in religious orientation that make a difference to someone significant in the life of the patient. For example, a person with a conventional, mainline Protestant background (e.g., Methodist or Presbyterian) who becomes involved with a person from a Pentecostal church may be regarded by the family of the latter person as not being a Christian. Similarly, the family of the former person may regard the person from the Pentecostal background as fanatical or un-Christian because of their exclusivistic attitudes. In the past, marriages that crossed major denominational lines (Protestant—Catholic—Jewish) regularly generated tensions, and although this is still true, it tends to be somewhat less intense, on the average. Although one is less likely to hear of Jewish families sitting *shiva* for a child who has married a non-Jew, intermarriage between Jews and non-Jews is likely to cause discomfort, anger, feelings of betrayal, and the emergence of latent prejudice on both sides.

Depending on the developmental level, the patient may be attempting to stave off fears of merger or even symbiosis. Alternatively, avoidance of oedipal impulses through selecting a very different object may be the patient's aim. Hostility may also be involved in the selection of a mate likely to antagonize significant people in the patient's family—or the intended spouse may have this motive. Whatever is involved, intermarriage represents a threat to group and family survival, although it may also reflect specific individual motives in those persons objecting to the marriage. Although the therapist must consider the individual motivations in the various people that are involved in the situation, sociological factors are also likely to be significant.

Homosexuality

In Chapter 7, homosexuality is considered at some length as it relates to the Bible, and thus it will not be discussed here. The decision by the therapist to accept homosexuality as a choice or to treat it as a problem or to be neutral and "just do therapy" is also not at issue. The Bible is quite explicit in prohibiting male homosexuality, although it may be argued that the sexual aspect of idolatry is really the issue. Arguing that a particular clergyman has misinterpreted the Bible is not likely to get very far. Homosexual patients will often have religious needs that they may not be able to have met in the locally available churches. There are some church or synagogue groups that will accept homosexual members, and some, in larger cities, that will welcome them. One such is the Universal Fellowship of Metropolitan Community Churches. Perhaps all that is needed is to point this out.

Other Therapeutic Issues

Interpretation and Resistance

Interpretation, resistance, and transference are central to dynamic therapy as primary vehicles of change. Most interpretations are constrained by the material present and the patient's ability to tolerate anxiety, but additional limits may be encountered with the religious patient. Most patients experience their religion as both true and exclusively so, and true on the level on which it is presented or described. Thus, an interpretation of the dynamic meaning of some religious concept may be experienced as an attack, or the interpretation may be so used by the patient.

J., a member of a very conservative denomination that was oriented around the Revelation of John, mentioned this Book in passing. Cast in vivid, cataclysmic imagery, Revelation is one of the most difficult and obscure books of the Bible. I commented that it had probably been written during a period of Roman persecution and was likely meant as a message of hope. He immediately came back with "Does that mean it isn't true?"

> After about a dozen sessions, Ms. H. expressed the fear that therapy would damage her theology. This was connected to certain secrets kept in the family. Her resistance was noted, but I pointed out that this was not disobedience. Shortly thereafter, she expressed a reaction to a wordy church service that seemed directly connected to her father's tendency to "lecture." She was relieved that the problem was in her family and not her theology. About a month later, she had an anxiety attack at a Bible study group, which, at first, seemed an intellectual reaction to a simplistic, dogmatic presentation, but developed into fears of loss of intellectual autonomy. Finally, late in therapy she began to discuss her theology. I drew a parallel between her theology and her relations with her parents. She immediately saw the parallel and asked if that meant her theology was invalid. I replied that I could not make such a judgment, although it pointed to the personal contribution of her experience to her view of the cosmos.

Stolorow and Atwood's (1979) discussion of the contribution of experience to the metapsychology in personality theory is most relevant here. At such points, however, the therapist is in a very powerful position to go from interpretation to conclusion. Because this or that concept or attitude has roots in a particular set of experiences, therefore that is enough to explain the concept or attitude fully. One is not in a position to know if an interpretation is complete, only if it is sufficient to produce an effect.

> Near the end of therapy, Mrs. F. had made a good deal of progress in most areas of her life, except her marriage, the reason she came to therapy in the first place. She felt that sex spoiled relations and it was possible to connect this to her father's attempted seduction of her when she was a young adolescent. Her fear of closeness with her husband and with me was then brought together. This was followed by an intense session that revealed that the price for her parents' acceptance and her consequent good self-esteem was her accession to her parents' demands to accept Jesus as her personal savior and to follow the other

behavioral constraints of their church. For her to accept my positive (but realistic) remarks and interpretations was to risk salvation, as well as conversion by me. The following session revealed a marked positive shift in her relationship with her husband.

The above case illustrates how religious and dynamic factors can be interrelated, as well as the limited degree to which the therapist has to intervene directly when religious issues arise. It would seem that when the dynamic issues are resolved, there is likely to be a concomitant shift in theology.

Resistance can take many forms. If the patient knows that the therapist is interested in or knowledgeable about religious or theological matters, theological discussions or questions may surface. I find it more useful to let this flower a bit before asking whether this is what the patient really wants to discuss or wondering aloud why this is being discussed now. If both the therapist and patient happen to share the same denominational membership, the expectation of a collusion between "us insiders" can be used to subvert treatment (Spero 1981). A more difficult problem may emerge when the therapist and the patient do not share the same orientation, when the therapist does not disclose his or her orientation, or when the therapist is, or appears to be, secular. Then the therapist is easily made into the "other," the opponent, and this view may be facilitated by family or church members. It is easy to see the resistance here, but it is much harder to expose it, and directly labeling this to the patient most often intensifies the resistance. Temporarily accepting the patient's negative ascription, while tactfully, but persistently inquiring into the feelings and their sources in the patient's experience of the therapist's behaviors, is slower, but more likely to be effective.

Another phenomenon that can readily feed into resistance in therapy is existential anxiety. Life is meaningless or absurd. The therapist may be challenged to prove that life is worth living. Also, it may be hard to distinguish between these expressions and suicidal impulses. Chessick (1969) suggested that existential anxiety is often fed by pathological anxiety and is hard to treat as such, although improved object-relations tend to reduce this, as does courage, moderate Stoic teachings, or religious faith. When expressed religiously, however, such anxiety may be even less directly accessible. Perhaps directing therapy onto those things that are actually going on in the person's life will open the issues to therapeutic intervention. It may be useful for the therapist to observe that he or she does not find life meaningless without insisting that the patient agree.

Forgiveness and Service

A common trajectory in therapy begins with the patient's positive view of some significant person, such as a parent, even though, inexplicably, the patient has angry feelings toward the parent. As therapy proceeds, the reasons for the patient's anger will emerge, and sometimes a great deal of anger will be expressed by the patient about the significant other. Still later, as these feelings are worked through, the patient may develop a more balanced view of the parent. There will be realistic, partly or largely positive feelings left in the patient who will come to better understand the parent's motives, behaviors, and limits. The patient will likely experience rapprochement and forgiveness, to the extent possible, and can re-experience valuable qualities worth identifying with. In a word, the patient can forgive the parent. All this may go on even if the parent is dead.

Forgiveness is emphasized in both Judaism and Christianity, both of which have rituals for reconciliation. The Christian emphasis on turning the other cheek, the sacrificial practices in the Temple in Jerusalem, and *Yom Kippur* or Day of Atonement are all metaphors for forgiveness. The process of reconciliation in a religious sense involves a genuine effort to change and to make restitution (even if only sincere apology), but is readily debased to empty ritual or empty verbalization. Psychotherapy is also vulnerable to a similar process. A good deal of experience may have to be remembered, much feeling expressed, and much pain recalled before the patient can genuinely resolve the hurt and anger. To evade this difficult task, the patient may seek a less than full recall, and the therapist's task is to evoke as fully as possible the buried material. The facile, but evasive religious ritual or verbalization can readily serve the patient's resistance, too. To see the evasion as just resistance misreads the similarity in aim of both the theological and the therapeutic enterprises.

Pattison (1965), working from both a theological and a therapeutic position, listed six steps in the process of forgiveness: "guilt, confession, remorse, restitution, mutual acceptance, reconciliation" (p. 107). For each of these he discussed various neurotic distortions. *Confession* may lead to the denial of responsibility or the defense against hostility or other impulses, whereas *remorse* can allow masochistic self-punishment to obtain sympathy. *Restitution* can be a payment to avoid punishment, whereas in *mutual acceptance*, the forgiver may retaliate or forgive too easily (enacting omnipotent fantasies or defending against anger). Pattison concluded that psychotherapy deals with guilt as a partial salvation, but that complete salvation requires "reconciliation of the existential estrangement" (p. 113). This last point largely sets him within a religious frame-work, but does not keep the therapist from examining a patient's religiously motivated forgiveness for depth and authenticity without assuming that a religious motivation either provides or precludes genuineness.

One of the hallmarks of effective therapy is an increased capacity, as Freud remarked, to work and to love. Concern for the other person in the form of nondestructive caring is certainly one such marker. However, one also sees people who show strong generalized concern for the welfare of others and who derive significant gratification out of service to others. In extreme instances, there are delusional salvation fantasies (Atwood 1974) of the person being Jesus Christ or some similar figure, and these can be traced to the traumatic loss of a loved parent who is not replaced by other loving individuals. Atwood detailed two such cases in which the lost parent was introjected to solve the unresolved grief, which led to lives devoted to intense service to others, yet was also marked by eruptive anger. Unless the symptomatology is clearly pathological, as it was in Atwood's two cases, it is possible to see the attitude of service as representing an unusual degree of humane concern and sensitivity. When such attitudes are not well integrated or when strong, incompatible impulses are also found, then one must question the bases of the patient's concern and sensitivity. The therapist will have to acquire a good deal of data on the patient's interactions before this becomes reasonably clear.

Termination

For patients with significant religious problems, past or present, a successfully concluded therapy should contain some indications that these matters have been resolved in one way or another. Mr. C., in attempting to resolve his strict Catholic upbringing, found a book critical of the Early Church Fathers that supported his wish to break away from this part of his past.

For Mrs. G., in the eight months prior to her termination, the wish to resolve matters with the Catholic Church surfaced in various ways. Two months later she had a dream, in which one incident concerned the theft of $30 from her purse. In part, this appeared connected to feelings of betrayal of her old attachment to the Catholic Church (Jesus betrayed for 30 pieces of silver). This was followed by a discussion with her husband over divorce and her strong feelings of guilt. Pointing out that she had "confessed" and had done "penance" (that is she had worked on it in therapy and would be unlikely to get into this sort of difficulty again) both eased her feelings of guilt and led to a fuller, more detailed investigation of the factors contributing to her marital difficulties. She then began to make some moves of a socially useful and appropriate sort. At the very end of therapy, she was able to resolve her feelings about her church and began to explore the possibilities in a church that was not too distant from the one of her childhood.

COUNTERTRANSFERENCE

Various facets of the therapist's reactions to religious issues have been dealt with earlier, although they may not have always been labeled countertransference. Here the topic will be discussed with more direct reference to therapeutic matters. Transference was early recognized by Freud as not only an obstacle to therapy, but also as a major source of therapeutic leverage and data about significant formative experiences. Countertransference was acknowledged as a problem somewhat later (Freud 1910, 1912), but here, too, a careful reading of his comments indicates that Freud regarded this as not only a problem when the analyst's personal reactions hindered understanding of the patient, but also that the analyst's unconscious was the means by which the patient's communications were apprehended (Epstein and Feiner 1979). Until the 1950s, countertransference was regarded only as the analyst's unresolved problems that required further analysis or supervision. At this time, there was an increasing awareness that countertransference reactions might also contain data about the course or content of therapy or about the patient's dynamics. Nevertheless, even in the latter case, such feelings must be scrutinized and understood so as to determine whether or how the therapist should use these materials in treatment.

In the past 30 years, the tendency to ignore countertransference in therapy has changed, but not when the literature is examined with regard to religious issues. Henning and Tirrell (1982) noted a number of general sources of practitioner resistance to what they called, more generically, spiritual issues. In addition to those discussed earlier (negative attitudes, limited or distorted knowledge, rigid and no longer adaptive doctrines), they also noted

1. The fear of religious therapists that their personal, unresolved doubts will be aroused

2. The fear of the affective aspects of the knowledge of one's mortality
3. The fear of not just the unknown, but also of those matters in our existence that may be entirely unknowable.

Henning and Tirrell reviewed the issues facing the therapist, whether religious or nonreligious. Spero (1977, 1981) more specifically considered the therapeutic problems, with particular reference to countertransference difficulties in the religious therapist. After stipulating the general necessity for self-examination of the therapist's attitude to religious issues and values, Spero pointed out that the therapist must be alert to

1. Apparent similarities in religious values and beliefs that do not have the same origins and functions in the patient
2. Shared religious values and traditions that may lead to collusive avoidance rather than therapeutic investigation
3. Situations in which the newly converted therapist's enthusiasm may lead to overlooking the dynamic significance of the patient's religious issues
4. Intrusions of interested third parties (clergy, teachers, relatives) that further complicate treatment

In dealing with countertransference, Spero (1981) made a number of recommendations. In addition to distinguishing between mature and immature forms of religious belief, the need for therapist self-scrutiny, and self-acceptance of the therapist's own feelings, which have been discussed elsewhere, Spero noted the necessity for coherently viewing neurotic and normal religious needs, accepting the patient's religious struggles, and tolerating the patient's need for a transitional or nonrational belief system. Further, Spero indicated that therapy should not depend upon a religious similarity between therapist and patient.

Like transference, countertransference may have many manifestations. With religious patients, there are several fairly direct forms, including

1. Extended "philosophical" discussions that have no therapeutic aim
2. Arguing with patients about their doctrine because the therapist regards it as destructive or theologically incorrect, even though it is normative for the patient's denomination
3. Avoiding religious topics if the patient raises them or labeling them to the patient as "resistance"
4. Interpreting too quickly, and without sufficient exploration, religious matters in dynamic terms
5. Failing to explore significant shifts in the patient's religious orientation thoroughly, particularly, an affinity for the therapist's denomination

6. Interpreting the patient's acquisition or rejection of a religious orientation as a sign of progress or as regressive without adequate investigation

In one instance I observed, a Protestant patient working with a therapist who had a nominal Protestant background began wearing a Jewish symbol. Since it was not something very obvious, such as a star of David, it may have merely been overlooked. Knowing the patient in a nonprofessional capacity, I was surprised by the appearance of this piece of jewelry and, in the ensuing discussion, the patient volunteered that the therapist had never asked about the item and no information had been offered. Nevertheless, I thought this piece of jewelry was sufficiently unique to have elicited inquiry. Knowing the therapist's proclivity to ignore all data that patients had not offered, I suspected that the therapist may have known of the symbol and waited until the patient raised the matter. The patient never did, as far as I know. This may not have been a serious omission, since the patient seemed to weave this interest smoothly into other aspects of living.

A more serious example was that of Ms. K., an experienced therapist, working with a woman raised in a Christian Science home. Although the home was adequate socioeconomically, the patient's mother seemed both intrusive and emotionally unavailable. There was much emphasis on right thought and right behavior, but love, support, and affirmation of the patient's worth and effectiveness were absent. Not surprisingly, the patient's adult relationships were characterized by intense needs vaguely expressed and poorly communicated, difficulties in maintaining reasonable intimacy, and expectations of rejection and abandonment. During the course of therapy, Ms. K. was able to effect considerable improvement in the patient's capacity for intimacy, clarity of communications, and level of self-esteem. After an interruption for a vacation, Ms. K. was both startled and dismayed to find that her patient had returned to therapy to announce that her prior religious yearnings had coalesced into a connection with an evangelical religious group and that the patient had "accepted Jesus as her personal savior." Ms. K. regarded this as a therapeutic setback, although I perceived it as a comment on the improvement the patient had made in being able to find a good object in her world, both with the members of this particular religious community and in relation to a good, non-hurtful male image (i.e., Jesus). Nevertheless, Ms. K. experienced a strong negative reaction to this development in therapy and I was not able to help her. She consulted another supervisor and was able to contact significant issues in her early life. Ms. K. was of Jewish background and had an older brother who the family designated as the "messiah." Once she was able to recognize this, she was able to see that her reaction to the patient's preference for Jesus Christ (Christ is Greek for Messiah) was a repetition of her experience in her own family. This enabled her to resume a therapeutic stance with her patient.

The practicing therapist may not receive much aid with countertransference on religious issues from other professionals, such as peers or supervisors, unless it is self-identified. Unless one works in an agency with a substantial connection to some religious organization or is part of a team that includes clergy, the therapist may be the only one able to identify the problem. In organizations that have a strong religious affiliation, or with therapists who are personally and enthusiastically religious, positive religious countertransference may be easily overlooked. Such countertransference may be easier to identify, but the therapist may then appear to attack religion rather than the inappropriate intrusion of the therapist's or agency's agenda into therapy. One therapist in a state-funded, mental health agency held prayer and fellowship meetings in his office, which he defended as being on his own time. When he included the patient of Ms. K., referred to above, in these meetings, this created considerable divisiveness in the therapeutic alliance, even though he, nominally, was not in a therapeutic role. If the matter were confronted with him directly, it would only have seemed to the patient as an attempt at thought control, similar to that experienced as a child, and his intrusion had to be tolerated and worked with more slowly and indirectly in therapy.

WORKING WITH THE CLERGY AND FAMILY

The impending rapprochement between religion and psychotherapy is coming soon, according to recent forecasts. It has been impending and forecast for a long time. When a patient's significant others include a conservative or fundamentalist minister or a devoutly religious parent or spouse, the therapist is more likely to experience these people's distrust of, opposition to, or attack on therapy, secular humanism, and other modern evils. When the minister, religious parent, or spouse is unobtrusive or supportive, the therapist may not give much notice or appreciate this. When these people do create difficulties in therapy, it is useful to recognize that they have, in addition to unconscious motives, realistic and partly justifiable reasons to be wary of therapy. From the perspective of the conservative religious person, reading Freud's analyses of religion or Albert Ellis' vehement critiques conveys the image of a massive attack on vitally important values. The emphasis on self-actualization, liberation, and growth in humanistically oriented therapists brings implicitly, in its train, an erosion of traditional Christian values of self-abnegation, obedience to God, and unconditional moral standards (Adams 1970, Bergin 1980a, Ellis 1970, 1980, Vitz 1977, 1978). Further, the emphasis on the individual by many therapies has an ill-considered impact on the networks of social relations in the lives of patients (London 1980, Vitz 1977). Thus, the minister, or religious parent or spouse, has reason for real concern.

There are also territorial issues (Haas 1967). The counseling function of the clergy is quite ancient (Moss 1978), and if it had been partially surrendered in the first part of this century, the clergy seem to want some of it back. There is more systematic training in counseling in many seminaries, as well as sophisticated thought and training among people whose primary base is in the clergy (Jackson 1975, Moss 1977, 1978, Wise 1980). Further, the patient's emotional attachment to the therapist is likely to deepen, which may threaten others in the patient's life and thus contribute to their wariness of the whole therapeutic process. In brief, these are the issues the therapist is likely to face, particularly if the patient is a member of a more traditional church. Of course, there are many conservative as well as liberal clergy who welcome and support psychotherapeutic aid (Larson 1969, Rockland 1970) for their congregants, but a modicum of tact is necessary on the therapist's part to enlist that support if it is not present. Conversely, a liberal theological orientation does not ensure a favorable attitude to psychotherapy. Although Freud thought there was no help for relatives, it is possible to do better than that with both relatives and the clergy. They can even be quite helpful if the therapist is willing to work with them in ways that do not negatively affect therapy. Once these issues emerge in therapy, offering to meet with clergy can lead to discussion. Meeting with family members would be guided by the therapist's overall view of the requirements of the case.

The Role of the Clergy in the Treatment Process

The Referral

Priests, ministers, and rabbis are all occasional or frequent referral sources. For simplicity, they will all be designated here as clergy, unless a specific instance is being discussed. Further, such a referral is as professional as one from a physician or a school counselor. Nevertheless, the therapist has to exercise appropriate judgment as to what is fed back to any referral source and also be aware that all referral sources are not created equal. One physician of my acquaintance regarded himself as quite a therapist, as well as a skilled diagnostician of emotional disorders. By the time he made a referral, the field was not inconsiderably more complicated, and therapy was usually a good deal harder. Some ministers see themselves as providers of sacramental rituals, whereas others are more interested in people-centered activities, church organization, outreach, evangelical activities, or scholarly work. Hence some knowledge of what the referring professional is like is useful additional data. In one study (Larson 1969), it was expected that a liberal New England clergy would be more sensitive to emotional problems, but that a more conservative Southwest clergy would be more likely to refer because of less training in cases that involved both emotional and religious problems. These expectations were largely confirmed, although mainline Protestant clergy in the Southwest did not differ much from the New England clergy. Ministers from more conservative denominations in the Southwest could recognize emotional difficulties, but were somewhat less likely to refer.

In my experience, the referring clergy is quite willing to grant the therapist competence and to be helpful if asked. One should be alert to the covert presence of religious issues or to the clergy's concern over how therapeutic activity affects faith. This sort of concern is less likely to surface with rabbis in two main divisions in Judaism (Conservative or Reform), but is more likely to appear among some very Orthodox or Hasidic groups (Gersten 1979). Similarly, among Catholic priests and mainline Protestant denominations, there is less likely to be concern about therapy affecting religion. Conservative Christian churches, Latter-Day Saints (Skidmore 1973), and perhaps Seventh-Day Adventists may evince more caution and try to sound out the therapist's stance if it is not already known. Very conservative and fundamentalist churches are more likely to oppose secularly based therapy, as are Jehovah's Witnesses and Christian Scientists. Seeing a patient from one of these denominations is more likely to signal the patient's own questions about his or her affiliation (Cohen and Smith 1976, Halleck 1976, London 1976) or referral may be through court order or intense school pressure.

Cooperation with the Clergy

Cooperative efforts on behalf of the patient may range from just the initial referral contact and discussion to the patient's obtaining religious interpretive or spiritual guidance at appropriate points in the course of therapy to consultations between the therapist and clergy to co-therapy in which the clergy's religious or moral valence becomes a deliberate part of the treatment. In the latter instance, Kagan and Zucker (1970) reported on a family with two adopted children in which the family values and relations were distorted and the son was diagnosed as sociopathic. The father was described as competitive, macho, and self-centered, whereas the mother had high status needs and concealed her assertiveness. The struggle for control was mainly over money and sex. The rabbi (Kagan) was also a certified psychologist and treated the parents, the psychiatrist (Zucker) treated the son, and both therapists conducted joint family sessions. The rabbi's function was "a concretized superego" (p. 31), and he also worked toward ego growth and self-developed moral principles. The parents learned to stop undercutting, and the son improved behaviorally, eventually being seen as a socialized sociopath. The therapists noted real risks in co-therapy because of disciplinary differences, competition between therapists, splitting of the therapists by family members, and transferences regarding religion and psychological determinism. Some of the reported difficulties are typical problems seen in co-therapy and do not seem to be related to religious issues. Since the rabbi in this report was also a trained psychologist, some of the working difficulties probably were reduced. For a therapist to attempt co-therapy with clergy without formal training or with only a modicum of pastoral counseling training is considerably more difficult.

Little has been reported regarding collaborative efforts between therapists and clergy who have limited training, but mental health professionals who have tried to provide consultation have noted a more or less extended feeling-out process leading to useful mutual exchanges (Hathorne 1966, Rockland 1970). In smaller communities, in which a limited number of trained professionals are available, and when the therapist is faced with serious superego deficits of the sort described above, one may have to weigh carefully the problem of involving clergy in the treatment process.

The Family in the Treatment Process

Therapists vary widely in their view of contact with the family of the patient. With children, there is, of necessity, much more contact than with adults, but even this varies. In psychoanalysis with adults, some analysts may not even accept calls from relatives, and most will hold such people at a distance. In other therapeutic modalities, there may be collateral contacts with family or other professionals, depending on the patient's intactness, the nature and severity of the behavior outside treatment, the reason for the referral (e.g., as a condition of probation), etc. Where there is a good deal of sophistication, such as among relatively well-educated people, the work of the therapist and the need for a private field is much better understood and accepted. In smaller, more rural communities, or with less sophisticated people, this is less well understood.

Religion involves a community. The not-uncommon phrase "the people of God," referring to a church, is founded in the concept of a social group bound by adherence to a common faith and a set of rituals. This has its roots in the survival needs of the group or community, which is vulnerable. The investment and even the intrusion of the patient's relatives needs to be understood from this perspective, as well as from the purely dynamic one. Working in a relatively small community, albeit one with a university, I sometimes find it useful to meet the relatives after a period of work with an adult. At the least, I am interested in eventually seeing pictures not only from the present, but from childhood if the patient will share them. If asked by relatives about training, attitude toward religion, or such, I am willing to tell the relatives much of what I would tell the patient. Naturally, such an encounter is best managed by prior discussion and genuine approval by the patient. One makes clear that a secret communication from the relative will not be accepted and that whatever is said will likely be communicated to the patient if he or she is not present. In part, I have come to accept this as a permissible practice when I realized how strange a creature the psychotherapist is to many people. Some of the "flak" that occurred in therapy from relatives was based, in part, on the degree to which someone important to them was intimately involved with a stranger. By having a face, place, voice, and character, it made matters easier for the patient and the therapy. Then, if there were continued intrusions from the relatives, these were more easily examined in a psychodynamic context in therapy.

7

Translations—Obstacle and Opportunity in Therapy

At certain points in psychotherapy, a patient may defend a particular attitude by pointing out its biblical basis. It is wrong to masturbate, to have homosexual impulses, to be angry with someone, or to resist in the face of aggression, and the Bible says so. Perhaps, if pressed, the patient may be able to cite the sin of Onan (Gen. 38), the prohibition against homosexuality (Lev. 18, Rom. 1), the commandment to love your neighbor as yourself (Lev. 19, Matt. 5), or the injunction to turn the other cheek (Matt. 5). Often a therapist will feel blocked at this point and either must retreat, argue with the biblical message, or find some other way to deal with a "religious" resistance (Lovinger 1979). Yet the patient who has cited such biblical support has either misread the text cited, or is not using an accurate, modern translation or else the text itself is open to alternative, legitimate interpretations that can have rather different meanings. Further, the texts that are emphasized and overlooked, as well as the rationale for these choices, can sometimes be a fertile field for inquiry. The aim of this chapter is to provide ways for the therapist faced with these sorts of problems to read the cited material in alternative, but legitimate ways so that therapy can move forward, and thus this chapter should be read as a companion to Chapter 6. Before we can consider these alternatives, some background on what the Bible is and is not will be presented. Since there will be many references to specific material in the Bible, it may help to read this chapter with one or two Bibles at hand.

THE BIBLE: ORIGINS, LANGUAGE, AND STYLE

The Bible, the most widely published book in the world, has been translated into the most languages and has had a notable effect on English, in such phrases as "the skin of our teeth," "the sweat of your brow," "sour grapes," "the signs of the times," and "the apple of your eye." Yet if one were to sample the definitions and descriptions offered for the Bible, there would be little if any unanimity. In order to understand how to deal with biblical material in therapy, some definitional framework is necessary; that developed here takes into account the needs and problems of the therapist. There are, of course, other ways to look at the Bible.

The Bible in Hebrew and Greek

To talk glibly of the Bible as a single thing is to begin with confusion and, with a religious patient, one needs to be aware that there are several Bibles. For Jews, the Bible includes the *Torah* (the first five books: Genesis, Exodus, Leviticus, Numbers, Deuteronomy), the Prophets (*Nevi'im*), and the other writings (*Ketuvim*) (such as Psalms, Proverbs, Job, and Ruth). The tenth century B.C.E. may be roughly taken as the time when the oldest portions were set down in writing, but it is most likely that some parts circulated orally or in writing up to a thousand years before that. Some parts are perhaps even more ancient. Hence, some of this material is three or four thousand years old (or even older) and other parts were composed a few centuries before the birth of Jesus. Some of the books that circulated were not finally accepted into the Hebrew canon (i.e., the approved Bible for Jews), even though they existed in the Septuagint.[1] They were taken up by the Early Church and added to the New Testament. Jerome referred to these parts as the Apocrypha (hidden, in Greek) although their treatment as a separate section dates to the early sixteenth century. Appendix 1 lists all the books of the Bible, along with an indication as to what part of the Bible each one belongs. For our usage here, *Old Testament* will refer to the Bible in the Jewish usage, *New Testament* will also include the Apocrypha (where it does not actually belong), and *Bible* will refer to both the Old and New Testament.

Since the writing of the Bible (both Old and New Testament) spans more than 12 centuries, three languages (Hebrew, Aramaic, and Greek),

---

[1]Also called the LXX (i.e., 70) from a legend about 72 scholars who separately, but identically translated the Old Testament from Hebrew to Greek.

and many cultures (nomadic Hebrew tribes, settled pastoralists in a tribal federation, Philistine domination, and Canaanite influences, a briefly powerful kingdom, plus Assyrian, Babylonian, Persian, Hellenistic, and Roman domination), it is not surprising that any attempt to render in modern language the meaning of a text that may have arisen at any point along this time line is a complex and difficult enterprise. Further, the two main languages (Hebrew and Greek) are different and are native to peoples with rather different world-views. Since much of the New Testament was written in Greek by people who spoke both Greek and Aramaic (a close cognate of Hebrew), the Greek text may contain cross-currents of both Jewish and Greek languages and cultures. Added to this, Hebrew was written without vowels, capital letters, or in early times, spaces between words. This does not cover all the difficulties inherent in translating the words and grasping the meanings of the biblical text, but it sketches in some of the high points for the therapist.

Hebrew: Language and Literary Style

"And it came to pass" is a common phrase that begins with the prefix *ve*. This is usually translated as "and," although it may mean "now," "but," "however," or it may be untranslatable (Daiches 1970), thus requiring much astuteness and sensitivity on the translator's part. Greek, on the other hand, has many conjunctions, which gives it a precision and specificity that is largely missing in Hebrew. This technical issue is only mentioned to illustrate why a patient's heavy emphasis on a particular word may have no justification. Some of the translated words may actually not exist in the original. Hebrew does not possess the auxiliary verb "to be," so that in the dramatic denouement of the Joseph story, when Joseph finally reveals that he, the Pharaoh's chief minister, is also their brother, he literally says "I Joseph" (Gen. 45:3), although in every translation this is "I *am* Joseph." Incidentally, in the King James Version, the italicized words do not indicate emphasis, but rather the fact that they are *missing* in the original text.

The Bible is commonly referred to as "the Word of God," and this may be taken quite literally by some more conservative or fundamentally oriented people. Somehow, every word is not just divinely inspired, but also divinely set down. Even certain translations (e.g., the King James Version) may be regarded as divinely sanctioned. Given what is known of the long history of the composition of the Bible, the vigorous debates over which parts to accept and which to reject (there is still no unanimity), and the contradictions within the text as a whole, many people find it difficult to take the literalist or inerrancy stance of certain conservative churches seriously. In spite of this, calling it "the Word of God" captures something important. The ancient Hebrew writers saw speech as a powerful force that most vividly separated humans from animals. Within the first two dozen words of the Hebrew text, the world was created by God's spoken word (Gen. 1:3). Then, in the next chapter, all the animals were brought before Adam to be given names. Similarly, the Gospel of John starts with "In the beginning was the Word."

Jaynes' (1976) ingenious theory about human bicameral mental organization is predicated on the concept that people lived in relatively small groups and that each person experienced a hallucinated voice of their own personal god directing them in the course of the day. He saw this as derived from spoken language, but with the advent of writing in the second millennium, people began to develop a subjective consciousness and their gods grew silent. He stated that the origin of names was a major step in the rise of language and the development of consciousness, which is consistent with the description in Genesis. The patterning of name usage in psychotherapy is a current example of the power relations inherent in naming.

The Bible as Literature

"The Bible as Literature" is a common enough English course which many students have taken. Such courses risk trivializing the Bible unless the teacher has a profound grasp of both the text and the settings in which it was written. As taught in many religion departments, biblical studies often provide the scholarly apparatus to study the Bible. Bible study groups, either sponsored by churches or initiated by groups of individuals, may study the text in less disciplined ways, which can both extend and cloud the individual's understanding. For the therapist trying to find his way through a thicket of biblical references from a patient, recourse to a religion department may be helpful if the material here is not. The academic study of religion has been in the forefront of efforts to clarify the Bible. Bible commentaries and concordances are also useful, and a number of these are listed in the Bibliographic Sources. But how can one approach these materials? What attitude is useful to take?

The King James Version of the Bible makes for difficult reading, but a good modern translation is often rather engaging. The narrative portions of the Bible have a not inconsiderable charm. The story of the obnoxious, arrogant, adolescent Joseph, flagrantly favored by his father Jacob, who both tells his brothers dreams of narcissistic adolescent grandiosity and tattles on them rings true even today. The brothers' decision to kill him or sell him off certainly fits many fantasies held by siblings. And yet as one reads the Bible, one may sometimes feel a faint, teasing sense that there is something else here. Like the movie *Rashomon*, a tale told from four different perspectives, biblical narrative has puzzling inconsistencies, repetitions, and silences. One scholarly explanation is that the Bible was compiled from multiple sources by editors (redactors) who did not feel free to edit their texts. There are variant manuscripts, so there may well have been multiple sources. "Higher Criticism," as it was called, flourished in the nineteenth century and is still a major way to explain the disjunctive qualities of the Bible, although the more extreme manifestations of Higher Criticism have collapsed under their own weight.

Although attractive, this explanation could imply that these ancient redactors were not smart enough or not aware enough to recognize these textual problems—but that we are. As therapists, we do not find it useful to assume that errors and inconsistencies are foolish. On the contrary, errors, misstatements, and inconsistent actions represent meaningful motives. Alter (1981), among others, has suggested a mode of analysis compatible with this therapeutic stance. Consider the two stories of creation of man and woman in Genesis. In the first chapter it reads "And God created man in His image, in the image of God He created him; male and female He created them" (J.P.S. 1967, p. 4). Man and woman are created by God as equals. In the second chapter, the famous rib of Adam is taken and the woman is clearly secondary. This is still further emphasized in the denouement of the story of the serpent and the fruit where man is placed as dominant over woman. Alter suggested this represented multiple, alternative views on male–female relations. Although women could sometimes be worthy and powerful people (cf. Rebekah or Deborah), they were often under male control. Alter used several examples that make the Old Testament coherent, but structured differently from current literary conventions, to say nothing of the political aspects of women's issues.

But after all, isn't the Bible about religion, not literature? Actually biblical Hebrew did not contain a word for religion in anything resembling the modern sense. The spare, laconic narratives imply (and sometimes focus on) the impact of God in history, but often the moral and theological point is made indirectly and through what is said in one place and not said in another. As Alter (1981) stated,

> The ancient Hebrew writers . . . seek through the process of narrative realization to reveal the enactment of God's purposes in historical events. This enactment, however, is continuously complicated by a perception of two, approximately parallel, dialectical tensions. One is a tension between the divine plan and the disorderly character of actual historical events . . . the other is a tension between God's will, His providential guidance, and human freedom, the refractory nature of man. (p. 33)

Further, whereas the Bible stories presented to children or made into movie spectaculars will present two-dimensional characters as fully formed, the major figures in the Bible are likely to present a character that develops and grows in time. Character contains "a center of surprise" (Alter 1981, p. 126) that makes the narratives interesting. The development of personality in the Bible narrative may offer the therapist a way to approach the religious patient who is not psychologically minded. The sibling rivalry of Joseph and his brothers (Gen. 37, 39, 42-46) and David's callousness after the death of his first child by Bathsheba (2 Sam. 11-12), compared with his anguish over the death of another son (2 Sam. 13-18), are but two examples of character complexity. This could be reviewed with a patient to give some insight into the dynamics of human motivation.

Specific Literary Conventions

At a distance of 2,500 years or more from the time and culture in which the Old Testament was written, the opportunities for misinterpreting the text are substantial. There are a number of literary conventions that readers are often unaware of. There is much word-play. For example, the first man Adam (*Adom*) was formed out of the dust or ground, the word for which is *adomah*. Idiomatically, we might better recognize him in translation if he were named "Dusty" or "Earthy," but probably not "Rocky."

Numbers also had a convention. The number 40 meant a generation or a sizable or typical period of time. It rained for 40 days at the flood (Gen. 7), Isaac married at 40 (Gen. 25:20), and Moses died at 120 (Deut. 34:7), meaning that he had grandchildren. That is, at "40" one married, at "80" one had children, and at "120" one had grandchildren. The fabulously long lives of the very early figures in Genesis also deserve comment. These numbers cannot be taken literally, but they are meaningful. First, "the idea that men in primeval times lived extraordinarily long lives is common to the traditions of most ancient peoples" (Hertz 1960, p. 17). Second, in contrast to modern American culture, age was valued, whereas youth was not. In addition, there was a long-standing propensity to exaggerate one's age in the Middle East (Patai 1960), in order to garner greater honor and prestige. Thus, if a patient argues humanity's fallen state as evidenced by the shorter lives now lived, it may be useful to indicate that this was a mode for honoring these ancient progenitors. Concerns about the life-spans reported in the Bible may reflect fears of death.

It was a common ancient belief that if something untoward happened, a god was displeased. If a person died young, a god was angry. Some of the narratives recount someone's death and state God killed the person, whereas other accounts will detail the person's offensive behavior. In the former, we see a general explanatory convention automatically invoked, in the latter a specific explanation fitted to a circumstance. This ancient causal connection is still common, although perhaps not so blatant. A religious patient may suppress feelings of anger toward parents or God out of fear of reprisal. Straightforward therapy is usually the appropriate tactic, but if such patients cite these kinds of biblical statements, then it may be useful to reread these materials to show that persons in the Bible are never killed for their feelings, only for their behavior. Sometimes this is clearer in a more literal translation, such as the King James Version.

Other conventions of writing refer to encounters with God. On the exodus from Egypt, the Hebrews were led by God's presence in a pillar of fire during the night and a pillar of smoke during the day. We now know that a smoke signal at the head of a marching column of soldiers was commonly used in the ancient Middle East. Similarly, there are a number of accounts of people asking God questions and receiving answers. To answer these queries, they often used two objects (Urim and Thummim) in the breastplate of the High Priest. These were likely lots, perhaps like dice (Hallo 1983), used to obtain answers to questions. Some religious patients may expect divine guidance or report the feeling of contact with God or Jesus, which is not the same as frankly hallucinatory experiences in which God (or the devil) issues clear verbal directions. Too great a reliance on divine guidance may indicate a loss of agency (Pruyser 1977) or infantile hopes for care and nurturance, but such expectations do not automatically mean severe pathology or psychosis.

General Literary Conventions

The discussions above deal with specific aspects of the text and are not exhaustive. There are also more general conventions. Certain scenes are type-scenes (Alter 1981), which, according to how they are played out, connote an overall commentary on the main characters. For example, there are repetitive encounters at a well, where a protagonist (or his agent) meets a maiden and draws water for the animals, and she hurries to tell her father who invites the man to a feast. Another is the loved, but barren wife who gives birth after divine intervention. Nor did Hebrew literary construction lend itself to the expression of a person's inner thoughts. These thoughts may sometimes be given in some modern translations, but the older, more literal translations will likely show a person speaking with no one else present or speaking to himself or herself.

More generally, the ancient Hebrew writing style in the Bible was both vivid and earthy. For example, after the Hebrews left Egypt, they complained to Moses that they wanted meat, and God promises they will eat so much meat it will come out of their nose and be disgusting (Num. 11:20). I think one implication may be they will eat until they get sick and vomit through their noses. Terms like "neighbor" or "brother" may be used either literally or generally, since biblical Hebrew did not have generic terms for humanity.

Another convention worth noting is the diffidence with which writers took authorship. Often the writer attributed authorship to earlier times and figures; a form of reverse plagiarism. The Song of Songs or Songs of Solomon were almost certainly not written by him, but seem to be a collection of marvelous, erotic wedding poetry that was nearly excluded from the Hebrew Bible when it was closed in the second century, C.E. This book is now often regarded as an allegory describing God's relationship with humanity. Job "seems manifestly a philosophic fable," whereas Jonah "looks like a parabolic illustration of the prophetic calling and of God's universality" (Alter 1981, p. 33). Alter's remark echoes ancient Rabbinic opinion, in which the entire Old Testament was not taken literally either. The Book of Ruth, which was attributed to the time of the Judges, was most probably composed after the Babylonian captivity and exile (i.e., *ca* 586 B.C.E.). It appears to be a public relations attack on Ezra's requirement that the returning exiles to Judaea divorce their foreign wives by representing a woman from Moab (a foreign country) as the ancestor of King David.

Although there is reason to believe that the Bible has generally been accurately transmitted (Millard 1982, Thiele 1965), authorship is often not as certain. Some of the letters of Paul are now thought to contain only Pauline elements and to be the work of his disciples or even to have been written after his death. The Book of Isaiah is now widely regarded as having been written by two (and possibly three) authors. The first part

(Chapters 1–39) was written when Judah was an independent state, the second (Chapters 40–66) was written some 150 years later, after the Babylonian exile. The former part is a warning to change, the second part provides hope and comfort. This change from warning to comforting may be cited as a prophecy of the future, which is not warranted in the text and is unnecessary in order to appreciate the message. The message is in the content and not in whether Isaiah ever really existed. Excessive concern for a specific story element or set of elements may relate to their idiosyncratic symbolic value or perhaps with the patient's need to deny doubt, or for other defensive purposes. In Hebrew literature, philosophical issues were dealt with by narrative and parable, rather than abstract exposition. Greek, as a language from Classical times on, was much more amenable to abstraction, but even here the New Testament, which was probably written originally in Greek, has a direct, immediate quality even in its more abstract portions. More of this shortly.

Literal belief is an unbiblical stance for the religous patient, although he or she may not be aware of it. Teaching and study are clearly implied (Deut. 6:6-7), as are interpretation and translation (Neh. 8:7-8). In the New Testament, statements that are translated as being about belief are better understood as being about trust. Irony, sarcasm, word-play, and humor are all significant aspects of biblical narrative and often are significant for their moral and theological message. Approached from this perspective, the therapist is in a better position to understand and deal with specific portions of the Bible a patient may bring into therapy.

Greek: Language and Literary Style

Like Hebrew, Greek is a highly inflected language in which the form of the word is affected by tense, mood, voice, and number (Mickelsen 1963). A large number of verb conjugations and noun declensions do not appear in the English translation. Since Greek is even more inflected than Hebrew, and since it has more particles, more precision of expression is possible. Further, there were several stages of Greek, ranging from the Homeric to Modern, and since Attic (or Athenian) Greek was considered highly literary, much attention was paid to style and convention by later writers. The Greek of the New Testament was long considered a sacred language because it was somewhat different from the other known styles. About the turn of the century, many ordinary papyri from that time were discovered in Egypt and it was realized that the language of the New Testament was written in *koine* or common Greek, the *lingua franca* of the Roman Empire. Jesus probably spoke Aramaic, rather than Greek, and most if not all of the writers of the New Testament were bilingual, for some of the Greek has an Aramaic quality.

Unlike many of the religions then current, which were mythological in their foundations, both Judaism and Christianity are historical religions founded on events that occurred at a particular time and place. A central element of Judaism is the Exodus from Egypt, of Christianity, the Crucifixion and Resurrection of Jesus. The common question is did these events happen and what evidence is there for them? There is no clear evidence either for the Exodus or the Resurrection other than in the Bible, so one must consider secondary evidence. Although not all the historical references in the Bible have been confirmed, the record is rather impressive (Keller 1981). Further, in the face of the despotic proclivity of the times to rewrite history to flatter the ruler, the Old Testament's judgments on the rulers of Judah and Israel are startlingly frank and often severe. This does not prove the Exodus happened, but rather it is consistent with a tendency to write accurate accounts. The Resurrection of Jesus does not appear in accounts outside the New Testament, but Pontius Pilate was an historical figure and Christianity was well recognized within the first century, C.E. Within the New Testament, there is the empty tomb in which the body of Jesus had been laid after the Crucifixion, as seen by two or three women. Such testimony is inconvenient; women could not testify in a Jewish court (Robinson 1977).

The question of fact and evidence in these events is so natural to the modern mind that it is hard to realize that there could be a different mind-set when these texts were written. People did not ask what a thing *was* but what it was *for* (Küng 1976). Hence, events were viewed in terms of their meaning in the lives of people. As far as can be discerned, the narratives of the Old Testament seem aimed at revealing God's intersections with humanity and with His intentions and directions. Acceptance of these events and of their meanings was aimed at bringing about behavioral changes. In the New Testament, the narratives of the Gospels are not disinterested histories, but rather "committed testimonies of faith meant to commit their readers" (Küng 1976, p. 153). If it could be stated without pejorative connotations, the Gospels were propaganda; that is, "good news about God" (Robinson 1977, p. 21). To put the matter to the point, the Resurrection is not argued on the basis of modern physical evidence, but rather on the *basis of the revivifying experience in the life of the communicant* (Küng 1976, Robinson 1977).

As with the Old Testament, narrative or story is a major form in the New Testament. The use of the address or essay (as in the Pauline letters) is another form. The narrative contains both stories that carry an implicit message, as well as proverbs and parables given directly by Jesus. The Beatitudes appear to be a special form of the proverb, connected to the more general Wisdom literature (Beardslee 1970). This comparison obscures the radical nature of these sayings of Jesus. For example, in Luke (6:27), Jesus states "Love your enemies, do good to those who hate you" (Jones 1966, p. 102). Beardslee noted that, typically, this would be expanded in the Wisdom literature as something like "Love those who hate you *and you will not have an enemy*." Küng (1976) also noted the radical quality of Jesus's statements, but he held that these are not a systematic program or just an intensification of the law of the Old Testament, as commonly thought. Rather, the total of Jesus's message is aimed at making the law of the Old Testament immediate, inward (as an experience), and a preparation for the imminently expected Kingdom of God. This can be directly seen in his statement on adultery. "'You have learnt how it was said: *You must not commit adultery*. But I say this to you: if a man looks at a woman lustfully, he has already committed adultery with her in his heart'" (Matt. 5:27–28; Jones 1966). One could easily take this to mean that if you have sexual thoughts, then you might as well act sexually; it is no worse, for Jesus says the sin is the same. Reading the entire statement in context makes it clear that it is an attempt to go beyond formal behavior in order to confront matters of attitude and feeling.

But Is It Still the Word of God?

We know a great deal about the ancient Middle Eastern societies partly because of their written records: chiseled inscriptions, clay tablets, leather scrolls, and papyri. Correspondingly, we know much less about the Inca and Maya because of the destruction or lack of such records. Still the ancient Middle East was a very oral society, in which much was transmitted through oral repetition, but with a great deal more fidelity than we are accustomed to. Jewish teachers around the beginning of the Common Era were known as *tannaim* (repeaters). Large portions of text were memorized and taught to students who carefully memorized and taught them. Although few manuscript copies of the Masoretic (traditional) text of the Old Testament exist, and these only go back a thousand years, they are quite similar to the Dead Sea scrolls, which are a thousand years older (Geisler and Nix 1968).

The New Testament manuscripts have a good many more variant texts, although a few go back to perhaps the second century. Much careful study seems to have yielded a largely consistent text. There are more variant readings of different passages than in the Old Testament, but fewer portions are unreadable because the text is damaged or because a word is unknown. Most of the modern emendations and improved translations do not significantly affect the meaning of the text, but some are important. Some of these proof-texts (see below) have been modified by better translations. For example, in the King James Version, Psalm 2:11-12, one reads "Serve the Lord with fear, and rejoice with trembling. Kiss the Son." As Barr (1968) pointed out, "Son" here was an Aramaic word in an otherwise all-Hebrew text. Most probably this was a copying error. Thus, where a patient is overly concerned with the literal accuracy of the text, I would first suspect the patient may be trying to defend against or restitute awareness of a parent's unreliability, unless specific material indicates otherwise.

Proof-texts are sections of the Old Testament taken as predictions of the coming of Christ. A very conservative patient who is concerned that the therapist is not "saved," may introduce these proof-texts to convert the therapist. Such an introduction may be understandable from the ongoing situation in the therapy, but before that may be accessible, the specific material brought in by the patient may have to be dealt with. Some 40 segments of the Old Testament may be cited as proof-texts. If a patient brings in a particular citation, it is worth examining it for its projective qualities. An important text is Isaiah 53, in which the "Suffering Servant" is despised and rejected and suffers mistreatment without protest, and it is God who was pleased to hurt him. This parallels an abused childhood endured without effective protest. One such patient who was battered by her mother would, at the worst of these times, fantasize being a little girl Jesus, fastened to the cross. Her grandfather was a Methodist minister, which helped give form to this reparative fantasy. Oates (1950) likened the Bible to a projective test with good reason.

TRANSLATIONS AND THERAPY

The most visible aspect of Judaism and Christianity is the institutional structure of the synagogue or church (clergy, congregation, hierarchy, etc.), but much of the Bible was originally written for the people in their vernacular and not for the institution. Ironically, as time passed, the vernacular became a sacred language, often the property of the institution. Aramaic, in the later portions of the Old Testament, was the vernacular, as was Hebrew in earlier times. The Greek of the New Testament (*koine*) was the common language of the day, and the famous Septuagint was a translation of the Old Testament from Hebrew to Greek so that Greek-speaking Jews could read their Bible. Jerome's translation of the Bible into Latin was called the Vulgate from the Latin *vulgus*, meaning "the common people." It again brought the Scripture to the people in their own language. Subsequently, there were other translations and among the most famous in more modern times was the King James or Authorized Version.

The King James or Authorized Version

The sonorously majestic quality of the language in the King James Version was far more clear when it was first issued in 1611 than it is today. Not only has the English language changed, but many linguistic, archaeological, and sociological studies have immeasurably added to our understanding of the Scriptures compared with what was known in the early seventeenth century. Still, many Americans view the King James Version as authoritative, and for some it is divinely sanctioned. Faced with a patient who is bound to a particular statement from a particular translation, the therapist needs to be aware that words and phrases all have multiple meanings and this is entirely true of the Bible. Further, the Bible was written in the language of the people and meant to be understood by everyone. If a patient is fixed on a particular reading, sometimes one can convey to the patient that one has the duty to understand the Word of God in as many ways as God has spoken.

Older translations, such as the King James, were likely to render the text literally, and the form of expression is stilted. Semitic peoples had a startlingly direct manner of address to their deities, albeit with elaborate courtesy as befits dealings with a sovereign power. There was not really any equivalent to "Thou" as a form of address to God in the Bible, nor were such terms capitalized. These are relatively modern conventions and even the chapter and verse divisions are relatively late, having been added during the late Middle Ages or the Renaissance (Geisler and Nix 1968). Thus, many of the features of English translations that are taken for granted reflect late additions and modifications that alter the original. In spite of these limitations, the sonorous majesty of the King James Version is very powerful, although it filters out the pungent directness of the original text. What is more problematic, however, is that the meanings of words have shifted in the nearly four centuries that have elapsed since it was published. For example "careful" always meant much anxiety and never meant cautious, "charity" as a noun meant love but never alms, and "conversation" may mean citizenship or conduct (Elliot 1967). More of these are given in Appendix 2.

Problems with Modern Translations

A number of modern translations are clearer, more readable, and more accurate than the King James, yet here, too, theological considerations can overtake the plain text. For example, in Exodus, Moses is told to go to Pharaoh to demand that the Hebrews be freed, but Moses makes several objections. Moses demurs because Pharaoh is a god, and Moses lacks this status. Then in Exodus (7:1) it states literally, "And the Lord said unto Moses: See, I have made thee a god to Pharaoh" (Magil 1905, p. 17). In a less literal rendering, it is "And the Lord said unto Moses: 'See, I have set thee in God's stead to Pharaoh" (J.P.S. 1917, p. 79), and a modern rendition has it as "The Lord replied to Moses, "See, I place you in the role of God to Pharaoh" (J.P.S. 1967, p. 108). All three translations are within the Jewish tradition, wherein the idea that *any* person or thing could be a god is abhorrent—but that is what the text literally says and Magil's (1905) linear translation so renders it. Similarly, Mary was subsequently declared to be a virgin at the time of Jesus's birth (Matt. 1:18-25) based, at least partly, on a prophecy in Isaiah (7:14) that reads, in the King James Version, "Behold, a virgin shall conceive, and bear a son" (New York Bible Society ND, p. 629). The word translated as virgin into the Greek of the Septuagint, on which the King James Version relied, means young woman in the Hebrew and is more or less rendered in this sense in modern translations. Further, the context and wording in current translations make it clear that the statement refers to the immediate future, rather than to an event several centuries hence (see the discussion on proof-texts, above).

Uses of Comparative Translations

A translation will usually represent a specific word or phrase in one language by another specific word or phrase in another language, which often means that the connotations of the translated word or idea will not be an exact match for the original, even if that original is well understood. Some Bibles contain explanatory footnotes that significantly aid the reader in determining what else was meant in the original or how this statement connects or contrasts with others. Translations can filter or distort meanings, and although this cannot be completely reversed, for many of the reasons given above, we can recover somewhat more than is usually done without becoming experts in other fields. An example of this, with practical implications for therapy, is given below.

One of the frequent statements cited by Christians regarding marriage and the role and status of women comes from Paul (Eph. 5:21-29), which directs wives to submit to their husbands for he is the head of the wife. Commonly used to justify the domination and mistreatment of women, there is another and rather different meaning in the text, but it requires a little exegesis (interpretation of biblical texts) as well as the consideration of an entire block of text. The same text from four different translations is presented on pp. 228-229 to show how similar originals[2] are rendered differently. The four Bibles are the King James Version, the Jerusalem Bible, the New American Bible, and the Anchor Bible. These four are among many that are available. The King James is still the standard for many conservative Protestant denominations. The Jerusalem Bible is a scholarly French edition translated into English and the New American Bible is a popular American translation; both are Catholic. The Anchor Bible is a highly scholarly version representing an international effort among Catholic, Protestant, and Jewish scholars.

A survey of these four parallel passages will indicate several things. First, the wording is rather different in the parallel verses. For example, in verse 21, the two operative words there are "submitting" and "fear" in the King James Version, which parallel "give way" and "obedience," "defer" and "reverence," and "subordinate" and "fear." There are important differences in nuance between "submit," "subordinate," "give way," and "defer" in terms of degree of helplessness, with "submit" implying most helplessness and "defer" perhaps the least. Thus, if a specific biblical text is important to the patient, the therapist may be able to introduce more flexibility into therapy by also reviewing other authoritative interpretations with the patient. Second, translations may reflect subtle theological doctrine or cultural differences. The Jerusalem Bible and the New American Bible were both produced under Catholic auspices; the former in Europe and the latter in the United States. The former capitalizes Church, the latter does not. In Christian thought, the church is the assembly

---

[2]Continued scholarship has refined the accuracy of the Hebrew and Greek texts, but some variations in translation depend on which original is used as the source text.

King James	Jerusalem Bible
21 Submitting yourselves one to another in the fear of God.	21 Give way to one another in obedience to Christ.
22 Wives, submit yourselves unto your own husbands, as unto the Lord.	22 Wives should regard their husbands as they regard the Lord,
23 For the husband is the head of the wife, even as Christ is the head of the church: and he is the savior of the body.	23 since as Christ is head of the Church and saves the whole body, so is a husband the head of his wife;
24 Therefore as the church is subject unto Christ, so let the wives be to their own husbands in everything.	24 and as the Church submits to Christ so should wives to their husbands in everything.
25 Husbands, love your wives, even as Christ also loved the church and gave himself for it;	25 Husbands should love their wives just as Christ loved the Church and sacrificed himself for her
26 That he might sanctify and cleanse it with the washing of water by the word,	26 to make her holy. He made her clean by washing her in water with a form of words,
27 That he might present it to himself a glorious church, not having spot or wrinkle, or any such thing; but that it should be holy and without blemish.	27 so that when he took her to himself she would be glorious, with no speck or wrinkle or anything like that, but holy and faultless.
28 So ought men to love their wives as their own bodies. He that loveth his wife loveth himself.	28 In the same way, husbands must love their own bodies; for a man to love his wife is for him to love himself.
29 For no man ever yet hated his own flesh; but nourisheth and cherisheth it, even as the Lord the church:	29 A man never hates his own body, but he feeds it and looks after it; and that is the way Christ treats the Church,
30 For we are members of his body, of his flesh, and of his bones. (New York Bible Society, p. 200).	30 because it is his body—and we are its living parts. (Jones 1966, p. 336).

(*ekklesia*) of believers, whereas the Church may be more the visible structure. This distinction is not a sharp one, but may accord with the parallel to Europe's tradition of established national churches and the American tradition of separation of church and state. The main theme of this section deals with the nature of marital relations as Paul was discussing it. We will consider this in broader terms in the next section, which deals with marriage. Subsequent sections will deal with specific topics that are likely to appear in therapy, along with alternative, legitimate ways to view the text.

New American	**Anchor Bible**
21 Defer to one another out of reverence for Christ.	**21** Because you fear Christ subordinate yourselves to one another—
22 Wives should be submissive to their husbands as if to the Lord	**22** wives to your husbands—as to the Lord.
23 because the husband is head of his wife just as Christ is head of his body the church, as well as its savior.	**23** For in the same way that the Messiah is the head of the church—he, the savior of his body—is the husband the head of his wife.
24 As the church submits to Christ, so wives should submit to their husbands in everything.	**24** The difference not withstanding, just as the church subordinates herself to the Messiah, so wives to your husbands —in everything.
25 Husbands, love your wives, as Christ loved the church. He gave himself up for her	**25** Husbands, love your wives, just as, The Messiah has loved the church and has given himself for her
26 to make her holy, purifying in the bath of water by the power of the word,	**26** to make her holy by word and clean by the bath in water,
27 to present to himself a glorious church, holy and immaculate, without stain or wrinkle or anything of that sort.	**27** to present to himself the church resplendent free from spot or wrinkle or any such thing so that she be holy and blameless.
28 Husbands should love their wives as they do their own bodies. He who loves his wife loves himself.	**28** In the same manner also husbands owe it to love their wives for they are their bodies. In loving his wife a man loves himself.
29 Observe that no one ever hates his own flesh; no, he nourishes it and takes care of it as Christ cares for the church—	**29** For no one ever hates his own flesh, but he provides and cares for it—just as the Messiah for the church
30 for we are members of his body. (Confraternity of Christian Doctrine 1970, pp. 231–232).	**30** because we are members of his body. (Barth 1974, p. 607).

SPECIFIC PROBLEM AREAS AND ALTERNATIVE TRANSLATIONS

Marriage, Family, and Children

Marriage

The nature of marriage; the role, extent, and power of the family; and the position of children and their relations to their parents have fluctuated widely over the three to four thousand years since the oldest parts of the

Bible were set down. These intensely important matters appear recurrently, so there are both some general attitudes within the Bible as well as some countervailing trends.

Marriage, as choice residing in the couple to be married, is largely a recent development in Western society and runs contrary to prevailing social practice in many non-Western societies. Some exceptions are partly suggested in the Bible, too, as in the case of Samson (Judg. 14:1-4), who tells his parents to arrange a marriage with a woman of his choice. Ironically, the entire story of Samson may have been an allegory (Greenstein 1981). Marriages connected families and thus there were a number of interested parties who had impelling and wide-ranging practical interests, but there was an erotic and affective side to ancient marriage as well, at least as recorded in the Bible. In the Old Testament, we see families as power groups, which were endogamous, patrilineal, patriarchal, patrilocal, extended, and polygynous (Patai 1960). A marriage brought the bride into the groom's father's household, unless the groom was the head of the household already. In the oldest portions of the Bible, as in Genesis, the head of the house effectively had the power of life and death over the children and women; a husband could divorce his wife largely at will; inheritance was largely in the father's line; and the law of primogeniture applied (although it was repeatedly upset in the narrative). This was the prevailing theme or direction. Some counterpoint is shown by a statement (Gen. 2:24) in the Adam and Eve story "Hence a man leaves his father and mother and clings to his wife, so they become one flesh" (J.P.S. 1967, p. 6), but, in fact, this was not the practice (Patai 1960). Similarly, there are several instances of men declaring or enacting their love, care, and affection for their wives (e.g., Gen. 29:18, 34:3, Exod. 21:5, Judg. 16:4, 1 Sam. 1:5), but there is only one recorded instance of a woman expressing love toward her husband (1 Sam. 18:20, 18:28), that of Michal, Saul's daughter, who loved (but later despised) David.

Initially, to a considerable degree, marriages were contractual arrangements, which set down the agreements and remedies for the various parties. In a world in which there was little law outside what a family or tribal group could enforce, survival imperatives take a prominent role. Later in the Old Testament, and still later in the New Testament, the rights of the weaker person (the woman) were increasingly protected, but equal status or power for women was not made structural. There were women throughout the Bible who acquired notable power or influence, but they were the minority. Although this paints a rather grim picture, the status of wives was actually somewhat ambiguous throughout the Bible. Those elements that emphasize male control and negative attitudes toward women can readily be made prominent. Rebekah, who was to marry

Isaac, for example, is asked if she will go with Abraham's messenger, Eliezer, although this occurred after the marriage agreement between Eliezer and Rebekah's family was negotiated. Her choice was really *when* and not *if* she would go. Nevertheless, this verse forms the basis for the Rabbinic conclusion that a woman must consent to a marriage. Similarly, the rules of separation during the menstrual period (*niddah*; see Chapter 3 on women) involve the use of the term "unclean," which evokes repellent images. "Unclean" there referred to ritual, not hygiene (see also Douglas 1966). There are many other such references to women as unclean (Job 25:4), seductive (Job 31:9, Pro. 6:24-26, 7:5-10, Koh. 7:26-29, Sir. 9:2-13, 26:8-12), unfaithful or weakening (Hos. 1, Pro. 31:3), foolish (Pro. 9:13-17, 11:22), quarrelsome (Pro. 21:9, 21:19, 27:15), or the source of sin (Sir. 25:24, 1 Tim. 14) and death. Alternatively, women are also represented as wise, brave, clever, or skilled (Exod. 35:25, Judg. 4, 9:53, Esth., Ruth, 1 Sam. 25, 28:7-24, Pro. 14:1, 31:25-27); helpful or generous (Exod. 35:29, Josh. 2:4); self-assertive (Gen. 38:14-26, 1 Sam. 15-16, Pro. 31:16-18); or gracious and virtuous (Pro. 11:16, 12:4, 31:10-13).

For Christians, there is a powerful impact from statements by Jesus and Paul on marriage, family, and children. As with the Old Testament, there is a range of statements that, depending on one's selections, will tilt the view of marriage and relations between women and men as well as parent and child. Both Jesus and Paul clearly felt they were living in an eschatological period. The end of the world as they knew it was coming—soon. Both were unmarried and neither saw marriage as important to their teaching in light of the overwhelming nature of what was soon to happen. Paul also (in contrast to Jesus) seemed averse to marriage, although he made it clear that this was his personal feeling and that others might have different attitudes and practices. Later in Paul's writings, this attitude began to change when the expected eschatological crisis did not occur. Marriage, the importance of work, and the organization of the Church began to receive positive attention.

Jesus's prohibition of divorce (Matt. 19, Mark 10) is readily construed as oppressive, but it actually fits within the ongoing development of Rabbinic or Pharisaic Judaism toward a continuous improvement in women's rights by progressively limiting the husband's right to divorce more or less at will. Similarly, Paul (Gal. 3:28) took the radical position that within the Christian community all were equal; Jew and Greek, slave and free, male and female. These efforts to enhance the dignity and status of women in relation to their husbands were, at best, only partly implemented. More typically, women were directed to be silent (1 Cor. 14:34, 1 Tim. 2:11-15) and submissive to their husbands (Eph. 5:24, Col. 3:18), but these statements are also balanced by others that assert that wives have rights to their husbands' bodies in the same ways that husbands have rights to their wives' bodies (Col. 3:8-19, 1 Cor. 7:3-6). Although this idea of reciprocal ownership might not sit well with many modern views, it both represents a major advance from the then-current views of women as possessions and provides openings to discuss with a patient the right to sexual satisfaction or a wife's right to good treatment (Eph. 5:28-33, 1 Pet. 3:7, 1 Cor. 7:33, Col. 3:19). The *Talmud* also noted a wife's right to sexual satisfaction. A man could not change his occupation to the detriment of these rights without her permission.

Some Interpretations of Ephesians

With the above as background, let us continue with the comparison and interpretation of the section from Ephesians compared in the four translations. The main issue here is contained in how one reads Verse 22, which is "Wives, submit yourself unto your husbands, as unto the Lord" in the King James Version. Perhaps husbands are like gods and wives have no choice but to submit (in terms of sex, autonomy, or any other way). This is an extreme reading, although not far from normative for some very conservative churches, in theory, at least. Before accepting such an interpretation, one should note issues of translation and culture, as well as the statement in the context of other defining passages in the New Testament. The translation of the Anchor Bible is probably the most accurate, although, stylistically, it is not always the easiest to read. Barth (1974), who translated and produced the commentary on Ephesians, made it clear how Verse 21 is connected to the rest of the chapter and how the intent of Paul's letter was both mutual consideration of husbands and wives for each other and how women were not to be second-class citizens to men, in general. Barth denied that a leading or executive role was assigned to men, although that seems harder to sustain from this text. Other letters (Col. 3:18, Titus 2:5, 1 Tim. 2:11-12, 1 Pet. 3:1-7) do not contain the same counterbalance, and place women in a specific, but largely subservient role. Further, the term "subordinate" (Verse 21, Anchor Bible) limits both the degree of differential between men and women and confines this to relations between husband and wife. In both Greek and Jewish culture, men had leading and controlling roles both at home and in their polity. Thus, this statement seems to be an attempt to limit the man's control of his wife, both by the obvious text as well as the connection to Christ.

Jesus is the head of the church as the husband is the head of the wife. What is the nature of this headship? The apparent answer is domination and control, but this is not correct. In Mark (10:41-45), Jesus defined his relationship with his followers and those leaders who would come after him. After a squabble over favoritism, Mark recorded Jesus as saying "anyone who wants to be first among you must be slave to all. For the Son of Man himself did not come to be served but to serve, and to give his life as a ransom for many" (Jones 1966, p. 80).[3] In sum then, *headship involves service* and the use of this in therapy with the dominated wife or controlling husband who relies on this text will depend on where in the therapeutic process one is.

Children and Parents

The treatment of children, their roles in relation to their parents and families, and the quality of their relationships to siblings and parents are all recurrent biblical themes. As with other topics, one can find more or less what one wants, from the murderous rivalry of Cain and Abel through the daughter-initiated incest of Lot (Gen. 19) to Jacob's extravagant favoritism of Joseph (Gen. 37) and the loyalty of Ruth, Naomi's daughter-in-law (Ruth). The narrative material, the bulk of which is in the Old Testament, contains useful material. However, many patients who use biblical texts regarding children will draw upon either legal material from the Old Testament (e.g., the Ten Commandments), the Wisdom writings, such as the Proverbs, or prescriptive material from the letters attributed to Paul.

The *Torah*'s central function in Jewish religious life makes it akin to the Constitution in its core legal strictures. Some 613 commandments or statutes have been identified in the *Torah* although the Ten Commandments are not infrequently taken as the essence of the law in the Old Testament by some Jews and many Christians. They might better be regarded as an index. The main theme of relations between children and parents may be summarized in the fourth (or fifth)[4] of the Ten Commandments, which is "Honor your father and your mother, that you may long endure on the land which the Lord your God is giving you" (Exod. 20:12, J.P.S. 1967, p. 134). What might this mean? The traditional understanding is that to "honor" one's parents means obedience, respect, love, service, and reverence. Honor (*kaved*) can also mean "to make heavy," "weighty," or perhaps "glorify" (Ben-Yehuda and Weinstein 1961). Since there were

---

[3]I am indebted to Dr. Paul Vitz who first pointed this out to me.
[4]Jews and Christians number the Ten Commandments slightly differently. For Christians this is the Fourth and for Jews the Fifth Commandment.

words for obedience, respect, love, and reverence in Hebrew, which were not used, something else may be implied. Recall our characterization of the laconic nature of Hebrew and its communication through silence as well as explicit statement. Honor is perhaps an ambiguous term, which has evoked a penumbra of meanings and elaborations so that the core or central implications are clouded over. *Kaved* seems to mean here to regard one's parents as weighty (i.e., with respect) or perhaps to act in a way to bring glory (honor) to one's parents. Respect is a two-sided word, referring to an internal state, on the one hand, and to external polite behavior, on the other. Since biblical Hebrew rarely attended to interior states directly, the latter is the more likely meaning. Thus, the patient who takes this part of the Bible as a warrant for total obedience and love of the parents is extending the meaning beyond the text. However, of all the many commandments in the *Torah*, few are explained. This one was explained (that you may long endure on the land), so it was clearly regarded as a very important issue, since it is implied that the quality of parent–child relations affected the society's survival.

Parental discipline of children is repeatedly touched on in the Old Testament, mostly in Proverbs (13:24, 19:18, 22:15, 23:13-14, 29:15), and also in Sir. (30:1–13). In general, physical punishment is recommended for the child's own good. Two examples will do. "He who spares his rod hates his son, but he who loves him takes care to chastise him" (Pro. 13:24, Confraternity of Christian Doctrine 1970, p. 714). Or, "withhold not chastisement from a boy; if you beat him with the rod, he will not die. Beat him with the rod, and you will save him from the nether world" (Pro. 23:13-14, Confraternity of Christian Doctrine 1970, p. 724). The book of Ecclesiasticus (Sir.) contains the harshest of such material, but it is canonical only for Catholics; Protestants put it among the Apocrypha. There is not much in the Old Testament to ameliorate these kinds of material, although their repetition suggests a reluctance on the part of Jewish fathers to use corporal punishment. Harsh physical punishment is not typical of Jewish families. Even when wife-beating was a popular indoor sport, it was relatively uncommon among Jewish husbands.

The strictures of the Old Testament are moderated by the New Testament. In a few places (Eph. 6:1-4, Col. 3:20-21) Paul exhorted children to obey their parents, but parents are warned not to anger, cause resentment, or nag their children so as not to frustrate or discourage them (Eph. 6:4, Col. 3:21, 1 Thes. 2:11-12). These latter admonitions may not receive much attention among religious parents who are continuously angry with their children, but the therapist needs to be aware of them.

Parents are held to have an important role as teachers, models, and guides for their children (Deut. 6:7, Pro. 1:8, 6:20). Further, whereas the main form of control was corporal punishment. there is some recognition of the differences among children and between children and adults. Again in Proverbs (4:3), "I too was once a son with a father, in my mother's eyes a tender child, unique" (Jones 1966, p. 937) or "I too have been a father's son, tender in years, my mother's only child" (Joint Committee on the New Translation of the Bible 1970, p. 750). Similarly in Proverbs (22:6), in the King James Version, "Train up a child in the way he should go: and when he is old he will not depart from it" (New York Bible Society ND, p. 605). Similarly, in the Jerusalem Bible it begins, "instruct a child in the way he should go" (Jones 1966, p. 962). This particular verse is commonly understood as permitting the parent to determine the child's course in life, yet the literal reading is something like "instruct (or train) a child in the beginning of his way" or "instruct a child according to his dispositions." This variant, but acceptable translation can be understood to mean the recognition of unique differences in children. Similarly, Paul (1 Cor. 13:11) said "when I was a child, I used to talk like a child, and think like a child, and argue like a child" (Jones 1966, p. 304).

Some Limits in Therapy

Perhaps this is a suitable place to repeat an essential premise. Arguing Bible verses with patients is not likely to be an effective therapeutic strategy. Rather, if a patient bases a particular issue squarely on a specific biblical statement, the dynamic underpinnings may not be accessible at first. Taking the client's biblical concerns as a reasonable way to organize one's life (even if the therapist proceeds differently) leaves room for discussion and the consideration of alternatives. If the therapist first tries to understand rather than undermine the patient's view of the Bible, the patient may be open to hearing other things the Bible has to say. However, the therapist must, I think, keep within certain boundaries.

At least three limits seem worth observing in using biblical materials in therapy. First, arguing is rarely effective as it tends to intensify defenses. Second, the basic stance is one of respectful interest in the patient's world without necessarily agreeing or disagreeing with the patient who wants to live differently from the therapist. Third, there are limits as to how far the textual material will stretch. As an example, the phrase "Spare the rod and spoil the child" is commonly attributed to the Bible and is probably based on Proverbs (13:24), cited above, although I have never seen it written just that way in a Bible. When used to justify abusive treatment of children, many professionals are deeply and justifiably troubled and frustrated. One interpretation recently offered (Huber 1981, p. 2) cited a manual on family violence that stated

> the image referred to in this Proverb is probably that of shepherd and the rod is the shepherd's staff (see Psalm 23:4: "thy rod and thy staff shall comfort me"). A shepherd uses his staff to guide the sheep where they should go. The staff is not used as a cudgel.

This is a very attractive interpretation; unfortunately, the text will not support it. The "rod" (*shevet*) in Proverbs 13:24 is the same as in Psalm 23, but the "staff" in Psalm 23 is *mishnet*. The words are not etymologically related in the Hebrew; they only have one letter in common, not the two letters shown in the transliteration. Using this apparently persuasive connection is risky. If the patient or the patient's minister has access to an analytical concordance,[5] the difference in spelling will be apparent and the therapist may be viewed as dishonest or perhaps just ill-informed.

Divorce

As with marriage, divorce involves a number of interested parties other than the couple, and includes the families, the children, and the community, which has to deal with the disruption caused, children to support, and so on. Among Jews, divorce is quite easy, in theory. Although Judaism discourages divorce, it is permitted and simple if there is an irreconcilable breakdown in the relationship. This includes physical abuse, a repellent physical condition, or long-standing sexual deprivation. Basically, these rights protect the wife who cannot initiate a divorce, although she can compel her husband to grant one through a Rabbinic court or *bet din*. A Jewish divorce is not hard to obtain if the couple is determined, but it carries the prohibition of the couple ever remarrying each other. As with most other matters in Judaism, there are disagreements about divorce, too, but the position summarized here is the one that prevailed, following the tradition of Hillel. His opponent Shammai held that a divorce should only be granted for adultery, a position also seen in Matthew (5:32, 19:9), but not in Mark or Luke.

Jesus flatly prohibited divorce in Mark (10:11-12) and Luke (16:18), but Matthew gave the exception noted above. A further exception was

[5]A concordance is a guide to the location of themes or words in the Bible. Some give the Hebrew and Greek words in the original spelling, as well as a transliteration.

given by Paul (1 Cor. 7:12-16) involving a person married to an "unbeliever," when a divorce is permissible if the other spouse is not content to live with the spouse who is a Christian. Paul also opposed divorce (Rom. 7:3, 1 Cor. 7:10-11). Remarriage after the death of a spouse was permitted, although Paul preferred that people refrain, if possible. The traditional position of the Roman Church has been to strictly oppose divorce except under very restrictive conditions. In practice, divorce has become somewhat more acceptable under conditions of severe marital difficulty, but this does not carry with it the right to remarry within the Roman Church. An annulment is the other alternative and is feasible under specific conditions. These include that the marriage was not consummated or that one or both parties were not competent to understand fully or to live out the nature of what was involved in marriage. Such incompetence is not easy to demonstrate to the diocesan Marriage Tribunal and involves a lengthy procedure. If accepted there, in certain cases a final decision may have to be made at a review level or even in Rome. The new code of Canon Law (promulgated in 1983) may also have some effect, but this will take some time to become clear. Other grounds for an annulment include a lack of valid consent (undue pressure or actual force) or a clear reservation in the mind of one or another spouse as to the purposes of marriage. This latter typically involves a refusal to have children, but with all these situations, substantial evidence is needed to make a case, and these proceedings may take six months to a year.

Perhaps 15 to 20 years ago a civil divorce and remarriage by a Catholic typically led to excommunication, but this has now changed. A remarriage will now not usually lead to excommunication, but the remarriage is not recognized by the Church. The person can attend Mass and participate in a variety of church activities, but cannot take part in communion (Eucharist) or certain other ritual activities, such as being a godparent. There is probably some variation from parish to parish and diocese to diocese. Confession is permissible, but because the person is continuing to sin, it may be perfunctory or limited. A divorced Catholic who is planning to remarry may sometimes have the marriage blessed or conducted by a priest who is doing a private favor. This does not mean that the marriage is approved by the Church. Occasionally, one may still encounter the view that the Roman Church is a monolithic structure. Although it may have appeared so in the first half of this century, it was never really true, and the Roman Church is now much more diverse than before. For a patient living in a strict parish or diocese, judicious consultation with a priest from another parish or diocese may be helpful. Strictly speaking, one is not supposed to "shop" for an opinion, but if a Catholic patient wants to remain within the Church, a move to a more liberal diocese may be a workable answer.

The mainline Protestant churches typically accept divorce without demur. Among these churches, as well as among the more conservative individual churches, there are likely to be pastors and/or members who will object to repetitive divorces among their congregants, and members of these churches will likely be under pressure to modify their behavior or leave. Among many very conservative, fundamentalist and evangelical churches, the basic stance is likely to be that marriage is for life and this will be enunciated clearly from the pulpit. In individual counseling, such pastors may well be a good deal more flexible and understanding. Patients who are members of such a church may find it useful to consult with their ministers privately and not rely on pulpit pronouncements. It is a rather basic rule (cf. 1 Cor. 5), however, that those members within the church whose behavior cannot be modulated to meet community standards should be excluded, but the community is also obligated to try to help the offending member before excluding them (Rom. 14, Col. 3:12-14).

Sin and Salvation; Guilt and Therapy

A religious patient may at first be reluctant to talk of sin to a therapist whose setting is clearly secular, but the idea of sin is likely to emerge sooner or later. Guilt or shame may be more readily expressed, and it is easier for the therapist to deal with these familiar topics that avoid facing the issue of sin in the patient's experience and attitudes. This is a twofold error. First, it says to the patient that there are areas of the patient's life that the therapist is afraid of or disinterested in, a priori. Second, it bypasses a very useful aspect of therapy touching on a wide range of topics. Most secularly based therapists would see an even wider gap between salvation and therapy than sin and guilt. Ironically, their origins are essentially the same: salvation comes from a Greek word meaning healing and it was for this latter purpose that the people in the New Testament sought Jesus (Bonnell 1969, Hegy 1978). Therapy, too, comes from the Greek *therapeia* and also means healing. The patient who wants to separate salvation from therapy in their generic senses is making a common division. The patient may also be compartmentalizing for defensive purposes.

What is sin? In the *Oxford Universal Dictionary* (Onions 1955, p. 1897), sin is defined as "A transgression of the divine law and an offence against

God; a violation (esp. willful or deliberate) of some religious or moral principle." The common Hebrew word for sin is *chet*,[6] I have told patients, and it is a technical term from archery. *Archery?* This surprising disclosure is likely to interrupt temporarily any struggle that may be going on between patient and therapist over the therapist's effort to "take away the patient's sin." Most simply, *chet* means to miss the mark; it means to make an error. Similarly, in New Testament Greek, the common term *hamartema* or *hamartia* means sin or error. In Hebrew, one may sin unwittingly (*shagag*) or deliberately (*pesha* or transgression; *avon* or iniquity). Similarly in Greek, an offense or trespass (*paraptoma*) may be deliberate, but these terms are relatively infrequently used. Thus, the Bible is somewhat ambiguous about exactly what sin means in most cases, leaving ample room for error rather than malice. This is useful for the therapist to know and may, at times, be helpful in therapy.

Construing sin in the Bible as always willful is only one aspect. Some patients will focus on specific sins they have committed, either from an organized list, such as the Ten Commandments, the "Seven Deadly Sins," a catechism, or from a list of their own. For Jews, a detailed list is at least congruent with the overall behavioral thrust of the Old Testament. For Christians, however, this is really at odds with a core concept of the New Testament. The statements and injunctions of Jesus in the Gospels are not a newer, stricter, and more detailed legal code, but a call for inner change. Similarly, Paul attacked the idea that scrupulous observance of the detailed Law (i.e., *Torah*) would bring salvation. Rather, "faith in Christ rather than fidelity to the Law is what justifies[7] us" (Gal. 2:16; Jones 1966, p. 324). Similar statements appear elsewhere (Gal. 2:21, 3:11-12, Rom. 3:28, 7:4-13). The patient who is harassed by a sense of having committed specific sins can, at an appropriate point, be faced with having missed the message from the New Testament. Specific texts, such as 1 Cor. 4:3, may help patients to step back from their relentless self-criticism to explore what this means.

It is useful to keep in mind that there are actions for which guilt feelings are quite appropriate. If the patient has really injured someone, attacking a sense of sinfulness is not likely to be effective, even if other factors are at work. If, for example, a patient has had an extramarital affair and is concerned with the sin of adultery, the guilt feelings are reality based, even if overgeneralized or a defense against anger toward

[6]*Chet* is pronounced "het" with a strongly aspirated *h*.
[7]"Justify" here means to relieve the person of original sin. See Appendix 3, regarding the Lutheran Church as well as the topic of grace in Chapter 3.

the spouse. This may not be accessible in treatment until the issue of sin is dealt with. Depending on how entrenched the sense of sinfulness is, one may resort to countervailing material, such as "Be not righteous over much, neither make thyself over wise: why shouldest thou destroy thyself?" (Koh. 7:16) in the King James Version. Actually this is a problematic translation and better concludes "Why make yourself a laughing-stock?" in the *New English Bible* (Joint Committee on the New Translation of the Bible 1970, p. 793) or "Why drive yourself too hard?" in the *Jerusalem Bible* (Jones 1966, p. 986). "Shopping" among different renderings may be useful if the patient will permit it. Similarly, a bit further on (Koh. 7:20), it states "The world contains no man so righteous that he can do right always and never do wrong" *or* "prospers without ever making a mistake" (Joint Committee on the New Translation of the Bible 1970, p. 793). Romans (2:1-3) also contains similar material.

Although the whole Bible is the Word of God for many people, its various parts are not, as a practical matter, all taken as of equal weight. Ecclesiastes does not count as much as the Gospels. A therapist using some of the textual material mentioned here, which is aimed at self-acceptance, may collide with the patient's need to be perfect and this can be tied to a specific text (Matt. 5:48): "You must therefore be perfect just as your heavenly Father is perfect" (Jones 1966, p. 23). There is a parallel text in Luke (6:36): "Be compassionate as your Father is compassionate" (Jones 1966, p. 102). It is commonly thought that the Synoptic Gospels (Matthew, Mark, Luke) drew largely from the same source, a hypothetical document referred to as "Q." The New Testament was written in Greek, the *lingua franca* of the Roman Empire, but Robinson (1977), in common with many other scholars, maintained that there was probably an Aramaic base to much of the New Testament. Jesus most probably preached in and spoke Aramaic and the words "perfect" and "compassionate" (or merciful) in these nearly parallel statements in Matthew and Luke could well be alternative translations of a single Aramaic word meaning "whole" or "generous," which Robinson (1977) hypothesized as being in "Q." Thus, the patient who strives for perfection and ties this to these two Gospels may be working with only part of Jesus's message. It is certainly compatible with therapy to accept as a goal the desire for wholeness or generosity, and to be whole one needs to know and accept that which is rejected (i.e., unconscious). Perfectionist strivings are often the patient's antidote for feelings of worthlessness or perhaps to avoid guilt or punishment for unacceptable wishes. The meanings or motives behind such strivings may not be readily accessible in the very religious client before the religiously based resistances (Lovinger 1979) have been loosened. Meeting such resistances in their own idiom is what is suggested here.

In Jewish tradition and practice, sins are specific acts toward God or others and the remedy is equally specific: changes in behavior and restitution for damage. The Bible makes numerous references to repentance, both by God and humans (particularly in older translations), but this is not a good rendition of *nicham*, which is better translated as "to regret" or "to be sorry." It was less a change of mind than of a feeling or attitude, and the changes were expected to lead to reconciliation. This is made a good deal more specific in Christian thinking. Menninger (1973) put it succinctly when he described "sin in the sense of alienating oneself from God; for believers this was, is, and will continue to be THE sin" (p. 46). This is quite consistent with Pauline theology, which opposed compulsive attention to minutia to achieve salvation, but emphasized faith or trust in Jesus. One example of how this can work in therapy comes from a patient who was struggling to extricate herself from a failing marriage. Strongly religious, she agonized over the sin of divorce (cf. Mark 10:9-12). Her therapist was both a clinician and a minister and was aware of her historic feeling of having never won her father's approval. He reminded her of what THE sin (alienation) was. This allowed her to recognize the core issues and to move on.

For therapy, then, sin can easily be construed as an error, a goof, or a glitch. Intent makes a difference, and this was recognized. Moses directed the establishment of "cities of refuge" for people who caused accidental death (Num. 35:6) to disrupt the practice of reflexive revenge. It was also recognized that, although punishment for error was not needed, recompense was. Sacrifices are often regarded as a form of punishment, but a sacrifice for an unintentional sin (*shagag*) was not a punishment. It was perhaps roughly equivalent to civil damages in modern terms. Lists of sins are, in a sense, non-Christian, although caution is needed with some, such as certain Catholics and Baptists[8] and fundamentalists whose backgrounds heavily emphasize detailed behavioral prescriptions. Too early or too direct a confrontation on this issue will likely be experienced as an attack. Finally, sin can be an idiom for alienation, for feeling unloved by important significant others. Therapeutic explorations of the meaning and sources of these attitudes to the self are appropriate.

In treatment, therapy and salvation have real equivalences in spite of

---

[8]This has changed considerably, but Catholics reared under the older practices emphasize detail more. Nor do all Baptists fit the image of Southern Baptists, for example.

differences in source (therapist or God), location (office or church), or mode (collaborative effort or divine intervention).[9] The similarities have been touched on earlier, and in Chapter 3 under the topic of Grace. Traditional Judaism had no doctrine of salvation, for the world was good, but Greek-oriented Jews, who viewed the material world as evil, saw a need for salvation (Sandmel 1957). Such needs were reinforced by the progressive deterioration of the conditions of Jewish life and focused on the hope for the *mashiach* or messiah, a leader appointed by God. Thus although salvation has rather different meanings for Jews and Christians, theologically, it can refer to generously given aid and healing more or less out of the person's direction. As such, the parallels to effective psychotherapy may lead some patients to invest the therapist with quasi-religious qualities. One patient described her therapy with me as her salvation, when speaking to another professional who related this remark to me. Ironically, I considered her therapy to have been only modestly successful, since her basic narcissistic character was largely untouched. Another patient, who was moderately religious, had a series of dreams that contained the figure of a minister. Associations suggested this figure related to her views of her therapist. Although interpreting this sort of idealizing transference with neurotic clients is often appropriate, less well-structured personalities may need to maintain their idealization for an extended period of time.

Sexuality and Pleasure

Not uncommonly, one finds the view of the Bible as anti-sex and anti-pleasure. Although there is enough material in the Bible to support such a view, if one chooses carefully, the overall thrust is in favor of *legitimate* sexuality and pleasure. Eating, drinking, having adequate possessions, and the satisfaction associated with these are repeatedly presented in a positive light (in the Old Testament), if the activity is permissible. This is less clear in the New Testament, but the eschatological framework made such planning for the future irrelevant, not impermissible. This attitude begins in the story of Creation, when God looked on the world and saw it was good, except on the second day (Monday) where there was no such statement. Traditionally, Jews will not marry on that day, but they will go to work. Esteem for Mondays has not generally increased in recent times.

---

[9]Knowledgeable clergy recognize that salvation nearly always entails human mediation, and the distinction made here is artificial.

Although there are certain restrictions in the Old Testament on what was permissible to eat, this applied to animal, seafood, and fowl. Plants were all permissible and there was no prohibition of poisonous plants any more than people had to be told to come in out of the rain. The Bible is quite reticent about sexual pleasure (but see Deut. 24:5); what is opposed are impermissible sexual activities, such as incest, adultery, male homosexuality, bestiality, religious/sexual idolatry, or prostitution. With regard to the last of these, the rules are somewhat inconsistent. However, actions, not thoughts or impulses, were prohibited. The apparent exception in Jesus's statement about looking at a woman lustfully (Matt. 5:27-28) is to commit adultery in the heart (i.e., mind) has been turned into the slogan "to think is the same as to do." As discussed earlier, the intent was to reach matters of attitude, and this is clearer if one reads it closely in a more literal translation, such as the King James Version.

Homosexuality is clearly and explicitly prohibited—in men (Lev. 18:22, 20:13, Rom. 1:19-27), but regarding women, the Old Testament is silent. Since women are mentioned (sometimes at length) as to incest, adultery, bestiality, and prostitution, it is not likely that women were omitted here because they were unimportant. What is probably at issue is the unproductive (homosexuality, bestiality, male prostitution) or impermissible (incest, adultery) discharge of semen, a matter of real concern for an agricultural society. There may be some sort of magical thinking behind this. In the New Testament (Rom. 1:26-27, 1 Cor. 6:9-10), male homosexuality is strongly and clearly condemned, but this passage in Romans does not make an unambiguous reference to female homosexuality. Some translations are more definite than others, but the original language is less explicit.

It is important to read a biblical passage in the immediate *context of its times.* Thus, the specific context of Paul's comments on homosexuality in Romans indicates that he was not just prohibiting homosexuality, he was specifically prohibiting sexual activity connected with religious activities. In Hebrew, an ordinary prostitute was a *zonah*, whereas a man or woman who engaged in sexual intercourse as a function of a religious rite or cult was a *kadesh* (male) or *k'deshah* (female). These terms are derived from *kadosh*, or holy, indicating their religious connection although this is not always made clear (cult-prostitute is a common translation). Still, the Bible prohibits male homosexuality. Paul urged that Christians should avoid Christians leading an immoral life (1 Cor. 5) and listed several categories. With the patient who is both religious and homosexual or so inclined, pointing out that thoughts are not prohibited or that homosexual idolatrous practices are likely the main issue may not help. Two other alternatives may be suggested. One is that Jesus is not recorded as ever commenting on homosexuality. The nearest relevant incident seems to be of the woman accused of adultery and Jesus, in the famous dramatic incident (John 8), says that whoever is without sin should throw the first stone. Jesus was described as hanging around with a variety of disreputable people, such as tax collectors,[10] and he used the telling analogy (Matt. 9:10-13) that one need not send a physician to someone who is healthy. His message was that salvation was for everyone, especially those who needed it most and felt they did not deserve it (Luke 18:9-14). Hence, Jesus is available to the homosexual Christian who needs him. Again, in a number of large metropolitan areas there are churches that accept or are oriented to gay congregants. The local gay community is probably the best resource to locate these churches. "Perversion" is a common translation of many of the terms related to homosexuality. One common meaning for "perversion" in Hebrew is confusion or mixing, others are spice, seasoning, or lewdness. Thus certain prohibitions can be understood as basically offenses against order (see Clean and Unclean, Chapter 3).

The idea that sexuality was reserved only for procreation is a well-ingrained attitude among many older Catholics and among some very conservative Protestant denominations. The origins for this are, in part, in one of Paul's letters (1 Cor. 7:5-9), in which he makes an allowance for individual differences, and although he prefers celibacy, he recommends marriage to avoid the risk of impermissible sexual activity. Jerome translated the word for "allowance for individual differences" (*sungnomen*) into Latin as *veniam*, meaning "requiring pardon," the basis of the concept of venial sins. It was Augustine who argued that sex was only for procreation (Cole 1959), but this is not really in the New Testament in any clear way. Further, Paul opposed permanent discontinuation of sexual relations among married couples, partly to avoid sex outside of marriage, but without the implication that sex should not be enjoyed. This can be supplemented by an injunction (Exod. 21:10-11) whereby, if a man marries an additional wife, he may not reduce the first wife's food, clothing, or conjugal rights or the wife could leave. This specifically applied to the situation in which the first wife had once been a purchased slave and whose rights were specially protected in this passage. Presumably, wives who were free had such rights as a matter of course. Sex is equated here with food and clothing as a *basic necessity*.

Paul is not infrequently perceived as being against sensuality because of his criticisms of the "flesh" (*sarx* in Greek). This word sometimes

---

[10]Tax collectors at that time paid the government a fixed sum and then took as much as they could from the area assigned to them. They were even more unpopular then than now.

means sensuality and sometimes refers to a contrast between flesh and spirit or real and ideal, which is consistent with Greek modes of thought. Seen most clearly in Romans 6–8, the "flesh" meant the Law (i.e., *Torah*), which he was opposed to following as the sole means to salvation. I am not suggesting that Paul encouraged sensuality or pleasure; his attention was fixed on other matters. Comparing the King James Version with a modern translation makes clear how the literal quality of the former distorted Paul's intent, which is clearer in the latter.

Love, Anger, Assertion, and Meekness

In Hebrew, there is basically one word for love, *ahavah*, and it is used in a variety of ways. In Greek, there are three words, *agape, philia,* and *eros,* and they are typically taken to mean (1) love of God for man, (2) love between friends, and (3) romantic love, respectively. Sometimes a good deal is made of these distinctions, although it has been noted (Cole 1959) that *philia* also refers to misdirected love and *agape* can refer to love between Christians and sometimes to love that is an error.

To love your neighbor as yourself (Lev. 19) is often taken to mean that one should put up with abuse and is often linked to the statement to turn the other cheek. What do these really mean? The context makes it clear. Leviticus 19 is considered by Jews as the central ethical code of the *Torah* and it reads, "you shall not hate your kinsman in your heart. Reprove your neighbor but incur no guilt because of him. You shall not take vengeance or bear a grudge against your kinsfolk. Love your neighbor as yourself: I am the Lord" (J.P.S. 1967, p. 217). The phrase "I am the Lord" occurs 16 times in this chapter and seems to serve both as an emphasis and as a sort of punctuation that brings related verses together. Thus, this says that loving one's neighbor is composed of not hating someone secretly and taking revenge, but rather reproving them openly if they deserve it. There is nothing to suggest one must even *like* one's neighbor or relatives.

One of the most common human problems is the appropriate management of anger. Assertion is different from anger, with which it is often confused. As with most other vital human matters, the Bible speaks to this, but not with a single voice. On the one hand, there is the injunction to love your neighbor as yourself (Lev. 19:18, Matt. 19:19, 22:39, Mark 12:31), and the statement that the meek (humble, mild) shall inherit the earth (Psa. 37:11, Matt. 5:5). On the other hand, Moses could express anger both at the Israelites (Exod. 32:1–20) and at God (Num. 11:10–15), and Jesus threw the money changers out of the Temple (Matt. 21:12-13, Mark 11:15-17, Luke 19:45-46). Anger is legitimate, but should be resolved if possible (Matt. 18:15-16, Luke 17:4, Eph. 4:25-27). Resistance to injustice or not following group opinion are noted in both the Old and the New Testament (Exod. 23:2, Deut. 16:18-20, John 18:19-24).

The expression to "turn the other cheek" (Matt. 5:38-42, Luke 6:27-35) is stated in the context of achieving a higher standard of performance and altruism and repudiates giving merely to obtain a return. It should be noted that Jesus was brought for interrogation before the high priest (John 18:19-24) and his answers are somewhat defiant. He is slapped (on the cheek) by a guard and although tied up, Jesus protests the injustice. The toleration of abuse is not the intent of this statement. Rather, it seems to reflect a radical approach to the problem of evil by saying that love, not violence, is the way to deal with evil. Love here seems to mean strength without brutality and concern for others and is analogous to civil disobedience or nonviolent protest in current times. Analogous material is given elsewhere (Pro. 15:1, 15:18, 16:32, 19:11, 27:4). There are some very hot, angry statements in various places (Psa. 58, 68:21-23, 69:22-28, 79, Eph. 4:25-27). Many churches and ministers tend to downplay anger or romanticize or rationalize it (Jackson 1972), and for some patients, it may be useful to point out that it was not only God that was angry, but that people in the Bible also had legitimate, intensely angry feelings.

Body and Soul; Flesh and Spirit

Body and soul is such a familiar phrase that it was used as the title of a movie issued in 1947, starring John Garfield and Lili Palmer. This entirely familiar distinction actually did not exist in the Old Testament in the way we currently use it. *Nefesh* can be translated as soul, but refers to the whole person. The term body is often a translation of belly, back, carcass, bone, thigh, or flesh. The New Testament writers also did not seem to make the sharp distinction we make between body and soul, although the references to *soma* and *psyche* are roughly equivalent in number compared to the primary use of *nefesh* in the Old Testament. As discussed above, "flesh" (*sarx*) for Paul generally meant following the detailed prescriptions of the Law (*Torah*), which he contrasted to the "spirit" (*pneuma*) and reliance on God's aid. *Pneuma*, and the Hebrew equivalent *ruach*, can also mean "wind," "breath," or "spirit"; the context usually indicates the meaning.

The modern word for "mind" also appears problematic when translated from Hebrew or Greek into English. For many ancient peoples, the heart was considered the seat of the mind, although without the sharp division between cognition and affect. In Hebrew, mind may be translated from words that also mean imagination, heart, and mouth, as well as from *nefesh* and *ruach*. Similarly, mind may be translated from words that also mean knowledge, decision, intellect, purpose, thought, will, or inclination, as may *psyche*. Jaynes' (1976) discussion of the growth and change in meaning of these concepts in Greek from Homeric to Classic times is very interesting. It would appear that the idea of consciousness, volition, and mind were largely absent from the Iliad, but began to appear in the Odyssey.

If a patient emphasizes such divisions as body and soul, body and mind, mind and soul, or other such combinations, one might think of disconnections between awareness and defense, impulse and prohibition. If this is based on some reading of the Bible, pointing out that the translation the patient relies on is doing its best to render into English rather different concepts will probably not resolve a defensive position, but it may help the patient see that the position is personal, not biblical.

Retrospect

We have covered a good deal of material here, with many citations from the Bible. My aim has been to equip the therapist to put a patient's biblical statements into some sort of historical framework; to see the Bible as a series of voices arising at different times and speaking to their contemporaries; to grasp the gulf that separates us from these people in language, culture, and world-view; and to understand the problems that have faced translators who have struggled to convey all that in a word. I also hope that I have conveyed the idea that the religious patient has a meaningful world-view, which can be both respected and investigated in the service of therapeutic growth.

Appendix 1
The Books of the Bible and
Their Abbreviations

Jews, Catholics, and Protestants recognize somewhat differing sets of writings as canonical or sacred. Jews do not accept any part of the New Testament as part of the Bible, and some parts of the Old Testament are accepted by Christians, but not Jews. There are, as well, certain writings called the Apocrypha, from Greek meaning *hidden* (things), which may have been part of the Jewish collection before this was finally organized and closed. The Apocrypha are not specially distinguished in the Catholic canon, but are set apart in the Protestant Bible. The listings to follow are taken from three authoritative Bibles. The Jewish canon comes from *The Holy Scriptures According to the Masoretic Text* (J.P.S. 1917), the Catholic canon comes from *The Jerusalem Bible* (Jones 1966), and the Protestant canon comes from *The New English Bible with the Apocrypha* (Joint Committee on the New Translation of the Bible 1970).

The organization of the books of the Bible varies. Jews divide them into the *Torah*, or first five books (also called the Pentateuch), the *Nevi'im*, or Prophets, and the *Ketuvim*, or Writings (such as Psalms, Proverbs, and Job). An acronym is sometimes formed of the initials (T N K) and called the *Tanakh*, which is a Jewish term for the Bible, since for them there is not an *Old* Testament, but rather only the Covenant. Catholics divide the Old Testament into the Pentateuch, the Historical books (from Joshua to Maccabees), the Wisdom books (from Job to Eccliasticus), and the Prophets. The New Testament contains the Gospels, Acts of the Apostles, various letters from Paul and others, and ends with the Revelation of John. *The New English Bible* has a sequence similar to

Table 1

Acts	Acts of the Apostles	Jon.	Jonah (J)
Amos	Amos (J)	Josh.	Joshua (J)
Bar.	Baruch (A)	Jude	Jude
1 Chron.	1 Chronicles (J)	Judg.	Judges (J)
2 Chron.	2 Chronicles (J)	Koh.	Ecclesiastes[2]
Col.	Colossians	1 Kng.	1 Kings (J)
1 Cor.	1 Corinthians	2 Kng.	2 Kings (J)
2 Cor.	2 Corinthians	Lam.	Lamentations (J)
Dan.	Daniel (J)	Lev.	Leviticus (J)
Deut.	Deuteronomy (J)	Luke	Luke
Eph.	Ephesians	1 Mac.	1 Maccabees
Esth.	Esther (J)	2 Mac.	2 Maccabees
Exod.	Exodus (J)	Mal.	Malachi (J)
Ezek.	Ezekiel (J)	Mark	Mark
Ezra	Ezra (J)[1]	Matt.	Matthew
Gal.	Galatians	Mic.	Micah (J)
Gen.	Genesis (J)	Nah.	Nahum (J)
Hab.	Habakkuk (J)	Neh.	Nehemiah (J)
Hag.	Haggai (J)	Num.	Numbers (J)
Heb.	Hebrews	Obad.	Obadiah (J)
Hos.	Hosea (J)	1 Pet.	1 Peter
Isa.	Isaiah (J)	2 Pet.	2 Peter
Jam.	James	Phm.	Philemon
Jdth	Judith (A)	Php.	Philippians
Jer.	Jeremiah (J)	Pro.	Proverbs (J)
1 Jn.	1 John	Psa.	Psalms (J)
2 Jn.	2 John	Rev.	Revelation of John
3 Jn.	3 John	Rom.	Romans
Job	Job (J)	Ruth	Ruth (J)
Joel	Joel (J)	1 Sam.	1 Samuel (J)
John	John (Gospel)	2 Sam.	2 Samuel (J)
Sir.	Ecclesiasticus (A)[3]	Titus	Titus
SSgs.	Song of Songs (J)[4]	Tob.	Tobit (A)
1 Thes.	1 Thessalonians	Wis.	Wisdom of
2 Thes.	2 Thessalonians		Solomon (A)
1 Tim.	1 Timothy	Zech.	Zechariah (J)
2 Tim.	2 Timothy	Zeph.	Zephaniah (J)

[1]Parts of Ezra and Nehemiah are in 1 & 2 Esdras in the Apocrypha.

[2]The abbreviation is of *Kohelet*, or Speaker in an assembly.

[3]This is attributed to Ben Sirach.

[4]The Song of Songs is also sometimes referred to as the Songs of Solomon.

that of *The Jerusalem Bible*, except that the Apocrypha are grouped separately.

Table 1 is a list of books in the Old and New Testaments in alphabetical order of their abbreviations as used in this book. Those books in the Jewish canon are followed by a J; those in the Apocrypha for the Protestant canon are followed by an A.

In addition, certain other materials are included in the Apocrypha, and any standard Bible that has a commentary should provide information on these materials. Further reference materials are listed in Bibliographic Sources.

Appendix 2
Modern Vocabulary of the King James Bible

The power and extent of current usage of the King James Version makes it important to understand its meaning if a religious patient relies on this translation. Such phrases as "We do you to wit" are nearly uninterpretable, until one finds out that it means "We cause you to know." For this reason, a relatively brief glossary is given here of words that may cause difficulty because their meanings have changed in the more than 350 years since this translation was done. This is based on Elliot's (1967) useful manual, although the presentation here is much less detailed. For material not covered here, the reader is referred to the original monograph.

The following abbreviations will be used: *Ad*, adjective; *Av*, adverb; *C*, conjunction; *IA*, indefinite article; *N*, noun; *P*, preposition; and *V*, verb. A word may not be given in this list because it is close enough to the current meaning or because, although now different, the word seemed unlikely to be of therapeutic relevance.

a, *IA*. As now, but also *an*
a, *P*. On, in, at, by, etc.
abide, *V*. To wait for, to endure, or to remain
acquaint, *V*. To familiarize
admiration, *N*. Astonishment or wonder, but does not connote pleasure
advise, *V*. Ponder or consider
affection, *N*. Feeling, emotion, inclination, or disposition
affectionately, *Av*. Earnestly, strongly, zealously

against, *C*. So as to be prepared for an event
amen, Hebrew, signifying agreement, as "so be it"
amiable, *Ad*. Attractive or lovely
anon, *Ad*. Immediately
approve, *V*. To test, prove, or commend
argue, argument, *V*, *N*. To reason, reasoning
attendance, *N*. Attention or service
avoid, *V*. To leave or to stay away from

banquet, *N*. Nearly always a feast, with drinking
because, *C*. In order that
behave, *V*. To regulate or control
believe, *V*. To have faith or trust, or as now
beside, *P*. In addition to, or as now (less frequent)
boisterous, *Ad*. Turbulent, stormy, or violent
botch, *N*. A boil

cabin, *N*. A prison cell
care, *N* and *V*. As is used today, but more anxiety is implied
careful, *Ad*. Always means anxiety-laden, never cautious
carefulness, *N*. Anxiety, distraction, or diligence
carnally, *Av*. In the Old Testament, it usually refers to the physical, in the New
   Testament, it usually means an attitude
celebrate, *V*. To praise, to observe (as in a holy day)
chance, *N*. An accident, or as used now
charity, *N*. Strong or noble love, although not excluding fondness. Never means
   alms, as such
cherish, *V*. To keep warm, or as now
clean, *Ad*. Clean or pure, either figuratively or literally; also completely
comely, *Ad*. Suitable, decent, as well as the usual meanings. Context is important
   in determining meaning
conclude, *V*. To enclose or assemble
conscience, *N*. Knowledge of right and wrong (in the New Testament only)
convenient, *Ad*. Becoming, proper, suited, or well-timed
convert, *V*. To turn or return, as to turn away from sin
crafty, *Ad*. Skillful or cunning
cunning, *Ad*. Acquainted with, intelligent, or skillful

declare, *V*. Explain, show, make known, or put before someone
defy, *V*. To reproach or to be indignant
delicacy, *N*. Wantonness or indulgence
deliciously, *Av*. Voluptuously or pleasurably, in a negative sense
despite, *N*. Hate, anger, contempt, or scorn
discipline, *N*. Instruction or chastisement
divers, *Ad*. Various or of different kinds
divine, *N*. In the title of Revelations, it means a preacher, and as now

doctor, *N.* Teacher
doubt, *V.* To be without resource or to stand divided
doubtful, *Ad.* Apprehensive, hesitant, or uncertain in judgment

earnest, *N.* Surety or pledge
enjoy, *V.* To belong to, possess, or have pleasure
envy, *N* or *V.* Jealousy, malice, or spite
experience, *N.* Proof or testing

fame, *N.* A report or reputation
faulty, *Ad.* Guilty
feebleminded, *Ad.* Fainthearted
flesh, *N.* Used in a variety of ways, including meat in the current sense. Meat, in
       the King James Version, means food and not flesh
flower, *N.* In addition to the usual meanings, menstrual impurity (Lev. 15:24, 33)
       or one's prime
froward, *Ad.* Perverse, cross, or to be a wrestler
furious, *Ad.* Hot, also as now
furiously, *Av.* Heatedly and also madly

gender, *V.* To breed or produce
gift, *N.* A bribe in certain places, elsewhere as now
glutton, *N.* A vile person, lightly esteemed (in the Old Testament). In the New
       Testament, the meaning is as now
godly, *Ad.* Kind or of God (Old Testament), reverent or pious (New Testament)
guilty, *Ad.* To deserve, or as now

handful. *N.* Generally implies abundance rather than scarcity
hard, *Av.* Strong, heavy, wonderful, or as now. With "by," it means near by
hip and thigh. *N.* Without reserve
honest, *Ad.* Respectable, decent, suitable
hurt, *V.* To strike or to shame, or as now

ill, *Ad.* Evil or bad. *N.* Evil deed
imagination, *N.* Formation, stubbornness, or thought
iniquity, *N.* Vanity, perversity, or lawlessness
inquisition, *N.* Inquiry or investigation
intelligence, *N.* Communication
invention, *N.* Device, deed, or plan, usually in a negative sense
inventor, *N.* One who finds out something

jealousy, *N.* Zeal, indignation, and as now, in both positive and negative senses

lawyer, *N.* Refers to someone knowledgeable in Jewish law (New Testament), but
       does not mean an attorney, the term for which is orator
leasing, *N.* A lie or deceit
leprosy, *N.* Refers to a variety of skin diseases. In regard to houses or clothing,
       probably refers to mildew or fungus

let, *V.* Although generally means to permit or cause, occasionally means to prevent or hinder (Isa. 43:13, 2 Thes. 2:7, Rom. 1:13)

Lucifer. *N.* Shining one, referring to the king of Babylon. Does not refer to Satan

lust, *N.* Although usually has approximately the current meaning, may also refer to soul, sweetness, pleasure, or suffering

mammon. *N.* An Aramaic word, transliterated through Greek into English, riches

martyr, *N.* A witness

mean, *Ad.* Obscure, humble, or ordinary

meat, *N.* Anything to eat. See "flesh" above

meek, *Ad.* Humble, mild, or kind

meet, *Ad.* Suitable, qualified

mercy seat, *N.* A mistranslation of ark cover, which refers to atonement (literally, covering) for one's sins

mischief, *N.* Injury, accident, vanity, or evil, never a prank

modest, *Ad.* Orderly or becoming

mortify, *V.* To kill

motion, *N.* Emotion, affection

naughtiness, *N.* Evil, worthless, or bad. Never mischief

nought, *Av.* Nothing, connoting bad or worthless. Spelled "naught" to distinguish it from "nought," which is always negative

officer, *N.* In the Old Testament, an agent or a minister. In the New Testament, a police officer

orator, *N.* An attorney or advocate, or as now

paradise, *N.* Literally, a fenced garden or park

passion, *N.* Suffering, feeling, or emotion

perfect, *Ad.* Complete, full, mature, accurate, or readied

piss, *N.* Urine. Implies a grown male. Although now considered vulgar, it illustrates how usage has changed (see 2 Kng 18:27, Isa. 36:12)

pleasant, *Ad.* Desirable, delightful, precious. Connotes a more intense feeling than as now used

power, *N.* Strength, arm, force, hand (Old Testament). Authority is a common meaning in the New Testament, also as now

prevent, *V.* To anticipate a time, a question, or help. Also to appear before someone or to precede, or as now

prophecy, *N.* The words and activities of a prophet, but not necessarily predictions. See different spelling below.

prophesy, *V.* To speak through God's inspiration

protest, *V.* To assert or declare

prove, *V.* To test or to show to be true

quick, *Ad.* Alive

reins, *N.* The kidneys as the seat of the feelings, rather than the heart as in modern usage

repent, *V.* To change one's mind. Often though not exclusively used with regard to sin

revenge, *V.* To inflict punishment on someone without the connotation of malice or resentment. Means "avenge," as is currently used

reverend, *Ad.* Entitled to respect or honor, but not a religious title

road, *N.* A raid

rude, *Ad.* Uneducated, but not discourteous

rumor, *N.* A message

saint, *N.* Kind, pious (*chasid*), or set apart (*kadosh* or *hagios* in the Old or the New Testament, respectively)

science, *N.* Knowledge, without any of the modern connotations of the term

scribe, *N.* Originally meant scribe or writer, it gradually came to mean a person learned in the *Torah*

several, *Ad.* Separate, distinct, or relating to an individual

slime, *N.* Bitumen

solemn, *Ad.* A prescribed festival (i.e., holy day) on a fixed annual cycle. Not necessarily a lack of joy, it often implies the contrary

suffer, *V.* To allow, give, or let alone, or as now

temper, *V.* To mix or mingle

thing, *V.* To feel, reason, or remember

thought, *N.* Worry or anxiety, or as now

try, *V.* To test, assay, refine, or purify

unbelief, *N.* Stronger than current usage, it implies disbelief, disobedience, or distrust

unicorn, *N.* Buffalo, wild ox, or roaring animal

virtue, *N.* Strength of body or mind, or power

Appendix 3
Supplementary Information on
Protestant Denominations[1]

Lutheran

American Lutheran churches are members of one of four major organizations that vary in doctrinal strictness and conservatism and literalness of interpretation. Church governance is between episcopal and presbyterian: there are bishops, but there are also councils or representative assemblies. The clergy are ministers, oral confession is no longer regular, but infant baptism, the Eucharist, and absolution are seen as sacraments; marriage, ordination, confirmation, and unction are sacraments with a secondary position (Piepkorn 1978, Vol. 2). A key tenet of the Protestant Reformation was the acceptance of the Bible as the full authority; in rejecting the Roman Church's authority and control over the teaching function, however, authoritative creeds or confessions were developed to supplement the Bible and to guide and direct interpretation. Thus, to be a Lutheran in good standing, it is rather difficult to also entirely steer one's own course in biblical interpretation. In other words, the reliance on the Bible as sole authority was supplemented by teaching functions from other sources. Still, there is some freedom of choice.

"Justification by faith alone" is important. Divine aid, in the form of grace, can relieve the person of original sin (injustice) and produce justification through faith, which is irresistible. This concept is related to predestination (divine election). Predestination recognizes that there are

[1]The Protestant denominations are also discussed in Chapter 5 in the context of personality, and how they affect progress in therapy.

no constraints on God's power or that God's choices are not subject to human behavioral shaping, but Lutheran doctrine denies that God chooses "a predestination to damnation" (Piepkorn 1978, Vol. 2, p. 72). Human depravity (predilection to sin when guided by will or intellect) and availability of salvation only through faith in Jesus is balanced against the universality of God's love for humanity. However, in many denominations, there are varying degrees of assertion that outside of Jesus there is no salvation.

Practically, Lutherans will support a strong social welfare orientation; are active in missionary work; and emphasize education, having a strong scholarly tradition in keeping with their Roman Catholic origins. Some fundamentalism is seen, but it is leavened by scholarship, compared with certain Baptist and Pentecostal denominations. A highly conservative approach is not the only, or even the dominant position.

Presbyterian and Reformed

Lutherans consider themselves as separate from the Presbyterian and Reformed churches, even though, for the purposes of the taxonomy presented in Chapter 5, they were so grouped. If one reads only the works of Martin Luther or John Calvin, one is apt to be misled about the modern functioning of Lutheranism or Presbyterianism, respectively. Calvin is often regarded as a dour, cheerless man who produced a theology and a civil practice to match, but Piepkorn (1978) suggested the contrary, and although his picture of Calvin is three-dimensional, it is difficult to see much cheer in a person who would burn someone alive.

The Reformed churches have a presbyterian or eldership form of governance. A district is governed by a council of elders, so that the church has a representative governance; creedal positions vary, although Presbyterian and Reformed churches are not as non-creedal as are Baptists or Disciples of Christ, for example. Trials for heresy are not common, although they have occurred in this century, and there is pressure for doctrinal conformity, particularly among ministers. Piepkorn (1978) listed 22 separate Presbyterian and/or Reformed church groups.

Calvin's doctrines as they eventually developed are severe. They include total depravity, predestination, irresistible grace, and the Bible as the inerrant and infallible authority, but are ameliorated by his system of church governance, his opposition to schism over extreme efforts at purity, and the concept that God's revelation was progressive and geared to people's capacity to grasp it. Calvin also emphasized community through the church rather than monastic solitariness, and a thread of God's love and justice runs through his writings. Churches within this group thus span a rather broad and diverse range of positions. Some are very liberal, theologically and interested in social welfare and education and scholarship. Others are middle-of-the-road, and still others are rather conservative, theologically, although a scholarly bent tends to be common in all, but the most fundamental churches.

In terms of ritual, these churches practice baptism and the Lord's Supper, but whereas Lutherans hold that the Real Presence of Jesus occurred in the consecration of the bread and wine, the Reformed church sees the Lord's Supper as containing the spiritual presence of Jesus. Practically, however, few parishioners are likely to be concerned about such theological issues.

Protestant Episcopal

Because the break with Rome was primarily for dynastic rather than religious reasons (Henry VIII wished to divorce his wife), the Anglican church considers itself Catholic and the differences in thought and practice between Roman Catholic and English Catholic may be quite small. The clergy are priests, but are allowed to marry. The two sacraments of baptism and Eucharist (Lord's Supper) are observed, whereas confirmation, ordination, marriage, absolution, and anointing the sick (unction) are considered either rites or sacraments. The Thirty-Nine Articles and a central creed embody a core position, but the Anglican church and the American branch, or Protestant Episcopal church, vary widely in theological concepts and ritual. For example, for some the bread and wine in the Eucharist are the body and blood of Christ, for some the body and blood are present in the recipient's heart, and for some the bread and wine are symbolic, but there is no Real Presence. The range of differences can also be expressed as High, Broad, and Low Church or Anglo-Catholic; Liberal; and Evangelical. High Church tends to emphasize sacraments, vestments, and rituals as external signs of Christ's presence; the Liberals emphasize intellectual enterprises and oppose fanaticism, and the Evangelicals emphasize the vitality and spirituality of union with God through faith.

The Apostles and Nicene Creeds are accepted, but some of the severity of earlier Lutheran and Calvinist theology has moderated considerably. Henry VIII and Elizabeth I both followed theological matters, which led to considerable state involvement in the Church of England. This is not the case in America, for although the governance of the church is episcopal, there is a good deal of independence. Women have been ordained as priests, but some churches refuse to accept them. Social welfare activities figure prominently in the church's national activities and education and scholarship are emphasized.

Baptist

The churches in the Free Will and Salvation group are generally characterized by intense devotion, direct religious experience, personal involvement and free choice in salvation, and the Bible as sole authority. Often theologically conservative and behaviorally strict, Baptists tend to be democratic in governance and relatively non-doctrinal. Individual Baptist churches have considerable freedom: they can hire and fire their ministers and can request that an individual be ordained. They emphasize freedom of religious belief, separation of church and state, the authority of the Bible, direct communication with God, the role of faith and repentance in receiving grace, and the baptism of adult believers. Infant baptism is strongly rejected. The Lord's Supper and baptism are not sacraments, but rather memorials.

In general, social welfare involves combating such evils as the use of alcohol and other drugs, nonobservance of the Sabbath, gambling and dancing, or movies, in some instances; individual salvation and family life are promoted.

The governance structure tends to limit the leadership role of the elected officials to what individual churches will accept. Northern Baptists are usually more liberal than Southern Baptists. The teaching of evolution has been opposed, but there has been more emphasis on education recently. Many ministers can receive a good education, but this is not as highly valued as it is among the denominations discussed above.

Methodist

In an effort to revitalize a stale, politicized church, John Wesley reached out to the many people to whom the religious services offered by the Anglican church were not available. He preached where the people were, and commissioned lay preachers to do the same. Since he did not intend to found a new church, the theological content of Methodism is not its most striking feature. Basically cheerful and hopeful, Methodism emphasized behavior and church structure; thus, the United Methodist Church held in America the bulk of the members in 1977 with nearly ten million, and some two and one-half million more Methodists in several Black denominations, such as the African Methodist Episcopal Church and the African Methodist Episcopal Zion Church (Piepkorn 1978).

Wesley taught that grace for salvation and justification are freely available, that people can fully accept or reject grace, and that the justified sinner should continue on to seek perfection or freedom from deliberate sin. Perfection has a specific technical meaning and is sometimes called holiness. The emphasis on perfection or holiness has declined in Methodism. Although Wesley held that faith alone was necessary for salvation, he also held that holy living was also needed. Methodism is able to contain this apparent contradiction. This led to belief in and dependence on God, but also left room for continued efforts at renewal and improvement, which fitted the American temper. The substitution of grape juice for wine in the Lord's Supper, however, was an American innovation, apparently not known to Wesley.

Methodism in America is active in missionary efforts, although perhaps not as intensely as other more active denominations. Social welfare is important, shown in terms of allocated funds. Although governance is episcopal, bishops are elected and have definite, but limited power. Women are ordained as ministers, and one was recently elected bishop. Education is valued, but not typically scholarly.

Holiness and Pentecostal

Holiness churches are relatively fragmented, but Pentecostal churches are even more prone to schism, separation, and division. Piepkorn's *Profiles in Belief* (1977, 1978, 1979) lists 55 Holiness churches, some with memberships as few as a hundred and with two or three congregations. They are (in decreasing size) the Church of the Nazarene, Church of God (Anderson, Indiana), Wesleyan Church, and Free Methodist Church, with a total membership over three-quarters of a million members. A church with the name Holiness in its title may be in this category, although some are actually Pentecostal. The name Pentecostal is not found among Holiness churches, which often reject glossolalia.

Traditionally Protestant, these churches see the Bible as a full and final authority, often literally without error or inerrant in the original texts, which opens the possibility of an improved translation. Man's sinful nature and the person's possession of free will in accepting salvation and grace are emphasized. If accepted, the person is still sinful, but is expected to continue on toward entire sanctification or perfection. Sacraments vary and are usually regarded as memorial or symbolic, and most churches baptize in different ways (sprinkling, pouring, immersion) and give the Lord's Supper. Church governance varies from episcopal to congregational, but schism is common, so in practice, control is basically congregational. These churches are active in missionary or evangelical work, but less active in social welfare work except as it relates to evangelical activities. Alcohol, tobacco, drugs, and secret societies, as well as gambling, dancing, theatre, movies, and television are generally prohibited, but the mix varies. Some churches oppose military service; others permit it. Training for ministers and preachers varies, but most denominations cannot support seminaries. Education under church control may be valued, and opposition to teaching evolution is common.

Pentecost (Greek, for fiftieth) is derived from the second of the three Hebrew harvest festivals, the Feast of Weeks that came seven weeks and a day or fifty days after Passover. Associated with the barley harvest, it also figures in the book of Ruth. For many Christians, the important aspects of their experience are contained in two key parts of the New Testament (Acts 2:4, 1 Cor. 12:4-10). In Acts, speaking in tongues is described as happening on Pentecost, hence the name. The description makes it clear that the "speaking in tongues" was speaking in *languages* known to other peoples. Glossolalia, as it now occurs, has usually not been found to be any known foreign language. Some churches encourage spontaneous glossolalia; others require a translator to be present. Some ministers have recognized that this intense emotional experience is not for everyone and will discourage glossolalia in people who are seen as unstable.

These groups are generally close, theologically, but there are differences. Piepkorn (1979, Vol. 3) identified 75 Pentecostal churches (not all American) that accept the Trinity more or less traditionally, whereas another 27 churches have a modified unitarian or "Oneness" conception. Piepkorn also identified an additional 27 churches, so this general rubric covers some very diverse groups. The four largest trinitarian Pentecostal churches are (in decreasing size) the Assemblies of God, Church of God in Christ, Church of God (Cleveland, Tennessee), and the Pentecostal Holiness Church, Inc., with a total membership of well over two million. The four largest in the "Oneness" camp are (in decreasing size) the United Pentecostal Church International, Apostolic Overcoming Holy Church of God, Inc., Pentecostal Assemblies of the World, Inc., and The Church of Jesus Christ, with a total membership of well over one-half a million. The Pentecostal movement may also be seen in churches usually considered mainline: in Methodism, from which it arose, and as the Charismatic Movement in Catholic and Protestant (Episcopal, Baptist, Lutheran, and Presbyterian and Reformed) churches.

Pentecostals who have come out of a Wesleyan or Methodist background tend to see the baptism of the Holy Spirit as a third blessing after sanctification and conversion (baptism); those who have come out of a non-Methodist background tend to see the baptism of the Holy Spirit as a second blessing.

Governance of these churches varies, but the mix is episcopal and congregational, although some call the senior head a superintendent, or by some similar title. Other groups are either too small for such an apparatus or may have an entirely congregational organization. Sacraments also vary, but are generally seen as memorial. Missionary activities are generally important and the larger Pentecostal churches emphasize social welfare. Education for members and clergy is important for the larger groups; although the attitude toward the Bible may sound fundamentalist, study is generally welcomed. The Bible is inerrant—in their originals, which leaves room for study to modify translations.

Salvation Army

Governmentally funded social support programs tend to obscure how recent a development "welfare" is. Until the 1930s and the Great Depression, most American social relief and aid was private. The Salvation Army originated in the efforts of William Booth to provide for the inhabitants of the worst slums of London. Although the Army was originally organized along the lines of Methodist governance, Booth found the system too sophisticated for his converts, and changed to a military organization, with considerable success. The local unit, the corps, is equivalent to a congregation, and converts who wish to join sign the Articles of War and volunteer for needed work. The simple services are not intellectual, and encourage emotional involvement and expression. The Salvation Army is well within its Methodist tradition, but sanctification or holiness are emphasized. The sacraments are not observed, and the focus is on the spiritual side of the experience. American membership is somewhat under one-half million.

One of the most visible and distinctive aspects of the Army is its programs for social action. It operates hospitals, homes for unwed mothers, camps and clubs for children, lodging centers, alcoholic service centers, centers for prisoners and their families, and other community centers. The street band and street preaching reflect a very active, effective social outreach to individuals and families who have limited, or no resources. A secure, comfortable therapist may resent the "hook" in a bowl of soup, but the Army meets important emotional and physical needs. The structured organization, the provision of care for its members, the requirement of providing services for others are all psychologically reparative to deprived people who may never have experienced adequate giving or receiving.

Mennonite

The Inner Light churches are a relatively small group, totaling perhaps some 190,000 members, divided among some 13 church organizations; the Brethren have a similar number of church groups, with some 250,000 members. With fewer than 150,000 Quakers in nine church groups, there are about 600,000 people in thirty-five groups, just slightly more than the Salvation Army. Although Mennonites are related historically, and in some external characteristics, to Baptists, there are important differences. In addition to separatism, avoidance of oaths, and pacifism, Mennonites downplay Original Sin, but emphasize man's sinful nature and the need for faith in, and acceptance of, Jesus as savior. Faith (Mayer 1961) is seen primarily in obedience; the outward signs of this include distinctive garb (women cover their heads, for example), plain clothing, following a ban placed on a member, and avoidance of worldly activities or amusements. In addition to baptism and the Lord's Supper, washing the feet of the saints (i.e., other community members) and a sign of fellowship in a kiss are also memorial sacraments.

The Mennonites do not usually reach out to those outside their group, although sincere converts appear to be accepted. Hard work and a closed community suggest that social welfare is likely to be just within the group. Education is often at home, although some groups (the General Conference Mennonite Church and the Conference of the Evangelical Mennonite Church) are more receptive to education and training for their ministers.

Brethren

Although separatist, the Brethren are involved in social action and welfare outside the group, particularly the Church of the Brethren. The Mennonite and Brethren churches may vary, although both have espoused various eschatological concepts as to the end of the world and Christ's return. If this appears an issue in therapy with a patient, the therapist should explore the specific church's position. Generally conservative, theologically, churches do vary, and education is esteemed to differing degrees.

Quakers or Friends

Some Quaker churches hold fairly traditional Christian concepts, such as the Trinity, the divinity of Christ, and human depravity. Other churches are non-Trinitarian and may regard the Bible as symbolic. Sometimes fundamentalism is seen, but the low level of dogma has not fostered an anti-scientific position, even on such touchy issues as evolution. Education is emphasized (Hardy 1974). Individual experience of a direct contact with God (or oneself) also is emphasized, the structure is almost creedless, with little authority in the usual sense, war is opposed, and social concern and action make this group attractive to many therapists.

Millennialism

Millennialism appears in a number of Christian denominations, and is central for Seventh-Day Adventists and Jehovah's Witnesses. For Christians, the biblical basis comes from Psalms 2 and 11, 2 Samuel 7:12, Isaiah 11, Daniel 7:13 and 14, and Revelation 20. The Old Testament says that the Davidic dynasty will endure and emerge triumphant and glorified (this apparently written during a time of political decline). The New Testament indicates the hoped-for early return of Jesus to usher in a world of peace and justice for the righteous and punishment for the wicked. Cataclysmic imagery of a battle between Jesus and Satan occurs in the Revelation of John. Since Jesus was described as a descendant of the line of David, the Old Testament remarks about the Davidic dynasty are important. Two other factors must be borne in mind. First, the hopes for a Messiah (*meshiach*) have roots in Jewish thought and may have lesser or different divine connotations. In the Jewish conception, the world must be thoroughly rectified *before* the Messiah comes, but most Christian constructions see things becoming much worse before Jesus returns as the Messiah. Second, both Greek and Hebrew used letters for numbers before the introduction of Arabic numbers; *alpha* or *alef* were

"1," *beta* or *bet* were "2," etc. Words were converted to a numeric value and the process was called *gematria* (from geometry) in Hebrew. Some imagery in Revelation is directly in line with this practice; more generally, the practice has been continued to foretell the future or to extract hidden meanings from biblical texts.

Three different stances are seen within this group. Most common is *premillennialism*, which holds that Christ will return before the millennium to revive and save the dead believers, and save the living believers; the rest of the peoples will suffer; the Jews will accept Jesus; and the other biblical prophecies will be fulfilled. At the end of this period, Satan will be released to make a final attack on Christ and will be completely destroyed. Very similar to premillennialism, *dispensationalism* divides all history into seven eras (dispensations); each is a test imposed by God on the people. *Postmillennialism* holds that Christ will return after the millennium. The premillennial position is currently interpreted (Mayer 1961) as a reaction to modernist Christian reinterpretations, and premillennial positions are found in creedal statements of Fundamentalist, Holiness, and Pentecostal groups.

Seventh-Day Adventist

Here are considered a group of denominations that arose out of a remarkable religious ferment in nineteenth-century America. The history of each denomination is related to European religious developments, but these churches, which include the Adventist, Jehovah's Witness, Latter-Day Saints (Mormon), and Christian Science, had their most significant development then. The Witnesses and Adventists are millennial. Based on the predicted return of Jesus in March 1844, they did not disband when the prophesy failed, but concluded that the process had begun—in Heaven. Ellen White and her husband were early Adventist leaders; and her writings provided a substantial body of secondary literature that contained much of the basic views of the group. Adventists are Trinitarian; hold the Bible to be God's inspired word; and accept the Incarnation and atoning death of Jesus, the virgin birth, the Resurrection of Jesus, and his return. They also hold that although people can accept or reject salvation, the Ten Commandments are binding on all people, that the soul has conditional immortality, that the Sabbath should be observed on the seventh day (Saturday) rather than on the first day (Sunday), and that the Old Testament dietary restrictions apply, at least with regard to slaughter-

ing practices,[2] whereas foot washing during the Lord's Supper was instituted by Christ. Baptism and tithing are practiced, and modest and
dignified clothing is expected.

The denomination is growing rapidly in this country, with over a half-
million members by 1977, a 64 percent increase since 1960. Some seven
other splinter groups in this movement are all small. Of the total of
2,500,000 members, 80 percent are in other countries (Piepkorn 1979).
Local church governance is congregational. The Adventist church is
stronly missionary, with a strong educational and social welfare program;
hundreds of secondary schools are operated, as well as some 5,000 ele-
mentary schools and a large number of medical treatment facilities.

Core positions and concepts are diverse. A great deal of support is
offered in being among those who are saved, and thus elect, and aggression
is directed toward those who are damned. Some members may feel a
special distinction in being among the elect. A clear, detailed plan of
living is educed from the behavioral practices of the Old Testament.

Jehovah's Witnesses

Founded by Charles Russell in 1872, the approach of the Witnesses is
dispensational, with the world seen as divided into three eras (dispensations). The first era ended with the Flood, the second ended in 1914, and
we are currently in the third and last era. Now about as large as the
Adventists, with some 550,000 American members in 1977, this denomination has grown 122 percent since 1960. The Witnesses take the spelling
of the name of God as a key issue.

Because it is such an issue, a short digression is in order. In the Old
Testament, God is referred to in several ways: *El Shaddai* or God Al-
mighty, *El* or God, *Elohim* or God (literally Gods, although the grammar
makes it clear that the use is singular), *Adonai* or my Lord, and *YHWH*.
This latter is a proper name written in consonants, since all Hebrew is
written without vowels. As reverence surrounding the name of God
increased, the Jews put up barriers to ever pronouncing God's name. In
writing God's name, the consonants were spelled correctly (Yhwh), but
the vowel markings (introduced when Hebrew was no longer a vernacular)
were changed to those appropriate to *Adonai*. A deliberate mispronuncia-

[2]Kosher meat is used if available, but otherwise Adventists are vegetarian. Tobacco and
alcohol are avoided.

tion was introduced to preserve the consonants, hence *Yehowah*. Since the *w* sound was now pronounced *v*, it would be *Yehovah*, but transliteration into English yielded a *j*, so we have *Jehovah*. The actual pronunciation was lost with the end of the priesthood, but *Yahweh* was the probable one. The Witnesses hold that the Papacy wickedly mistranslated the Bible.

The main evils in modern life are attributed to religion, commerce or finance, and government. Witnesses reject the Trinity, and Jesus is not God, but only god and the Holy Spirit is the power of God. Blood transfusions are prohibited as eating blood (Gen. 9:4). Voting or using tobacco is rejected (Whalen 1972), and so is saluting the flag or bearing arms (Mayer 1961). Only 144,000 people have earned immortality (Rev. 6:3-8) and belong to a "great mystery class." A second class, of Old Testament believers, will be given a lesser reward, a third class of "other sheep" will aid or defend the Witnesses, and a fourth class will be created after the rule of God has been established. The soul is mortal, since otherwise God could not impose the death penalty on a sinner.[3] Eternal punishment for sin is denied, but death may be visited on the recalcitrant.

Extensive financial contributions are expected from members, and there is an active missionary effort. There is less involvement in social welfare, and education seems to be less important. The degree to which the Bible is interpreted literally seems to vary.

Church of Jesus Christ of Latter-Day Saints

In the mid-1820s, the angel Moroni appeared to Joseph Smith and told him to translate *The Book of Mormon*, written in a script called Reformed Egyptian on golden plates buried on Mt. Cumorah near Palmyra, New York. With the aid of the mysterious spectacles Urim and Thummim,[4] Smith and an Oliver Cowdery translated and published this book. *The Book of Mormon* recounts how a group of people came to America after the confusion of the tower of Babel, but became extinct about 600 B.C.E. About the same time, Lehi and his family, including Lehi's son Nephi, left Jerusalem and came to America. The descendants of Nephi were advanced, and Jesus appeared to the Nephites after his resurrection and established a church among them. They were opposed by

[3]This translation from the Hebrew is inconsistent with common usage, whereby soul is translated as *person*.

[4]These are the two objects (literally "lights and perfections") on the breastplate of the High Priest in the Temple (Gen. 28:30) used to ascertain the divine will.

wicked people who destroyed them about 385 C.E.; these people became the Indians. Moroni completed the history his father Mormon had begun before this disaster, however, and it was this that Joseph Smith dug up and translated. It has been alleged that *The Book of Mormon* was based on a novel written by a Presbyterian clergyman named Spaulding (Mayer 1961).

Smith and his associates organized a church in 1830 and established a series of social-religious settlements. Although successful in some ways, the church's doctrine of polygamy, among other factors, aroused so much hostility that Smith and his brother were murdered. Many in the church came under Brigham Young's leadership, but a smaller number followed Smith's son, Joseph Smith, Jr., to constitute The Reorganized Church of Jesus Christ of Latter-Day Saints, with a membership in 1977 of some 185,000. The church that developed under Young, however, had a membership of nearly 2,500,000 in 1977, up 67 percent from 1960. It is reported that Joseph Smith promised his son the leadership of the church in writing about six months before his death, but this will make no difference as to how the church leadership is transferred. This illustrates how arguments as to the historical correctness or error of some significant religious event miss the mark—at issue is psychological validity, not historical accuracy.

Although commonly grouped with other Protestant denominations, the Latter-Day Saints do not consider themselves in that tradition (Rosten 1975), since Joseph Smith was not a member of a church and received a new and direct revelation that supplemented the Bible. The Latter-Day Saints see the process of revelation as ongoing and the *Book of Mormon* as only part of it; other parts include *The Pearl of Great Price* and *Doctrines and Covenants*. The Bible is accepted in the King James Version insofar as it is correctly translated.

Latter-Day Saints theology is often similar to general Protestant thinking; accepted are the Trinity, the atoning death and resurrection of Jesus, the virgin birth, adult baptism (after age eight), confirmation, and the Lord's Supper (bread and water) as a memorial. Tobacco, alcohol, and hot drinks (tea and coffee) are avoided. Latter-Day Saints revelations are aimed at the Western world, just as the Bible was aimed at the Eastern. God, a loving father, would not restrict his revelation to only one time, place, and people. Concepts of heaven and of the soul are rather concrete; heaven is a place and the soul is indestructible, having always existed and continuing to exist after death. God and Jesus are also concrete, and there appears to be a concept of a plurality of gods, wherein God was once like man is now and man may progress to the level of God.

At one point, Adam was viewed as a god, although this is now rejected (Mayer 1961), and there are signs that Latter-Day Saints theology may be edging toward mainstream Protestant thinking. This theology may raise the hackles of more traditional theologians, so secondary material about the Saints should be viewed cautiously.

There is no professional priesthood or clergy, but most males have some priestly duties and the church organization seems episcopal. Women have an important, but subordinate position, and Blacks can be members and occupy some church positions, but at this writing cannot become "priests." Progressive revelation is accepted as a principle, so there is a mechanism for change. Polygamy was once an accepted principle for Latter-Day Saints, but this was prohibited when Utah joined the Union. It was never accepted in the Reorganized Church under Smith's son's leadership. The Latter-Day Saints are active missionaries, and their industry and the practice of tithing have enriched the church. They are not entangled in fundamentalist agitation over evolution and other scientific concepts (Rosten 1975).

Compared to the Adventists and Witnesses, imagery and theology is much less aggressive. A doctrine of "blood atonement" has led to at least one massacre in the nineteenth century, but the Latter-Day Saints had also been subjected to brutality. The doctrine is much modified now.

Christian Science

The origins of Christian Science were described in part in Chapter 5. Mary Baker Eddy's book, *Science and Health with Key to the Scriptures*, was first published in 1875, and the Church of Christ, Scientist was founded in Boston in 1879. Now known as the Mother Church, its governance is tightly run from the central church to the point of having uniform worship. Weekly readings from the Bible and *Science and Health* are prescribed by the Mother Church. The size of the membership is unknown (statistics are not reported, in accord with Mrs. Eddy's rules).

There are certain parallels between the Latter-Day Saints and Christian Science. Both reject alcohol, tobacco, coffee, and tea, and Christian Science also rejects medication. Both are disliked by some theologians (e.g., Mayer 1961) and other writers (Whalen 1972); both seem to view human possibilities for development with hope. A major difference appears to be along the material–ideal dimension; Latter-Day Saints emphasize the material world as a present and future experience, Christian

Scientists view most things in abstract, nonphysical terms. "Material" here does not mean materialistic, as greedy, but rather a view of outcomes as having concrete-sense aspects similar to the experiences of the congregants.

Outsiders make much of Christian Science as faith healing or as a "medical" system that uses prayer, but this is a vulgarization. It is held that "health is a spiritual reality, not a physical condition; therefore true health is eternal. Disease is an aspect of falsehood—a delusion of the carnal mind that can be destroyed by the prayer of spiritual understanding" (Stokes, in Rosten 1975, p. 71). Evil is a lie about God and the world as a result of incorrect thinking; and Christian Science healing in the hands of trained practitioners will help the person correct his or her errors through prayer and right thinking. Recent studies involving meditation and visualization in the treatment of cancer suggest that this matter is not as simple as was once thought. Stokes also noted that "God is divine Mind, the source and substance of man's true being. Mind, or Spirit, is cause; man and the universe are effect. . . . Matter itself is only a false sense of substance" (p. 70). This differs considerably from most Christian theologies, although Christian Science considers itself Protestant.

The differences are important. *Science and Health* is considered to be divinely inspired, biblical terms are interpreted differently; for example, "*Jacob*. A corporeal, mortal, embarrassing duplicity, repentance, sensualism. Inspiration" (from *Science and Health* glossary, cited in Mayer 1961, p. 535). Sin is seen as the belief in a life separate from God, but any material-mindedness is sinful, which is not necessarily consistent with most Christian and Jewish formulations. Heaven and Hell are held to be states of mind. Jesus is considered as divine, but the Trinity is seen as a unity of Life, Truth, and Love; that is, three aspects of a single divine Principle. Baptism is a spiritual cleansing, not an actual rite, and the Eucharist is a spiritual communion with God experienced in silence and without bread or wine.

There is a fairly active missionary orientation, and education is well regarded. *The Christian Science Monitor* appears to have considerable independence in factual reporting, and is well regarded, journalistically. Christian Science sanitaria exist, as do Christian Science nurses and practitioners, but medication is not used. Medical assistance at birth, in bone setting, and in the use of mortuary facilities is permissible. Payments to Christian Science practitioners are reimbursable expenses under most insurance policies and are deductible as medical treatment under Internal Revenue Service regulations.

Unitarian Universalist Association

Although normative Christianity takes a clearly marked path in the Synoptic Gospels (Matt., Mark, Luke), Jesus is not seen as making a statement that is unequivocally readable as meaning the Trinity in its modern interpretation. Some idiomatic expressions are readable in that direction, but that is not the only direction. As a Jew preaching to other Jews, the assertion that one is God is not consistent with Jewish thought. In those days, it would have been considered blasphemy, for which you would have been stoned to death. Debates over what came to be considered unitarian views are ancient; the "Oneness" Pentecostal churches are another manifestation of this issue, although they take a considerably different view. The Universalists originally accepted the Trinity, but they drew closer to the Unitarians, and the two groups united in 1961. They numbered some 180,000 in 1977, an increase of 5 percent from 1960, but they have been influential. Jefferson and both Adamses were members, as were Madison, Franklin, and Thomas Paine, among others.

Creedal statements are avoided and modern Unitarian Universalist thinking includes more freedom of belief than is true of the Christian groups discussed. There is a concept that people are imperfect, but not inherently bad, and capable of improvement, and a sense that wisdom is obtainable from many sources, including the Bible. Jesus is considered divine in the sense that all people are; that is, good and of value, but belief, faith, ritual (sacraments), or such in themselves do not convey salvation or remove sin. Prayer, sometimes called meditation, expresses feelings aimed at improving the person, not at affecting God. Many associations are not churches, but rather fellowships, and conduct their own services, so church governance is congregational. There is a long history of women as ministers, but the percentage is small. The Association is hospitable to people who do not believe in God; typically, members espouse politically liberal causes. The Association is not missionary, but accepts members. Many people are regarded as members because of their outlook, although they have not yet joined a group. Education is very much an individual value, as is social welfare, which is expressed officially through the Unitarian Universalist Service Committee.

Unionist

Three fairly similar churches come under this heading: the Disciples of Christ (Christian Church), the Churches of Christ, and the United Church of Christ. Altogether there were about 5,500,000 members in 1977, down 11 percent since 1960, only the Churches of Christ posted a gain in membership; the other two noted declines. These unionizing churches had diverse backgrounds in the Protestant spectrum (Baptist, Presbyterian, Unitarian), so the overall stance is diverse. Although the Trinity, baptism, formal worship services, and the Lord's Supper are emphasized, creeds, doctrinal tests of acceptability, and an organized church hierarchy are avoided. Jesus Christ is generally seen as "Lord and Savior," but this varies, too. Because of congregational control, individual churches range from liberal to fundamental. Clergy are seminary-trained, and a few women are ordained. The missionary orientation ranges from low to moderate, as does social welfare orientation, consistent with the system of governance and the overall resistance to external control.

References

Adams, J.E. (1970). *Competent to Counsel.* Nutley, NJ: Presbyterian and Reformed Publishing Co.

—— (1973). *The Christian Counselor's Manual.* Nutley, NJ: Presbyterian and Reformed Publishing Co.

Agel, J. (1971). *The Radical Therapist.* New York: Ballantine Books.

Allen, R.O., and Spilka, B. (1967). Committed and consensual religion: A specification of religion-prejudice relationships. *Journal for the Scientific Study of Religion* 6:191–206.

Allport, G. W. (1950). *The Individual and His Religion.* New York: MacMillan.

——, and Ross, J.M. (1967). Personal religious orientation and prejudice. *Journal of Personality and Social Psychology* 5:432–443.

Alter, R. (1981). *The Art of Biblical Narrative.* New York: Basic Books.

Anon. (1977). The therapist and Christian client relationship. *Journal of Psychology and Theology* 5:30–33.

APA (1967). *Casebook on Ethical Standards of Psychologists.* Washington: American Psychological Association (updated, 1974).

Appelbaum, S.A. (1976). The dangerous edge of insight. *Psychotherapy: Theory, Research and Practice* 13:202–206.

Argyle, M., and Beit-Hallahmi, B. (1975). *The Social Psychology of Religion.* London: Routledge & Kegan Paul.

Atwood, G. (1974). The loss of a loved parent and the origin of salvation fantasies. *Psychotherapy: Theory, Research and Practice* 11:256–258.

Ausubel, N. (1964). *The Book of Jewish Knowledge.* New York: Crown.

Balsiger, D., and Sellier, C. (1976). *In Search of Noah's Ark.* Salt Lake City: Schick Sunn Classic Books.

Barkman, P.F. (1977). The relationship of personality modes to religious experience and behavior. In *Current Perspectives in the Psychology of Religion*, ed. H.N. Malony, pp. 201–208. Grand Rapids: Eerdmans.

Barr, J. (1968). *Comparative Philology and the Text of the Old Testament*. London: Oxford University Press.

Barth, M. (1974). *The Anchor Bible: Ephesians*, eds. W.F. Albright and D.N. Freedman. Garden City: Doubleday.

Batson, C.D., Naifeh, S.J., and Pate, S. (1978). Social desirability, religious orientation and racial prejudice. *Journal for the Scientific Study of Religion* 17:31–41.

Beardslee, W.A. (1970). *Literary Criticism of the New Testament*. Philadelphia: Fortress Press.

Beegle, D.M. (1982). What does the Bible say? Translations speak in many tongues. *Biblical Archaeology Review* 8(#6):56–61.

Beit-Hallahmi, B. (1974a). Salvation and its vicissitudes: Clinical psychology and political values. *American Psychologist* 29:124–129.

——— (1974b). Psychology of religion 1880–1930: The rise and fall of a psychological movement. *Journal of the History of the Behavioral Sciences* 10:84–90.

——— (1975a). Encountering orthodox religion in psychotherapy. *Psychotherapy: Theory, Research and Practice* 12:357–359.

——— (1975b). Religion and suicidal behavior. *Psychological Reports* 37:1303–1306.

——— (1976). Sacrifice, fire and the victory of the sun: A search for the origins of Hanukkah. *The Psychoanalytic Review* 63:497–509.

——— (1977). Curiosity, doubt and devotion: The beliefs of psychologists and the psychology of religion. In *Current Perspectives in the Psychology of Religion*, ed. H.N. Malony, pp. 381–391. Grand Rapids: Eerdmans.

——— (1979). Identity and religion in psychotherapy. Colloquium presentation at the Psychological Training and Consultation Center, Central Michigan University, February 19, 1979.

Bellah, R.N. (1967). Civil religion in America. *Daedalus* 96:1–21.

Benson, P.L., and Spilka, B.P. (1973). God-image as a function of self-esteem and locus of control. *Journal for the Scientific Study of Religion* 12:297–310.

Ben-Yehuda, E., and Weinstein, D. (1961). *Ben-Yehuda's Pocket English-Hebrew Hebrew-English Dictionary*. New York: Washington Square Press.

Berger, P.L. (1974). Some second thoughts on substantive versus functional definitions of religion. *Journal for the Scientific Study of Religion* 13:125–133.

Bergin, A.E. (1980a). Psychotherapy and religious values. *Journal of Consulting and Clinical Psychology* 48:95–105.

——— (1980b). Religious and Humanistic values: A reply to Ellis and Walls. *Journal of Consulting and Clinical Psychology* 48:642–645.

Bertocci, P.A. (1971). Psychological interpretations of religious experience. In *Research on Religious Development*, ed. M.P. Strommen, pp. 3–41. New York: Hawthorn Books.

Beutler, L.E. (1979). Values, beliefs, religion and the persuasive influence of psychotherapy. *Psychotherapy: Theory, Research and Practice* 16:432–440.

———, Jobe, A.M., and Elkins, D. (1974). Outcome in group psychotherapy: Using persuasion theory to increase treatment efficiency. *Journal of Consulting and Clinical Psychology* 42:547–553.

———, Pollack, S., and Jobe, A. (1978). "Acceptance," values and therapeutic change. *Journal of Consulting and Clinical Psychology* 46:198–199.

Bibby, R.W. (1978). Why conservative churches *really* are growing: Kelly revisited. *Journal for the Scientific Study of Religion* 17:129–137.

Bixby, W. (1964). *The Universe of Galileo and Newton*. New York: American Heritage Publishing Co.

Blanck, G., and Blanck, R. (1974). *Ego Psychology: Theory and Practice*. New York: Columbia University Press.

Bockoven, J.S. (1963). *Moral Treatment in American Psychiatry*. New York: Springer.

Bonnell, G.C. (1969). Salvation and psychotherapy. *Journal of Religion and Health* 8:382–398.

Boulding, K.E. (1980). Science: Our common heritage. *Science* 207:831–836.

Bowers, M.K. (1963). *Conflicts of the Clergy: A Psychodynamic Study with Case Histories*. New York: Thomas Nelson.

Brettler, M. (1982). The Torah, the Prophets and the Writings: A new Jewish translation. *Biblical Archaeology Review* 8(#6):63.

Broad, W.J. (1979). Paul Feyerabend: Science and the anarchist. *Science* 206: 534–537.

Brock, T.C. (1962). Implications of conversion and magnitude of cognitive dissonance. *Journal for the Scientific Study of Religion* 1:198–203.

Bugental, J.F.T. (1965). *The Search for Authenticity*. New York: Holt, Rinehart & Winston.

Buhler, C. (1962). *Values in Psychotherapy*. Glencoe, IL: The Free Press.

Butcher, H.J. (1968). *Human Intelligence: Its Nature and Assessment*. London: Methuen.

Campbell, C. (1971). *Toward a Sociology of Irreligion*. New York: Herder & Herder.

Caporale, R., and Grumelli, A. (1971). *The Culture of Unbelief*. Berkeley: University of California Press.

Chafetz, M.E., and DeMone, H.W. Jr. (1962). *Alcoholism and Society*. New York: Oxford University Press.

Chessick, R.D. (1969). *How Psychotherapy Heals*. New York: Science House.

Clark, R.A. (1980). Religious delusions among Jews. *American Journal of Psychotherapy* 34:62–71.

Cohen, R.J., and Smith, F.J. (1976). Socially reinforced obsessing: Etiology of a disorder in a Christian Scientist. *Journal of Consulting and Clinical Psychology* 44:142–144.

Cole, W.G. (1959). *Sex and Love in the Bible*. New York: Association Press.

Confraternity of Christian Doctrine. (1970). *The New American Bible, St. Joseph Edition*. New York: Catholic Book Publishing Co.

Coyle, F.A., Jr., and Erdberg, P. (1969). A liberalizing approach to maladaptive fundamentalist hyperreligiosity. *Psychotherapy: Theory, Research and Practice* 6:140–142.

Coyne, J.C. (1978). Sources of difficulties in handling religious material in psychotherapy: Some myths of psychotherapy. Paper presented at the American Psychological Convention.

Cullen, J.B. (1974). On the methods, rationale and unanticipated consequences of Soviet atheistic "upbringing." *Religious Education* 69:72–87.

Daiches, D. (1970). Translating the Bible. *Commentary*. May. pp. 59–68.

Davidson, J.D. (1977). Socio-economic status and ten dimensions of religious commitment. *Sociology and Social Research* 61:462–485.

Dearman, M. (1974). Christ and conformity: A study of Pentecostal values. *Journal for the Scientific Study of Religion* 13:437–453.

DeJong, G.F., and Ford, T.R. (1965). Religious fundamentalism and denominational preference in the Southern Appalachian region. *Journal for the Scientific Study of Religion* 5:24–33.

de la Torre, J. (1977). Psychoanalytic neutrality: An overview. *Bulletin of the Menninger Clinic* 41:366–384.

de Santillana, G. (1955). *The Crime of Galileo*. Chicago: University of Chicago Press.

Dimont, M. (1962). *Jews, God and History*. New York: Simon and Schuster.

Dittes, J.E. (1969). Psychology of religion. In *The Handbook of Social Psychology*. Vol. 5, eds. G. Lindzey and E. Aronson, pp. 602–659. Menlo Park, CA: Addison-Wesley.

——— (1971). Religion, prejudice and personality. In *Research on Religious Development*, ed. M.P. Strommen, pp. 355–390. New York: Hawthorn Books.

Douglas, M. (1966). *Purity and Danger: An Analysis of Concepts of Pollution and Taboo*. New York: Praeger.

——— (1970). *Natural Symbols: Exploration in Cosmology.* New York: Pantheon.

Eissler, K.R. (1971). *Talent and Genius*. New York: Quadrangle Books.

Ekstein, R. (1962). Reflections on parallels in the therapeutic and the social process. In *Values in Psychotherapy* by C. Buhler, Glencoe, IL: The Free Press.

Eliade, M. (1959). *The Sacred and the Profane: The Nature of Religion*. New York: Harcourt, Brace & World.

Elkind, D. (1964). Age changes in the meaning of religious identity. *Review of Religious Research* 6:36–40.

——— (1970). The origins of religion in the child. *Review of Religious Research* 12:35–42.

——— (1971). The development of religious understanding in children and adolescents. In *Research on Religious Development*, ed. M.P. Strommen, pp. 655–685. New York: Hawthorn Books.

Elliot, M. (1967). *The Language of the King James Bible*. New York: Doubleday.

Ellis, A. (1970). The case against religion. *Mensa Journal* #138.

—— (1973). Rational-emotive therapy. In *Current Psychotherapies*, ed. R. Corsini. Itasca, IL: Peacock.

—— (1974). Experience and rationality: The making of a rational-emotive therapist. *Psychotherapy: Theory, Research and Practice* 11:194–198.

—— (1978). Untitled paper read at a symposium on Religion and Psychotherapy at the American Psychological Association Convention.

—— (1980). Psychotherapy and atheistic values: A response to A.E. Bergin's "Psychotherapy and religious values." *Journal of Consulting and Clinical Psychology* 48:635–639.

Epstein, L., and Feiner, A.H., eds. (1979). *Countertransference*. New York: Aronson.

Evans, H.S. (1973). The Seventh-Day Adventist faith and psychotherapy. In *Religious Systems and Psychotherapy*, ed. R.H. Cox, pp. 89–97. Springfield, IL: C.C. Thomas.

Fackenheim, E.L. (1970). *God's Presence in History: Jewish Affirmations and Philosophical Reflections*. New York: Harper & Row.

Fairbairn, W.R.D. (1952). *Psychoanalytic Studies of the Personality*. London: Routledge & Kegan Paul.

Fantz, R.L. (1961). The origin of form perception. *Scientific American* 204:66–73.

Farson, R.E. (1961). Introjection in the psychotherapeutic relationship. *Journal of Counseling Psychology* 8:337–343.

Feifel, H. (1958). Symposium on relationships between religion and mental health. Introductory remarks. *American Psychologist* 13:565–566.

Ferreira, P., and Ferreira, M.L. (1978). Barriers and therapeutic impasses encountered when both client and therapist share a similar cultural base. Paper presented at the American Psychological Association Convention.

Fisher, S., and Greenberg, R.P. (1977). *The Scientific Credibility of Freud's Theories and Therapy*. New York: Basic Books.

Flannery, E.H. (1965). *The Anguish of the Jews*. New York: Macmillan.

Frankel, M. (1967). Morality in psychotherapy. *Psychology Today* 1(3):25–29.

Frankl, V.E. (1968). *The Doctor and the Soul*. 2nd ed. New York: Alfred Knopf.

Freud, A. (1946). *The Ego and the Mechanisms of Defence*. New York: International Universities Press.

Freud, S. (1909). Analysis of a phobia in a five-year-old boy. In *Collected Papers of Sigmund Freud*. New York: Collier.

—— (1910). The future prospects of psychoanalytic therapy. In *Collected Papers*. New York: Collier.

—— (1912). Recommendations for physicians practising psychoanalysis. In *Collected Papers*. New York: Collier.

—— (1913). Further recommendations on the technique of psychoanalysis. In *Collected Papers*. New York: Collier.

—— (1919). Turnings in the ways of psychoanalytic therapy. In *Collected Papers*. New York: Collier.

—— (1923). A Seventeenth Century demonological neurosis. In *Collected Papers*. New York: Collier.

—— (1927). *The Future of an Illusion*. New York: Norton.

—— (1930). *Civilization and its Discontents*. New York: Norton.

Fromm, E. (1941). *Escape from Freedom*. New York: Rinehart & Co.

Fromm-Reichmann, F. (1950). *Principles of Intensive Psychotherapy*. Chicago: University of Chicago Press.

Gartner, J.D. (1982). Christians need not apply: Religious discrimination in Clinical Psychology graduate admissions. Paper read at the American Psychological Convention.

Geiser, R.L., and Rheingold, P.D. (1964). Psychology and the legal process: Testimonial privileged communications. *American Psychologist* 19:831-837.

Geisler, N.L., and Nix, W.E. (1968). *A General Introduction to the Bible*. Chicago: Moody Press.

Gersten, L. (1979). The mental health needs of the pious. *Sh'ma* 9(167):52-55.

Gibbon, E. (1776). *The Decline and Fall of the Roman Empire*. Vol. 1. New York: The Heritage Press (1946).

Gilmore, S.K. (1969). Personality differences between high and low dogmatism groups of Pentecostal believers. *Journal for the Scientific Study of Religion* 8:161-164.

Ginsburg, S.W. (1950). Values and the psychiatrist. *American Journal of Orthopsychiatry* 20:466-478.

Glasser, W., and Zunin, L.M. (1973). Reality therapy. In *Current Psychotherapies*, ed. R. Corsini. Itasca, IL: Peacock.

Glock, C.Y., and Stark, R. (1966). *Christian Belief and Anti-Semitism*. New York: Harper & Row.

Greeley, A.M. (1963). A note on the origins of religious differences. *Journal for the Scientific Study of Religion* 3:21-31.

——, and Gockel, G.L. (1971). The religious effects of parochial education. In *Research on Religious Development*, ed. M.P. Strommen, pp. 264-301. New York: Hawthorn Books.

Green, A.W. (1946). Social values and psychotherapy. *Journal of Personality* 14:199-228.

Greene, R.J. (1978). Psychotherapy with hard science professionals. *Journal of Contemporary Psychotherapy* 8:52-56.

Greenstein, E.L. (1981). The riddle of Samson. *Prooftexts* 1:237-260.

Grolnick, S.A., Barkin, L., and Muensterberger, W., eds. (1978). *Between Reality and Fantasy: Transitional Objects and Phenomena*. New York: Aronson.

Guntrip, H. (1971). *Psychoanalytic Theory, Therapy and the Self*. New York: Basic Books.

Haas, H.I. (1967). Relations between clergymen and psychiatrists. *Psychiatric Quarterly Supplement* 41:40-56.

Halleck, S.L. (1976). Discussion of "Socially Reinforced Obsessing." *Journal of Consulting and Clinical Psychology* 44:146–147.

Hallo, W.W. (1983). The first Purim. *Biblical Archaeologist* 46:19–29.

Hardy, K.R. (1974). Social origins of American scientists and scholars. *Science* 185:497–506.

Harris, M. (1977). *Cannibals and Kings: The Origins of Cultures*. New York: Random House.

Hartmann, H. (1951). Ego psychology and the problem of adaptation. In *Organization and Pathology of Thought*, ed. D. Rapaport. New York: Columbia University Press.

—— (1960). *Psychoanalysis and Moral Values*. New York: International Universities Press.

Hathorne, B.C. (1966). Frontiers in religion and psychiatry. *Journal of Religion and Health* 5:296–306.

Haugen, C.D., and Edwards, K.J. (1976). Religious values and their effect on the perception of a therapist in a psychotherapy analogue. *Journal of Psychology and Theology* 4:160–167.

Hegy, P. (1978). Book review. *Journal for the Scientific Study of Religion* 17: 181–184.

Heitler, J.B. (1973). Preparation of lower-class patients for expressive group psychotherapy. *Journal of Consulting and Clinical Psychology* 41:251–260.

Helfaer, P.M. (1972). *The Psychology of Religious Doubt*. Boston: Beacon Press.

Henning, L.H., and Tirrell, F.J. (1982). Counselor resistance to spiritual exploration. *Personnel and Guidance Journal* 61:92–95.

Henry, W.E., Sims, J.H., and Spray, S.L. (1971). *The Fifth Profession: Becoming a Psychotherapist*. San Francisco: Jossey-Bass.

Hertz, J.H. (1960). *The Pentateuch and Haftorahs*. 2nd ed. London: Soncino.

Hine, V.H. (1969). Pentecostal glossolalia: Toward a functional interpretation. *Journal for the Scientific Study of Religion* 8:211–226.

Hobbs, N. (1962). Sources of gain in psychotherapy. *American Psychologist* 17:741–747.

—— (1981). The role of insight in behavior change: A commentary. *American Journal of Orthopsychiatry* 51:632–635.

Hodges, D. (1974). Breaking a scientific taboo: Putting assumptions about the supernatural into scientific theories of religion. *Journal for the Scientific Study of Religion* 13:393–408.

Hoffnung, R.A. (1973). Patterns and relations of personality and dogmatism among selected groups of Orthodox Jews. Unpublished doctoral dissertation, Fordham University.

Hoge, D.R., Perry, E.L., and Klever, G.L. (1978). Theology as a source of disagreement about Protestant church goals and priorities. *Review of Religious Research* 19:116–138.

Holt, R.R. (1973). On reading Freud. In *Abstracts of the Standard Edition of Freud*, ed. C.L. Rothgeb. New York: Aronson.

Homans, P. (1970). *Theology After Freud: An Interpretive Inquiry.* Indianapolis: Bobbs-Merrill.

Hood, R.W., Jr. (1974). Psychological strength and the report of intense religious experience. *Journal for the Scientific Study of Religion* 13:65–71.

Hooker, D. (1978). Some contributions of Christianity to Psychotherapy. Paper presented at the American Psychological Association Convention.

Huber, M. (1981). The church as resource. *Family Life Developments: Region II Child Abuse and Neglect Resource Center* August–September.

Humanist Manifesto II. (1973). *The Humanist* 33:4–8.

Hunt, R.A., and King, M.B. (1971). The intrinsic–extrinsic concept: A review and evaluation. *Journal for the Scientific Study of Religion* 10:339–356.

Hux, S. (1979). Affection: Beyond philo-Semitism. *Moment* 4 (#3):20–23.

Immergluck, L. (1964). Determinism-freedom in contemporary psychology: An ancient problem revisited. *American Psychologist* 19:270–281.

Ingram, L.C. (1981). Leadership, democracy and religion: Role ambiguity among pastors in Southern Baptist churches. *Journal for the Scientific Study of Religion* 20:119–129.

Jackson, E.N. (1975). *Parish Counseling.* New York: Aronson.

Jackson, G.E. (1972). The problem of hostility psychologically and theologically considered. *Journal of Religion and Health* 11:73–93.

Jacquet, C.H., Jr., ed. (1979). *Yearbook of American and Canadian Churches, 1979.* Nashville: Abingdon.

Jaynes, J. (1976). *The Origin of Consciousness in the Breakdown of the Bicameral Mind.* Boston: Houghton-Mifflin.

Jeffries, V., and Tygart, C.E. (1974). The influence of theology, denomination, and values upon the position of clergy on social issues. *Journal for the Scientific Study of Religion* 13:309–324.

Johnson, P.E. (1973). Protestantism and psychotherapy. In *Religious Systems and Psychotherapy*, ed. R.H. Cox. pp. 46–55. Springfield, IL: C.C. Thomas.

Joint Committee on the New Translation of the Bible. (1970). *The New English Bible, with the Apocrypha.* 2nd ed. New York: Oxford University Press.

Jones, A., ed. (1966). *The Jerusalem Bible.* Garden City, NY: Doubleday.

Jones, E. (1951). The psychology of religion. In *Essays in Psychoanalysis.* Vol. 2, ed. E. Jones. London: Hogarth Press.

—— (1955). *The Life and Work of Sigmund Freud.* Vol. 2. New York: Basic Books.

J.P.S. (1917). *The Holy Scripture According to the Masoretic Text.* Philadelphia: Jewish Publication Society (reissued with corrections, 1955).

—— (1967). *The Torah: the five books of Moses*, 2nd ed. Philadelphia: Jewish Publication Society.

Kagan, H.E., and Zucker, A.H. (1970). Treatment of a "corrupted" family by a rabbi and psychiatrist. *Journal of Religion and Health* 9:22–34.

Kanfer, F.H., and Grimm, L.G. (1978). Freedom of choice and behavioral change. *Journal of Consulting and Clinical Psychology* 46:873–878.

Kaplan, H.S. (1974). *The New Sex Therapy.* New York: Brunner Mazel.

Karon, B.P., and VandenBos, G.R. (1977). Psychotherapeutic technique and the economically poor patient. *Psychotherapy: Theory, Research and Practice* 14:169–180.

——— (1981). *Psychotherapy of Schizophrenia: The Treatment of Choice.* New York: Aronson.

Keller, W. (1981). *The Bible as History*, 2nd rev. ed. New York: Morrow.

Kelley, D.M. (1978). Why conservative churches are still growing. *Journal for the Scientific Study of Religion* 17:165–172.

Kernberg, O. (1975). *Borderline Conditions and Pathological Narcissism.* New York: Aronson.

Kidorf, I.W. (1966). The Shiva: A form of group psychotherapy. *Journal of Religion and Health* 5:43–46.

Klein, M. (1975). *The Psychoanalysis of Children.* New York: Dell.

Kluckhohn, C. (1951). Values and value-orientations in the Theory of Action. In *Toward a General Theory of Action*, eds. T. Parsons and E.A. Shils. Cambridge: Harvard University Press.

Kluckhohn, F.R. (1956). Dominant and variant value orientations. In *Personality in Nature, Society and Culture*, 2nd ed. eds. C. Kluckhohn, H.A. Murray, and D. Schneider. New York: Alfred Knopf.

———, and Strodtbeck, F.L. (1961). *Variations in Value Orientations.* New York: Row, Peterson.

Kohlberg, L. (1964). Development of moral character and moral ideology. In *Review of Child Development Research.* Vol. 1, eds. M.L. Hoffman and I.W. Hoffman. New York: Russell Sage Foundation.

Kohut, H. (1968). The psychoanalytic treatment of narcissistic personality disorders. *The Psychoanalytic Study of the Child* 23:86–113.

Kopp, S.B. (1972). *If You Meet the Buddha on the Road, Kill Him.* Palo Alto: Science and Behavior Books.

Kramer, S.N. (1983). The weeping goddess: Sumerian prototypes of the *Mater Dolorosa. Biblical Archaeologist* 46:69–80.

Küng, H. (1976). *On Being a Christian.* New York: Doubleday.

——— (1979). *Freud and the Problem of God.* New Haven: Yale University Press.

Larson, R. F. (1969). Clergymen's subjective feelings of competence when dealing with emotionally disturbed people. *Review of Religious Research* 10:140–150.

Lazarus, A.A. (1971). *Behavior Therapy and Beyond.* New York: McGraw-Hill.

Lefcourt, H.M. (1973). The function of the illusions of control and freedom. *American Psychologist* 28:417–425.

Lepley, R. (1943). The identity of fact and value. *Philosophy of Science* 10:124–131.

Lieberman, M., Yalom, I., and Miles, M. (1973). *Encounter Groups: First Facts.* New York: Basic Books.

Liefer, R. (1964). The psychiatrist and tests of criminal responsibility. *American Psychologist* 19:825–830.

London, P. (1976). Psychotherapy for religious neuroses? Comments on Cohen and Smith. *Journal of Consulting and Clinical Psychology* 44:145–146.

—— (1980). The Rabbi as therapist. *Moment* 5:57–60.

Lovinger, R.J. (1979). Therapeutic strategies with "religious" resistances. *Psychotherapy: Theory, Research and Practice* 16:419–427.

Lowe, C.M. (1976). *Value Orientations in Counseling and Psychotherapy: The Meanings of Mental Health*, 2nd ed. Cranston, RI: Carroll Press.

MacNutt, F. (1974). *Healing*. Notre Dame, IN: Ave Maria Press.

Maesen, W.A. (1970). Watchtower influences on Black Muslim eschatology. *Journal for the Scientific Study of Religion* 9:321–325.

Magil, J. (1905). *Magil's Linear School Bible*. New York: Hebrew Publishing Co.

Mahler, M.S. (1979). *The Selected Papers of Margaret S. Mahler*. Vol. 2. New York: Aronson.

Mallenbaum, V. (1973). Toward a value orientation in the psychology of religion. *Dissertation Abstracts International* 34(2-B):860.

Marty, M.E. (1971). Religious development in historical, social and cultural context. In *Research on Religious Development*, ed. M.P. Stommen. pp. 42–77. New York: Hawthorn Books.

May, R. (1939). *The Art of Counseling*. New York: Abingdon.

Mayer, F.E. (1961). *The Religious Bodies of America*, 4th ed. St. Louis: Concordia Publishing House.

McDonald, W.J., chief ed. (1967). *New Catholic Encyclopedia*, 16 vols. New York: McGraw-Hill (including supplement to 1974).

McFadden, W. (1969). Psychology and unbelief. *Religious Education* 64:491–498.

McGaw, D.B. (1979). Commitment and religious community: A comparison of a charismatic and a mainline congregation. *Journal for the Scientific Study of Religion* 18:146–163.

McGuire, M.B. (1977). The social context of prophecy: "Word-gifts" of the spirit among Catholic Pentecostals. *Review of Religious Research* 18:134–147.

McNamara, R.J. (1967). Catholics and academia. *Review of Religious Research* 8:81–95.

Meehl, P., Klann, R., Schmieding, A., Breimeier, K., and Schroeder-Slomann, S. (1958). *What, Then, Is Man?* St. Louis: Concordia Publishing House.

Mendelsohn, G.A. (1966). Effects of client personality and client–counselor similarity on the duration of counseling. *Journal of Counseling Psychology* 13:228–234.

——, and Geller, M.H. (1963). Effects of counselor-client similarity on the outcome of counseling. *Journal of Counseling Psychology* 10:71–77.

Menninger, K. (1973). *Whatever Became of Sin?* New York: Hawthorn Books.

Mickelsen, A.B. (1963). *Interpreting the Bible*. Grand Rapids: Eerdmans.

Millard, A.R. (1982). In praise of ancient scribes. *Biblical Archaeologist* 45:143–153.

Miller, D.F. (1959). *How to Explain What You Do as a Catholic*. Liguori, MO: Redemptorist Fathers.

Miller, R.L'H. (1976). The religious value system of Unitarian Universalists. *Review of Religious Research* 17:189–208.

Montague, H. (1977). The pessimistic sect's influence on the mental health of its members: The case of Jehovah's Witnesses. *Social Compass* 24:135–147.

Morris, W.W. (1955). The place of religion in the training of a medical psychologist. *Religious Education* 50:374–378.

Moss, D.M. III. (1977). Doctoral nomenclature and some misconceptions in need of reevaluation. *The Psychotherapy Bulletin* 10:24–26.

—— (1978). Priestcraft and psychoanalytic therapy: Contradiction or concordance. Paper read at the American Psychological Association Convention.

Mowrer, O.H. (1960). "Sin," the lesser of two evils. *American Psychologist* 15:301–304.

—— (1961). *The Crisis in Psychiatry and Religion*. New York: Van Nostrand.

Muhammad, E. (1965). *Message to the Blackman in America*. Chicago: Muhammad Mosque of Islam No. 2.

Muhammad, W.D. (1980). *As the Light Shineth from the East*. Chicago: W D M Publishing.

Muller, H.J. (1958). *The Loom of History*. New York: Harper.

—— (1961). *Freedom in the Ancient World*. New York: Harper.

Myrdal, G. (1944). *An American Dilemma: The Negro problem and modern democracy*. New York: Harper.

Nawas, M.M., and Landfield, A.W. (1963). Improvements in psychotherapy and adoption of the therapist's meaning system. *Psychological Reports* 13:97–98.

New York Bible Society. (ND). *The Holy Bible, King James Version*. New York: New York Bible Society.

Nudelman, A.E. (1971). Dimensions of religiosity: A factor-analytic view of Protestants, Catholics and Christian Scientists. *Review of Religious Research* 13:42–56.

Oates, W.E. (1950). The diagnostic use of the Bible. *Pastoral Psychology* 1(9):43–46.

Oetting, E.R. (1964). The treatment of interpersonal relationships in psychotherapy as a function of religious socialization. *Journal for the Scientific Study of Religion* 4:100–101.

Onions, C.T., ed. (1955). *The Oxford Universal Dictionary*, 3rd ed. Oxford: Clarendon Press.

Opler, M.K. (1957). Schizophrenia and culture. *Scientific American* 197:103–110.

Ostow, M. (1958). The nature of religious controls. *American Psychologist* 13:571–574.

——, and Scharfstein, B-A. (1954). *The Need to Believe*. New York: International Universities Press.

Parenti, M. (1967). Political values and religious cultures: Jews, Catholics and Protestants. *Journal for the Scientific Study of Religion* 6:259–269.

Parsons, T., and Shils, E.A. (1951). *Toward a General Theory of Action*. Cambridge: Harvard University Press.

Patai, R. (1960). *Family, Love and the Bible*. London: MacGibbon and Kee.

Patterson, C.H. (1959). *Counseling and Psychotherapy: Theory and Practice.* New York: Harper.

Pattison, E.M. (1965). On the failure to forgive or to be forgiven. *American Journal of Psychotherapy* 19:106–115.

——, Lapins, N.A., and Doerr, H.A. (1973). Faith Healing: A study of personality and function. *Journal of Nervous and Mental Disease* 157:397–409.

Perls, F.S. (1969). *In and Out the Garbage Pail.* Lafayette, CA: Real People Press.

Peteet, J.R. (1981). Issues in the treatment of religious patients. *American Journal of Psychotherapy* 35:559–564.

Peterson, J.A. (1970). *Counseling and Values: A Philosophical Examination.* Cranston, RI: Carroll Press.

Piaget, J. (1948). *The Moral Judgment of the Child.* Glencoe, IL: Free Press.

Piepkorn, A.C. (1977). *Profiles in Belief.* Vol. 1. New York: Harper & Row.

—— (1978). *Profiles in Belief.* Vol. 2. New York: Harper & Row.

—— (1979). *Profiles in Belief.* Vols. 3,4. New York: Harper & Row.

Pope John Paul II. (1980). Address of Pope John Paul II (to) Einstein Session of the Pontifical Academy. *Science* 207:1165–1167.

Pruyser, P. (1968). *A Dynamic Psychology of Religion.* New York: Harper & Row.

—— (1971). Assessment of the patient's religious attitudes in the psychiatric case study. *Bulletin of the Menninger Clinic* 35:272–291.

—— (1974). *Between Belief and Unbelief.* New York: Harper & Row.

—— (1977). The seamy side of current religious beliefs. *Bulletin of the Menninger Clinic* 41:329–348.

Ragan, C., Malony, H.N., and Beit-Hallahmi, B. (1980). Psychologists and religion: Professional factors and personal belief. *Review of Religious Research* 21:208–217.

Rahner, K., ed. (1975). *Encyclopedia of Theology: The Concise Sacramentum Mundi.* New York: Seabury Press.

Redlich, F.C. (1960). Psychoanalysis and the problem of values. In *Psychoanalysis and Human Values, Science and Psychoanalysis* series. Vol. 3, ed. J.H. Masserman. New York: Grune & Stratton.

Rexroth, K. (ND). In *The Holy Kabbalah* by A.E. Waite. Secaucus, NJ: Citadel Press.

Rice, C.A. (1971). The relationships of intrinsic and extrinsic religious orientations to selected criteria of mental health. Unpublished doctoral dissertation. Boston University.

Richardson, J.T. (1973). Psychological interpretations of glossolalia: A reexamination of research. *Journal for the Scientific Study of Religion* 12:199–207.

Rieff, P. (1959). *Freud: The Mind of the Moralist.* New York: Viking.

—— (1966). *The Triumph of the Therapeutic: Uses of Faith after Freud.* New York: Harper & Row.

Rizzuto, A-M. (1979). *The Birth of the Living God: A Psychoanalytic Study.* Chicago: University of Chicago Press.

Robinson, J.A.T. (1977). *Can We Trust the New Testament*. Grand Rapids: Eerdmans.

Rockland, L.H. (1970). Psychiatric consultation to the clergy. *Pastoral Psychology* 21 (#200):51–53.

Rogers, C.R. (1942). *Counseling and Psychotherapy*. Boston: Houghton Mifflin.

——— (1951). *Client-Centered Therapy*. Boston: Houghton Mifflin.

Rokeach, M. (1969). Value systems in religion. *Review of Religious Research* 11:3–23.

Rosenthal, D. (1955). Changes in some moral values following psychotherapy. *Journal of Consulting Psychology* 19:431–436.

Rosten, L., ed. (1975). *Religion in America*. New York: Simon & Schuster.

Rubins, J.L. (1955). Neurotic attitudes toward religion. *American Journal of Psychoanalysis* 15:71–81.

Rümke, H.C. (1962). *The Psychology of Unbelief*. New York: Sheed & Ward.

Russell, G.W. (1975). The view of religions from religious and non-religious perspectives. *Journal for the Scientific Study of Religion* 14:129–138.

Salzman, L. (1953). The psychology of religious and ideological conversion. *Psychiatry* 16:177–187.

Samler, J. (1960). Changes in values: A goal in counseling. *Journal of Counseling Psychology* 7:32–39.

Sandmel, S. (1957). *A Jewish Understanding of the New Testament*. Cincinnati: Hebrew Union College Press.

Sanua, V.D. (1969). Religion, mental health and personality: A review of empirical studies. *American Journal of Psychiatry* 125:1203–1213.

Schwartz, G. (1970). *Sect Ideologies and Social Status*. Chicago: University of Chicago Press.

Sclabassi, S.H. (1973). Literature as a therapeutic tool. *American Journal of Psychotherapy* 27:70–77.

Sexton, R.O., and Maddock, R.C. (1978). The Adam and Eve syndrome. *Journal of Religion and Health* 17:163–168.

Shapin, S. (1980). A view of scientific thought (Book Review). *Science* 207: 1065–1066.

Siegel, M. (1979). Privacy, ethics and confidentiality. *Professional Psychology* 10:249–258.

Silverman, H. (1969). Determinism, choice, responsibility and the psychologist's role as an expert witness. *American Psychologist* 24:5–9.

Silverman, L. (1976). Psychoanalytic theory: "The reports of my death are greatly exaggerated." *American Psychologist* 31:621–637.

Simkin, J.S. (1962). Comments as discussant. In *Values in Psychotherapy* by C. Buhler. Glencoe, IL: The Free Press.

Skidmore, C.J. (1973). Mormonism and psychotherapy. In *Religious Systems and Psychotherapy*, ed. R.H. Cox. pp. 98–107. Springfield, IL: C.C. Thomas.

Skolnick, J.H. (1958). Religious affiliation and drinking behavior. *Quarterly Journal of Studies on Alcohol* 19:452–470.

Sloane, R.B., Staples, F.R., Cristal, A.H., Yorkston, N.J., and Whipple, K. (1975).

Psychotherapy versus Behavior Therapy. Cambridge: Harvard University Press.

Smith, H. (1958). *The Religions of Man.* New York: Harper & Row.

Smith, M.L., and Glass, G.V. (1977). Meta-analysis of psychotherapy outcome studies. *American Psychologist* 32:752-760.

Smith, W.H. (1978). Ethical, social and professional issues in patients' access to psychological test reports. *Bulletin of the Menninger Clinic* 42:150:155.

Snook, J.B. (1974). An alternative to church-sect. *Journal for the Scientific Study of Religion* 13:191-204.

Sollod, R.N. (1978). Psychotherapy and religion: Some ethical issues. Paper read at the American Psychological Association Convention.

Spero, M.H. (1977). Implications of countertransference for the religious therapist and client. *Journal of Psychology and Judaism* 1:39-51.

—— (1981). Countertransference in religious therapists of religious patients. *American Journal of Psychotherapy* 35:565-575.

Spiegel, J.P. (1959). Some cultural aspects of transference and countertransference. In *Individual and Familial Dynamics, Science and Psychoanalysis* series, Vol. 2. ed. J.H. Masserman. New York: Grune & Stratton.

Spilka, B., and Werme, P.H. (1971). Religion and mental disorder: A research perspective. In *Research on Religious Development*, ed. M.P. Strommen. pp. 461-481. New York: Hawthorn Books.

Srole, L., Langner, T.S., Michael, S.T., Opler, M.K., and Rennie, T.A.C. (1962). *Mental Health in the Metropolis: The midtown Manhattan study.* Vol. 1. New York: McGraw-Hill.

Stamey, H.C. (1971). The "Mad at God" syndrome. *American Journal of Psychotherapy* 25:93-103.

Stark, R. (1965). A taxonomy of religious experience. *Journal for the Scientific Study of Religion* 5:97-116.

—— and Bainbridge, W.S. (1979). Of churches, sects and cults: Preliminary concepts for a theory of religious movements. *Journal for the Scientific Study of Religion* 18:117-131.

—— Foster, B.D., Glock, C.Y., and Quimby, H.E. (1971). *Wayward Shepherds: Prejudice and the Protestant clergy.* New York: Harper & Row.

Stolorow, R.D., and Atwood, G.E. (1979). *Faces in a Cloud.* New York: Aronson.

Strunk, O., Jr. (1972). Bibliotherapy revisited. *Journal of Religion and Health* 11:218-228.

Sullivan, H.S. (1953). *The Interpersonal Theory of Psychiatry.* New York: Norton.

—— (1954). *The Psychiatric Interview.* New York: Norton.

Szasz, T. (1965). *The Ethics of Psychoanalysis.* New York: Dell.

Tamayo, A., Pasquali, L., Bonami, M., Pattyn, M-R., and Custers, A. (1969). Concept of God and parental images. *Journal for the Scientific Study of Religion* 8:79-87.

Tashurizina, Z.A. (1974). Les Superstitions, mystification des relations quotidiennes. *Social Compass* 21:153-169.

Thiele, E.R. (1965). *The Mysterious Numbers of the Hebrew Kings*, 2nd ed. Grand Rapids: Eerdmans.

Thomas, L.B. (1965). Sacramental confession and some clinical concerns. *Journal of Religion and Health* 4:345–353.

Tomkins, S.S. (1962). *Affect, Imagery, Consciousness*. Vol. 1. New York: Springer.

Vayhinger, J.M. (1973). Protestantism (Conservative–Evangelical) and the therapist. In *Religious Systems and Psychotherapy*, ed. R.H. Cox. pp. 56–71. Springfield, IL: C.C. Thomas.

Vitz, P.C. (1977). *Psychology as Religion: The Cult of Self-Worship*. Grand Rapids: Eerdmans.

—— (1978). Religion and Psychotherapy: Conflict over the concept of the self. Paper presented at the American Psychological Association Convention.

Walker, M. (1976). *Alone of All Her Sex*. New York: Alfred Knopf.

Walls, G.B. (1980). Values and psychotherapy: A comment on "Psychotherapy and religious values." *Journal of Consulting and Clinical Psychology* 48: 640–641.

Warburton, T.R. (1969). Holiness religion: An anomaly of sectarian typologies. *Journal for the Scientific Study of Religion* 8:130–139.

Wardwell, W.I. (1965). Christian Science healing. *Journal for the Scientific Study of Religion* 4:175–181.

—— (1973). Christian Science and spiritual healing. In *Religious Systems and Psychotherapy*, ed. R.H. Cox. pp. 72–88. Springfield, IL: C.C. Thomas.

Weintraub, W., and Aronson, H. (1974). Patients in psychoanalysis: Some findings related to sex and religion. *American Journal of Orthopsychiatry* 44: 102–108.

Welkowitz, J., Cohen, J., and Ortmeyer, D. (1967). Value system similarity: Investigation of patient-therapist dyads. *Journal of Consulting Psychology* 31:48–55.

Werner, E. (1959). *The Sacred Bridge*. New York: Schocken. Reprinted 1970.

Whalen, W.J. (1972). *Separated Brethren*. Huntington, IN: Our Sunday Visitor.

Wigoder, G., ed. (1974). *Encyclopedic Dictionary of Judaica*. Jerusalem: Keter Publishing House.

Williams, D.L., and Kremer, B.J. (1974). Pastoral counseling students and secular counseling students: A comparison. *Journal of Counseling Psychology* 21: 238–242.

Williams, J.P. (1969). *What Americans Believe and How They Worship*, 3rd ed. New York: Harper & Row.

Wilson, S.J. (1981). A Piagetian-based analysis of insight and the interpretive process. *American Journal of Orthopsychiatry* 51:626–631.

Winnicott, D.W. (1951). Transitional objects and transitional phenomena. In *Through Paediatrics to Psychoanalysis*. New York: Basic Books.

Wise, C.A. (1980). *Pastoral Psychotherapy*. New York: Aronson.

Wouk, H. (1960). *This Is My God*. Garden City, NY: Doubleday.

Yassky, A. (1976). Active use of counter-transference. *Journal of Clinical Issues in Psychology* 7:13–16.

Zuk, G.H. (1978). A therapist's perspective on Jewish family values. *Journal of Marriage and Family Counseling* 4:103–109.

Bibliographic Sources

BIBLES

Many Bibles are now on the market, but only a few of the more important and popular ones will be reviewed here. Many of the available Bibles will have introductory material bearing upon the theological orientation of the translators, the source texts used, explanatory introductory materials, and clarificatory footnotes. Others (Bible in Basic English, Good News Bible, Living Bible Paraphrased) dispense with much of this, render the text freely into current English, and may even modify the text to a particular theological position. A brief but informative history of biblical translation is available in Beegle (1982) from whom some of the following material in this section was derived.

King James Version (Conservative Protestant). Many publishers, including the American Bible Society. First published in 1611, with subsequent revisions, the King James Version has become a standard. The language is now considerably antiquated and words that were not in the original texts are italicized, which gives a confusing emphasis. More accurate source texts than the one used for this translation now exist.

New King James Version (Conservative Protestant). Thomas Nelson. This new translation was supported by the publisher who assembled a team of more than 130 Christian scholars. The goal was equivalence with the King James Version, so that changes or deletions indicated by modern scholarship or more recently discovered manuscripts are indicated in a footnote, not in the text. Punctuation has been clarified, archaic usage has been modernized ("thee" and "thou" are now "you"), words whose meaning has changed have been updated, quotation marks to indicate the speaker have been added, long sentences have been broken down into shorter ones, but italics for words not in the original text have been retained.

Revised Standard Version (Mainline Protestant, Roman Catholic). Thomas Nelson, Moody, and others. Published between 1946 and 1957, this is a revision of the King James and the American Standard Version issued in 1901. The latter was supposed to be more accurate, but its literal, stiff style did not give it much appeal. A study version of the Revised Standard Version that appeared in the early 1960s is known as the Oxford Annotated Bible. The translators utilized the Masoretic (traditional Jewish) text as their basic source for the Old Testament.

New American Standard Bible (Conservative Protestant). Cambridge University Press, Creation Press. Also a revision of the King James Version and the American Standard Version, this Bible emphasized the inerrancy of the original texts. Published in 1971, this Bible is preferred by conservative and evangelical Protestant churches.

New English Bible (Mainline Protestant). Cambridge and Oxford University Press. The aim of this translation, published between 1961 and 1970, was to take advantage of modern scholarship and also to render the Bible into stylistically good, modern English. In a joint effort, a team of scholars was used to review a draft of a book produced by a single translator; when this team was satisfied, it was passed on to a team of literary stylists. Since the Bible has many layers of composition, the relentlessly modern approach of the stylists did not render this well, and subtle connotations were lost (Daiches 1970). Nevertheless, it generally reads well. Two study versions exist in the Oxford Study Bible and the Cambridge Bible Commentary.

New American Bible (Roman Catholic). Catholic Bible Publishers. This is a standard current (published 1970) Bible for Catholic use. It is generally regarded as accurate, but not very elegant or literary. The illustrations give a dimension lacking in many other Bibles. Unfortunately, the title is similar to the New American Standard Bible, which sometimes causes confusion.

The Jerusalem Bible (Roman Catholic, Mainline Protestant). Doubleday. Translated from the French *Bible de Jerusalem*, this Bible was published in 1966. A very readable rendition into elegant English, it has attracted interest and is used by mainline Protestant denominations.

Soncino Books of the Bible (Jewish). Soncino Press. This English translation (King James style) has a parallel Hebrew text (Masoretic) and commentaries. Published in the mid-1940s, each of the 14 volumes is done by a Judaic scholar under general editorship. Although designed for the general reader, it is scholarly and detailed. A knowledge of biblical Hebrew is useful, but not necessary.

The Holy Scriptures, according to the Masoretic Text (Traditional Jewish). Jewish Publication Society. This, as with the Bible above, only contains what is otherwise regarded as the Old Testament. Published in 1917, it represented the consensus of Jewish scholarship at that time and the English is rendered in King James style. The *haftarah*, or Prophetic reading, that parallels the appointed weekly reading from the *Torah* is indicated.

New Jewish Edition (Jewish, Mainline Protestant). Jewish Publication Society. Also based on the Masoretic text, this modern, idiomatic translation appeared over two decades, with the third, and last volume issued in 1982. Although the translation was based on the Masoretic text, better renditions or uncertain texts are indicated in footnotes. Also, the parallelism and repetitive qualities of certain word usages in various passages is retained, rather than the common literary usage of avoiding repetition for the sake of variety. This makes the text more faithful to the original (Brettler 1982).

The Interpreter's Bible (Mainline Protestant). Abingdon Press. This 12-volume Bible is a detailed exegesis of the King James and the Revised Standard Version. Published in 1952 under the general editorship of George Buttrick, and written from an avowedly Protestant position, the contributors included some well-known scholars, but it was not a new translation.

The Anchor Bible (Protestant, Roman Catholic, Jewish). Doubleday. So far, nearly 40 volumes have been published in this series for which recognized scholars prepared fresh translations utilizing the latest textual and archaeological studies. Under the general editorship of William F. Albright and David Noel Freedman, and aimed at the general reader, the Anchor Bible is widely regarded as one of the most authoritative translations available for general use. There is no specific theological perspective in the series and the individual translators may be Protestant, Catholic, or Jewish.

REFERENCE WORKS

In addition to being the most published book, the Bible is also the most studied book. There are commentaries of all sorts on the Bible itself, on translations, cognate languages, archaeology, personalities, and places mentioned in the Bible, as well as general works at all levels of specialization. Most of these have a specific point of view or faith position, which, if kept in mind, can illuminate the meaning of the material presented. Technical aids, such as concordances, enable one to find the location, translation, and spelling of just about all the words in the Bible. What follows is a brief, annotated list of books that may be useful to the reader.

General Sources

Allport, G.W. (1950). *The Individual and His Religion*. New York: MacMillan. This has been a popular book among some writers, perhaps because it has rescued religion from the charge of promoting immaturity. Allport's discussion of maturity and immaturity in religion is worth reading and has generated a fair amount of research. His discussion of doubt is interesting, but his understanding of psychotherapy is simplistic. The book appears to have been written from a Christian perspective, but some points regarding Islam, Buddhism, Hinduism, and other religions are noted. Curiously, Judaism is never mentioned. Overall, I thought the book had a mushy quality, as though a religious man were trying to write an "objective" book.

Douglas, M. (1966). *Purity and Danger: An Analysis of Concepts of Pollution and Taboo*. New York: Praeger. This seems to be a thoughtful, useful discussion of ritual, pollution (in a religious sense), and purity in a variety of cultures. Although Douglas does not deal very much with modern cultures, some connections can be made by the reader. She is incisively critical of some past anthropologists for major errors, including not understanding the practices they discuss from within the culture, disparagement of "primitive" societies, and misunderstanding the symbolic facets of magic. She herself does not idealize the cultures discussed. Her later book, *Natural Symbols*, is also well worth reading.

Kosnik, A., Carroll, W., Cunningham, A., Modias, R., and Schulte, J. (1977). *Human Sexuality: New Directions in American Catholic Thought*. New York: Paulist Press. This radical book, by thoughtful, humane, and scholarly Catholics, seems to have gone to the limits in openly exploring the Roman Church's teachings and comparing them to current knowledge in anthropology and human and animal behavior. I found it useful and interesting. One or more of the writers incurred the displeasure of their superiors.

Menninger, K. (1973). *Whatever Became of Sin?* New York: Hawthorn Books. A wise and sophisticated consideration of the interrelated issues of sin and crime, morality and law, and change and responsibility.

Pruyser, P.W. (1974). *Between Belief and Unbelief*. New York: Harper & Row. This book is a thorough, thoughtful, wide-ranging, scholarly, and humane discussion of many complex issues relating to belief, unbelief, mystery, fantasy, reality-development, and identity-formation. Although psychoanalytically trained, Pruyser is very open to alternatives. The book is not directed toward therapeutic concerns, but he deals with some interesting matters that have applicability to treatment.

Understanding the Bible

Alter, R. (1981). *The Art of Biblical Narrative*. New York: Basic Books. Although Alter has knowledgeable roots in the rabbinic literature, his ways of describing the intertwining of narrative and God's action in the Hebrew view of history are novel and even radical. Some are derived from talmudic and rabbinic sources. He gives a new luster and vivid perspective to old, sometimes timeworn stories. Although he does not directly address the concerns of the practicing therapist, there are a variety of nuggets that become useful with only a little reflection. Unfortunately, he does not deal with the New Testament.

Asimov, I. (1968). *Asimov's Guide to the Bible: The Old Testament.* New York: Avon Books; Asimov, I. (1969). *Asimov's Guide to the Bible: The New Testament.* New York: Avon Books. These two volumes, available in relatively inexpensive paperback editions, do not represent advances in scholarship but, Asimov, mostly using the King James Version, summarizes standard thought on biblical texts. His commentary and notes proceed through the text starting with Genesis. He includes maps, materials drawn from various sources, and illustrations. The writing proceeds at an interesting, readable pace.

Chase, M.E. (1955). *Life and Language in the Old Testament.* New York: Norton. Although no longer current, this is a fair introduction to the topic. The "golly, gee-whiz" quality of the writing suggests that idealization may have overtaken the critical stance necessary to approach the text for maximum understanding.

Cole, W.G. (1959). *Sex and Love in the Bible.* New York: Association Press. This book, like that of Koznik et al. (1977), attempts to extend the usual limits of Protestant thought through a detailed examination of the biblical roots of many Christian attitudes. Not quite as daring as the Koznik book (it is also 20 years earlier) and without the survey of relevant social science data, it seems thorough. It can provide therapists with useful material.

Hahn, H.F. (1966). *The Old Testament in Modern Research.* 2nd ed. Philadelphia: Fortress Press. As an introduction to seven approaches to understanding the Old Testament (Higher Criticism, anthropology, religio-historical school, form criticism, sociology, archaeology, theology), this book serves its purpose. Based largely on German, Protestant sources, this is more a history of Old Testament studies than a detailed examination of the issues. Hahn's range of sources is limited, and although the book deals with the Old Testament, relevant Jewish writers (Buber, Heschel) are hardly cited.

Patai, R. (1960). *Family, Love and the Bible.* London: MacGibbon and Kee. In this companion to the Cole and Koznik volumes, Patai, although apparently Jewish, does not hold a rabbinic stance, but rather is using his scholarly background in the Old Testament to elucidate how it bears upon the issues in the title.

Sandmel, S. (1957). *A Jewish Understanding of the New Testament.* Cincinnati: Hebrew Union College Press. Writing primarily for a general Jewish audience, Sandmel attempts to help Jews understand the New Testament. His stance toward the New Testament is interested, respectful but not reverential. His analysis and critique is not severe. Sandmel is a highly respected scholar, but the New Testament was not his major area. He does, however, provide a thoughtful perspective from a somewhat different angle. There is some material that can aid the therapist.

Stacey, D. (1977). *Interpreting the Bible.* New York: Hawthorn Books. A good beginning for thoughtful readers without an extensive background, Stacey presents a number of disparate positions from the inside. He deals concisely with important issues in interpretation, while still illuminating them. His stance on the Bible (positive, Christian) is unobtrusive. Although not directly relevant to the therapist's concerns, this book would make a good starting point for someone wanting to understand the ways the Bible is viewed.

Young, R. (1970). *Analytical Concordance to the Bible.* 22nd Am. ed. Grand Rapids: Eerdmans. A concordance is a guide to specific material within the Bible. Many concordances are keyed to a particular translation, and therefore not very flexible. Young's concordance, although apparently using the King James Version in showing the context of the word or name being listed, will usually help the reader find any name or just about any word desired without depending on a particular translation. There are other concordances, but I have found this very useful, since it gives the original Hebrew or Greek, as well as alternative definitions.

Encyclopedias

Ausubel, N. (1964). *The Book of Jewish Knowledge.* New York: Crown Publishers. Although set in the format of an encyclopedia, this book is a set of shorter or longer discussions of a wide variety of topics. It is a knowledgeable and readable one-volume reference source on the many facets of Jewish life.

Hastings, J., ed. (1955). *Encyclopaedia of Religion and Ethics.* New York: Scribners. Although dated as being published in 1955, this is actually the date of the reprinting. It was edited by James Hastings, who died in 1922 as he was working on the index. Although it is not up to date in a number of aspects, it contains useful information from a Protestant perspective.

McDonald, W.V., editor-in-chief (1967). *New Catholic Encyclopedia.* New York: McGraw-Hill. This 16-volume work (including a supplement to 1974) appears to be thorough, supported by good scholarship, and designed for general home and school use. Though the emphasis is Catholic, it treats general culture, too.

Rahner, K., ed. (1968). *Sacramentum Mundi: An Encylopedia of Theology.* New York: Herder and Herder. Produced under Catholic auspices, under the general editorship of Karl Rahner, a respected scholar, this 6-volume work is highly scholarly and has the goal of being open to other Christian denominations and to non-Christian religions as well.

——— (1975). *Encyclopedia of Theology: The Concise Sacramentum Mundi.* New York: Seabury Press. A one-volume condensation of the above.

Roth, C., ed. (1972). *Encyclopaedia Judaica*. Jerusalem: Keter Publishing House. This is an extensive, modern reference work under a respected editor. With sixteen volumes and two supplements, it is enlivened by both color and black and white illustrations.

Wigoder, G., ed. (1974). *Encyclopedia Dictionary of Judaica*. Jerusalem: Keter Publishing House. Edited by Geoffrey Wigoder, this was designed to complement the much larger Encyclopedia Judaica in a single volume. Primarily a compendium of facts and brief summaries and descriptions, it is meant for general use in schools and homes.

There do not appear to be any other general encyclopedias from a Protestant perspective. A variety of specialized books dealing either with a specific denomination in an encyclopedia format or with an individualized topic (e.g., Bible dictionaries, *Who's Who in The Old Testament*) can be located in any reasonably well-stocked library or in the library of a particular church or its pastor.

Denominations

Smith, H. (1958). *The Religions of Man*. New York: Harper & Row. There are many descriptions of the major religions. This one is reasonably concise, covers seven of the world's religions (Hinduism, Buddhism, Confucianism, Taoism, Islam, Judaism, Christianity), and is available in paperback. It appears to be accurate and is well regarded.

The following three books analyze a wide range of individual denominations.

Mayer, F.E. (1961). *The Religious Bodies of America*. 4th ed. St. Louis: Concordia Publishing House. Mayer was a Lutheran theologian in the Missouri synod. His systematic description of denominations in the United States is interesting, but biased, and it is clear that Lutheranism is best. Some of his characterizations exceed the bounds of fair comment.

Piepkorn, A.C. (1977). *Profiles in Belief*, Vol. 1. New York: Harper & Row; Piepkorn, A.C. (1978). Vol. 2. New York: Harper & Row; Piepkorn, A.C. (1979). Vols. 3, 4. New York: Harper & Row. Also a Lutheran theologian, Piepkorn, in his four-volume study, could not be more different in his balanced, thorough presentation. The study is incomplete, since it was published after Piepkorn died so not all the denominations in the United States are represented. It is unique in containing so many individual small denominations, some with only a few churches. Faced with a patient from a small denomination, there does not appear to be a more useful and fair source.

Whalen, W.J. (1972). *Separated Brethren*. Huntington, IN: Our Sunday Visitor. In this book designed for Roman Catholics, Whalen surveyed eleven major and seven minor Protestant groups, four "cultists," six other Christian groups, and several others (Jews, Muslims, Bahai, Buddhists). Although some cognitive background is presented, a breezy style, as well as a Catholic slant, limits the book's usefulness as a source of objective data.

Psychotherapy

Bowers, M.K. (1963). *Conflicts of the Clergy: A Psychodynamic Study with Case Histories*. New York: Thomas Nelson. Although it deals primarily with therapy with clergy, it presents a positive but psychodynamic attitude toward religion in therapy. The book is a bit dated, but it has interesting case histories and therapeutic tactics.

Buhler, C. (1962). *Values in Psychotherapy*. Glencoe, IL: The Free Press. A thoughtful discussion by a practicing therapist that does not seem dated, even though it is more than 20 years old. Interesting commentary by Rudolph Ekstein and James Simkin.

Cox, R.H., ed. (1973). *Religious Systems and Psychotherapy*. Springfield, IL: C.C. Thomas. An interesting collection of articles from a number of positions, by psychotherapists well acquainted with, or within, varying faith positions.

Rizzuto, A-M. (1979). *The Birth of the Living God: A Psychoanalytic Study*. Chicago: University of Chicago Press. Rizzuto, a trained analyst, examines the connections between dynamics and religious imagery. Unfortunately, her methodology is poor when it comes to statistical analysis and renders her conclusions suspect.

Strommen, M.P., ed. (1971). *Research on Religious Development*. New York: Hawthorn Books. Extensive, thorough reviews of the relevant literature by recognized authorities. Although somewhat old, it is a good summary up through the 1960s.

Index of Biblical Citations

This index is organized thematically to enable the reader to find more rapidly those references to the Bible discussed in the text (page numbers are given in the parentheses following each citation). Not all statements in the Bible that relate to the indexed material have been cited in this book. An asterisk (*) indicates that the text discussion should be reviewed.

MEN, WOMEN AND LOVE

MIRACLES

PARENTS AND CHILDREN

RELATIONS AMONG CHRISTIANS

SEX AND PLEASURE

Index